D1559610

Affecting Fictions

Affecting Fictions

 MIND, BODY, AND EMOTION IN
AMERICAN LITERARY REALISM

JANE F. THRAILKILL

HARVARD UNIVERSITY PRESS
Cambridge, Massachusetts, and London, England   2007

Library of Congress Cataloging-in-Publication Data

Thrailkill, Jane F., 1963–
    Affecting fictions: mind, body, and emotion in American literary realism / Jane F. Thrailkill.
        p. cm.
    Includes bibliographical references and index.
    ISBN-13: 978-0-674-02512-7 (alk. paper)
    ISBN-10: 0-674-02512-1 (alk. paper)
    1. American fiction—19th century—History and criticism—Theory, etc. 2. Body, Human,
in literature. 3. Emotions in literature. 4. Realism in literature. 5. Mind and body in
literature. 6. American fiction—20th century—History and criticism—Theory, etc. 7. United
States—Intellectual life—19th century. 8. United States—Intellectual life—20th century.
I. Title.
    PS374.B64T48 2007

    813'.409353—dc22   2007007007

For Hawley

Contents

Introduction

The "Affective Fallacy" Fallacy

This book is a sustained argument in defense of the Affective Fallacy. The term was coined in 1946 by the literary critics W. K. Wimsatt and Monroe Beardsley, who contended that "affective criticism"—criticism that took seriously literature's effects on readers—led to impressionism and relativism.[1] They pointed out that emotional responses to different objects, especially but not only literary works, varied wildly across cultures, historical periods, and even one individual's lifespan (21). At the heart of this problem was emotion itself, for as articulated by Wimsatt and Beardsley, feelings were not only private and subjective but also distorting of reason and cognition. "Emotion," they wrote, ". . . has a well known capacity to fortify opinion, to inflame cognition, and to grow upon itself in surprising proportions to grains of reason" (26). Feelings, manifested in the "'shiver down the spine,' the sensation in 'the pit of the stomach'" (30), were rooted in the body—therefore, for these critics, they occluded the operation of cognition and the ascription of meaning, processes centered in the mind.

Reproduced in a book by Wimsatt entitled *The Verbal Icon: Studies in the Meaning of Poetry* (1954), the essay entitled "The Affective Fallacy" was presented for the explicit purpose of stabilizing and making public the meanings conveyed by works of literature. While any given literary work might have a multitude of idiosyncratic, "physiological and psychologically vague" (34) effects on particular individuals, these influential New Critics argued that dispassionate, objective, cognition-based interpretation might overcome the material differences of bodies, societies, and historical periods. Their argument against affective criticism sought to affirm the primacy of interpretation, and indeed culture itself, over the unpredictable and potentially solipsistic motions of the body. Wimsatt and Beardsley would assent to anthropologist Catherine Lutz's observation that "nothing . . . appear[s] more natural and hence less cultural than emotions, nothing more private and hence less amenable to public scrutiny, nothing more inchoate and less compatible" with the collective study of culture and the interpretation of its artifacts—especially (as they refer to works of literature) its "Verbal Icon[s]."[2] In an unstable world, in which "cultures have changed and will change" (39), the New Critics cast the verbal icon as a solid levee holding back "mob psychology, psychosis, and neurosis" (27). For Wimsatt and Beardsley, affective response involved precultural visceral reactions that threatened coherent principles of order and epistemological stability.

Yet Wimsatt and Beardsley's argument produced a tantalizing paradox: why, in an essay urging the irrelevance of feeling to literary studies, is the rhetorical register of such emotional intensity? Despite its brevity, "The Affective Fallacy" offers up a lengthy inventory of perils associated with emotion: including such "obsolete or exotic customs" as "exposing babies"; a variety of menaces, such as "a cyclone, a mob, a holdup man"; viciousness and vice ("robbery, fornication, horse racing, war"); predatory nature ("the crow that kills small birds and animals or feeds on carrion"); and barbarism as such ("murder . . . atrocity . . . wholesale butchery") (39, 26, 27, 33, 36, 37). This intensity, I believe, directs us to an important fear motivating the New Critics' discussion of literary interpretation: that a world without a stabilizing principle—whether that "world" is a work of literature, or the culture of literary studies, or a broader geopolitical entity—would have no foundation for discussion, much less agreement, about the validity of acts of interpretation. Their use of metaphor suggests that such a world, fractured by material and perceptual differences (and ruled by the very entity, the body, that encapsulates these essential divisions), would amount to a Hobbesian state of nature.

Recognition of this underlying anxiety helps to explain the ominous terms Wimsatt and Beardsley use to describe the problems attendant on the Affective Fallacy, as when they hint that attentiveness to what literature "does" to us (its corporeal appeal) and not just what it means (its cognitive aspect) might authorize vivisection as a form of criticism: "If animals could read poetry," they muse, "the affective critic" might be tempted to experiment on animal bodies to monitor "the increased liberation of sugar from the liver, the secretion of adrenin from the adrenal gland" (21, 31). A literary/interpretive world governed by feelings could, they indicate, devolve into a grim battle of wills, producing a situation where "cognitively untranslatable" (34) meanings could only be passed along corporeally. The critics' figures for this sort of corporeal communication range from unpleasant to gruesome: meanings, on this model, must be understood as "communicated to the reader like an infection or disease, . . . inflicted mechanically like a bullet or knife wound, . . . administered like a poison, . . . expressed as by expletives or grimaces or rhythms" (38).[3] (Notably, the meaning of a literary work is never "absorbed like sunlight," "passed along as by the clasp of a hand," or "imbibed like a fine wine.") The metaphors underscore that, for Wimsatt and Beardsley, not just literary interpretation but something like civilization itself was at stake.

The critic Walter Benn Michaels, in *The Shape of the Signifier* (2004), has recently taken up the New Critics' line of reasoning. Like Wimsatt and Beardsley, he distinguishes between the meaning of a literary work, which is attainable through reason and cognition (i.e. a person's interpretation), and an individual's actual reception of a literary work (i.e. a person's experience). Michaels's formulation suggests that while *interpretations* may be cast into language and reasonably conveyed to others, the *experience* of a literary work—its "physiological and psychologically vague" effects ("Affective Fallacy," 34)—cannot. To imagine that it could, Michaels suggests, is to think of textual meaning as a material entity capable of entering a person's body without cerebral engagement, on "the model of a virus."[4] Or on the model of a nail gun: Michaels echoes Wimsatt's and Beardsley's comments regarding knife wounds and grimaces as exemplary affective modes of communication when he observes that in Brett Easton Ellis's *American Psycho* (1991) "the moan of pain from the woman the psycho shoots with a nail gun really does give him information about how she's feeling" (123). Michaels argues that the actions of Ellis's narrator betray something like a commitment to the Affective Fallacy, for the psycho requires that "meanings" transpire experientially, which is to say corporeally, bypassing the mind and evading the vicissitudes of both speech and interpretation.

While Michaels's point in bringing up Ellis's novel is that one has to go to extraordinary lengths to imagine interpretation without cognition,[5] I would venture a different reading: that the rather sanguinary examples of critics who argue against committing the Affective Fallacy suggest the extraordinary lengths one must go to imagine that the experience of a literary work—how it makes us feel—is irrelevant to its interpretation. In the chapters that follow, I elaborate the ways in which, for writers, readers, and theorists of the late nineteenth century, affective experience was conceptualized as both rooted in the body and as mindful. To put this point in terms pertinent to current debates over the role of affect in literary studies: attentiveness to the experience of a literary work need not eradicate meaning (or its concomitant, civilized society) if we come to accept that feeling is not opposed to interpretation but is part of it.

The Entanglements of Two Cultures

Since the 1980s, work by scholars and theorists interested in the history of the body can be seen as a response to the anxieties first expressed by the New Critics. Whereas Wimsatt and Beardsley understood the body—with its unspecifiable, idiosyncratic, and irrational emotional responses—to be at odds with culture and interpretation, influential thinkers such as Catherine Lutz, Judith Butler, Thomas Lacqueur, Elaine Showalter, Jane Tompkins, and Julie Ellison have argued that the body's textures, habits, and responses (especially those pertinent to sex and gender) must themselves be understood as the expressions of culture.[6] As the psychoanalytic critic Julia Kristeva puts it, these accounts acknowledge *"the relativity of [a person's] symbolic as well as biological existence."*[7] Catherine Lutz has written, "After deconstruction, emotion retains value as a way of talking about the intensely meaningful as that is culturally defined, socially enacted, and personally articulated" (5). While Lutz acknowledges that emotion is experienced as "something that rises and falls within the boundaries of our bodies" (5), she recasts feelings as essentially cultural and interpretive modes of "negotiation over the meaning of events, over rights and moralities" (5). "Talk about emotions," Lutz affirms, "is simultaneously talk about society" (6). Whereas Wimsatt and Beardsley cast the body as dangerously antithetical to culture, more recent thinking about the constructed character of biological existence—a position underwritten by, among others, the theories of Sigmund Freud and Michel Foucault—has cast the body and its attendant emotions as eloquent expressions of culture. For a range of cultural critics, the study of the body, even in its material form, must indeed attend to meanings rather than (as the New Critics had predicted) adrenal secretions. The body was reconceived as a text that could be read without recourse to scientific knowledge or methods of inquiry.

Yet the ascendance of the culture concept in literary and historical study appears to have shifted, rather than solved, the essential problem that preoccupied Wimsatt and Beardsley: that "cognitively untranslatable" reactions to literary works were an index of the larger problem of incommensurability of meaning and value from "culture to culture" (38). In 1959, just five years after The Verbal Icon was published, C. P. Snow in the Rede Lectures coined the term "two cultures" to encapsulate the widening gulf between scientists and scholars in the humanities.[8] Judging by today's widespread discussion of the "Science Wars" (a close cousin of the "Culture Wars") in academic and popular media, the critical work of the past few decades has if anything exacerbated rather than assuaged the anxiety, vividly expressed a half century earlier, about the problems of relativism, the stability and communicability of knowledge, and the incommensurability of the disciplines. This incommensurability took dramatic form in 1996, when physicist Alan Sokal submitted a sham article to the "Science Wars" issue of the critical theory journal Social Text.[9] The piece was published, Sokal repudiated it, and a storm of controversy followed. So while the emphasis on the cultural construction of biological and physical entities may have dissolved the strong distinction between the biological body and culture as such, it has nonetheless helped to drive a wedge between the sciences and the humanities.

As Wai Chee Dimock and Priscilla Wald have argued, institutional collaboration and communication are somewhat rare between the humanities and the sciences. Yet, they observe, the spheres that humanities scholars have claimed as their own—the realms of literary production, cultural practices, and historical meanings—are now saturated with the practical consequences of specialized scientific knowledges, "from reproductive technologies to electronic archives, from bioterrorism to gene therapy."[10] "Science illiteracy," Dimock and Wald affirm, "[is] no longer an option. Scholars in the humanities simply have to come to terms with these forces of change. Unpersuaded by the language of crisis with which some cultural observers have responded to the current situation, we see an opportunity for creative and productive responses to the emergence of new forms of knowledge, of cross-disciplinary conversations and collaborations, all born of the necessity to address the growing *entanglement* of culture, technology, and science" (705–706; emphasis added). Literary study has been slow to import the insights of these other fields, and not without good reason: traditionally, biological accounts of the body have been wielded with a heavy hand, used to justify existing social inequalities based on sex and race, or to produce reductive and deterministic accounts of human behavior.

In discussions of emotion, however, the entanglement Dimock and Wald delineate is unusually knotty—and for this reason, as I have found, especially productive. This book engages with scientific work, not only through analyzing its rhetorical and ideological force but also by taking seriously its range of ideas, models, and practices pertinent to the biological human body. There are historical grounds for such a project, for literary realism in the United States reached its height during the dynamic, post–Civil War decades, when a range of sciences of the human mind and body were in the process of disaggregating into discrete disciplines: neurology out of/alongside physiology, scientific medicine out of/alongside other healing practices, psychology out of/alongside philosophical pragmatism. Such an approach may also, however, have broader theoretical and practical salience. Certain literary-critical paradigms of the twentieth century, sponsored by both New Critics and poststructuralists, have had the paradoxical effect of helping to alienate the humanities from the sciences even as they have fostered critical work that in many ways draws on the sciences: methodologically, in the emphasis on "rigor," arcane terminology, and expertise; in the object of study, which frequently attends to the rhetorical and cultural impact of scientific discourses; and institutionally, in our credentialing procedures and emphasis on research over teaching, and specialization over general knowledge. It is the premise of this book that, by tracing the complex allegiances among discourses that are focused on the human interaction with others and with the material world, we can align without conflating the work of literary scholars with that of investigators in other fields.

So instead of simply disparaging scientific knowledge of the body (as with the New Critics) or deconstructing it (as with poststructuralists), a reenergized attentiveness to the distinctions between the sciences and the humanities opens up exciting possibilities for substantive cross-fertilization. In recent years, critics in the humanities have actively taken up findings of researchers in fields such as evolutionary biology and artificial intelligence, even as writers and literary critics are increasingly making contributions to an understanding of human perception, production, and flourishing that are valuable to other fields of inquiry, such as cognitive neuroscience and medicine.[11] In other words, while necessarily respectful of the important differences in our objects of inquiry, methodologies, and institutional histories, investigators in the humanities and in the sciences can find common ground. This common ground, in the words of Donna Haraway, must embrace both "an account of radical historical contingency" and the "no-nonsense commitment to faithful accounts of a 'real' world, one that can be partially shared and friendly to earth-wide projects of finite freedom, adequate material abundance, modest meaning in suffering, and limited happiness."[12] Approached from such an orientation, the study of literature and our responses to it could be an occasion for connection and conversation, both within and across disciplines.

Literature and Neurology, 1860–1910

The central claims of this book are, in short, theoretical as well as literary and historical; they also gesture toward a methodological imperative. This study advances the proposition that the literature of the late nineteenth century requires us to commit to the Affective Fallacy. Read in the context of discourses focused on sensory perception, emotional receptivity, and the embodied mind, these works of fiction contribute, both experientially and conceptually, to our understanding of the nature of aesthetic experience and, more generally, to our appreciation of the human engagement with the material world. This literary examination of mind-body connections is centered on the historical period when emotion itself emerged as an object of scientific as well as philosophical inquiry. With the illumination provided by work being done in the twenty-first century, we can see how writers of realist fiction actively engaged with ideas about the mindful corporeality of affective experience, as theorized by Charles Darwin, William James, and John Dewey. A focus on the exemplary realist emotions of pity, fear, nervousness, pleasure, and wonder reveals how attention to bodily response placed literature and aesthetic experience at the center of nineteenth-century explorations into human consciousness. As the physiologist Thomas Laycock announced in 1860, "It is the man in his twofold constitution who is conscious, not the mind as apart from the man."[13]

This inquiry is situated in the conceptual space designated by the philosopher and psychologist William James, who was writing in the late nineteenth century, and the literary scholar I. A. Richards, writing early in the twentieth. In "What Is an Emotion?" (1884) James noted that physiologists, while "industriously exploring the functions of the brain," had not yet attended to "the *aesthetic* sphere of the mind, its longing, its pleasures and pains, and its emotions."[14] Richards, in *Principles of Literary Criticism* (1924), offered the flip side of James's point, urging that literary critics had themselves overlooked scientific hypotheses about the human nervous system, including findings pertinent to "the understanding of poetic, musical, and other experiences."[15] So while James suggested that neurology had not attended sufficiently to the aesthetic aspects of experience, Richards indicated that aesthetics could profit from more attentiveness to neurology. Both men deputized these concerns to future generations of investigators, whose knowledge about the operations of mind embedded in the human nervous system would fruitfully supplement the current understanding of the experience of literary works. Both anticipated a time when scientists and scholars might collaborate to give a more satisfactory account of what happens when, for instance, we feel our way into works of fiction. The novelist and critic Richard Powers has recently posed the question this way: "Why wouldn't a literary scholar want to know everything that neurologists are discovering about the way the brain works?"[16]

This book affirms that the time is ripe for such an endeavor, and that the stimulating half century of William James's adult life, roughly 1860 to 1910, is the most fruitful period in which to ground such an inquiry. The chapters that follow make the case for the centrality of emotion to American literary realism, and to literary study more broadly construed, by taking into account the affective enlistments of fictional works by Oliver Wendell Holmes, Mark Twain, S. Weir Mitchell, Charlotte Perkins Gilman, Kate Chopin, Harold Frederic, and Henry James. As we shall see, cultural developments of the late nineteenth century—including the emergence of evolutionary biology, physiological psychology, neurology, pragmatist philosophy, formalist aesthetics, comparative anthropology, and mental therapeutics—were crucial to a new way of thinking about the interanimation of the human mind and body, in which emotion was increasingly understood to mediate our experience of the exterior world. Realist writers, attentive to the corporeal components of human perception, sought both to represent in their work and to exemplify in their readers the way that, in the words of the contemporary neuroscientist Antonio Damasio, "emotions play out in the theater of the body."[17] Indeed, the recent work of Damasio and other twenty-first-century investigators of embodied emotion draws on ideas about the human nervous system that were developed during the second half of the nineteenth century.

I argue that literary realists were first and foremost committed to elaborating what William James (whose writing and thinking provide a cornerstone for this study) described as "feelings of reality."[18] The story fleshed out in these chapters is, therefore, integrally concerned with the philosophy and science of the period—to which the writers discussed made active contributions—as well as its literature and aesthetic theory. So while this study engages with a wide range of writings and genres, it is not properly a book "about" literature and science, or literature and philosophy. Its multidisciplinary nature emerges from the shifting historical and cultural topography of the late nineteenth century, a period in which—as figures such as Oliver Wendell Holmes and Charlotte Perkins Gilman attest—fields of knowledge were in a process of uneven disaggregation and emergent institutionalization.

After Chapter 1, which provides a theoretical and historical overview of the project, each chapter analyzes a set of texts from a specific historical moment that are united in treating a particular affective response. These "focal feelings" can be situated within the broad categories of emotional experience articulated by the turn-of-the-century psychologist Théodule Ribot, whose thinking was influenced by the writings of both James and Holmes. In *The Psychology of the Emotions* (1897) Ribot suggested that while we have myriad sorts of sensations, generally speaking, states of feeling can be grouped into four principle types: a *painful* state, a state of *fear,* a state of *excitability,* and an *agreeable* state. To the list of four anatomized in Ribot's text is added a fifth, to which he alludes: a state of *wonder,* the feeling that most vividly unites the aesthetic, the philosophical, and the scientific in describing a particular stance of open-ended interest in the world outside the self. Wonder is exemplary, to quote Ribot, as "not being provoked by, but, on the contrary provoking [the intellectual state]."[19]

Chapter 1 provides a conceptual genealogy for a new understanding of literary realism. This chapter argues that attentiveness to the neurological and affective components of human experience downplays the usual critical preoccupation with mimesis, referentiality, and fixity and instead emphasizes mediation, relationality, and above all *motion*. "From this standpoint," Ribot wrote, "feelings and emotions are no longer a superficial manifestation, a simple efflorescence; they plunge into the individual's depths; they have their roots in needs and instincts, that is to say, in *movements*."[20] This chapter examines how a set of founding dualisms, which became most firmly established for the humanities in the early decades of the twentieth century within the influential discourses of psychoanalysis and modernism, have tended both to structure and to limit our critical conversations about literary realism and, more broadly, the ends of literary studies and the nature of aesthetic experience. These include dichotomies between thoughts and things, between the physical and the psychological, between voluntary and involuntary actions, between thinking and feeling, between the public and the private, between realism and sentimentalism, and between the scientific and the aesthetic. New work in a variety of fields, including cognitive science, affect theory, aesthetics, and neuroscience, provides a set of tools for recovering the ways that literary realists, along with their contemporaries in philosophy and the emergent sciences of the body, actively challenged a number of conceptual divisions that had been central to the Western philosophical tradition.

Chapter 2, which centers on the "painful state" articulated by Ribot, and is the first of the affective case studies treated in this book, examines the earliest of the self-proclaimed "medicated novels" of Oliver Wendell Holmes Sr. Critics have puzzled over the generic status of *Elsie Venner: A Romance of Destiny* (1861), noting its focus on embodied feelings, even as it almost ludicrously undercuts sentimental conventions by creating a hot-tempered, part-snake heroine. By reading *Elsie Venner* in light of Holmes's proto-epidemiological study of women dying in childbirth, I show how the physician-novelist exposed the dangers of what Marianne Noble has called sentimental masochism, an epistemology predicated on too much fellow feeling.[21] Holmes revealed that for sympathetic doctors, "touching scenes" of maternal distress authorized actual touching, which in turn passed along deadly disease to parturient patients. In his fictional and scientific writings, Holmes demonstrated that the pity enlisted by statistical data, in being ontologically agnostic, provided therapeutic insight in spite of medical ignorance. Holmes, in short, developed a physically detached yet affectively engaged mode for "realizing" material connections among what appeared as disconnected, incomparable personal tragedies.

The seemingly oxymoronic conception of statistical pity brought together two ways of apprehending the world: the abstractly intellectual and the viscerally emotional. Both were for Holmes essential to human intelligence, and also to a literary realism predicated on preserving and treasuring, as well as representing, individual lives. Indeed, attentiveness to the compatibility of these modes of mindfulness forced nineteenth-century *accoucheurs* to turn their often pejorative attention away from their dying patients and diagnose themselves as unwitting murderers. This contributed to what I, following Ian Hacking, term a "forensics of self," in which the seemingly detached perceiver comes to recognize his involvement in what he had, ostensibly, been merely reporting.[22] The novelistic practice of Oliver Wendell Holmes, in emphasizing both the passive and the constructive aspects of "realization," troubles the distinction between objective and subjective experience that has subtended many critical accounts of American literary realism.

Chapter 3 explicitly engages Ribot's "state of fear" and its relation to knowledge. Emily Dickinson famously asserted, "I like a look of Agony / Because I know it's true"; or, in the words of the nineteenth-century physiologist Xavier Bichat, "If you wish to know whether the pain is real, examine the pulse."[23] Through a reading of the psychophysiology of thinkers such as Oliver Wendell Holmes, Thomas Laycock, and Herbert Spencer, and the medico-legal debate over a baffling injury known as "railway spine," this chapter argues that literary realists' conception of an unconscious embodied memory contributes to the historical construction of a modern understanding of trauma. In *The Senses and the Intellect* (1855) the physiologist Alexander Bain affirmed that "the organ of mind is not the brain by itself; it is the brain, nerves, muscles, and organs of sense." A memory does not, by this account, consist solely in the retrieval of a mental image: rather, "the train of feeling is re-instated on the same parts as first vibrated to the original stimulus."[24]

For writers and scientists, railway accidents provided the exemplary catalyst for such a "train of feeling": it both figured and enacted modernity's impingement on the body, producing fear that reverberated along the spinal column, mediating between body and mind. Only after the Civil War did neurologists begin to speculate that "male hysteria"—which, in lieu of a uterus, had seemed a contradiction in terms—was prompted not by wandering wombs or wounded body parts but by extreme fright. Realist literature, such as Holmes's *A Mortal Antipathy* (1885) and Kate

Chopin's "The Story of an Hour" (1894), used narrative to bring together the corporeal etiology of physical trauma (wombs and wounds) with its emotional counterpart (psychological fear) to produce a conception of "impression" that translated a physiological experience into a mental state by way of the autonomic nervous system. Nineteenth-century literary realists, in mapping the experiential terrain between private bodies and public events, helped to engender a new form of subjectivity in which external mediation—the forensic narrative—worked to authenticate and bring to consciousness bodily feelings.

Chapter 4 shifts the focus to Ribot's "state of excitability," as exemplified by the neurasthenic housewife and the apprehensive soldier, and analyzes how a range of writers and thinkers conceived of even the most banal actions as requiring physical exertion that was at once cerebral and corporeal. As the philosopher John Dewey wrote in his "Psychology of Effort," "Surely everyone is familiar, in dealing with unfamiliar occupations, . . . [with a sensation] of effort, out of all proportion to the objective significance of the end."[25] Mundane concerns, such as worrying over home decorations, are recast as miniature "struggle[s] for realization" (155) that are embodied, mindful, and constructive. Nervousness, in Darwinian terms, registered the creative attempt—often conservative, but potentially rebellious—to bring a person and her environment into harmonious relation. In elaborating the paradigm, at once evolutionary and neurological, that underlies this thinking, Chapter 4 unsettles the now traditional opposition of Charlotte Perkins Gilman and her nerve doctor, S. Weir Mitchell. They, in fact, agreed that the discordant design of the middle-class home damaged its inhabitants in ways analogous to the way war had injured the shell-shocked Civil War soldiers Mitchell had treated. Both housewife and soldier suffered from a discrepancy between a familiar image—a happy home, a noble field of battle—and jarring sensory stimuli: "The two sets of sensations," Dewey noted, "refuse to coincide," thereby producing "divided activity of the self" (154, 155).

In pathological cases of nervousness, therefore, the projections of mind and the experience of the body remain disparate, unsubsumed in a coherent "whole." The psychologist Pierre Janet, accordingly, instituted what could be termed art homeopathy: small doses of aesthetic work (such as learning to play the piano) that reintegrated a person's sensations, thereby producing the embodied experience of calm attendant on what Dewey called "effective realization" (155). Janet's attentiveness to mind-body connections led him to almost precisely the therapeutic regimen exemplified in Gilman's career as a writer and activist, while also suggesting ways of attending to the rhythms of dissociation and realization in nineteenth-century literary works that have been cast as too aesthetic to be realistic (e.g. *The Red Badge of Courage*) or too realistic to be aesthetic (e.g. "The Yellow Wallpaper").

Turning from the redesigning effort registered by nervousness, the "agreeable state" described by Ribot is at the core of Chapter 5, which argues that the novels of Kate Chopin and Harold Frederic, in exploring the psycho-sensuous phenomenology of rapture, complement the work of William James in psychology and Charles Sanders Peirce in semiotics. Moreover, in portraying characters who are intensely aroused by the sound of piano-playing, these authors reference an influential nineteenth-century debate over the representational status of instrumental or "absolute" music: music detached from any referential context (such as a battlefield or religious service) and unaccompanied by the human voice. Physiologists and psychologists of the day believed that melody offered a corporeal conduit to the wellsprings of emotion, giving it morally questionable access to the most intimate workings of the human body and mind. Music was understood to be an aesthetic mode that operated in terms of realization rather than referentiality: as the eclectic writer Edmund Gurney argued in *The Power of Sound* (1880), musical compositions "imply no external fact at all. Their function is to *present* not to represent, and their message has no direct reference to the world outside them."[26]

Chopin and Frederic tested out the formal features of music—the emphasis on repetition, rhythm, and the sound component of language—to produce prose that emulates music in its physiological effects on readers. While Frederic ends up depicting the ironic rhythm of illumination and damnation that characterized the Sick Soul (William James's term), Chopin, by contrast, was inspired by the poetics of Walt Whitman, the philosophy of Arthur Schopenhauer and Richard Wagner, and Darwin's theory of emotional expression in her association of music, sensual expansion, and literary production. Chopin's work, which cultivates relaxing transports in readers, is importantly placed in relation to the broader cultural interest in what James dubbed "mind cure": a psychophysical therapeutic movement, developed in the United States and promoted largely by women, which reached its most lasting institutional form in the Christian Science of Mary Baker Eddy.

The sixth and final chapter moves beyond pleasure to the "state of wonder." Philip Fisher has described the "horizon line" of wonder, a state that suspends the wonderer between "what we already know— our familiar world" and "what is potentially knowable, but not yet known."[27] In this chapter I argue that Henry James, the nineteenth century's deft literary geographer of this epistemological territory, maps the profound cultural and corporeal effects of aesthetic experience. James restores the strangeness to modern social relations through the receptive presence of Milly Theale, in whom reified social systems, ossified domestic relations, and deadened works of art become dangerously alive. It is the ripeness of the American heiress's wonder, and not just the heaviness of her purse, that leaves her prey to the occult intrigues of English society.

James, in short, isolates a potentially pathological form of one kind of aesthetic encounter: a social terrorism to which the eminent Harvard physiologist Walter Cannon gave the name "voodoo death," which he described as "the fatal power of the imagination working through unmitigated terror."[28] The Jamesian aesthetic mode—what Henry referred to as "merciful indirection" and what his brother William put down as the maddening refusal to actually tell the story—is from one perspective the only compassionate stance when words and even thoughts might impinge directly on the material of the world and the bodies of the persons who occupy it. The contemporary philosopher Daniel Dennett echoes James when he speaks of the uniquely human capacity "to wonder the wonders," to be compelled, rather than solely terrified, by the presence of otherness—especially other wonderers.[29]

The chapters proceed chronologically: the earliest literary works discussed were published just after Charles Darwin's study *The Origin of Species by Means of Natural Selection* in 1859, and the latest appeared in print a few years before Sigmund Freud gave his first U.S. lectures, at Clark University in 1909. The feelings that structure this book, along with the literary works discussed, can be situated along a continuum of increasing complexity: with the comparatively artless writing of Oliver Wendell Holmes and the primal responses of Elsie Venner at one end of the scale and at the other the sophisticated novels of the mature Henry James and the exquisite consciousness of Milly Theale. There may also appear to be an increasing disembodiment in this progression, from the rudimentary impulses of pain and fear, through the more "civilized" feeling of nervousness,[30] to the rarified experiences of pleasure and wonder. Yet, if we keep in mind the structure of preservation and emergence essential to an evolutionary perspective (a perspective shared by the nineteenth-century writers in this study), we can temper the impulse to translate such gradations into essential differences. Rather than outgrown or discarded, the modes of feeling described in earlier chapters can be understood to be modulated and layered, such that the primitive, embodied reactions of a snake-girl are discernible even in the subtle mind games of a Jamesian heroine.

Rethinking Emotion

To return to the essay with which I began: in "The Affective Fallacy," published over a half century ago, Wimsatt and Beardsley astutely noted that their anxiety about affective criticism rested on a set of assumptions about the nature of emotion, assumptions predicated on a strong distinction between mind and body, and between cultural processes and biological ones. "A question about the relation of language to objects of emotion," they observed, "is a shadow and index of another question, about the status of emotions themselves" (26). For Wimsatt and Beardsley, the status of emotions was structured by a paradox, one that yoked together the timeless and the contingent. In their view, the absolutely certain thing about emotion was that it was not stable: it did not stay still, from moment to moment, person to person, culture to culture. Yet in the past few decades, this equation has been undergoing revision. New scholarly and scientific work, in fact, comes close to reversing the New Critics' position on what is timeless about emotion (i.e. our understanding of it) and what is contingent (i.e. the bodily operations of emotion). Drawing on evolutionary theory, these emerging accounts suggest that while the cultural significance of feelings, along with rules about displaying them, may fluctuate over time, the actual corporeal architecture of emotional experience—almost universal to members of a species, and often highly similar across species—has evolved so slowly over the course of millennia as to be, in the limited timeframe of human history, practically stable.[31]

Findings in these fields, moreover, are challenging the received wisdom about the function of emotion that has subtended—often in unacknowledged form—accounts of the relations between feeling and culture: that, as for the New Critics, emotions are of the body, therefore precultural, hopelessly private and inwardly focused, opposed to or distorting of cognition, incommunicable; or that, as for cultural critics, emotions are of the body, therefore culturally constructed, essentially public and outwardly determined, expressive of social meanings, a site of social hegemony and control. In twenty-first-century work focused within but not limited to the sciences, emotion is being understood as embodied but not mindless; as culturally conditioned in its expression but not in its biological substrate; as a vital component of the operations of consciousness but not identical to thinking; as embedded deep within the body but nonetheless essential to an individual's flourishing in the external world.[32] Does emotion's role in mediating between body and mind, between thinking and doing, and between self and world produce cultural difficulties for expression, translation, communication, and the conveying of meanings? Of course. But, as the philosopher Daniel Dennett observes, "if you can't keep a secret there is little role for communication to play."[33] Far from posing a threat to culture, as Wimsatt and Beardsley feared, or exacerbating divisiveness within culture, as the Science Wars seem to have done, it is my contention that attentiveness to our emotional responses to experiences, aesthetic and otherwise, helps to provide the ground for—even as it sustains the need for—human collaboration and communication.

Moreover, as I discuss in the following pages, the insights of other disciplines can actually help us to revisit one of literary studies' intransigent questions. For if feeling is essential to thinking, then serious criticism must take into account the affective aspects of literary works. If our bodies, even across cultures, are more similar than different in their capacity to apprehend, reflect on, and modify our worlds, then scholarly accounts of our relationship to literary works must expand beyond an understanding of meaning narrowly construed and attend also to the corporeal textures of aesthetic experience. While challenging the New Critics' disciplinary jingoism, as when they assert that "the discerning literary critic has his insuperable advantage over the subject of the laboratory experiment and over the tabulator of the subject's responses" (34), a form of criticism that takes seriously what the sciences can tell us about our emotions does not abandon its essential concern with literature, interpretation, cultural practice, and historical contingency. It does, however, have an expanded body of knowledge, and a wider set of conceptual and methodological tools from which to select. By actively drawing on the findings of the sciences, an affectively attuned criticism is freed up to attend more rigorously, and with less embarrassment, to the emotional and aesthetic entailments of literary works. It is the premise of this book that these new ways of framing the relations among mind, body, and emotion, if employed judiciously and with the nuances made possible by cultural critique and the sorts of exegesis intrinsic to literary study, can enable an array of exciting new possibilities for critical study and promote potential collaborations across disciplines.

CHAPTER ONE

"The Zest, the Tingle, the Excitement of Reality"

In the mind's eye, neurobiology and art meet.

—DIANE ACKERMAN, *AN ALCHEMY OF MIND* (2004)

At first blush, it may seem puzzling that the aging Henry James included the early serialized novel *Roderick Hudson* (1876) in his collected works. Others were passed over, including his first novel *Watch and Ward* and the now classic *Bostonians*. Critics have noted *Roderick Hudson*'s melodramatic tendencies, and James himself acknowledged that the book, which traces the brief rise and protracted decline of a histrionic young sculptor in Rome, barely "escapes . . . with its life."[1] Yet escape it did, supplemented by the first of James's magisterial Prefaces, to serve as the inaugural volume of the author's authoritative New York Edition (1907–1909). What, then, did the Master of the realist novel see in this youthful "experiment" (45)?[2]

Its importance for James, intriguingly, resided in its most obvious flaw: that despite the titular centrality of Hudson, the novel's primary subject was in fact the sculptor's self-effacing sponsor. "The center of interest throughout 'Roderick,'" James wrote thirty years later, "is in Rowland Mallet's consciousness" (45). Mallet, however, provided more than a passive lens through which to view the action of the plot; the "total adventure," James discerned, was "the very drama of that consciousness" (45). Unlike the self-absorbed sculptor, who "was not remarkable for throwing himself into the sentiments of others" (384), Mallet was just like readers of novels: "what happened to him was above all to feel certain things happening to others" (45–46).

Looking back over a lifetime's work, James realized that in *Roderick Hudson* he had gotten something importantly right: he had recognized that feelings weren't simply *about* things or happenings. The feelings *were* things, or more precisely, they themselves were "happenings," effecting a transit between self and world: "this *movement* really being quite the stuff of one's thesis" (46; emphasis added). It wasn't just that Rowland Mallet, who "shrank from the imperious passions" (120), was "moved" in the manner familiar from sentimental novels; rather, Rowland was himself in motion, his international excursions indexing his itinerant consciousness. (Similarly, in the preface to *The Princess Cassamassima,* sister volume to *Roderick,* James acknowledged that "this fiction proceeded quite directly, during the first year of a long residence in London, from the habit and the interest of walking the streets"). James recognized in the preface to *Roderick,* "I was dealing after all, essentially with an Action" (4). Like the author's, Mallet's perceptions were not just cerebral but also motor and sensory: he embarked "with an irresistible tremor into the world," tracing a "sentimental circuit" (317) around Rome and among his friends. The creative center of James's early novel lay not with the aspiring artist but with the peripatetic perceiver.

Roderick Hudson's plot begins with the premise that Mallet, a man with money but without passion ("I am not inflammable"), would live vicariously by sponsoring a young genius (53). But it is Mallet's slow-smoldering feeling for the sculptor's rejected fiancée that brings about the novel's climax: Roderick Hudson, for the first time, registers the intense life of feeling of the diffident Mallet, who produces a "visible, palpable pang" (377) by revealing the object of his affection. The sculptor's new knowledge precipitates a unique moment of self-seeing, as he realizes how hideously oblivious he's been to his friend's feelings: "'It's very strange!' said Roderick presently. 'It's like something in a novel'" (377). Roderick Hudson, belatedly, learns to be a reader of feelings, which is to say a reader of himself—which is to say, a reader of novels.

James in *Roderick Hudson* had embodied what the philosopher John Dewey would later codify in *Art as Experience* (1934): the insight that in perception, as in art, "*Emotion is the moving and cementing force* . . . giving qualitative unity to materials externally disparate and dissimilar."[3] As Roderick Hudson's artistic production dwindled to a trickle and then stopped altogether, Rowland Mallet's affective life expanded: "He grew passionately, unreasoningly fond of all Roman sights and sensations. . . . It was a large, vague, idle, half profitless emotion, of which perhaps the most pertinent thing that may be said is that it brought with it a sort of relaxed acceptance of the present, the actual, the sensuous—of life on the terms of the moment" (159). Mallet's sensuous appreciation was not merely reflective but also compositional; it pulled together random bits of perception, sights and sounds and attitudes, into a unified, resonant experience. Detached neither from the body nor from the bustle of common life, the motions of a labile consciousness were both somatic and aesthetic, which is what John Dewey meant when he said that art is "prefigured in the very processes of living" (24).

The implication of common life and aesthetic experience helps to explain the generic strangeness of James's 1907 Preface, with its amalgamation of autobiography and critique, memory and manifesto. For despite the documentary promise of its first sentence, which suggests that James will report the details of the novel's original creation and publication, the Preface focuses instead on the present compositional moment, on the now-elderly writer's feelings, memories, associations, and regrets as he reengages with his first published novel. The Preface traces the "upheavals of his sensibility" (47) attendant on "renewing acquaintance with the book after a quarter of a century" (35). The Preface to *Roderick Hudson* is itself cast as a miniature adventure novel featuring the exploits of an exploring consciousness—James's— which "embarks, rash adventurer, under the 'star' of representation" (40), weathers the "ache of fear" (36) at the potential "wreck" (42) of its "vessel" (36), and finally basks in the "strange charm" "begotten within the very covers of the book" (46). The detached author is reborn as buffeted reader, judging the work through his evolving apprehension of its ability to generate "upheavals" yet bring about compositional "equilibrium" (45). John Dewey distinguished between works of art— which, like any emotive object, such as Rome was for Mallet, *provide* experience—and works of science, which "can be used as *directions* by which one may arrive at the experience" (84). James's Prefaces, remarkably, do both: they provide an aesthetic experience precisely by giving directions. Simultaneously enlisting readers to the narrative experience of the Preface and instructing them about his own experience of the novel, James "makes his criticism essentially active" (42). In the terms of the nineteenth century, in short, he makes his criticism *emotional*.

The New York Edition of *Roderick Hudson,* which textually shuttles the reader from 1907 to 1876, provides a flexible set of terms for an experience-based, full-bodied emotive realism that emerges in the literature and science of the late nineteenth century, as well as in its philosophy and aesthetic theory. In some respects, Henry James might seem an unlikely figure to inaugurate such a study. While undeniably aesthetic, his novels have been read as helping to codify elite as opposed to "common" culture, as concerned with the mind rather than the body, as detached from the chaotic urban scene in the United States and centered instead on the rarified social forms of English and European culture. James's pronouncements on the novel, moreover, have been seen as committed to a formalism that is oblique to the imperatives of realism, leading some to construe his work—especially his last three novels—as early instances of literary modernism.[4] Influential critics such as Leon Edel, Shoshana Felman, and Kaja Silverman have also nudged many readers toward Freudian readings of James's work and life, again situating his influence at the commencement of the twentieth century rather than the zenith of the nineteenth.[5]

As this glancing reading of *Roderick Hudson* suggests, however, there is another story to be unearthed, one that features James's work as a crucial site for correcting prevalent understandings of literary realism that associate it with "cultural work" rather than aesthetics, with objectivity rather than subjectivity, and with the rational mind instead of the feeling body. In her remarkable book *Psychosomatic: Feminism and the Neurological Body* (2004), Elizabeth Wilson has noted that "neurological theories have been considered too reductive, and evolutionary theories too interested in phylogenetic determinism" to be of use or interest to many feminist and cultural critics addressing questions of embodiment.[6] Yet serious attention to ideas and practices that emerged in the late nineteenth century, both aesthetic and scientific, enables a dynamic account of literary realism that places the neurologically networked human body, with its astonishing capacities for thought and appreciation, at its center. Henry James, in directly engaging with questions about the affecting nature of experience and art's privileged connection to the sources of human emotion and sensuality, provides literary studies with a productive challenge: to expand our account of realist works to encompass their sensory as well as their intellectual potency, and to tax our resistance to powerful ideas and discourses that have seemed alien to our commitment to culture and contingency. Serious engagement with work being done now in a range of fields helps to illuminate a central point: that the persistent attention to both the object world and to bodily feeling in the work of James and other realist writers is above all traffic in emotion.

This chapter is organized into three sections and lays the conceptual groundwork for demonstrating the centrality of feeling to literary realism. The first section condenses key findings on the links among emotion, embodiment, and aesthetics currently being developed not just in literary and cultural studies but also in the neurosciences, philosophy, and affect theory. This scholarship offers a way to rethink a set of dualisms that have structured critical conversations about literary realism. Contemporary thinkers such as Daniel Dennett and Elaine Scarry, with their nuanced conceptions of the relationship between mind and body, and mind and world, provide a framework for conceiving of the literature of the late nineteenth century as projections, rather than just representations, of human sentience. The second section turns to the volatile decades following the U.S. Civil War to examine how emotion was increasingly conceived in terms of physiological movement rather than psychological states. In the influential words of William James, professor of philosophy and elder brother to Henry James, "no shade of emotion, however slight, should be without a bodily reverberation."[7] Writers, scientists, philosophers, and physicians of the late nineteenth century understood the human nervous system to be analogous to, and indeed influenced by, systems of rapid communication and transportation such as the train and the telegraph. The commotion of modernity posed unique challenges to the delicate equilibrium of body and mind, while feelings were understood to provide a crucial conduit, albeit one that was easily damaged or derailed, through which individuals could negotiate a volatile environment.

The third and final section of this chapter discusses how these ideas underwrote the understanding of experience theorized most fully in the radical empiricism of William James, as well as in the philosophy of his University of Chicago colleague John Dewey. What Dewey called "the science of the realization of the universe in and through the individual" (what might be termed a psychophysical phenomenology) provides a way of thinking about how works of literary realism enlist rather than merely represent experiences.[8] The reverberative humor of Mark Twain's *Adventures of Huckleberry Finn* (1885) is here exemplary, for it replaces concerns about referentiality with an emphasis on *realization:* the coming to consciousness of an experience, which entails being "moved" in the dual sense of emotionally engaged and repositioned with respect to the world.[9] A constructive process, realization is dynamically present in the ups and downs of readerly emotion—what Dewey referred to as "the development or . . . mediation of an experience"[10]—that are depicted, elicited, and brought to consciousness by works of literary realism.

Toward a New Conceptual Genealogy for American Literary Realism

I begin with a simple premise: that critics have not taken embodied emotions seriously enough in their accounts of the cultural work of American literary realism, and that theorists of affect haven't taken the science (and to some extent, the literature) of the late nineteenth century seriously enough in their accounts of the role of feeling in aesthetic experience and practical judgment.

The first concern—that the study of literary realism has seemed immune to a renewed critical interest in aesthetics and emotional response—has obvious roots in the "Affective Fallacy" described by Monroe Beardsley and W. K. Wimsatt, who warned against reducing literary criticism to the study of "tears, prickles, or other physiological symptoms."[11] More recently, however, the tendency to eschew realism's emotional entailments has been reinforced by an alignment made between the epistemological status of realist works and a certain version of scientific positivism. Unlike eighteenth-century novels, which critics have examined in terms of sympathetic identification,[12] works of literary realism have been cast as immune to affective concerns. This critical position is exemplified by Lawrence Rothfield's *Vital Signs: Medical Realism in Nineteenth-Century Fiction* (1992) and George Levine's *Dying to Know: Scientific Epistemology and Narrative in Victorian England* (2002). In what Rothfield identifies as "medical realism," "a new, absolute gap, an ironic distance, must open up between the knowing subject (doctor or writer) and the object of knowledge (patient or character) . . . a silencing of one's sympathy so as to permit the disease to speak for itself."[13] In this account, affective disengagement was a prerequisite for objectivity, which in turn authorized the mimetic accuracy of realist fiction.

The central imperative of scientific inquiry, in these accounts, is the eradication of subjectivity—what Levine terms the "story of selflessness."[14] This pose of affective neutrality has, in turn, been mapped onto nineteenth-century fiction: the novelistic focus on detailed descriptions of objects and settings is likened to the scientist's detached observation of material facts, while intimate characterization is likened to a form of diagnosis. As Nancy Glazener argues in *Reading for Realism* (1997), "The particulars of a novel functioned like a scientific model, distilling each phenomenon down to its principles of operation."[15] Writers in these accounts are cast as scientists manqué, providing glimpses of facts and objects and miming a positivist commitment to detachment, disinterest, and dispassion.[16]

This formulation, however, led to an impasse: poststructuralist skepticism about the possibility of mimesis or disinterested knowledge consigned the project of literary realism, construed in these terms, to the dubious status of exemplary failure.[17] The failure, as discerned by scholars of the 1980s and 1990s, lay in two apparently unbridgeable gaps: one between mind and matter, what Eric Sundquist described as "an increasing discrepancy between the figurative life of the mind and the literal life of the material"; the other between representations and reality, what Louis Budd termed the "'disjunctures' between rhetoric and actuality in American life."[18] Out of the ashes of referentiality, however, rose the phoenix of ideology: a number of critics have argued that middle-class authors, writing under the sign of realism and ostensibly engaged in the (failed) quest to represent reality, were in fact (quite successfully) constructing it in the interest of their own class, gender, and race affiliations.[19]

The second problem in contemporary critical discourse—that renewed interest in affect and aesthetics has tended to bypass the late nineteenth century[20]—can be traced to a discomfort with the materialism of that period's emergent scientific practices: medicine's increasing commitment to a germ model of disease; physiology's distressing dependence on tortured dogs and decorticated frogs; neurology's overemphasis on reflex arcs, the therapeutic use of electricity, and brain localization; psychology's prurient focus on double consciousness, sexual inversion, and hysteria; mental healing's weird fascination with trance states, mesmerism, and spirit possession; and anthropology's fascination with the "exotic" practices of foreign cultures, such as voodoo death.

The relative shortage of critical work that takes seriously the insights of the late nineteenth century's sciences of the body is to some extent matched by a perception that the literature of the period, interesting for its incarnation of cultural practices, is itself somewhat epistemologically naïve, aesthetically crude, or biologically reductionist. (R. W. B. Lewis captured this sentiment in his aphoristic put-down of the novel *Elsie Venner:* "while Emerson and Whitman were trying their best to convert medical facts into inspirational poetry, [Oliver Wendell] Holmes was converting a literary form into a vehicle for a case history.")[21] Indeed, despite the republication in recent decades of hundreds of overlooked literary works, one must search library shelves to find copies of the once-popular novels of Holmes or Silas Weir Mitchell. A range of more critically acclaimed works, such as "The Yellow Wallpaper" and *The Awakening,* have been read less for their philosophical, affective, or aesthetic contributions than as provocative media for approaching cultural questions. Philosophers drawing on works of literature (or philosophically inclined literary critics) seeking to theorize the relationship between aesthetics and affect have tended to focus on the eighteenth century, or with Aristotle in the fourth century B.C., and to jump forward to the twentieth. This is the case in notable studies by Martha Nussbaum, Rei Terada, and Charles Altieri: Greek philosophy prepares us to consider James Joyce's *Ulysses (Upheavals of Thought),* Jean-Jacques Rousseau is preliminary to an analysis of Jacques Derrida *(Feeling in Theory),* and discussion of Immanuel Kant frames discussion of W. B. Yeats *(The Particulars of Rapture).*[22] The emphasis on modernist and postmodernist texts has tended to marginalize the science and literature of the nineteenth century and to sustain theorizations of affect that center on the mind.

With a few notable exceptions, the leap over the nineteenth century has entailed a leap over the demands, questions, and possibilities posed by an understanding of the emotions that is less focused on mental contents and capacities than on bodily reactions. Recently, scholars in a number of fields have begun to rethink this tendency. Elizabeth Wilson, in her study of the neurological underpinnings of psychoanalysis, asks the provocative question "How can a neurosis not be acquainted with the nervous system?" following her observation that cultural critics' interest in hysteria has tended to be matched by an equally intense aversion to talking about bodily pathologies in biological terms.[23] Similarly, Bill Brown has noted how "the fetishization of the subject, the image, the word" has tended to foreclose for literary studies precisely the sort of inquiry Wilson sketches.[24] There has been a troubling propensity, in short, to assert a disciplinary mind/body divide: to affirm an implicit division between rhetorical and cultural analysis on the one hand (the *modus operandi* of scholars in the humanities) and empirical and practical inquiry on the other (the province of investigators in the sciences).[25]

This study, therefore, makes its own historical leap, which is also a conceptual one: over the intellectual behemoth posed by Freud and modernism back to the unabashedly materialist nineteenth-century understanding of the embodied mind. For as Alexander Bain wrote in *The Senses and the Intellect* (1855), "The organ of mind is not the brain by itself; it is the brain, nerves, muscles, and organs of sense."[26] To that list we might add that the organ of mind includes objects of human construction and imagination, such as books. Drawing on the work of Charles Darwin, evolutionary biologists have pointed out that the brain evolved with a significant space limitation: the human skull, which—despite harboring novel aptitudes for such things as language and love—had to remain diminutive enough to pass through a woman's pelvis. As Diane Ackerman elegantly puts it in *An Alchemy of Mind* (2004), "What the brain really needed was space without volume. So it took a radical leap and did something unparalleled in the history of life on Earth. It began storing information and memories outside itself, on stone, papyrus, paper, computer chips and film. . . . 'Are you out of your mind?!' we sometimes demand. The answer is yes, we are all out of our minds, which we left long ago when our brain needed more room to do its dance" (10). Works of literary realism, despite the documentary promise of the term, are not photographic representations of a real world elsewhere; they are condensations and expansions of human thought, sentience, and experience. At the center of American literary realism is a conception of the intelligent, feeling human body that militates against overly simplistic distinctions between objective and subjective experience, and between everyday practical life and rarified aesthetic encounters. In a not insignificant way, works of literary realism contain real experiences.

Through analysis of literary works in relation to other scientific and cultural materials, this study focuses on a series of specific affective responses—pity, fear, nervousness, pleasure, and wonder—to trace an emotive realism that has tended to elude twentieth- and twenty-first-century readers. New scholarship in three often overlapping areas has helped to elucidate a historical, literary, and conceptual context for American literary realism: in *the neurosciences,* which draw on the insights of nineteenth-century science to alert us to the centrality of feeling to cognition, and the relevance of bodily response to the experience of reading; in *literary and cultural studies,* where the important feminist recovery of sentimental works in the 1970s and 1980s has been followed by an explosion of scholarship on affect and theories of emotional experience; and in *the history and philosophy of aesthetics,* where thinkers influenced by John Dewey are challenging conceptions of aesthetic experience that cast it as hopelessly elitist, private, transcendental, and apolitical, thus at odds with the contingencies of culture. In what follows I discuss how writers in these thriving fields have paved the way for rethinking a series of widely held antinomies: between subjects and objects, between mind and body, between emotion and reason, and between art and life.

1. *Subjects and objects.* The very concept of objectivity is predicated on a strong distinction between human agents and objects to be known. What Bill Brown has recently dubbed "thing theory," however, offers a way of rethinking the human engagement with the material of the world as mutually self-constituting. Subjectivity, from this perspective, is itself "objective"—or more precisely, object-oriented—in that it emerges in relation to things: "Our habitual interactions with objects both bring them to life and impose order on that life; our habits both mark time and allow us to escape from time, as we perform the present in concert with the future and the past."[27] The ground-breaking work in this area was Elaine Scarry's extraordinary book *The Body in Pain: The Making and Unmaking of the World* (1985). In it, Scarry articulates what she terms "the arc of making," the emergence of intentional objects—whether books or chairs or vacuum pumps—out of the bodily experience of human vulnerability. A made object, she argues, is not merely the material counterpart of the mind's vision, forever detached from the corporeally situated longings and fears that precipitated its creation. Rather, it "will be found to contain within its interior a material record of the nature of human sentience out of which it in turn derives its power to act on sentience and recreate it."[28] Such resonant objects Scarry calls artifacts, projections of the physical body: clothing, for example, embodies and distributes the attributes of skin, while the "print-

ing press . . . libraries, films, tape recordings, and Xerox machines are all materializations of the elusive capacity for *memory*" (283). "Aliveness" is not merely projected onto but infused into objects in the world—embodied in texts and tools—thereby *"depriv[ing] the external world of the privilege of being inanimate"* (285). Thing theory helps to illuminate literary realism's engagement with the material world as importantly sensory and affective.

From a neurological perspective, the animation of the nonhuman world is productive, and it embraces entities—such as plants—that might appear immune to such extensions of sentience. The philosopher of mind Daniel Dennett explains the tendency toward anthropomorphism in evolutionary terms, as an essential imaginative tool linked to the human capacity for language: "With the evolution in our species of language and the varieties of reflectiveness that language permits, we emerged with the ability to wonder . . . about the minds of other entities. These wonders, naively conducted by our ancestors, led to *animism*, the idea that each moving thing has a mind or soul."[29] Dennett urges that attributing subjectivity to such things as flowers (which we "trick" into blooming) should not be discounted as an atavistic throwback to primitive belief systems but should rather be understood as an active part of our neural makeup. It is a critical "aid to comprehension," a way of predicting what things will do and how we should handle them. As literary critic Lori Merish has observed, nineteenth-century culture was rife with homely instances of animistic thinking, which she terms "sentimental materialism": witness Harriet Beecher Stowe's belief that "domestic objects . . . should not be (merely) 'used' or displayed; they should be cared for, and loved."[30] What, from the point of view of everyday dualism, might look eccentric or wrongheaded, becomes visible—in light of Dennett's evolutionary perspective—as instructive "slips of mind," tiny cognitions that are also pocket-sized deconstructions of our customary ontological distinction between objects and subjects, and between meaningless materiality and meaning-bestowing human thought.

For nineteenth-century readers, things were neither essentially inert (a positivist position) nor merely fabrications of mind, whether human or divine (an idealist position). As William James urged, objects are precisely the "common property" of social life, the sine qua non for any "meeting of the minds": "Practically, then, our minds meet in a world of objects which they share in common, which would still be there, if one or several of the minds would be destroyed."[31] Simply to dismiss the mild animisms of everyday life as mistakes, or as instructive solely in individualized psychological terms, overlooks how literary realists and their audiences conceived of both intelligence and the world of objects.

2. *The mind and the body*. Critics, creating an implicit mind/body distinction, have tended to emphasize the "cognitive value of fiction" written under the rubric of literary realism, suggesting that other modes, such as sentimentalism and naturalism, were more attuned to the textures of the body.[32] George Lakoff and Mark Johnson, in their book with the audacious title *Philosophy in the Flesh: The Embodied Mind and Its Challenge to Western Thought* (1999), consolidate a strain of current thinking, in both academic circles and popular culture, that challenges the dualism between mind and body, a philosophical framework traditionally laid at the door of René Descartes. Lakoff and Johnson argue that the human capacity to be mindful—to cogitate, judge, abstract, remember, associate, hope, create—"is shaped crucially by the peculiarities of our human bodies, by the remarkable details of the neural structure of our brains, and by the specifics of our everyday functioning in the world."[33] Not only is the mind importantly embodied— philosophers and neuroscientists are affirming that, from an evolutionary standpoint, "[b]efore our ancestors got minds, they got bodies": that cognition itself developed along with the human nervous system, over vast stretches of time, from the material matrices of organisms coping with challenging environments.[34]

Bodies also are in possession of "mind"—a statement that usefully points up the implicit dualism, and semantic limitations, of these common terms. Practitioners of a variety of healing methods, such as behavioral therapy, affirm this idea, maintaining that the malleable structures of the brain and nervous system can house "somatic memories"[35]—a neurological application of Nietzsche's aphorism "There is more wisdom in your body than in your best wisdom."[36] In *The Vehement Passions*, Philip Fisher affirms that such "wisdom" has until recently been obscured by "the heavy shadow of Freud" (27), which suffuses our world with a "common-sense" interpretive imperative to construe the body's responses and experiences as penumbra of the mind's conflicts. To prevent the "contamination of the topic of the passions by this kind of strange, everyday, but theory-laden material," Fisher suggests, we are well advised to "turn back" to treatments of the vigorous intelligence of the body prior to the twentieth century (27). This is a salient reminder that literary realists were writing under the influence of James and Darwin, for whom emotions were crucially embodied as "actions . . . expressive of certain states of mind . . . determined by the constitution of the nervous system."[37]

3. *Reason and emotion.* The twinned notions that brains are crucially embodied and that bodies possess mindfulness can be misconstrued as grimly materialistic, undermining of human agency and intellect. Yet for many contemporary philosophers, these mind-body connections enable a different conclusion, one that is pertinent to the study of literary realism: that, in the words of philosopher Ronald de Sousa, there is a "rationality of emotion." Emotional response, de Sousa urges, provides the critical substrate for human action and decision: emotions both motivate response and constitute thoughtful ideas about particular circumstances. De Sousa resituates emotion "among the mechanisms that control the crucial factor of *salience* among what would otherwise be an unmanageable plethora of objects of attention, interpretations, and strategies of inference and conduct."[38] Without the subtle judgments enabled by such feelings as delight and dismay—which are the affective equivalent of natural selection, with its ability to fruitfully situate an organism within a potentially bewildering environment—the densely realized object worlds of realist novels would be about as compelling and coherent as a rummage sale.

In literary studies, the connection between feeling and thinking has been theorized most thoroughly by critics working on antebellum texts. As Philip Fisher has explained, the mode of knowing entailed by such works as *Uncle Tom's Cabin* depends on that crucial eighteenth-century affect, sympathy, which operates through mimesis and identification to efface distinctions between self and other: "The Sentimental Novel depends upon experimental, even dangerous, extensions of the self of the reader. . . . At its center is the experimental extension of normality, that is, of normal states of primary feeling to people from whom they have been previously withheld."[39] Sentimentalism provided a powerful reformist tool in the antebellum context of abolitionism and feminism, where the provocation of imagined identities between middle-class white readers and black slaves had obvious political entailments.[40]

Yet while sentimentalism in these accounts elides the strong distinction between thinking and feeling, it does not elude a dualistic understanding of mind and world. Michael Bell has taken up the epistemological association of sentimentalism with falsehood in *Sentimentalism, Ethics, and a Culture of Feeling* (2000). Addressing the problem of referentiality—that "spurious feeling" might be aroused by unreal objects, or that emotional response might be in excess of the precipitating cause—Bell argues for the essentially imaginative status of *everything* outside the self: "In responding to fictional beings, we acclimatize to the elusive and imaginative dimension of all objects of feeling."[41] Feeling, as Bell describes it, is equally adequate to reason—which is to say, equally imperfect and potentially delusional—in mediating between the perceiver and objects of emotion. Bell persuasively argues that sentimental works, informed by the associationist psychology of John Locke (*not* the physiological theories of the late nineteenth century), remain committed to a positivist ontology, which locates "realness" in material objects precisely as they are distinct from operations of mind.

The neuroscientist Joseph LeDoux urges, by contrast, that part of the power of emotional response is precisely its ontological agnosticism: one can have an emotive response to something, a sense of whether it is good or bad, even without knowing exactly what sort of a thing it is.[42] Acknowledging the epistemological nature of feelings, LeDoux gives an even stronger account than de Sousa: "Many emotions," LeDoux observes, "are products of evolutionary wisdom, which probably has more intelligence than all human minds together" (36). This facility can be literally life-sustaining—one can be jolted into action by vague noises and shadowy figures—but it also has a more equivocal function, as is the case with feelings aroused by certain kinds of literature. As James Dawes has shown in his work on the gothic novel, emotion's ontological agnosticism can be exploited (much as Pavlov did with the salivating dogs) to produce "fictional feeling." But, Dawes concludes, rather than invalidating the usefulness and frequent accuracy of the life of feeling, gothic fiction puts us in touch with corporeal capacities that extend well beyond the circumscribed zone of conscious thought.[43] As such, emotionally resonant fictions can be enjoyably revealing—if not always practical in their particular effects.

4. *Affect and aesthetics.* Although realist fiction has seemed largely immune to aesthetic concerns, recent work in neurology suggests a way of thinking about literary realism's emphasis on "the common" (the shared, the lowly, the quotidian) in terms of aesthetic experience. What LeDoux describes from a neurological perspective—individuals' capacity for judgment without concepts—and what Dennett explains in terms of evolutionary philosophy—the human tendency to ascribe intention even to objects such as flowers—has structural similarities to Immanuel

Kant's account of aesthetic judgment. In *The Critique of Judgment*, Kant anatomizes the human emotive response that extends to aesthetic objects and sublime nature a sense of wholeness or well-designed completeness (he calls this "purposiveness") while nonetheless setting aside conceptual concern with the object's ontological status (its nature or "purpose"). Kant explicitly addressed the problem of idiosyncrasy: if judgments are centered not in the object as such but in a person's feeling of delight, what makes them not merely private or personal? As Kant framed the problem: "How is a judgment possible which, going merely on the individual's *own* feeling of pleasure in an object, independent of the concept of it, estimates this as a pleasure attached to the representation of the same object *in every other individual* and does so *a priori*, i.e. without being allowed to wait and see whether other people will be of the same mind?"[44]

The answer, for Kant, lay neither in the material world of objects nor in regulative cultural norms but in what he called the *sensus communis*, the common sense (i.e. shared human capacity for such judgment), that provided the ground for a community of sense. As Elizabeth Maddock Dillon has explained, aesthetic judgment for Kant was an essential expression of human agency: "In response to the beautiful object . . . the subject's mental powers are set free—are able to 'play'—rather than conform to any fixed concept, and this mental play is precisely the evidence of our capacity for freedom in the material world."[45] The *sensus communis*, internal and essential to human beings, was an entity that Kant posited to protect against both solipsism and determinism, to provide the ground for a shared material world. Theorists in the twentieth century, however, have critiqued Kant precisely for this notion: for his inattentiveness to the contingencies of culture and history, and to the empirical particulars of individual taste.

The philosopher Suzanne Langer, in her book *Feeling and Form* (1953), elaborated one way to reconceptualize the relationship of affect and aesthetics in the wake of anti-Kantian sentiment. Feeling, she writes, has in its modern usage tended to be "associated with spontaneity, spontaneity with informality or indifference to form, and thus (by slipshod thinking) with *absence* of form."[46] Form, on the other hand, "connotes formality, regulation, hence repression of feeling, and (by the same slipshodness) *absence* of feeling" (17). Langer, critiquing the distinction between affect and aesthetics as a dubious legacy of modernism, argues instead that aesthetic objects themselves embody the dynamic structure of emotional life: "forms of growth and attenuation, flowing and stowing, conflict and resolution, speed, arrest, terrific excitement, calm or subtle activation and dreamy lapses. . . . Such is the pattern, or logical form, of sentience" (27). By locating the structure of sentience in aesthetic objects, Langer's important work reaffirmed the centrality of feeling for the philosophy of art.

Yet Langer's reconnection of feeling and form depended on the abstraction of feeling from individual experience. Echoing the New Critics in literature, Langer warned that attention to the effects of aesthetic objects in the lives or bodies of individuals would lead to a "neurological aesthetics" (38), dissolving the distinction between objects of art and other, lesser, creations: "Even chefs, perfumers, and upholsterers, who produce the means of sensory pleasure for others, are not rated as the torchbearers of culture and inspired creators" (28). Moreover, Langer believed a neurological aesthetics would be deterministic and hopelessly private, casting human beings as hardwired for specific responses to certain things and focusing solely on personal responses and associations. To avoid these pitfalls, Langer argued that works of art were addressed to the mind, not the body: they provided a *"nonsensuous apperception* of the feelings in question" (21–22; emphasis added). Thus dematerialized, it was the form of human feeling that was echoed in the form of the work: "Such formal analogy, or congruence of logical structures, is the prime requisite for the relation between a symbol and whatever it is to mean. The symbol and the object symbolized must have some *common logical form*" (27; emphasis added). These "verbally ineffable" (39) "symbols of sentience" (40), cut off from both their material origin in human effort and their embodied destination in human appreciation, constituted formal icons of feeling.

More recently, the literary critic Paul Gilmore has dubbed this kind of reverence for the aesthetic object "secular sacralization."[47] A sort of fossilization process, such sacralization limits the work's emotive dynamism to the narrow confines of the object itself, to the exclusion of both the human apprehension of a work and its continuities with other lived experiences. In *The Radical Aesthetic* (2000), Isobel Armstrong has also agitated against such thinking: "the components of aesthetic life," she affirms, "are those that are already embedded in the processes and practices of consciousness—playing and dreaming, thinking and feeling. . . . *These processes—experiences that keep us alive—are common to everyone, common to what early Marx called species being.*"[48]

While Armstrong details this commonality in conceptual terms, the neuroscientist Antonio Damasio is interested in the corporeal mechanisms that constitute aesthetic experience. Feelings in Damasio's account are indeed tied to the world, aroused by what he calls "emotionally competent objects," whether a compelling painting or a gorgeous seascape. The object of the *feeling,* however, is the *"body state that results from beholding that seascape"*; it comprises the awareness of those corporeal reactions elicited by the object.[49] Because it is the body state that is, neurologically speaking, at the origin of the feeling, and not the seascape, or a painting hanging on the wall, Damasio notes that "the object itself can be changed radically. In some instances the changes may be akin to taking a brush and fresh paint and modifying the painting" (92). As Kant elaborated in his Third Critique, and as Henry James discerned in *Roderick Hudson,* aesthetic experiences are far from deterministic: they house the potential for the sort of engaged play that might result in real transformations. While such enlistments are potentially available in common experience, they are condensed and made vividly available to consciousness in certain resonant objects.

So, while Kant's antiempiricist universalism has fallen out of favor in the light of the contemporary scholarly commitment to cultural specificity and historical contingency, when placed in the decidedly empiricist and materialist company of LeDoux and Damasio, and supplemented by the historicist and cultural studies perspective of Gilmore and Armstrong, it begins to look less rigid and potentially pejorative. The *sensus communis,* what Armstrong described in terms of "processes . . . common to everyone," might reasonably and nonreductively be traced to the human body, with its complex nervous system and capacity to engage with a rich world both within and beyond the skin. Lakoff and Johnson, in *Philosophy in the Flesh,* argue that it is precisely "our common embodiment that allows for common, stable truths" (6). Understood as "a full and intense experience," a work of art, John Dewey maintained, "keeps alive the power to experience the common world in its fullness."[50] In his neuroscientific work on feeling, Damasio argues that attention to the responses of the human perceiver must be at the heart of any understanding of the "reverberative process" between beholder and world that constitutes aesthetic experience (92). Modern neuroscience uses terms similar to those of Dewey, who wrote that "an act of perception proceeds by waves that extend serially throughout the entire organism" (53). What Langer disparaged as "neurological aesthetics"—attentiveness to the affective experience of literary and other works of art—is now emerging as an exciting area of study, one that extends well beyond isolate acts of appreciation.

Literary and cultural critics have been deepening our understanding of the human affective engagement with objects, tracing the corporeal links to other sorts of experiences and pointing toward potential new ground for human solidarity. Adam Frank has perceptively assessed the recent proliferation of such studies, remarking that "critical interest in emotion or feeling can be located, in part, as a response to specialization and an often felt lack of relation, a felt lack that a moralized version of 'the political' has been the major supplier for."[51] In his carefully historicized work on "romantic electricity" in antebellum literature and culture, Paul Gilmore shows how electrical impulses provided a material trope for imagining how exalting experiences could be both embodied and public, passing through a person's nervous system and connecting with that of others, much like a telegraph sending a similar message to different outposts. "The aesthetic's universalizing claims," Gilmore concludes, "imply a kind of egalitarianism that might be translated to the political sphere, where it can offer a starting point for building coalitions and communities across the lines of race, class, and gender reified by identity politics" (471). Pamela Thurschwell has argued that it was precisely the nineteenth century's interest in nerve-mediated transits between persons—aesthetic, technological, and occult—that drove Sigmund Freud to "distinguish psychoanalysis from telepathy" and to "privilege . . . fantasy over the real event."[52] Freud's repudiation of his seduction theory was the most influential instantiation of the privileging of fantasy, which Thurschwell sees as a manifestation of psychoanalysis's simultaneous anxiety about and fascination with "dangerous intimacy—bodies and minds which overlap in ways which are too close, too inextricable" (11).

A set of protective dualisms, in sum, were installed at the center of the founding psychological discourse of the twentieth century and perpetuated in critical approaches that have tended to fall, sometimes obliquely, under Freud's "heavy shadow." Now, with the emergence of embodied neuroscience, we can begin to adumbrate an alterative account of the relations among mind, body, and emotion to that established by psychoanalysis and perpetuated in literary theory. This new focus allows us to see how writers of the late nineteenth century situated the corporeal self at the heart of that "feeling of reality"—William

James's phrase—that saturates our daily lives but is often most acutely available for inquiry, as well as shock or delight, in certain kinds of aesthetic experiences.[53]

"Being Moved": Modernity, Evolution, and the Reflex Arc

In the late nineteenth century, the commotion of modernity was frequently cast as hard on the nerves: as one physician put it, "Civilization itself, with all that the term implies, with its railway, telegraph, telephone, and periodical press, [is] intensifying in ten thousand ways cerebral activity and worry."[54] Henry James depicted the edginess of the modern psyche in *A Small Boy and Others* (1913), where he describes the first rumblings of a consciousness (his own) "that was to be nothing if not mixed and a curiosity that was to be nothing if not restless."[55] Technologies that moved the physical body through space were matched by the ups and downs of an unstable economic market, fluctuations that also appeared to take a toll on the human mind and body. As the nineteenth-century neurologist Silas Weir Mitchell expressed it, "The industry and energy which have built this great city [Chicago] on a morass, and made it a vast centre of insatiate commerce, are now at work to undermine the nervous systems of its restless and eager people."[56]

Technological and economic changes altered the pace of life, while in the sciences, the innovative theories of Charles Darwin cast natural history as itself a narrative of incessant transformation. Darwin's potent linkage of mutability, deep time, and reciprocity between an organism and its environment produced a strong account of evolution, while suggesting to some, as Louis Menand has noted, that its engine, natural selection, was "a process without a mind."[57] Darwin's theory put to use the earlier geological theories of Charles Lyell and James Hutton; the latter famously stated that the earth itself was the product of inexorable change, with "no vestige of a beginning—no prospect of an end."[58] In these accounts, everyone was like Nathaniel Hawthorne's Clifford Pyncheon on a fast-moving train: "Looking from the window, they could see the world racing past them. . . . The spires of meeting-houses seemed set adrift from their foundations; the broad-based hills glided away. Everything was unfixed from its age-long rest, and moving at whirlwind speed . . . and the common and inevitable movement onward! It was life itself!"[59]

It is William James's conception of the stream of thought that scholars have lighted on as a model of thinking that seemed attuned to the rapidity of modern life and the interior motions of consciousness.[60] Yet James himself quickly became dissatisfied with the concept, which he developed relatively early in his career. As his biographer Gerald E. Myers has pointed out, consciousness as depicted in James's *Principles of Psychology* (1890) maintains a dualistic distinction between thoughts and things, or the purely psychical and the physical: Clifford's *thoughts* might be racing in the passage quoted above, but the church spires are standing still.[61] This position implied two sorts of division, both of which James came to see as misguided. First, it seemed wrong to divide what felt like a single experience into two seemingly irreconcilable parts: the nonphysical "stream of thought" (e.g. the moving spires) and the physical object (e.g. the stationary spires). James later corrected himself, affirming that *"experience, I believe, has no such inner duplicity"*: it was a misconstruction to think there was consciousness *and* content.[62] James came to believe that consciousness was not opposed to exterior, physical entities such as church spires—or, for that matter, interior, physiological events such as "heartbeats or temperature changes." Instead, James concluded that *"our entire feeling of spiritual activity, or what commonly passes by that name, is really a feeling of bodily activities."*[63]

The second division that dissatisfied James involved thinking and feeling. Centering attention solely on the "cognitive function" of mental states, James realized, "leads to a somewhat strained way of talking about dreams and reveries, and to quite an unnatural way of talking of some emotional states."[64] It is in James's notion of "the stream of our feeling," developed in later essays, that he begins to flesh out his radical empiricism. While cognition is the operation of mind that separates the flow of experience into parts and objects, it was the flow of feeling that James came to see as adequate to "the infinite chaos of movements" that constitute life, which is "in itself an undistinguishable, swarming *continuum.*"[65] If cognition provided snapshots, feeling offered a moving picture. It was just this picture, which emerges in the complex interaction of reader and text, that is embodied in works of literary realism.

The novelist/neurologist S. Weir Mitchell's short story "The Case of George Dedlow" (1866), depicting a man literally chopped into bits and then temporarily sutured back together at a séance, supplies a case in point. The tale portrays the experience of a Civil War surgeon who,

as a result of a series of battle injuries, has all four of his limbs ampu-
tated. Mitchell had himself treated nerve injuries of soldiers during the
war, working at the "Stump Hospital" outside of Philadelphia (so
dubbed by the soldiers housed there) and collecting material that was
published in a textbook entitled *Gunshot Wounds and Other Injuries of
Nerves* (1864).[66] Set at Mitchell's old hospital, "The Case of George
Dedlow" contains what most historians agree is the first fictional depiction of phantom limb—the experience of pain or sensibility or simply
"thereness" in a body part that has been surgically removed. "More remarkable," the narrator reports, "were the psychical changes which I
now began to perceive. I found to my horror that at times I was less
conscious of myself, of my own existence, than used to be the case. . . .
It was, as well as I can describe it, a deficiency in the egoistic *sentiment
of individuality*" (8; emphasis added). Dedlow traces the transformations in his consciousness to the loss of "half of the sensitive surface of
[his] skin": "and thus much of relation to the outer world [was] destroyed" (8). "A man," the surgeon concludes, "is not his brain, or any
one part of it, but all of his economy . . . [and so] to lose any part must
lessen this sense of his own existence" (8).

In his critique of Herbert Spencer's earlier theory of mind, William
James belittled the conception of an idealized, disembodied spectator as
itself a phantom: "simply a mirror floating with no foot-hold anywhere,
and passively reflecting an order that he comes upon and finds simply
existing."[67] In Mitchell's George Dedlow, this conceptual passivity and
lack of a "foot-hold" is gruesomely literal. To avoid such "amputations," nineteenth-century thinkers affirmed that a restless and interested attention, and not a deracinated, unsituated objectivity (e.g. a
brain in a bottle, or a man without a body), drove the human engagement with the world. Knowing and feeling, rather than being in necessary opposition, had a much more dynamic relationship; for James,
rationality itself was a full-bodied event entailing a "transition from a
state of puzzle and perplexity to rational comprehension" that was "full
of lively relief and pleasure."[68]

As a number of cultural critics have noted, nineteenth-century physiologists posed a challenge to distinctions between thinking and feeling,
and mind and the body, in their elucidation of the "reflex arc," a conception that dethroned the centrality of the brain in the reception and
processing of stimuli.[69] By the second half of the nineteenth century,
nerves in their material form were the object of study for a new set of

experimental scientists; no longer the sole property of upper-class men and women of feeling, or isolated to a tradition of analytic philosophy, nerves were scrutinized by physiologists like Marshall Hall, Thomas Laycock, and S. Weir Mitchell; pathologized by medical men and alienists such as George Beard and Henry Maudsley; and popularized by authors such as Oliver Wendell Holmes and Charlotte Perkins Gilman.[70]

The physiological breakthroughs of Charles Bell and Marshall Hall earlier in the nineteenth century had challenged the orthodox conception of the nervous system, inherited from the eighteenth century, as a homogeneous web of unitary nerve filaments. Bell argued that the system was composed of bundles of nerves that performed different functions, and he demonstrated that the spinal nerves had separate fibers for motion and sensation.[71] Subsequent research into the nervous system took this discovery as its foundation: the functional division of motor and sensory nerves was applied to successively higher parts of the central nervous system, including acts of cognition and volition. Marshall Hall extended the work of Bell with his investigations into the reflex action of the spinal cord. He found that responses to certain stimuli, such as a tap to the knee or a startling noise, bypassed the brain entirely, with the sensory stimulation passing directly, via the spinal ganglia, to the motor nerves to produce a kick or a flinch.

While Hall himself shrank from considering that the reflex arc might involve more than overtly corporeal, unconscious tasks such as circulation and digestion, thinkers such as Oliver Wendell Holmes, William Carpenter, and Thomas Laycock extended Hall's findings to consciousness itself. Here is Laycock, in *Mind and Brain* (1860):

> *It is the man in his twofold constitution who is conscious, not the mind as apart from the man.* As his states of body vary, so his states of mind vary— that is, his feelings, thoughts, motives, volitions, actions. Equally the practical man of common sense knows that these variations in the mental conditions depend, necessarily, upon variations in the bodily conditions; he guides his conduct accordingly . . . If he desires . . . to be wholly insensible to pain, he breathes the vapour of chloroform; if he wishes to be brilliant in imagination or glowing in diction, he swallows opium; if to be gay in spirit and joyous with a sense of vigorous life, he drinks wine.[72]

Laycock's list, which affirms that states of the body influence the mind, consists of a variety of affective states, both positive and negative: the desire to avoid pain, to exude brilliance, to relax, to seek solace, to cultivate a gay spirit. Holmes offers an amusing anecdote of precisely this sort of "doctoring" in *Elsie Venner,* in which a dogmatic Calvinist is softened by some good claret, so that his cup literally runneth over:

> "A little good wine won't hurt anybody," said the Deacon. "Plenty,—plenty,—plenty. There!" He had not withdrawn his glass, while the Colonel was pouring, for fear it should spill, and now it was running over.
> —It is very odd how all a man's philosophy and theology are at the mercy of a few drops of a fluid which the chemists say consists of nothing but C_4, O_2, H_6. The Deacon's theology fell off several points toward latitudinarianism in the course of the next ten minutes. He had a deep inward sense that everything was as it should be, human nature included.[73]

What Holmes refers to as the Deacon's "deep inward sense" is what physiologists and neurologists term the proprioceptive state.[74] Derived from the Latin word *proprius,* meaning "one's own," proprioception refers to one's sense of one's own body, the feeling from the *inside,* as opposed to those senses that involve exteroception, or sensory engagement with the outside world (sight, smell, taste, hearing, touch). In the case of the Deacon, the "deep inward sense" of calm, far from posing a problem, is expressed in the language of doctrinal health, in the churchman's newly balanced theological doctrine.

The English physiologist Alexander Bain (one of William James's "heroes" in psychology) also emphasized the centrality of the body to feeling.[75] In his 1859 text *The Emotions and the Will,* Bain asserted that "what we take merely as signs of the emotion are a part of its own essential workings, in whose absence it would be something else entirely."[76] He suggested that a look of terror is not a bodily "portrait" of fear but is essential to it. Moreover, emotion so defined was not isolated to the surface of the body but was evident in the "*diffusive action* over the system": "Every pleasure and every pain," Bain writes, "and every mode of emotion, has a definite wave of effects. . . . The organs first and prominently affected, in the diffused wave of nervous influence, are the moving members" (5). The physiologist Henry Maudsley, while employing the term "passion" where Bain referred to "feeling," asserted a similar process: "The passion that is felt is the subjective side of the cerebral commotion—its *motion* out from the physical basis, as it were *(e-motion),* into consciousness."[77] Crucial to this formulation is the notion of *movement,* in which a largely bodily event is translated into one that is increasingly conscious.

In the hands of late-nineteenth-century scientists of the body, "being moved" contained mindful elements that situated a person within the world and provided the conditions of possibility for the operations of the mind associated with consciousness. For thinkers drawing on Darwin, emotion was precedent to the operations of consciousness in two senses: (1) the apparatus of emotion was *evolutionarily prior,* meaning simply that the rudiments of a nervous system, existent in organisms without fully formed brains, developed before those organs and capacities necessary for consciousness; and (2) the experience of emotion was, as William James affirmed in what came to be known as the James-Lange theory, *temporally prior* to consciousness. In "What is an Emotion?" James writes, "Common sense says, we lose our fortune, are sorry and weep; we meet a bear, are frightened and run" (147). But, he affirms, "The more rational statement is that we feel sorry because we cry, angry because we strike" (148). Our very "sense of reality," as James sketched it, is dependent on *"excitement,"* which is cast along a continuum of "motor activities . . . perceptions . . . the imagination . . . reflective thought."[78] "But wherever it is found," he writes, *"there is the zest, the tingle, the excitement of reality;* and there is 'importance' in the only real and positive sense in which importance ever anywhere can be" ("Blindness," 844; emphasis added).

While James here seems to be making a pure value judgment in his comment on what makes life worth living, he is also, importantly, referencing a set of ideas that had their roots in nineteenth-century biology and physiology: (1) adaptive self-preservation, (2) homeostasis, and (3) psychophysical parallelism. The first concept, adaptive self-preservation, emerged in the context of Charles Darwin's theory of natural selection, in which he argued that, in the midst of unceasing variability, certain organisms survive (are "selected") because they function in the most advantageous way with respect to their environment. "Over all these causes of Change," Darwin wrote, "I am convinced that the accumulative action of Selection, whether applied methodically and more quickly, or unconsciously and more slowly, but more efficiently, is by far the predominant Power."[79] For James, the human organism was the product of natural selection and also a sort of internalization of it: our myriad responses provide ways of adjusting, in both the short and the long term, to our physical and cultural milieu.

The second influential concept, homeostasis, can be traced to the French physiologist Claude Bernard, who developed the concept of the *milieu interior,* or the "interior environment," of the body through his painful experiments on the nerves of animals. An organism's life, Bernard theorized, was dependent on its ability to maintain an internal balance despite (and in relation to) incessant movement, such as changes in its environment. In his *Introduction to the Study of Experimental Medicine* (1865), Bernard described the body not in static anatomical terms but as a dynamic system of interconnected functions that provide a bodily substrate for an organism's thriving: "The constancy of the internal environment is the condition that life should be free and independent. . . . So far from the higher animal being indifferent to the external world, it is on the contrary in a precise and informal relation with it, in such a way that its equilibrium results from a continuous and delicate compensation, established as by the most sensitive of balances."[80] The nervous system was merely the quickest means for achieving and monitoring this corporeal balance: lower organisms had to depend solely on such interior transportation systems as osmosis, which were significantly slower and less precise (one might think of a sunflower's unhurried tracking of the sun). The early-twentieth-century researcher Walter Cannon coined the term *homeostasis* to designate the intentionality of the physiological balancing act, the embodied commitment of all complex organisms to sustaining a life-supporting equilibrium even in the face of dangerous environmental fluctuations.

The third idea influencing James's comment about the centrality of excitement to human experience is psychophysical parallelism. Articulated by the British neurologist James Hughlings Jackson, whose work on the nervous system was influenced by Darwin's and Herbert Spencer's ideas about evolution, psychophysical parallelism insisted on a correspondence between the motions of the body and the operations of the mind. Hughlings Jackson theorized that the structure of the nervous system reflected its evolutionary origins from simple, inflexible, involuntary reactions to more complex, dynamic, voluntary responses. Moreover, according to Jackson, "the nervous system is a representing system," with the "lowest level" of the system (the brain stem and spinal cord, what has been termed the "reptilian brain") "represent[ing] all parts of the body most nearly directly." The "middle level" (including the limbic system, associated with the capacity for attachment and memory) "represents all parts of the body doubly indirectly," while "the highest sensori-motor centres" of the neocortex "make up the 'organ of the mind' or physical basis of consciousness . . . [and so] the

highest centres re-re-represent the body—that is, represent it triply indirectly."[81] The highest centers were, according to Hughlings Jackson,
also the most vulnerable; many pathological states emerged from the
"dissolution" of higher functions, which disrupted the balancing act
and allowed lower functions to predominate, as when someone suffering from a head injury loses the capacity for creative speech but pre-
serves the ability to repeat rote jingles.[82]

The conceptual framework that Hughlings Jackson brought to bear
on the human nervous system had obvious potential for pejorative uses,
with the "less human" capacities shared with reptiles and sunflowers
translated into moralistic terms and projected onto certain persons or
cultures, and the "more human" the special purview of, say, the white,
Protestant man of science. To return to a point made by Elizabeth Wilson: just as thinking about the body neurologically has seemed too reductive to many cultural critics, so has evolutionary thought seemed too
hierarchical, too value-laden, too deterministic.[83] Yet we can see that
the levels of the nervous system were understood to be more dynamic in
their operation, even in Hughlings Jackson's terms, than mere vestiges
of an animalistic past in need of top-down control. When brought into
contact with William James's own theories about the indispensability of
habit, even "reptilian" capacities such as rote imitation are resituated
not as primitive but essential to human flourishing. "The great thing,"
James urged, "is to *make our nervous system our ally instead of our enemy. . . . For this we must make automatic and habitual, as early as possible, as many useful actions as we can.*"[84] The brightest lights of the
rising generation (e.g. James's Harvard students) would do well, he
maintained, to cultivate the programmatic power of the "reptilian
brain." So rather than being reducible to an atavistic slide down the
phylogenetic ladder, the functions of all levels were, James believed,
daily operative in the life of the (future) cultural arbiter, whose "higher
levels" of cognition shared the burden of study with the lower, thereby
allowing him to "wake . . . up one morning, to find himself one of the
competent ones of his generation."[85] Although Hughlings Jackson
comes to the conclusion from the perspective of neurological functioning, his description of the tripartite arrangement of the nervous system,
coupled with the idea that the cerebrum re-re-represents the body, affirms James's conclusion, that, if anything, "the truer side is the side
that feels the more and not the side that feels the less."[86]

Laughter, Reflection, and Realization in *Adventures of Huckleberry Finn*

The crucial element connecting the scholarly work summarized in section one, the emergent sciences of the body of section two, and literary works of the late nineteenth century is a philosophically significant understanding of *experience*.[87] The term, as exemplified and put into practice in the work of William James, has a fourfold import that might be cast along a spectrum from passivity to activity: (1) *experience in the passive sense,* as "what happens to one," the quotidian events of human life, thought, and feeling; this was especially important to James in his role as originator of American psychology; (2) *experience in the empiricist sense,* as "the actual observation of facts or events considered as a source of knowledge"; this pertained to James, the trained medical doctor, pragmatist philosopher, and psychical researcher; (3) *experience in the constructive sense,* derived from the Latin root *experientia,* which meant "to put to test or trial"; pertinent to James the founder of the first psychological research laboratory in the United States; and (4) *experience in the phenomenological sense,* its most dynamic yet also most general instantiation, as simply "the interaction of organism and environment," elaborated in the radical empiricism of James in his later career and in the evolutionary philosophy of John Dewey.

For Dewey, "experience is primarily a process of undergoing: a process of standing something; of suffering and passion, of affection, in the literal sense of these words. The organism has to endure, to undergo, the consequences of its own actions. Experience is no slipping along a path fixed by inner consciousness. Private consciousness is an incidental outcome of experience of a vital objective sort; it is not its source."[88] This engagement or "undergoing"—what James calls "eagerness" and Dewey terms "affection"—was not a matter of the mind suppressing the body. Nor was it a matter of an unmediated corporeal experience that somehow bypassed the mind. Such receptivity arose, as James described it, precisely out of a continuum: "Sometimes the eagerness is more knit up with the motor activities, sometimes with the perceptions, sometimes with the imagination, sometimes with reflective thought."[89]

Dewey notes that one cuts off experience at the neck, limiting it to "reflective thought," at one's own risk: "The standing temptation of philosophy, as its course abundantly demonstrates, is to regard the results of *reflection* as having, in and of themselves, a reality superior to that of the material of any other mode of experience."⁹⁰ If, instead, one "start[s] with no presuppositions save that what is experienced . . . reverie and desire are pertinent for a philosophic theory of the true nature of things; the possibilities present in imagination that are not found in observation, are something to be taken into account."⁹¹ This last passage can be easily misread as naïve empiricism, but it is almost the opposite. Philosophy mustn't begin with the very end point of experience—with the sense that there are objects "there" in the world, with cognition's sense that cognition is best equipped to "know" these objects—but must rather take into consideration the entire experience that leads to this endpoint and indeed frames a quite small slice of the whole as what is real, irrefutable, foundational.

Dewey's insight provides a challenge for critics approaching works of literature, as well: what happens when we take into consideration the evolving experience of reading, rather than homing in solely on the endpoint of interpretation? It is useful to consider the experiential spectrum prompted by a novel that has over the years been both affirmed to be an exemplary work of American literary realism and an ultimately problematic instance of it.⁹² Mark Twain's *Adventures of Huckleberry Finn* (1885) recurs continually to moments in which texts elicit strong emotional reactions (though often not the intended ones), from Emmeline Grangerford's poetry to Tom Sawyer's chivalric playacting to the Duke and Dauphin's outrageous performances. Yet the paradigmatic "realist" moment—one that seems to turn on the distinction between what is really happening and the audience's subjective perception of the event—takes place when Huck visits the circus and has the experience of watching an act that is apparently disrupted by an intrusive audience member. A drunk in the audience makes his way into the circus ring, obstreperously criticizing the performers. As in a scene from the Roman Colosseum, the audience jeers the man and urges him on as he grabs a horse, clings frantically to its neck, and is dragged around the arena by the frenzied animal. For an audience interested in spectacle, the drunk's infiltration of the ring is merely an added bonus; perfectly willing to continue to treat these events as rollicking theater, "the whole crowd of people [stood] up shouting and laughing till the tears rolled down."⁹³ The act, as the narrative makes clear, is defined not by its realism or fictionality, or by its probability or improbability, but by the arena. For this audience, whatever enters the ring unproblematically counts as entertainment.

Huck's reaction, however, is different: he distinguishes an inside and an outside to the ring, casting the drunk's antics as real, not a part of the show. Huck's discrimination, while not exactly a thought, nonetheless entails an act of judgment that is registered through bodily feeling: "It wasn't funny to me, though; I was all of a tremble to see his danger" (*Huck*, 150). Importantly, Huck's inability to laugh and his bodily agitation do not arise from a sense of his own physical danger, for he is safely ensconced in the audience. The realism of this moment inheres not so much in the reality that penetrates the representational space of the circus ring; it inheres in the bodily trembling that registers the *internal* theater of Huck's imaginative engagement with the perceived danger of someone else. The bloodlust of the Colosseum, where the audience's physical detachment from the scene of brutality produces the thrill of pure spectacle, gives way in this understated moment to the force of identification.

This moment of civilized and discriminating sentiment is crucially a moment of naïve reading. For before Huck's eyes the wretched drunk is transformed into a dashing circus rider; doffing his layers of ragged clothes and leaping to the horse's back, the man appears "slim and handsome, and dressed the gaudiest and prettiest you ever saw" (*Huck,* 150). Huck had of course been taken in by a venerable circus trick, in which a performer disguised as an audience member appears to infiltrate the stage. What looked real, then, is revealed to be an act, a simulation of reality.

In this scene Twain poses the question of what it means to feel emotion for an "unreal" object. From a purely epistemological perspective, Huck's compassion appears, after the fact, to be predicated on an error. The feeling arose in the absence of complete information: that the man was an accomplished rider, that he was therefore in no great danger, that his infiltration of the ring was planned rather than spontaneous. Huck's final interpretation of the scene, corrected by experience, would likely affirm these "facts." Clearly, however, throughout *Adventures of Huckleberry Finn* Mark Twain presents Huck as a model for the work that feeling can accomplish in opposition to apparently irrefutable fact. Most famous in this regard is Huck's fellow feeling for the escaping slave Jim when, despite the boy's impulse to help the man, he "knows" that he is doing wrong by assisting a slave with his flight. Huck's final "interpretation" here—that he is going to hell for committing the crime of stealing Jim—is for the reader nugatory (and indeed in error): the meaning of the scene lies in the boy's affective struggle, the tension between what he *knows* he should do and what he *feels* he should do, and in his actions to harbor Jim despite this experiential discrepancy.

The boy's experience with the drunk turned rider ends not in discomfort but rather in delight. Huck dissolves in laughter, joining the rest of the audience, who are "just a-howling with pleasure and astonishment" (151). In this scene, feeling and knowledge, illusion and reality, are not set in opposition: rather, the emphasis on Huck's amusement registers what Dewey referred to as the mediation of an experience: Huck's was the pleasure of being "taken in." Simply knowing at the outset that the drunk was a performer would nullify the effect of the joke; merely feeling worried and then relieved would be equally insignificant. The point of the circus scene is that Huck *gets* the joke—his laugh is *essential to* both his experience of and interpretation of the scene, for it marks his own realization of the discrepancy between his earlier worries and his later relief. His laughter affirms the distance between his naïve self and his more knowledgeable self: suddenly aware that he has misread the earlier events in the ring, Huck sees himself through new eyes.

But the pleasure does not stop there, nor does the unfolding of the experience for the reader. Huck's enjoyment comes not merely from his own experience of first being duped and then being in on the joke but by imagining the experience of the ringmaster, whom he clearly believes was equally fooled: "I felt sheepish enough, to be took in so, but I wouldn't a been in the ring-master's place, not for a thousand dollars" (*Huck*, 151). Sacvan Bercovitch has spoken of the twists in Twain's humor, in which a reader experiences satisfaction and even glee upon seeing the author poke fun at the self-satisfied—only, of course, to have the joke reflect back onto the reader's own self-satisfaction at being "in on" the joke.[94] This is the structure of what transpires in this scene, for just as Huck gets pleasure out of not being the ultimate dupe (the ringmaster is), so the reader's amusement at the scene results from her position of greater wisdom (in relation to Huck), for the reader knows full well that the ringmaster would have been very much in on the joke, would have in all likelihood have been its choreographer. (Note that, unlike some versions of reader-response criticism, this analysis does not posit or require that the "ideal reader" or even the "historical reader" *will* feel pleasure or amusement at the circus scene. It simply points out that if one *is* amused, the delight inheres at least partly in the wise chuckle at Huck's feelings of superiority to the ringmaster. It's not a prescription, in other words: it is just how the joke works.)

As Bercovitch has shown, Twain's humor is reverberative. For just as Huck's laughter marks his feeling of superiority to the ringmaster—a feeling that the reader pleasurably reads as "wrong," out of line with the facts, predicated on an unreality—so the reader's amusement registers her own sense of superiority to a fictional character. The permutations of feeling, reflecting, and realization generated by Huck's response to the circus act elicit a parallel (but not identical) process in the reader, whose final amusement marks not her superiority to Huck but her complete consanguinity with him. Like Huck, her laughter arises from her sense of superiority to her previous self: in the case of the reader, the prior self is she who had privileged knowing over feeling. That is, the reader who laughs at Huck's expense (i.e., for knowing something about the ringmaster that Huck doesn't), precisely because of Huck's laughter at the ringmaster's expense, finally gives way to the reader who laughs at her own expense. It is essential to affirm that the reader's wisdom cannot be achieved by cutting to the chase. The meaning of the scene emerges, it unfolds, it evolves: the affective response—in this case, the laughter—is part of it.

Yet another question that Twain's text provokes is whether laughter is itself an emotion. It is, without doubt, a bodily event: notoriously hard to feign, laughter, like a sneeze, is often only imperfectly under a person's control, involving the sudden and sometimes explosive exhalation of air, facial contortions, and a range of bodily shakes and shudders (as suggested by the term "belly laugh"). When the laughter is particularly violent we refer to someone "dissolving" or being "doubled over," and a sustained bout of giggles may leave one in tears, red in the face, and gasping for breath. Thomas Hobbes emphasizes this physiological involvement when he speaks of "that distortion of the countenance that we call LAUGHTER" that is the sign of a passion "which is always joy, but what joy . . . hath not hitherto been declared by any."[95] There is, in other words, no unambiguous emotional concomitant to laughter; the "joy" it expresses is not precisely synonymous with happiness, the sensation of comfort and well-being that may be marked by a smile but rarely provokes such extreme bodily transformations. Nor is laughter occasioned solely by such positive engagements of the mind as delight in the good fortune of another or an elegant witticism, for "men [also] laugh at mischances and indecencies" ("Passions"). Happy to delineate nineteen other "passions of the mind," ranging from courage and anger to admiration and repentance, Hobbes in his taxonomy of affects distinguishes laughter from all others as the "passion which hath no name" ("Passions").

While tears may be unproblematically linked to grief or sorrow, the difficulty of naming in normal affective terms (e.g. joy, delight, happiness) the emotion affiliated with laughter is matched, as the nineteenth-century theater critic William Archer observed, by the actor's difficulty in producing convincing laughter on the stage. Archer, a good friend of Henry James (and one of the few to applaud James's poorly received venture into playwriting), published a study of emotion in acting, entitled *Masks and Faces* (1888). In it, he collated actors' responses to a survey he submitted, asking them to reflect in some detail on their bodily sensations as they feigned a range of emotions. While any third-rate player can muster tears, Archer notes, the ability to embody true mirth is reserved for the select few: "Every theatre-goer," Archer writes, "must have noticed the comparative rarity of good laughter on the stage."[96] Archer speculates that part of the difficulty resides in laughter's uncertain connection to joy and happiness. In the words of one performer Archer interviewed, "in truth my simulated laughter has never transfused itself into the audience, which has remained insensible to my gaiety" (*Masks*, 153). Indeed, Archer's investigations suggest that laughter is not only internally reverberative but externally so, involving the collaboration of actor and audience. Rather than a player conveying his own laughter to the gallery, most of Archer's actors referred to the central role of the audience in eliciting their authentic laughter, which in turn worked to catalyze the audience's delight: "In comedy," one respondent wrote, "the actor is more alive to his audience's humour than in tragedy. The effect is instantaneous, and a good-tempered house evokes the best qualities of a comedian *by placing him on good terms with himself*" (*Masks*, 152; emphasis added). A certain receptiveness on the part of the crowd, then, places the actor on good terms not only with the audience but also "with himself": the audience mirrors back to the player his own performative power, which he then proceeds to live up to.

But this description of the process, suggesting as it does an image that the actor then mimes or imitates, is actually more static than what Archer's actors report. Here Thomas Hobbes is helpful, for he also describes the experience of laughter in general, not just on the stage, as the marker of being placed "on good terms with oneself": "Men laugh often (especially such as are greedy of applause from every thing they do well) at their own actions performed never so little beyond their own expectation" ("Passions"). Note that the laughing man is his own audience—he performs beyond his *own* expectations. The actor is of course literally an applause-seeking person, and his laughter is dependent, on these terms, not on the long-practiced feigning of a series of gestures (what Archer's informant admits left his audiences "insensible to my gaiety") but on the novelty of experiencing himself afresh in the role of one who performs a role: "the passion of laughter proceedeth from a sudden conception of some ability in himself that laugheth" ("Passions"). The actor's talent is mimetic, the ability to pretend to be someone else. The audience warmly receives the actor's performance, and their receptiveness startles him into a sudden sense of outstripping himself. In Hobbes's terms, "the passion of laughter is nothing else but a sudden glory arising from sudden conception of some eminency in ourselves, by comparison with the infirmities of others, *or with our own formerly*" ("Passions"; emphasis added). *Comparison* is the crucial term here. In the case of the player, he realizes his success—in the dual sense of *brings about* and *becomes aware of*—through the laughter that marks, yet for the moment bridges, the differential between himself and the part he is playing.

Hobbes's "passion that has no name," we can now see, is precisely the *delightful* experience of self-discrepancy, of becoming aware of the unfolding of an experience. It marks the pleasure of being an appreciative audience to oneself (I emphasize delight since this experience has been theorized as anomie or alienation and associated in some writing on the subject with less positive affects such as pathos.) Moreover, this "sudden conception of some eminency in ourselves"—what theorists of humor have termed the "superiority theory" of laughter—is not just a version of *shadenfreude,* or positive feelings at another's pain, which might take the propositional form of "I'm better off than he is." (As Hobbes writes, "it is vain glory . . . to think the infirmities of another sufficient matter for his triumph" ["Passions"]) The pleasure marked by these instances of laughter strikes closer to home; it comprises the realization "I'm better than *I* am!" There is, in short, an implied doubleness in laughter, a delightful self-seeing that expresses wisdom without being precisely cognitive, that is deeply corporeal without being purely automatic, and that is personal without being antisocial. Indeed, for Mark Twain, such moments are not just breaks from the violence and monotony of human life: they form the ground of sociality as such and keep open the potential for transformation—they are, in short, the source of whatever redemptive possibilities human beings possess. This helps to explain Sacvan Berkovitch's observation, in spite of his powerful reading of Mark Twain's bleak depiction of human viciousness in *Huckleberry Finn* (his "wisdom without consolation"), that "Twain makes us laugh outright, with an almost childlike delight. Somehow the novel *does* cheer us up" (130, 123).

Michael Bell, drawing on the work of Janice Radway, has termed the affective enlistments of sentimental texts "double-feel": "The emotion is knowingly indulged in an unreal object. It may be, however, that we should think of it in the other way round. Instead of sentimental 'double-feel,' in relation to fiction, being the naïve version of the act of reading, it is the archetype."[97] As we have seen, this notion applies nicely to Mark Twain's circus scenario, which first enlists the reader to feel superior to Huck's emotional naïveté in reading the scene, only to then lead the reader to realize/laugh that her supposedly sophisticated, cognitive, and properly factual reading is actually just as "naïve" as Huck's, insofar as it involves feelings of superiority toward a child, and indeed toward a fictional character. Only the experience of delight can propel the reader out of being the ultimate dupe.

Yet what differentiates the work of the romance, as articulated by Radway, or the effects of sentimentalism, as elaborated by Bell, from the work of realist literature is the extent to which the former "mask the reader's active collaboration in the production of textual meaning. . . . The reader is never forced to recognize that it is indeed she who actively supplies the significance of the words she encounters."[98] The work of realism, we will see in the chapters that follow, contains the following nested elements: (1) the enlistment of readers not just to feel emotion for (and thereby lend ontological stability to) an unreal object, which is arguably the work of sentimentalism, but also (2) to engage in this process of reflection or double-feel, to realize one's creative participation in experiencing the text and indeed the world. Feeling, once again, is not at odds with or irrelevant to interpretation: it is part of it. Twain's work is productive in this fashion. Focusing on the emotional engagement and education of the reader—indeed, the reader's education *about* and *through* his emotional engagement—helps to make clear how

Twain's bleakly playful novel can be usefully cast as a realist work, despite critical concern that it partakes too much of sentimentalist or even romantic elements.

As with the realist novel, laughter is corporeal as well as cognitive, epistemological as well as aesthetic. As John Dewey affirmed, "The laugh is by no means to be viewed from the standpoint of humor," or of merely risible content. It is formal and functional, marking a "divided activity" that ends in a realization, a sudden and explosive "point": "the getting the point," Dewey observes, "is the unity, the discharge."[99] This helps to explain what Henry James meant when he famously asserted, after his urbane deadpan list of all the absent things in American life—"No Epsom nor Ascot!"—that the American novelist "knows that a good deal remains; what it is that remains—that is his secret, his joke, as one might say."[100] What remains for the writer of the late nineteenth century is the most important story of all: the vivifying form of human perception itself, without which the world appears as inert, lifeless, and bleak indeed.

Charles Darwin, in his book *The Expression of the Emotions in Man and Animals* (1872), noted that in human beings smiling and laughter are suggestive of playfulness. This paragon of nineteenth-century materialism affirms the poet Homer's description of the laughter of the gods as "the exuberance of their celestial joy after their daily banquet."[101] Neurologists have taken up Darwin's point in asserting that the "ludic sense" distinguishes mammals from animals such as birds, along with long-lasting maternal connection to their offspring. (The two capacities are of course linked, in the playful interchanges that transpire between parent and infant.) The centrality of play—of knowingly engaging in self-representation, and of receiving affirmation from an audience—is, needless to say, the sine qua non of the actor. A version of this playfulness is what Rei Terada, in her study *Feeling in Theory,* refers to when she writes that not just stage-emotion, but emotion as such "demands virtual self-difference—an extra 'you'" (31). Terada notes that while "the theatricality of self-representation might seem to cast doubt on the reality of experience . . . it does not suspend or weaken emotion" (31). Moreover, "the object of emotion must not only be represented: it must be apprehended as representation" (33).

The *successful* laughter of the actor, then, can be seen as a paradigmatic experience of self qua self: the experience of a volatile, embodied, mindful self that emerges as both subject and object, knower and known, representer and that which is represented. In my study, the term for this self-reflexive process shall be the *forensic self*: that productively divided state of being in which one seeks or receives insight into one's own perceptual experience. Laughter provides an exemplary instance of this structure of self, insofar as it is prompted through interaction with another (the audience) and registers the laugher's "glory" in the sudden awareness of oneself as engaged in relation with oneself, mediated through another. To use Terada's terms, the actor's laughter marks the pleasure the "you" takes in the "extra you"—it is precisely the satisfaction that the one laughing has of being "placed on good terms with himself." The aging Henry James experienced this complex pleasure as he worked on his New York Edition, feeling his way back into the novels of his younger years. Works of literary realism help us to realize that, when we read, we are all like Narcissus staring into a puddle: delighting in that "extra you" who, far from being a solipsistic illusion, is a neurologically nested affective companion keeping us from our isolation by suturing us, body and mind, firmly to ourselves and to the world in which we live.

CHAPTER TWO

Statistical Pity

Elsie Venner and the Controversy over Childbed Fever

> The love of man for woman, or the human mother for
> her babe, our wrath at snakes and our fear of precipices,
> may all be described similarly, as instances of the way
> in which peculiarly conformed pieces of the world's
> furniture will fatally call forth most particular mental
> and bodily reactions.
>
> —WILLIAM JAMES, "WHAT IS AN EMOTION?" (1884)

As both doctors and laypersons in the nineteenth century were painfully aware, a woman who suffered from a virulent case of childbed fever died a terrible death. Although there were many things to dread in childbirth during that time—a prolapsed uterus, a vaginal tear, or a forceps-maimed infant, among others—nothing was as unpredictable or as lethal as puerperal fever.[1] As professor of obstetrics Charles Meigs wrote in 1854: "Sometimes the pain, which is, at the onset of puerperal fever, felt in the [abdomen], is too intense to be borne by any human patience; and no exhortation or recommendation can prevent the woman from crying aloud, or even screaming in her agony. I have seen patients, who not only appeared to suffer intolerable pain, but in whose minds that pain appeared to excite the most unspeakable terror."[2] Medical textbooks of the period included heart-wrenching depictions of individual patients who suffered from childbed fever, as well as the anguished commentaries of their doctors. As Meegan Kennedy has noted, the physicians' rhetoric drew heavily on sentimental conventions of the time, often describing in loving detail the victimized woman, her desperate family, and the physician's heroic efforts, in the words of Meigs, "to save one whom no art could save."[3] The medical accounts, in other words, had much in common with novelistic portrayals of deathbed scenes. Their power not just to portray but also to evoke an affective response would appear to be predicated precisely on those particularizing elements that

Ian Watt believed essential to the realist novel: the proper name (though disguised to protect the patient's privacy), specifics of time and place, the common rather than exemplary life, and so on.[4]

Given the epistemological focus on individuation, the term "statistical pity" might appear to be an oxymoron, insofar as the abstracting and aggregating impulse of statistical analysis has seemed antithetical to both novelistic realism and emotional response. This chapter's coupling of "statistical" with "pity" appears especially incongruous in light of critical interest in narrative ethics.[5] According to scholars of nineteenth-century literature and culture such as Mary Poovey, Martha Nussbaum, and Wai Chee Dimock, the scientific and philosophical commitment to abstraction and normativity produces an "epistemological violence" that deadens and dehumanizes. By contrast, according to these critics, the novel's densely layered details vivify: its complex web of motives both sustains accounts of human agency and elicits compassion.[6] If, as Poovey argues of statistics, "the individual human being . . . is obliterated by the numerical average or aggregate that replaces him," the novel's particularizing language provides, in Dimock's words, a "supplement and a corrective" to the "descriptive thinness and experiential harshness" of those abstractions that are "palpably impoverishing of the world."[7] Nussbaum sums up this position in her book *Poetic Justice* (1995): "The novel shows . . . the economic mind is blind: blind to the qualitative richness of the perceptible world; to the separateness of its people; to their inner depths, their hopes and loves and fears; blind to what it is like to live a human life and to try to endow it with a human meaning."[8] In these accounts, aggregating representations do not simply overlook differences: they actually eradicate them and in doing so harm individual persons. If the "thinness" of abstractions is damaging and the novel's "thickness" is sustaining, the task of the literary critic becomes importantly therapeutic—ameliorating the noxious effects of the former by an infusion of the latter. There is, as Elaine Scarry has observed, an oddly interventionist slant to this sort of critical undertaking, "as though the persons and events contemporaneous with the literary text are themselves alive and subject to alteration—capable . . . of being healed, or hurt, or educated."[9]

Recent critical accounts that describe narrative as a humanizing, agency-affirming, and even healing force bear directly on my examination of a moment in the history of American literary realism when Oliver Wendell Holmes Sr., working as both a physician and a novelist, explicitly inquired into the relationship between medical science and the novel. An examination of Holmes's work allows us to consider the consequences, both logical and historical, of the literary-critical position that the human realm of appreciations, feelings, and intentions is essentially individuated: that the representation of a beloved thing in its "incommensurable particularity," supplemented by a rich account of the psychological motives of the actors involved, is constitutively resistant to other more formal modes of analysis.[10] For Holmes, as this chapter explains, the commitment to the novel as a solution to the abstractions of science was deeply problematic, for the doctor-novelist's great contribution to medicine was his pioneering use of statistical norms to discover that the childbed fever then epidemic in Massachusetts was indeed contagious and that its appearance had nothing to do with a woman's individual constitution or moral choices—and everything to do with the physicians' actions and decisions. For Holmes, depersonalizing illness was a profoundly ethical act.

By explicating the novelistic thinking of the doctors who resisted Holmes's conclusions, I wish to suggest that Martha Nussbaum's comment regarding blindness might in certain instances be leveled against narrative, as well as the valorization of subjectivity understood in solely novelistic terms. For by treating each woman's case individually, nineteenth-century physicians unwittingly spread the disease that, before the discovery of the microbe, could only be made "visible" by comparing numerous cases. This individuation also authorized a deadly sentimentality, in which the physicians wept copiously for the very women they had infected. For doctors like Charles Meigs, the belief that puerperal fever could not be a single transmissible "thing" spread by the practitioners themselves was not merely an exculpatory argument (although desire to spare physicians from guilt was certainly a motivation). It was also the impassioned defense of a medical art predicated on—in Nussbaum's words—"the passionate love of particulars,"[11] the belief that each person constituted a unique and coherent whole, and that the study and care of human life can only be rooted in individual experience. As historian Charles E. Rosenberg has written, "Contagion seemed morally random and thus a denial of the traditional assumption that both health and disease arose from *particular* states of moral and social order."[12]

This chapter examines Meigs's commitment to narrative and to human incommensurability in light of his determination, at once dogged and deadly, to both moralize and sentimentalize sickness—to link it to the moral character and choices of the afflicted woman and to the feelings of the physician.[13] Holmes, in advancing his case for the contagiousness of puerperal fever, was not simply serving as protector of imperiled women (although he willingly adopted this role); he was also promoting an unsettling argument for the commensurability of bodies, the epistemological efficacy of pooling persons into populations, and the independent existence of specific diseases.[14] By infusing the techniques of modern science into American medicine, Holmes helped to disassemble the morally integrated—albeit physiologically dangerous—conceptual world of traditional therapeutics.[15]

Analysis of Holmes's medical, scientific, and literary work helps to frame the nineteenth-century understanding of the mind's relationship to the body. This chapter explores how numerical analysis allowed Holmes to reconfigure the idea of intention into the concept of "intentionality," to expand the concept of agency beyond the circumscribed psychological realm of human goals and aspirations. In the hands of Holmes, this not yet fully theorized usage was at once philosophical and physiological: it entailed what the cognitive theorist Daniel Dennett has called "aboutness."[16] Holmes's conceptual move allowed him to translate doctors' impeccable intentions, the alleviation of suffering and preservation of life, into murderous outcomes: the transmission of infection to parturient women. This approach, like the full-blown pragmatism of the generation that followed Holmes (including his own son, the Supreme Court justice Oliver Wendell Holmes Jr.), was ontologically agnostic: rather than the ascription of particular beliefs, goals, and feelings to a particular person, it entailed the adoption of an intentional stance, the ascription of intentionality to objects and actions such that they could be understood to form a system. This model was fertilized by Charles Darwin's theory of natural selection, in which every attribute and action of an organism was understood to house "intentionality": as Darwin put it, in the 1872 edition of *The Origin of Species*, "We must suppose that there is a power, represented by natural selection or the survival of the fittest, always intently watching each slight alteration. . . . In living bodies, variation will cause the slight alteration, generation will multiply them almost infinitely, and natural selection will pick out with unerring skill each improvement."[17] Natural selection "watch[es]" and then "picks out with unerring skill" those variations that suit the environment: every aspect of an organism's body, in other words, is understood to be the result of selection that is specific yet impersonal and of "design" that is attuned to environmental conditions yet unmotivated. Bodies were for Darwin "mindful," in that they were indexical with respect to the world around them. In the words of William James that serve as the epigraph for this chapter, the "peculiarly conformed pieces of the world's furniture . . . call forth most particular mental and bodily reactions."[18]

Oliver Wendell Holmes's experimentation with rudimentary statistical analysis was also crucial to his work as a novelist. This chapter argues that Holmes's portrayal of the snake-girl Elsie Venner, in the eponymous novel serialized in 1859 (published as a book in 1861), combines a Darwinian evolutionary perspective with the neurological knowledge of the anatomist to express the crude form of intentionality possessed not just by reptiles but also the "reptilian brain"—the oldest (in evolutionary terms) part of the human nervous system. This system, Holmes discerned, operated with intentionality akin to that of an epidemic: not through psychological agency (e.g. murderous plotting) but through the most primitive embodied affects of aversion and affiliation. As further elaborated in Chapter 3, in Holmes's later novels, written after the neurologist John Hughlings Jackson published a full-blown evolutionary account of the nervous system, Holmes further refines the notion that an individual's body harbors intentionality by expanding what we mean by intelligence and agency. In the words of the psychologist and Holmes-admirer Théodule Ribot, every individual has an "organic memory," housed not in the brain proper but encased in "the acquired movements which constitute the memory of different organs—the eyes, hands, arms, and legs."[19]

Holmes's work provides a corrective to arguments that, poised on an implicit dualism, choose between and valorize either mind or body at the expense of the other. Certain accounts of literary naturalism urge that the preeminence of corporeal processes in late-nineteenth-century fiction articulated a "pessimistic determinism" by reducing human beings to animals or machines: all body, no mind.[20] In the case of a certain strain of trauma theory, this notion takes on an oddly positive spin: the body contains truths that trump the representations (and protestations) of the mind;[21] while in the case of some Freudians, the discourse of the body serves as a material metaphor for the conflicts of the psyche.[22] Holmes's writings help to show the dualistic kinship of these apparently dichotomous positions, and to challenge those accounts that affirm the necessary alignment of statistics with determinism and dehumanization, and the novel with agency and the ethical as such. Holmes's work resists the tendency to distinguish categorically between "brute" sensitivity and higher feelings and to divide passion from reason, self from environment, and body from mind. As both Holmes and Darwin recognized, the treasuring of endless particularity produced a circumstance in which nothing could be treasured, for the environment is too rich: it contains a paralyzing plethora of information leading to infinite possible futures. As Henry James perspicaciously wrote in the 1907 preface to *Roderick Hudson,* "Really, universally, relations stop nowhere, and the exquisite problem of the artist is eternally but to draw, by a geometry of his own, the circle within which they shall happily *appear* to do so."[23] Holmes's great achievement was to develop such a critical geometry: to put the mind in relation to the body, by taking seriously the notion that statistical representation might elicit the strong response of compassion. This is the first step, for Holmes, toward making substantial changes in how practitioners in the nineteenth century understood sickness and disease, how they conceived of human intentions and corporeal permeability, and how they might develop a representational method that could actively "realize" the complexity of human life— leading to such unspectacular yet life-affirming practices as doctors' handwashing between patients. Far from undermining the integrity of the individual, Holmes's conception of statistical pity was predicated on the centrality of bodily feeling to human intelligence, and of both to the preservation and treasuring of individual lives.

The Case against Contagion

While critics of Holmes's novels have overlooked the centrality of his work on puerperal fever, I argue that *Elsie Venner* (1861), his first novel, reprises the medical positions at issue in the debate over contagion. In the final scenes of the novel, Elsie lies in bed, slowly succumbing to a malady as mysterious as the suffering character it afflicts. Holmes's narrative presents Elsie Venner as an epistemological riddle: stories circulate about the mesmeric power of her glance, her midnight wanderings along ledges and into caverns, and her wild solitary dances. Hushed rumors intimate that Elsie is not fully human, having been infected in utero by the venomous bite of the snake that killed her mother. When Silas Peckham, the mercenary director of Elsie's school, inquires whether the girl's disease is "ketchin'" and might spread to his other students, Dr. Kittredge, the local physician, laughs incredulously, asserting that no disease of this particular girl could possibly be contagious.[24] This exchange reveals the competing accounts of selfhood in the novel. Kittredge bases his diagnosis of Elsie on her "peculiar constitution" (429): her illness is unique because *she* is. By contrast, the schoolmaster's concern that the disease might spread to others reflects his translation of persons into a population: "Silas Peckham kept a young ladies' school exactly as he would have kept a hundred head of cattle,—for the simple unadorned purpose of making . . . money" (48). As identical figures on a balance sheet, Silas's students are literally equivalent, therefore equally susceptible to the same disease. The schoolmaster's abstracting mode itself follows the logic of contagion, which Charles Meigs denounced for being "no respecter of persons . . . attack[ing] all individuals alike."[25]

In revealing their ways of conceptualizing disease, the school director and the doctor reenact the confrontation between the two representational modes—one operating on the principle of similarity to aggregate, one operating on the principle of difference to individualize—that were so starkly articulated in the medical controversy over puerperal fever. The literary critic James Dawes, in his analysis of Civil War writing, has noted that both modes were active in the nineteenth century: the "contrast between [Walt] Whitman and [Louisa May] Alcott," he writes, "might be described as the contrast between the statistical and the narrative imagination."[26] American practitioners of traditional therapeutics (the source of the fictional Dr. Kittredge's ideas) tended to draw on the latter mode. They were influenced by the eighteenth-century theories of Benjamin Rush and John Brown, who predicated their medical interventions on what Rush termed the "unity of disease," the notion that there were no specific diseases, just individual constitutions out of balance.[27] "The whole human body," Rush wrote, "is so formed and connected, that impressions made in the healthy state upon one part, excite motion, or sensation, or both, in every other part of the body. From this view, it appears to be a unit, or simple and indivisible substance."[28] Healing involved the restoration of an individual's equilibrium, and Rush urged doctors to bleed, purge, and blister their patients accordingly.

Historian Charles E. Rosenberg has argued that, in the absence of modern explanations for the source and nature of disease, the startling results produced by nineteenth-century doctors' often violent treatments were, for both patient and practitioner, reassuringly *visible:* a pool of blood in a bowl, an eruption of red blisters, or a drenching sweat all confirmed that the physician was doing something to bring the illness under control.[29] Even as the physician was bringing to bear a massive conceptual framework for interpreting the body's every symptom (symptoms that doctors often went to heroic lengths to produce), he could feel assured that the body was speaking its own irrefutable language. The representational counterpart of Rush's conception of disease was an empirical realism focused on particular individuals: the "unity of disease" meant that each person's condition, composed of potentially infinite elements, must always be a never-before-seen portrait of disease.

While contagionists noted that puerperal fever had the ominous tendency to arise in clusters, physicians in the anticontagionist camp insisted that each instance was an unrelated or "sporadic" case. Holmes's medical adversary, Charles Meigs, in his influential textbook *Woman: Her Diseases and Remedies* (1859), insisted that a doctor must attend solely to the unique, suffering person before him. "Method in medicine," Meigs wrote,

> is beneath contempt; because owing to the infinite variety and differences existing among the living molecules . . . there never were, nor can be two absolutely similar cases. Each instance of disease is an independent integer and should in strictness be so deemed, and studied, and understood, and managed upon a reference to it, and not to another integer. . . . It is true that the patient who is under care to-day may be *like* 'him who died o' Wednesday,' but is not *him:* hence, you perceive that I am no admirer of statistics.[30]

In 1854 Meigs published an entire text devoted to refuting Holmes's position that puerperal fever was contagious. In that work, he described puerperal fever as "a group of diverse inflammations within the belly, in women pregnant, or recently delivered."[31] Not a "thing" and without a seat in a single organ, puerperal fever for Meigs comprised a constellation of causes and effects as unique as a fingerprint.

When Meigs asserted that "there is no such thing as a childbed fever" (*Childbed Fevers,* 122), he meant that it was the identity of the person that directed the course of the malady. Diagnosis was always retrospective, for one could never predict what element of a particular woman's constitution might make her susceptible. Women's choices and actions were for Meigs at the center of the production and (to some extent) the eradication of puerperal fever. Potential sources of illness lurked everywhere: anticontagionists mentioned improper diet or drinks, excessive emotionality, fatigue, burns, cholera, cuts, cold, and exposure. Meigs suggested susceptible women were too "highly sensitive and aesthetic" (*Childbed Fevers*, 194); another physician maintained that "the scratch of a pin or an oyster shell" could make a woman sick.[32] In Meigs's words, "There is an almost infinite number of contingencies" that might bring on childbed fever, "purely because a newly-delivered woman, like a bundle of flax, or like a pistol-pan of powder, is likely to be inflamed and go off for the smallest spark" (*Childbed Fevers*, 114, 205).

This conception of disease was not only self-ratifying (a doctor might marshal any account to explain why it arose); it also tended to place responsibility with the woman patient, especially those who "superstitiously" dismissed doctors with a long list of puerperal deaths. In these cases, Meigs was intent on foregrounding and assuaging the pain of doctors: "Be not discouraged, however; for the fault will not be yours" (*Woman*, 646). In his textbook on women's diseases, Meigs denounced noncompliant patients: "Such signal disobedience of express directions, such enormous stupidity, is apt to be followed by the loss of the patient; a loss so great, that there are no words in which I can set forth the mental distress it occasions. . . . This it is that makes the life of an accoucheur more painful than that of any surgeon or mere general practitioner" (*Woman*, 645). Meigs recalled a puerperal fever patient he treated, whose placenta he had extracted manually: "She was a very rosy, most beautiful, and most healthy creature, when in labor. . . . Her mother, who nursed her, gave her too large a dose of castor-oil. I presume, that if she had not taken the dose she would not have become ill" (*Childbed Fevers*, 139). Luckily, Meigs concluded, he later saved her life through profuse bloodletting.

The anticontagionist camp disparaged as romantics those who thought puerperal fever was communicable, maintaining that this tendency to fabulate was in contrast to their own empirical realism, their attention to "facts." Meigs warned his students explicitly against "fighting with ontological shadows, instead of directing all the force of your intelligence and skill to the removal of a disease" (*Childbed Fevers*, 209).[33] Contagionists created, "by force of vivid imagination, an *ens* [essence] out of nothing; and then endow[ed] it with power to produce a disease like itself" (*Childbed Fevers*, 211). Advocates of contagionist theories were censured for detaching childbed fever from the material world with their speculations, or even fatally implanting it in the minds of their patients. In the words of Meig's Philadelphia colleague Dr. Hodge, "Fear alone has destroyed many valued lives."[34]

The notion that disease was a process and not an entity underpinned Meigs's commitment to "really paint" a case in mimetic detail, so that his audience would feel a "partaker in the incidents and sentiments" of the sickroom and "would seem to be present and witnessing the whole scene" (*Childbed Fevers*, 212). He devoted an entire chapter of his textbook on childbed fever to narrating the course of the disease in a single patient, beginning with character development: "She was a very small and delicately formed creature, of the most cultivated understanding, and . . . thoroughly well bred" (*Childbed Fevers*, 212). Throughout the case, he interspersed novelistic detail—descriptions of the weather, dialogue among family members, descriptions of a patient's manners and personal appearance—with physiological symptoms of the spreading fever: "black vomit; lessening pulses; increased respiratory efforts; cooling hands and feet" (*Childbed Fevers*, 215). As his patient sickened, Meigs increasingly emphasized his own reaction to the case: "What shall I say, in a weak vain hope of portraying the feelings with which the physician approaches the bedside of one so perilous?" (*Childbed Fevers*, 214). Gauging his patient's impending death as much by his increasing hopelessness as by the woman's symptoms, Meigs replaces the agony of the patient and the "tears and suppressed moanings" (*Childbed Fevers*, 215) of her family with his own anguish. He summed up in these words: "Why say all this? Why, a physician to practise Midwifery must be made of stone if he would not feel on these occasions; and, if he have a heart of flesh, he surely deserves the sympathy of all good people when he turns away a baffled man, after faithful, well-conducted efforts to save one whom no art could save" (*Childbed Fevers*, 215). The identification was made complete by the sympathetic reader (the medical student to whom these chapters were addressed), who was urged to identify with the physician's intense anxiety and exculpating sorrow.

In his drive to depict adequately the patient's individual experience in narrative, Meigs allowed the physician's need for sympathy to eclipse that of the patient. In the case of a student of Meigs named Dr. Rutter, who "had charge of seventy cases [of puerperal fever], of which he lost only eighteen" (*Childbed Fevers*, 106), Meigs transferred the suffering of the "unfortunate victims" onto the unflagging physician himself. Rutter, who performed almost penitential ablutions—paring his nails, burning his clothes, shaving his hair—was depicted as a man broken by the "repetition of such disheartening labors" (*Childbed Fevers,* 105) and tainted by criticism "both cruel and unjust, particularly as his success in the treatment was most brilliant" (*Childbed Fevers,* 105–106). Sharon Marcus has termed this type of sentimental identification *mimetic,* where the sympathizing subject elides the difference between himself and the object of his attention.[35] As Marcus analyses it, mimetic identification begins by affirming the irreducibility of individual experience but ends ironically with the same sort of appropriation it claims to be resisting. In Meigs's medical texts what was intended as a radical defense of particularity becomes the broadest of universalizing gestures: dying women need your sympathy, I need your sympathy, all good doctors deserve sympathy. The sorrow engendered by such cruel loss of life unifies patient, physician, and readers in an imagined bond of common humanity. In the case of Holmes and the debate over puerperal fever, narrative depictions of the illness further authorized the dangerous intervention of physicians into the precariously male-dominated domain of childbirth. Under the sign of compassion, these representations had fatal significance, insisting as they did that only physicians possessed the finely tuned sensibility to divine—and the therapeutic skills to alter— the terrible reality of the disease.

Representing "Ontological Shadows"

The inflammatory material in Holmes's article "The Contagiousness of Puerperal Fever" was not only his claim that puerperal fever was contagious but also his insistence that the illness was iatrogenic: caused by the doctors themselves. Holmes, in making his case, figured the physicians' actions not in terms of psychological intention but, instead, as analogous to the impersonal system of switches used by the railways:

> If I am right, let doctrines which lead to professional homicide be no longer taught from the chairs of those two great Institutions [the University of Pennsylvania and Jefferson Medical College, where Hodge and Meigs taught]. . . . Why a grand jury should not bring in a bill against a physician who switches off a score of women one after the other along his private track, when he knows that there is a black gulf at the end of it, down which they are to plunge, while the great highway is clear, is more than I can answer.[36]

The culpable physician operates a "private track," indicating individual responsibility for what happens along the "line." Nonetheless, the metaphor of the railway switching system shifts concern away from the specific intention of the doctor, as well as the specific details of the women involved (who, drawing out the trope of transportation, are mere "carriers"). Despite the impersonality of Holmes's critique—he refers only to the culpability of "chairs" at the Philadelphia colleges—Meigs responded in ad hominem terms, urging his readers to "disregard the jejune and fizzenless dreamings of sophomore writers" (113), answering Holmes's claims with character slurs and personal attacks. Further personalizing his case, Meigs's medical text on puerperal fever marshaled anecdotes of highly esteemed doctors—including himself—who encountered bouts of puerperal fever in their practices. Of the miserable Dr. Rutter, Meigs asserted, "He is a gentleman who is scrupulously careful of his personal appearance. . . . Did he carry it on his hands? But a gentleman's hands are clean" (104). Meigs concluded, "Seeing that I could never convict myself of being the means of spreading the contagion, I remain incredulous as to the contagiousness of the malady."[37] Just like good doctoring, the defense of good doctors was for Meigs a personal issue, about individuals, not diseases.

But Holmes's radical point was *not* that it was possible for good doctors to provide poor care, or even that incompetent doctoring could be fatal. It was Holmes's methodology that was pioneering, in its application of mathematical norms to the experience of any physician, regardless of individual contingencies. The 1855 introduction to Holmes's treatise on childbed fever distills his argument into twelve statements of "medical logic" (112) intended to carry the power of syllogism rather than mimetic accuracy. Holmes sought to "exhibit, in a series of propositions" (112), the "results of practice in more than six thousand cases" (110). For Holmes, critical expertise lay not in the seasoned accoucheur but in the statistician:

> I have had the chances calculated by a competent person, that a given practitioner, A., shall have sixteen fatal cases in a month, on the following data: A. to average attendance upon two hundred and fifty births a year; three deaths in one thousand births to be assumed as the average from puerperal fever. . . . It follows . . . [that] there would not be one chance in a million million million millions that one such series should be noted. . . . Applied to dozens of series of various lengths, it is obviously an absurdity. Chance, therefore, is out of the question as an explanation of the admitted coincidences. (114)

Before considering actual cases, Holmes established a mathematical rule that precluded the possibility of a doctor "'unlucky'" enough (Meigs's term) to treat multiple cases of puerperal fever. Holmes supplanted the persona of the sage doctor with matchless skills with a systematic analysis that might be applied to anybody, and, within limits, *by* anybody. Such an impersonal standard of comparison could make visible the reality of "professional homicide" (Holmes's words) regardless of a particular physician's professional stature, gentlemanly attire, or capacity for sorrow.[38] Holmes saw democratic promise in figures that aggregated personal feelings into potent data: "I conceive a Committee of Husbands, who can count coincidences and draw conclusions as well as a Synod of Accoucheurs, would justly . . . [effect] an *unceremonious dismissal* of a practitioner . . . after five or six funerals had marked the path of his daily visits" (107). Holmes believed that the fruits of numerical analysis would be perfectly compatible with—indeed, preserving of—human sentiments and affections.

Focusing too closely on individual cases, Holmes argued, led to a naïve empiricism, in which a physician misconstrued his "foregone conclusion" about disease and doctors (e.g. that gentlemen have clean hands) as the "teachings of his experience" (175). Holmes argued that the "numerical system" developed in Paris by Pierre Louis corrected this human tendency:

> The "numerical system" of which Louis was the great advocate, if not the absolute originator, was an attempt to substitute series of carefully recorded facts, rigidly counted, and closely compared, for those never-ending records of vague, unverifiable conclusions with which the healing art were overloaded. . . . Cases thoroughly recorded and mathematically analyzed would always be available for future use, and when accumulated in sufficient number would lead to results which would be trustworthy, and belong to science.[39]

The numerical system could short-circuit the distorting effects of one's expectations and track a phenomenon in the face of uncertainty about its ontology. If, in traditional therapeutics, meaning always preceded and determined what counted as data (such that a patient's symptoms were always explicable in terms of her prior behavior, status, or character) the numerical system reversed this arrangement: one might have data without meaning, information or "knowledge" without a representation. The philosopher Daniel Dennett has pointed out that the capacity to track phenomena "does not require the ability to *conceive of* this thing as an enduring particular entity, coming and going" (105). Holmes employed numbers as an epistemological cryogenics, preserving undigested experience for later interpretation. This rudimentary form of statistics was importantly pragmatic, making it possible for both doctors and patients to predict who was at risk for a disease.

Whereas Meigs's account of puerperal fever focused on particulars, Holmes's was crucially comparative. In "The Contagiousness of Puerperal Fever" Holmes shifted the scrutiny from the afflicted women to the doctors, analyzing documented cases solicited directly from physicians. He observed that attendants who didn't wash or change clothes between patients usually had multiple cases of puerperal fever. In one egregious instance, a physician fresh from an autopsy pocketed the viscera of a puerperal corpse before embarking on his obstetrical visits. Not himself an obstetrician, and unacquainted with the patients whose cases he collected, Holmes eyed the evidence from a position of detachment.

Yet, even for those most intimately involved with obstetrical patients, Holmes asserted that the numerical method itself could serve as a system of detachment. Holmes pointed to the example of Alexander Gordon, a Scottish physician who in the late eighteenth century had used mathematical analysis to discover his own culpability for spreading puerperal fever to his obstetrical patients. Holmes in his treatise is moved to quote Gordon's understated self-indictment: "'It is a disagreeable declaration for me to mention, that I myself was the means of carrying the infection to a great number of women'" (134–135). During a puerperal fever outbreak in 1789, Gordon had recorded which practitioners of midwifery came in contact with the disease; his final compilation of data, collected over a period of three years, condensed seventy-seven cases into a two-page chart. Gordon included only six pieces of information from each case: the date, the patient's age and name, where she lived, whether she survived or when she died, and who delivered her baby. These data set into relief a pattern obscured by the vagaries of individual practice, namely, that only certain attendants met with the disease, and that once they did, so did their subsequent patients. These diverse women, Gordon maintained, suffered from the exact same disease.

Daniel Dennett, offering examples of mystifying entities and events that can nonetheless be "tracked" or "seen," tellingly cites diseases and murderers: "An epidemic may be diagnosed by seeing—*seeing* thanks to color coding—that all the cases of one sort line up on the map alongside one or another inconspicuous or even heretofore undepicted feature— the water main, or the sewage system, or perhaps the route of the postman. A serial killer's secret base of operations may sometimes be homed in on—a variety of villaintaxis—by plotting the geographic center of the cluster of his attacks" (144). (The term "villaintaxis" is a creative use of the Greek root -*taxis,* which designates the responsive movement of a simple organism toward or away from a particular stimulus.) In the hands of Alexander Gordon, statistical analysis provided a means to "figure," in the numerical sense, the unimaginable: that a doctor could be an unwitting serial killer. Rather than fueling an oppressive naturalism and reducing persons to automata, Gordon's approach extended the concept of intention, attributing it beyond individual human beings. An "entity" or system, as Dennett has suggested, could be approached from the *intentional stance,* which is "the strategy of interpreting the behavior of an entity (person, animal, artifact, whatever) by treating it *as if* it were a rational agent who governed its 'choice' or 'action' by a 'consideration' of its 'beliefs' and 'desires'" (27). The point of doing this? Dennett's answer: "To treat an entity as an agent in order to predict its actions" (34). More precisely, in the case of puerperal fever, the point was to reduce suffering, enhance the chances of flourishing and, above all, avoid death—the same implicit "desires" that motivated the "choices" of Darwin's primitive organisms.

A prototype for twentieth-century clinical trials, Gordon's chart enabled chilling predictions about subsequent cases knowing only *one* particular (Holmes quoted Gordon in full capitals): "'I ARRIVED AT THAT CERTAINTY IN THE MATTER THAT I COULD VENTURE TO FORETELL WHAT WOMEN WOULD BE AFFECTED WITH THE DISEASE, UPON HEARING WHAT MIDWIFE THEY WERE TO BE DELIVERED . . . DURING THEIR LYING-IN: AND ALMOST IN EVERY INSTANCE, MY PREDICTION WAS VERIFIED'" (135). Almost one hundred years before bacteriology, Gordon isolated disease as an impersonal object of analysis separable from, yet intimately concerned with, both the patient and the doctor. As the historian Irvine Loudon writes, "It is no exaggeration to say that Gordon's treatise is an early masterpiece of epidemiology."[40] Though microbes wouldn't be identified under a microscope for decades, Gordon (and Holmes) helped to realize disease as an entity distinct from a person's corporeal balance. The Scottish physician recognized, to use Daniel Dennett's terms, "knowledge *in* the system" that was "not yet knowledge *to* the system" (132). Gordon's depersonalizing mode and his devastating professional honesty, which ruined his obstetrical practice, served for Holmes as a model of ethical medical inquiry. Embodying a distressing contradiction between healer and killer, Gordon traced a fracture within the coherent moral universe of traditional therapeutics, between the particular experience of one person and aggregate knowledge.

While Meigs's medical heroism lay in applying arcane skill—usually in the form of a lancet—to save a puerperal patient, Holmes's valor lay in advocating practices like handwashing, for he "had rather rescue one mother from being poisoned by her attendant, than claim to have saved forty out of fifty patients to whom [he] had carried the disease" (106). An indignant Holmes in 1860 lambasted anticontagionists who cast themselves as sympathetic saviors: "Do not some of you remember that I have had to fight this private-pestilence question against a skepticism which sneered in the face of a mass of evidence such as the calm statisticians of the Insurance office could not listen to without horror and indignation?"[41] In reconfiguring what counted as evidence, Holmes inverted Meigs's sympathetic alliance, transforming ostensible healers into murderous skeptics and "calm statisticians" into men of feeling. Contra Meigs, who was "no admirer of statistics," Holmes affirmed that numerical evidence could produce clarity of vision without sacrificing sympathy.[42] Indeed, Holmes's essay is fueled by a sense of outrage that makes it a startlingly effective, impassioned piece of rhetoric.

Although Meigs derided contagionist theories as fighting with "ontological shadows," thirty years later in France, Louis Pasteur isolated the objects casting the shadows—bacteria—under a microscope.[43] At the time Holmes wrote, however, the only visible manifestation of the disease was a baffling array of symptoms in the bodies of afflicted women. Holmes's treatise reversed the representational polarity, condensing patients into tables, while giving shape and intentionality to the previously unimaginable disease. In Holmes's scathing words,

> It does appear a singular coincidence, that one man or woman should have ten, twenty, thirty, or seventy cases of this rare disease following his or her footsteps with the keenness of a beagle, through the streets and lanes of a crowded city, while the scores that cross the same paths on the same errands know it only by name. It is a series of similar coincidences which has led us to consider the dagger, the musket, and certain innocent-looking white powders as having some little claim to be regarded as dangerous. (157)

Deploying statistics along with metaphor and analogy, Holmes sought a way to figure something that had eluded the mimetic sensibility of traditional therapeutics.

Holmes's "Algebra of Human Nature"

Holmes's 1861 novel *Elsie Venner* reveals a high degree of awareness that when representing persons, consequences attach to the mode one employs. On its surface, the novel rehearses Holmes's position in the debate over childbed fever, albeit in narrative form, with a healthy pregnant woman receiving a deadly inoculation prior to delivering her child:

> In the year 184–, a melancholy proof was afforded to the inhabitants of Rockland, that the brood [of snakes] which infested The Mountain was not extirpated. A very interesting young married woman, detained at home at the time by the state of her health, was bitten in the entry of her own house by a rattlesnake which had found its way down from The Mountain. Owing to the almost instant employment of powerful remedies the bite did not prove immediately fatal; but she died within a few months of the time when she was bitten. (45)

The woman died, that is, after giving birth to the baby she had been carrying at the time of the rattlesnake bite. Charles Meigs had used this very trope in 1854 to ridicule contagionist theories that claimed that doctors "poison [a patient] as by the bite of a rattlesnake and so make her sick . . . [with] a childbed fever" (*Childbed Fevers*, 211).

Holmes, however, centers his novel not on the tragedy of the mother's death but on the strange daughter who survives, and who attends the class of a part-time medical student working at Silas Peckham's school for young ladies while seeking to fund his own education. The two mentors of Bernard Langdon, the young schoolteacher committed to "solv[ing] the mystery of Elsie Venner" (204), offer divergent models for conceptualizing the singular young woman. His medical professor is the novel's quasi-omniscient narrator, representing Holmes's own position of detached analysis in the puerperal fever debate (in character and title akin to Holmes's alter ego in his column entitled "The Professor at the Breakfast Table"). The Professor wrote a textbook on Anglo-American anthropology and provides his student Bernard with ethnographic categories to contain the anomalous Elsie. Bernard's other mentor, Dr. Kittredge, is by contrast a sympathetic country physician who has tended generations of Venners. Espousing the clinical perspective familiar from Meigs's writings, Kittredge scorns the idea of "an algebra of human nature" (321), espousing instead a therapeutic creed adapted "to suit the need . . . of each individual soul" (452). This point also appears in the homespun argot of Elsie's nurse: "'If you knowed all the young gals that ever lived, y' would n' know nothin' 'bout our Elsie'" (353). The tension between the Professor and the physician and their divergent epistemological modes centers on the character of Bernard, whose official education came from the Professor but whose bedside training is overseen by the doctor. The Professor frames the issue thus: will Bernard impersonally diagnose Elsie or succumb to particular preference and marry her?[44]

The Professor appears to import Holmes's central insight from his paper on puerperal fever: that individuals are most accurately represented on the page by employing reduction and abstraction. As with the medical treatise, the novel begins with an algebraic formula that effectively condenses the intergenerational saga of Bernard Landon's family into a couple of sentences: "It is in the nature of large fortunes to diminish rapidly, when subdivided and distributed. It splits into four handsome properties; each of these into four good inheritances; these, again, into scanty competences for four ancient maidens,—with whom it is best the family should die out, unless it can begin again as its great-grandfather did" (2). Bernard himself is initially presented by the Professor/narrator as a specimen: "It was a handsome face,—a little too pale, perhaps, and would have borne something more of fulness [sic] without becoming heavy. I put the organization to which it belongs in Section B of Class 1 of my Anglo-American Anthropology" (8). Similarly, girls whom Bernard teaches serve as representatives of broad human categories: "The door opened, and three misses came in to take their seats: three types, as it happened, of certain classes, into which it would not have been difficult to distribute the greater number of the girls in the school" (76).

The spatial separateness of human beings, the Professor maintains, produces the misleading effect of uniqueness: "People, young or old," he explains, "are wonderfully different, if we contrast extremes in pairs" (173). Aggregation, however, had the power to defeat the dispersing and therefore distorting effects of time and space, to allow one to see similarities among individuals. The Professor continues, "[People] approach much nearer, if we take them in groups of twenty. . . . If we go a step farther, and compare the population of two villages . . . there is such a regularly graduated distribution and parallelism of character, that it seems as if Nature must turn out human beings like chessmen" (173). Here, the ascription of intentionality familiar from the debate over puerperal fever is made explicit, with "Nature" as the agent or designer.

Even courtship, for the Professor, lends itself to such formulations: "Remember that Nature makes every man love all women, and trusts the trivial matter of special choice to the commonest accident" (104). Romance thus becomes fodder for scientific scrutiny, for "the study of love is very much like that of meteorology" (282). Speaking as if to a starry-eyed belle, the Professor clinically dissects middle-class fashions and social rituals to reveal their essential Darwinian functionality:

> Society is inspecting you, and it finds undisguised surfaces and strong lights a convenience in the process. The dance answers the purpose of the revolving pedestal upon which the "White Captive" turns. . . . Look you, there are dozens, scores, hundreds, with whom you must be weighed in the balance; and you have got to learn that the "struggle for life" Mr. Charles Darwin talks about reaches to vertebrates clad in crinoline, as well as to mollusks in shells. (94)

The Professor's analogy between maidens and mollusks would appear to entail an eradication of agency: you may think you're dancing and enjoying yourself, he implies, but actually this elaborate ritual was designed to display you in a process that sidesteps individual choice. Upon reflection, however, it becomes apparent that the Professor is actually engaged in the extension of agency: the ritual precisely was designed, or at least acts as if it were. This is what Charles Darwin discerned as "natural selection." Dennett puts it this way: "Mother Nature, the process of natural selection, shows her appreciation of good reasons tacitly, by wordlessly and mindlessly permitting the best designs to prosper. . . . We late-blooming theorists are the first to *see* the patterns and divine these reasons—the free-floating rationales of the designs that have been created over the eons" (59–60).

The narrating Professor advocates the sort of perspective that is provided by detachment and abstraction, two crucial "late-blooming" capacities available to human beings. While these modes of appreciation seem to be the province of the man of science—as in the case of the Professor himself—they are nonetheless compatible with quotidian instances of pattern-discerning insight. A very basic form might be found in parents who, the Professor points out, are wont to observe physical similarities between their children and other relatives: "They notice the trivial movements and accents which betray the blood of this or that ancestry. . . . This boy sits with his legs crossed, just as his uncle used to whom he never saw; his grandfathers both died before he was born, but he has the movement of the eyebrows which we remember in one of them, and the gusty temper of the other" (271). Such observations, however, rarely extend beyond the delight of perceiving resemblance.

Yet there are, the Professor notes, other points of view that embody a more elaborated form of pattern-discerning, which can even take the form of rudimentary statistical analysis: "Here and there," he explains, "a sagacious person, old, or of middle age, who has triangulated a race, that is, taken three or more observations from the several standing places of three different generations, can tell pretty nearly the range of possibilities and the limitations of a child, actual or potential, of a given stock" (271–272). The claim of the passage, while grounded in empirical observation, begins to push beyond the known to include a predictive element: the capacity to account for persons not yet born, or perhaps never to be born. While firmly committed to specifying material connections among persons, the method being advanced by the Professor—what he here terms "triangulation"—is a system that could function in the absence of the material thing it is nonetheless able to realize.

In his "Professor at the Breakfast Table" series, Holmes disparaged the standard instruments of mimesis—the mirror and the photograph—as too static and therefore inaccurate: "No genuine expression can be studied by the subject of it in the looking glass."[45] Nor, Holmes asserted, can a person trust a portrait-painter to produce a telling picture off just one sitting: "Even within your own family, I am afraid, there is a face which the rich uncle knows, that is not so familiar to the poor relation" (191). Only a true artist can overcome this difficulty: "The artist throws you off your guard, watches you in movement and repose, puts your face through its exercises, observes its transitions, and so gets the whole range of its expression. Out of all this he forms an ideal portrait, which is not a copy of your exact look at any one time or to any particular person. Such a portrait cannot be to everybody what the ungloved call 'as nat'ral as life'" (191). "As nat'ral as life" is an apt vernacular translation of William Dean Howells's affirmation that "realism is nothing more and nothing less than the truthful treatment of material."[46] In Holmes's alternate mode—more aptly termed *realization*—the "ideal portrait" is still derived empirically, with the artist compiling multiple images by coaxing a model through her range of expressions and then fusing them. (Holmes, familiar with Francis Galton's photographic attempts to isolate human types, notes in the preface to *Elsie Venner* that the characters in the novel are "mostly composites, like Mr. Galton's compound photographic likenesses" [xii].) This process, as Holmes depicts it here, depends on the painter's extraordinary skill as psychologist as well as draftsman.

The implicit elitism of Holmes's formulation, however, clashed with his own democratic ethos, while the singularity of such an artistic enterprise conflicted with his anatomist's commitment to replicability. Holmes regarded the stereoscope as one answer to these problems. At roughly the same time that he wrote *Elsie Venner* and the "Professor at the Breakfast Table" series, he composed articles for the *Atlantic Monthly* praising the representational power of this device, which, by holding two slightly different images before a person's eyes, produced for the viewer a three-dimensional effect. "The mind," Holmes wrote, "feels its way into the very depth of the picture."[47] Holmes advised that eventually every household would possess this tool of perception. (Elsie Venner had one, and particularly enjoyed "studying the stereoscopic Laocoon" [313].) The stereoscope, which Holmes described as "a mirror with memory" (739), was at once a metaphor and an instrument for rendering an image that, to achieve its richly detailed evocation of the object world ("we have the same sense of the infinite complexity which Nature gives us" [744]), required the active participation of the viewing subject. The stereoscopic image, as it was fused in the mind's eye, was unique to the viewer yet replicable, and it distilled a differential perspective (the two images in the device) into a singular one. In the stereograph Holmes had discovered an instrument of realization akin to statistics in its twinned commitment to and abstraction from the material world.

Pathological Particularity in the Novel

The "one of a kind" figure of Elsie Venner, however, is initially offered as a rebuke to the Professor's detachment and abstractions. "She was, indeed, an apparition of wild beauty, so unlike the girls about her that it seemed nothing more than natural, that, when she moved, the groups should part to let her pass through them. . . . In the midst of the crowd she made a circle of isolation around herself" (99, 100). Her intrigued schoolteacher, Bernard, muses over why he finds her so compelling: "'Elsie interests me,' said the young man, 'interests me strangely. She has a wild flavor in her character which is wholly different from that of any human creature I ever saw" (213). Her singularity, for Bernard, aligns her with Romanticism: "'She has marks of genius. . . . She read a passage from [John] Keats's "Lamia" the other day. . . . I declare to you

I thought some of the girls would faint or go into fits'" (213–214). The novel bristles with an abundance of stories, rumors, hints, and allusions about the girl, who is herself physically evocative: "She was dressed to please her own fancy, evidently, with small regard to the modes declared correct by the Rockland milliners and mantua-makers. . . . There was no end to the tales which were told of her extraordinary doings. . . . Her temper was singular, her tastes were anomalous, her habits were lawless, her antipathies were many and intense, and she was liable to explosions of ungovernable anger" (99, 192). Dr. Kittredge explicitly warns Bernard against categorizing Elsie Venner: "'I don't want to undervalue your science, Mr. Langdon, . . . but I know these people about here, fathers and mothers, and children and grandchildren, so as all the science in the world can't know them, without it takes time about it, and sees them grow up and grow old, and how the wear and tear of life comes to them. . . . You can't tell a horse by driving him once, Mr. Langdon, nor a patient by talking half an hour with him'" (211). Kittredge later radicalizes this point: "God opens one book to physicians that a good many of you don't know much about,—the Book of Life. That is none of your dusty folios with black letters between pasteboard and leather, but it is printed in bright red type, and the binding of it is warm to the touch. . . . [Physicians] will insist on reading you lessons out of it. . . . These will always be lessons of charity" (325). So what begins as a claim that a particular form of representation is dangerously inadequate turns into a critique of representation as such. Within this radically mimetic mindset, words, as much as figures, are inadequate substitutions for the thing itself, impotent actually to lift the irreducible human body into language.

The novel *Elsie Venner* thus links its philosophy of particularity to the almost mute figure of Elsie, who, speaking only a few lines in the entire novel, resists the substitutions implicit in any use of language. In his depiction of Elsie, Holmes literally casts her as "reptilian": her snake-like actions reflect the simplest of neural machinery, which produces stereotyped, indiscriminate, repetitive behavior. When Elsie's cousin, bitten by her once, "was rash enough to lean towards her . . . she threw her head back, her eyes narrowing and her forehead drawing down so that Dick thought her head actually flattened itself. He started involuntarily; for she looked so like the little girl who had struck him with those sharp flashing teeth, that the whole scene came back, and he felt the stroke again as if it had just been given" (159–160). Darwin noted that the behavior of snakes was indiscriminate and mindlessly replicated: "the rattling of the rattle-snake, and of the tail of the Trigonocephalus,— the grating of the scales of the Echis,—and the dilatation of the hood of the Cobra,—all subserve the same end, namely, to make them appear terrible to their enemies."[48] In a novel obsessed with the details of "family inheritance" (102), Holmes emphasizes that Elsie's aggressive behavior, her obsessive dancing, her sluggishness during cool weather, and her passion for rocky ledges derive from the prenatal snakebite: "In our pictures of life, we must show the flowering-out of terrible growths which have their roots deep, deep underground" (243).

The affinity for (or fear of) cliffs operates according to what Herbert Spencer called the "doctrine of hereditary transmission": the result of "accumulated experiences" inscribed in the body over "successive generation[s]," certain responses reflect "an automatic connection of nervous actions, corresponding to the external relations perpetually experienced."[49] As a kindhearted cleric says of Elsie in Holmes's novel, "'She may have impulses that act in her like instincts in the lower animals'" (257). Daniel Dennett draws on the doctrine of hereditary transmission when he observes (aptly, given Elsie's proclivity for precipices) that a human baby, unlike a newborn snake, "has an innate aversion to venturing out onto a pane of supportive glass, through which it can see a 'visual cliff.' Even though its mother beckons it from a few feet away, cajoling and encouraging, the infant hangs back fearfully, despite never having suffered a fall in its life. The experience of its ancestors is making it err on the side of safety" (90–91). Neither Elsie nor the infant "knows" what it is doing in conceptual terms; their knowledge is embodied in neural and visceral responses. This explains why in late summer Elsie's body "seemed fullest of its malign and restless instincts" (261). The girl has an almost preternatural bond with her nurse, Sophy, but they rarely speak, communicating instead by "a kind of dumb intercourse of feeling, such as one sees in the eyes of brute mothers looking on their young" (419). The "dumb feeling" connecting Elsie and Sophy, while cast in animalistic terms, also defines the more rarified "interpenetrative consciousness" shared by her aristocratic father and his confidant, Dr. Kittredge: "There are states of mind which may be shared by two persons in presence of each other, which remain not only unworded, but unthoughted, if such a word may be coined for our special need" (194–195).

In Elsie's case, such "unthoughted" moments are importantly affective: Elsie "loved, in her own way, the old black woman, and seemed to keep up a kind of silent communication with her, as if they did not require the use of speech" (432). The researcher Paul MacLean has in recent decades, observed that the "reptilian brain" of human beings has the same archaic modes of response as snakes and lizards, controlling autonomic functions such as digestion and heartbeat, as well as functions of muscular control, such as balance. Functional even in sleep, it is responsible for behaviors that appear to be compulsive and ritualistic; taken alone, the reptilian brain cannot learn from experience.[50] (The rattlesnakes Bernard obtains in his quest to understand Elsie exemplify these qualities: "The expression of the creatures was watchful, still, grave, passionless, fate-like" [208].) By contrast, Elsie's relationship to her nurse is, in MacLean's terms, "mammalian," for it includes attachment and affection. Yet without the capacity for abstraction, Elsie's feelings remain irreducibly particular, isolating her from "the common consciousness" of human beings, which the novel's narrator describes in these terms:

> Whereas an emotion which can shape itself in language opens the gate for itself into the great community of human affections; for every word we speak is the medal of a dead thought or feeling, struck in the die of some human experience, worn smooth by innumerable contacts, and always transferred warm from one to another. By words we share the common consciousness of the race. . . . The language of the eyes runs deeper into the personal nature, but it is purely individual, and perishes in the expression. (419)

The purely individual is, by its nature, untransmissable, while language, precisely because of its substitutions—"worn smooth by innumerable contacts"—is essential to human communality. Even the devoted nurse Sophy espouses this position, as when she tells Dr. Kittredge that Elsie "'a'n't like no other woman in none of her ways. She don't cry 'n' laugh like other women. An' she ha'n' got the same kind o' feelin's as other women'" (350). Dennett, drawing on modern neuroscience and cognitive psychology, concurs that language is essential to the "prosthetically enhanced imaginations" (146) of human beings: "Words make us more intelligent by making cognition easier, in the same way (many times multiplied) that beacons and landmarks make navigation in the world easier for simple creatures. Navigation in the abstract multidimensional world of ideas is simply impossible without a huge stock of movable, memorable landmarks that can be shared, criticized, recorded, and looked at from different perspectives" (146–147). The distinction between language users (those with what MacLean labels "neomammalian" abilities) and others, however, is far from essential: evolutionary thinkers such as Spencer traced human language to the capacities of other mammals, and Darwin even discerned rudimentary vocal communication in a snake's rattle, which "developed to serve as an efficient sound-producing instrument" (45).

Yet Elsie's near inability to use language places her outside the realm of human sympathy: "Poor Elsie! She never sang nor played. She never shaped her inner life into words: such utterance was as much denied to her nature as common articulate speech to the deaf mute. Her only language must be in action" (342). The girl's mute singularity renders her a figure so specific she couldn't be classed in even the most capacious category of the professor's Anglo-American anthropology: human being. It seemed as though "there was something not human looking out of Elsie's eyes" (434). Or, as the caregiver Sophy broadly hints, "'Who tol' you Elsie was a woman, Doctor?'" (349). The girl's neurasthenic teacher Helen Darby admits of her strange student that "'there are mysteries I do not know how to account for'" (73). Even Elsie's father affirms the "essentially solitary and uncommunicative" nature of his daughter: the otherwise kindhearted Dudley Venner had never loved his child, for "his task was not merely difficult, but simply impracticable to human powers. A nature like Elsie's had necessarily to be studied by itself" (441).

But as Dr. Kittredge maintains throughout, Elsie's distinctiveness and extreme particularity—that which makes her "wholly different from . . . any human creature" (213) and raises her above "the broad sea-level of average" (272)—are directly traceable to the prenatal snakebite that she suffered: "Through all this rich nature there ran some alien current of influence, sinuous and dark, as when a clouded streak seams the white marble of a perfect statue" (397). Holmes suggests that Elsie's anomalous behavior, including her venom for those who displease her, can be understood as "automatic action in the moral world; the reflex movement which *seems* to be self-determination" (227). And, Holmes concludes, "until somebody shall study this as Marshall Hall has studied reflex nervous action in the bodily system, I would not give much for men's judgments of each other's characters" (227). As a sort of a priori experience, the snakebite shapes the details of Elsie's life—her muteness, her hypnotic gaze, her strange birthmark, as well as rumors that she poisoned her wet nurse and now has an ominous antipathy for her cousin. It would be too crude to conclude simply that Elsie *is* a snake, for the novel with its suspicion of taxonomy wants the link to be less

categorical, more suggestive: "It would be needless to repeat the particular suggestions which had come into his [Bernard's] mind, as they must
probably have come into that of the reader who has noted the singular-
ities of Elsie's tastes and personal traits" (397). Elsie's snakiness is, in
other words, her very own.

But in this the novel sets up a conundrum, for what makes her *Elsie*
and therefore distinct from everyone else makes her not human; to
make her human would be to deny or even destroy what makes her
Elsie—and to affirm the continuities between snake and girl, mollusk
and maid, the reptilian and the neomammalian. The relationship the
novel establishes between particularity and abstraction is structured,
then, by an uncompromising opposition, one that places the novel in an
ethical bind. For it would appear that to humanize Elsie (the sort of
thing a novel does, according to Dimock, Poovey, and Nussbaum)
would be to make her just like everybody else: as this sentimental ontology is cast in the novel's final pages, "All true hearts are alike in the
hour of need" (452). In the novel's terms, such a move would of necessity
reduce her to a common specimen of girlhood and in doing so engage in
"epistemological violence." But to leave Elsie as radically particular is
precisely to *de*humanize her, to occlude her indisputable corporeal and
affective similarities to the girls around her. Perfectly resistant to the
substitutions and reductions of categorization, she is what Dennett
refers to as a "languageless mammal" with "no way of considering [a
concept] 'in general' or 'in itself'" (159), a state Holmes describes as
outside "the common consciousness of the race." Holmes's novel, in
other words, uncouples the equation of the particular and the ethical:
Elsie can be human, but not particular, or particular, but not human.
When scholars writing about Holmes's novel sum up Elsie as a simple
"hybrid"—part girl, part snake—they ignore the novel's own logic,
which leads to this impasse.[51]

What, then, is the relationship between Holmes's medical innovations
and the realism of *Elsie Venner?* Insofar as the novel reprises the opposed positions in the debate over puerperal fever, Holmes appears to
switch sides and endorse the particularism of Meigs and the anticontagionists: by discrediting the schoolmaster's reduction of girls to fungible
sums of money, by obsessively individualizing the central figure of Elsie,
and by endorsing the Meigs-like Dr. Kittredge, who in refusing to
"judge [Elsie] by any formula" (452) benevolently defends the girl

against all attempts to categorize her as sinful or crazy—or even as just a normal girl. Holmes the novelist, here incarnated as his adversary Meigs, seems to occupy the perspective he had attacked in the debate over puerperal fever. In generating such a proliferation of competing and overlapping narratives to explain Elsie Venner's oddness—hysteria, genetic influence, insanity, moral depravity, prenatal poisoning, verbal incapacity, morbid sexuality, poor parenting—the novel seems to replicate the model of disease within traditional therapeutics and to affirm that health and human flourishing are never reducible to a single source.

The novel's final scenes, however, trouble this Meigsian reading and enact the logic of Holmes the medical scientist. By stretching its mimetic logic to the breaking point, the novel affirms that in the end, for Elsie to be fully human, she must at once be and not be herself. And indeed the novel accomplishes this: Elsie's nurse says of the dying girl, "'It's her mother's look,—it's her mother's own face right over again'" (442). In the name of "restor[ing] her to that truer self," that which is "most truly human" (437), the novel effects a gothic substitution: Elsie not only looks like her mother, she in essence becomes her. Surrounded by the same people who attended her mother, Elsie dies at the same time of year and is buried next to Mrs. Venner under the headstone bearing only her mother's name. As Elsie's father proclaims, "my daughter is . . . restored to me,—such as her mother would have had her,—such as her mother was" (444). Elsie, in short, dies giving birth to Elsie. In fact, the novel hints that Bernard's sympathy bouquet, which contained leaves fatal to snakes, is what poisoned the girl. So while Holmes the novelist may appear to endorse a Meigsian particularism, the novel makes it look as if Elsie dies a puerperal death at the hands of her devoted attendants. As Elsie's body lies in state, she becomes imaginatively interchangeable with all the other girls at Silas Peckham's: "The young girls from the school looked at her, one after another, and passed on, sobbing, carrying in their hearts the picture that would be with them all their days. The great people of the place were all there with their silent sympathy" (457). The novel finally reveals that the only place where Elsie can be both herself and not herself—a paradox requiring that the irreducibly particular experience of two individuals be absolutely identical—is the cemetery. The novel, in both reprising and exposing the killing logic embedded in the radical commitment to particularity, brings Holmes the novelist and Holmes the medical scientist into stunning convergence.

In *Elsie Venner*, Holmes dramatizes how a resistance to abstraction translates a character into a species of one, in opposition to (rather than evolutionarily and affectively linked to) the human beings around her, placing her outside the realm of human compassion. The very last paragraph of the novel, however, recuperates Elsie Venner while also indicating the direction Holmes will take in his later novels. The professor, who as narrator, has remained detached from the action for most of the novel, takes bodily form in its conclusion, entering the plot as he witnesses a young woman walking down the street on the arm of his old student Bernard, the newly accredited "Professor Langdon." After "feasting [his] eyes with the sight of them for a few minutes," the narrator discerns a bracelet encircling the woman's wrist. "'My eyes filled with tears,'" he reports, "'as I read upon the clasp, in sharp-cut Italic letters, E. V. They were tears at once of sad remembrance and of joyous anticipation; for the ornament on which I looked was the double pledge of a dead sorrow and a living affection. It was the golden bracelet,—the parting-gift of Elsie Venner'" (486–487). Bernard, who once seemed in danger of marrying Elsie, seamlessly substitutes another girl for his deceased student, confirming the novel's comedic structure with the promise of a marriage. While this weepy scene lends itself to a sentimental reading it is certainly, at best, a vexed ending. Is this the Professor's doctrine of indiscrimination at work, where any woman might substitute for another since "nature makes every man love every woman"? If so, what should we make of the narrator's sorrowful tears? And why the disconcerting phrasing in which the narrator "feasted" on the two lovers? In the context of the debate over puerperal fever, the odd assortment of elements—the doctor's cannibalistic gaze, his uncharacteristic weeping, the lingering presence of a dead girl, and a personalized keepsake passed along to another young woman—has sinister overtones.

The clasping of Elsie's bracelet on the other woman's wrist, I would suggest, indicates Holmes's interest in extending the notion implicit in the novel: that Elsie Venner was not a unique, incommensurable figure. Rather, she embodied a mode of affective responsiveness that Holmes believed was operative in even the most refined human beings. In the next chapter I examine how Holmes extends the insights of his early statistical inquiry: that there can be intentionality without intention, and intelligence in the absence of knowledge expressed through mimetic representation. What appears in *Elsie Venner* as pathology, Holmes later articulated, was the common condition of human beings: "the mystery of unconscious mental action is exemplified, as I have said, in every act of mental association. What happens when one idea brings up another? Some internal movement, of which we are wholly unconscious, and which we only know by its effect. . . . There is a Delphi and a Pythoness in every human breast."[52] The "reptilian brain," in short, is operative inside all human beings, men as well as women; it is an evolutionary marker not just of the human connection to animals, but finally of the capacity of human beings to be connected to each other, as well.

Coda: Anecdote and Abstraction

Judging from the introduction to a historical study published in 1992 entitled *Death in Childbirth: An International Study of Maternal Care and Mortality 1800–1950*, the problem of how to represent persons both ethically and adequately is still a vexed one. Irvine Loudon begins this massive scholarly work with an account of one particular woman who died after an apparently normal childbirth: "Mrs K, who was born in 1849, was a woman of exceptional talent."[53] Loudon goes on to note Mrs. K's numerous academic honors before recounting the circumstances of her fatal delivery, including a portrayal of her husband's anguish and the doctor's solemn bandaging of the corpse. Loudon then explains his rationale for beginning a sweeping historical analysis, committed to the exhaustive study of mortality tables and population data, with this affecting anecdote:

> I have begun with the story of Mrs K as a reminder that behind the analysis of numbers, trends, causes, and factors lie such tragedies. It would be easy to compile a list of similar case-histories. To do that and nothing else, however, would be an empty exercise, for the story of Mrs K provokes a whole series of questions. Why did she die? Can we accept it as sheer, unavoidable bad luck, due to the primitive state of obstetric knowledge at the time, and the absence of modern obstetric techniques? Or was it, as [Registrar General of England] William Farr believed, a gross example of medical incompetence? (3)

"To answer these questions," Loudon concludes, "we need statistical data on populations rather than individual case-histories" (4).

Loudon's point, I suggest, is deeply compatible with Holmes's work. Loudon's purpose in briefly narrating the death of Mrs K is not to capture in mimetic detail the life of an actual woman but to personify all the other case-histories in a way that a table of mortality statistics cannot. But the power of narratives, like that of charts and tables, is limited. Mrs. K's exceptional talents and her advanced degrees may arouse interest or identification, but the study's exposure of the terrible normality of such deaths during the nineteenth century provokes the deeper pathos. Loudon's book, with its exhaustive statistics, serves to heighten the impression made by the anecdote; indeed, as Holmes first suggested, the sheer weight of the numerical evidence may elevate pity to the level of outrage, making feeling an engine of reform.

What Loudon captures is both the epistemological conflict and ethical interdependence of two different ways of representing persons, the narrative and the statistical. Loudon remains deeply committed to the scientific aspect of his enterprise while offering the anecdote of Mrs. K as an explanation for, or perhaps even the driving force behind, the text he goes on to write. What narrative cannot always do on its own, Loudon suggests, is answer epistemological questions; the answer to the question "how can we discover why did she died?" lies, as Holmes revealed more than a century earlier, in the distillation of hundreds of instances. Yet without some sort of devotion to the preciousness of individual personhood one has no reason to mobilize abstractions to save a life. I. A. Richards expressed this fertile tension in *Principles of Literary Criticism* (1924) when he wrote, "Clear and impartial awareness of the nature of the world in which we live and the development of attitudes which will enable us to live in it finely are both necessities, and neither can be subordinated to the other" (264). The vexed legacy of Holmes's role in the nineteenth-century debate over the contagiousness of puerperal fever is that while we still turn to narrative to honor individual lives, we must frequently draw on the impersonal methods of modern medicine to save them.[54]

CHAPTER THREE

Fear and Epistemology

Tracking the Train of Feeling in
A Mortal Antipathy

> Memory is a material record; . . . the brain is scarred
> and seamed with infinitesimal hieroglyphics, as the
> features are engraved with the traces of thought and
> passion.
>
> —OLIVER WENDELL HOLMES, "MECHANISM IN
> THOUGHT AND MORALS" (1871)

For the character of Clifford Pyncheon in Nathaniel Hawthorne's novel *The House of the Seven Gables* (1851), a man who has been housed in the past, the experience of plummeting into modernity on a passenger train is an exhilarating, mind-expanding event. The rush of movement lets loose in Clifford a torrent of rapturous predictions about how modern technologies will liberate the human mind from the limitations of the material body: "'These railroads—could but the whistle be made musical, and the rumble and the jar got rid of—are positively the greatest blessing that the ages have wrought out for us. They give us wings; they annihilate the toil and dust of pilgrimage; they spiritualize travel!'"[1] This "spiritualization," he notes, is contingent on eradicating "the rumble and the jar" of train travel, presumably because they return one to the discomforts of the body and restrain the free play of the mind.

By contrast, a passage written twenty years later by Oliver Wendell Holmes indicates that "some sudden jar," rather than obstructive of the mind's operations, is a critical way of making them visible: "We know very little of the contents of our minds until some sudden jar brings them to light, as an earthquake that shakes down a miser's house brings out the old stockings full of gold, and all the hoards that have hid away in holes and crannies."[2] Invoking the brain's structural fissures in his reference to a miser's "holes and crannies," the Harvard professor of anatomy returns attention to the mind's corporeal seat. As Holmes was writing those words, there was already a great deal of public discussion, both optimistic and anxious, about the impact of technology on the minds and bodies of Americans. Concerned about the physical costs of train travel, the medical journal the *Lancet* formed a commission whose 1862 report, published in a series of eight articles, was entitled "The Influence of Railway Travelling on Public Health." At the center of this medical discussion was the structure of the human nervous system, which was increasingly described by research physiologists of the nineteenth century as a dispersed, information-bearing system of communication analogous to the telegraph and the railroad. Operated by relatively autonomous companies, these systems of transportation and communication were not in the mid–nineteenth century nationalized or run by a central agency. Similarly, physiologists in the 1820s and 1830s had begun to "decentralize" the human mind, to dislodge it from its unifying role and to distinguish between two nervous systems: the central nervous system, consisting of voluntary nerves that respond to sensation and dictate muscular movement; and the autonomic nervous system, composed of nerves devoted to involuntary functions such as respiration, digestion, and circulation.

Despite the analogies between the human nervous system and the new technologies, the body was also understood to be vulnerable to these devices for speeding communication and movement. In the *Lancet*'s first installment on the health effects of rail travel, the commission quoted one politician who proclaimed, "'The very power of locomotion keeps persons in a state of great nervous excitement. . . . I have ascertained that many persons who have been in the habit of traveling by railway have been obliged to give it up in consequence of the effect on the nervous system.'"[3] In turn, the body's structures provided a trope for the material interconnections produced by modern technology: "The whole nation," Holmes wrote in 1861,

> is now penetrated by the ramifications of a network of iron nerves [the telegraph] which flash sensation and volition backward and forward to and from towns and provinces as if they were organs and limbs of a single living body. . . . The vast system of iron muscles [the train] . . . move the limbs of the mighty organism one upon another. . . . This perpetual intercommunication, joined to the power of instantaneous action, keeps us always alive with excitement.[4]

Nowhere in post–Civil War civilian life was the intercommunication of technological "nerves and muscles" with their human counterparts more vividly expressed than in the consummate nineteenth-century disaster, the train wreck, with its most puzzling passenger, the mildly injured male survivor who over time developed far-flung, debilitating bodily symptoms.

The perplexing figure of the hyper-symptomatic man was taken up in both fiction and medical debates of the 1880s. If a question posed by Oliver Wendell Holmes's first novel was "what's the matter with Elsie Venner?" the problem his third addresses is how to discern the story embodied in the protagonist, Maurice Kirkwood: "Everybody was trying to find out what his story was,—for a story, and a strange one, he must surely have—and nobody had succeeded"[5] (149). This chapter examines how Holmes in *A Mortal Antipathy* (1885) draws on contemporary theories about the human nervous system, reflex physiology, and the body's susceptibility to shock as he negotiates the compromising diagnostic categories of insanity, effeminacy, and hysteria. A person's prior experience, Holmes affirmed, could be encased in the structure of the nervous system and expressed affectively through such feelings as fear. The problem of a man whose character was radically illegible and whose symptoms exceeded initiating causes is solved—in Holmes's novel, and in the medical debate over the existence of "railway spine"—by the neurological equation of extreme emotions such as terror with physical concussion rather than congenital weakness or mental infirmity. Thus we see in *A Mortal Antipathy* a real seat of disease, infantile terror, in the absence of a visible physical injury. The role of the narrative, then, was to realize—in the dual sense of bringing about and bringing to consciousness—this connection: to elucidate the train of events that led from trauma to symptom, and to determine the structure of the nervous system that provided the physiological "track" for exterior impressions to become registered in interior corporeal states.

Through a reading of the psychophysiology of thinkers such as Herbert Spencer, Henry Maudsley, and Théodule Ribot, and the medicolegal debate over railway spine, this chapter argues that Holmes's conception of unconscious embodied memory offers an important prehistory to the Freudian conception of trauma, which would construe traumatic experience as a primarily psychic rather than physiological wound. Yet, while the physiology of affect that emerged in the 1880s indeed saved a certain version of masculinity from hysteria understood in specifically feminine terms, it also elevated the testimony of the body, posing a challenge to traditional conceptions of willpower and rationality on which masculine character had been built.[6] Whereas the influential British physiologist Marshall Hall had in 1841 described the mind as a potentate "sitting enthroned upon the cerebrum, . . . deliberating and willing, and sending forth its emissaries and plenipotentiaries, which convey its sovereign mandates, along the voluntary nerves, to muscles subdued to volition," by the 1870s Holmes would describe the mind as "a parliament of little men together, of whom, as also happens in real parliaments, each possesses only one single idea he is ceaselessly trying to assert."[7] Holmes, in *A Mortal Antipathy*, offered a solution to the problem of fractured corporeal authority, however: the central and centralizing role of the medical expert who, with his ethos of detachment and expertise, is able to help the parliament of the body to speak with one voice.

The physician, then, became an essential part of an apparatus of authentication that eschewed the incoherence, elisions, and outright fabrications increasingly associated with a person's testimony and facial expressions, and instead excavated affective truths from the body's hidden depths. As one surgeon instructed doctors who examined nervous claimants against railway companies, "A perfectly steady pulse throughout the whole examination tells its own tale . . . the pulse is often the only sign we have to guide us to a right estimate of a patient's condition."[8] The act of calibrating a person's conscious narrative with the unconscious testimony of his body produced what I term a forensics of self, for it installed the use of science and technology, along with an authoritative expert, as essential for bringing to consciousness experiences pertaining to the most intimate aspects of a person's life.

Historians and theorists have analyzed the emergence of organized medicine in the nineteenth century, with its aspirations to scientific status, as a site of disciplinary power and prestige.[9] Central to this work is the sociologist Paul Starr's book *The Social Transformation of American Medicine* (1982), which charts the rise of the healing profession in U.S. culture. More influential for literary and cultural studies, however, has been the work of Michel Foucault, in particular his books *The Birth of the Clinic: An Archeology of Medical Perception* (1963) and *Discipline and Punish: The Birth of the Prison* (1975). In the former work, Foucault describes the modern positioning of doctor and patient at opposite ends of the "transparent gaze." In his account "the clinic" is not so much a professional space as a disciplinary apparatus that attenuates the agency of the patient—who is transmogrified into the host of newly individuated diseases—as well as the agency of the physician, whose perceptions are structured by a "new outline of the perceptible and statable. . . . What counts in the things said by men is not so much what they may have thought or the extent to which these things represent their thoughts, as that which systematizes them from the outset."[10] *Discipline and Punish* gives an account of the history of punishment in which the site of discipline moves from the body to the "soul," such that the apparatus of the state is intimately inscribed on consciousness rather than exhibited in the spectacularly dismembered bodies essential to premodern forms of punishment.[11]

Unlike Foucault, whose account of power leaves no room for a strong account of human agency, the literary and medical writings of Oliver Wendell Holmes suggest that late-nineteenth-century practitioners tended to conceptualize corporeal processes as both affective and intelligent. Agency as it emerges in the work of Holmes and other thinkers of the period is conceived in more humble terms as the active commitment (always embodied, if not always explicit) to human survival and flourishing. This chapter attends to the modest humanizing possibilities in these nineteenth-century extensions of selfhood. Mark Seltzer, in *Serial Killers: Death and Life in America's Wound Culture* (1998), emphasizes the more sensational, less affective aspects of what he terms "*the double-logic of prosthesis.*"[12] Discussing Henry Ford's comment that many tasks on the factory assembly line could be accomplished by amputees, Seltzer writes, "If, from one point of view, such a fantasy projects a violent dismemberment of the human body and an *emptying out of human agency,* from another it projects a transcendence of the natural body and the *extension of human agency through the forms of technology that supplement it*" (69). Yet when one considers not just technologies traditionally understood (e.g. machines) but also aesthetic objects (e.g. music and novels) these sorts of extensions become less disturbing, indeed everyday sorts of events. Rather than seeing the incursions of professional medicine as unidirectional, such that the body is "medicalized" or transformed from a more natural state, this chapter investigates how the figure of the expert and his apparatus of medical knowledge are precisely "humanized" by being integrated into individual lives and bodies, thereby transforming traditional conceptions of subjectivity, agency, and knowledge.

Recent work in neurology and evolutionary biology, influenced by the materialism of the nineteenth century, provides a way to understand Holmes's revised, relational understanding of agency. As the researcher John R. Skoyles has suggested, "[Though] the brain on its own often lacks the experience to know our own condition . . . fortunately, other people can, particularly those that have studied health and illness. Human evolution . . . changed illness by offloading decisions about deployment whenever possible on to professionals. . . . Therefore [it made] doctoring more than just a science and a question of prescribing the right treatment. It made it also an art by which a doctor persuades the patient's body to offload its decision making onto them."[13] Rather than circumscribing the operations of the mind, in other words, Holmes's neurological perspective provided a way of expanding them. Just as memory might be housed in the tissues and neural circuits of the body as well as the structures of the brain, so expertise and knowledge could be "offloaded" onto the experienced physician—making the caregiver a collaborator with the body's innate intelligence and healing processes.[14] Holmes, as both novelist and physician, imagined that works of literature might effectively realize these sorts of corporeal collaborations. This chapter, moreover, continues work being done by contemporary scholars who argue against a reified understanding of separate spheres in the nineteenth century, for the cultural representation of nervous shock both solidified the interface between private bodies and public events and helped to produce a new way of experiencing the self in which external mediation was understood to be a way of authenticating and making available certain internal feelings.

From Physiognomy to Physiology

Holmes begins his third novel, *A Mortal Antipathy*, with a "personal reminiscence" (3) that, in tracing the arc of his literary career, marks a shift from the writings of "literary butterflies"—mere "bubbles of reputation" (6)—to the group of *Atlantic Monthly* writers cultivated by the editor William Dean Howells.[15] Playing on the floral motif associated with the pseudonyms of midcentury women writers, Holmes writes that littérateur Nathaniel Parker Willis was "in full bloom" when Holmes first entered the literary scene. Holmes turns his anatomist's eye on the earlier writer's dandified person: "He came near being very handsome. He was tall; his hair, of light brown color, waved in luxuriant abundance; his cheek was as rosy as if it had been painted to show behind the footlights, and he dressed with artistic elegance. He was something between a remembrance of Count D'Orsay and an anticipation of Oscar Wilde" (4). Sexually ambiguous in Holmes's portrayal, Willis is marked by an excessiveness that extends from his body (copious hair, flaming cheeks) through his fashionable dress to his theatrical persona.

In his work on nineteenth-century masculinity, Glenn Hendler has argued that Willis, in the role of literary dandy and sentimental author, "reproduces and simultaneously complicates the claims about the relation between appearance and identity that had been developed in contemporaneous pseudosciences such as physiognomy and phrenology."[16] First developed by Johan Caspar Lavater in the eighteenth century, physiognomic theory affirmed the correspondence of facial features and deep character. This was not, however, as marginal a practice as Hendler suggests, and elements of physiognomy appear in the work of prominent scientists such as Sir Charles Bell. As the historian Paul White has shown, Bell's influential text *The Anatomy of Expression* (1844) theorized facial expression as "'a window [placed] before the heart, in order to render visible human thoughts and intentions.'"[17] What Hendler aptly terms Willis's "aestheticized masculinity," his flamboyant, audience-oriented performance of sentiment, did indeed produce a problem for physiognomy, for it masked the correspondence of features and feeling.[18] Just as Holmes had condemned the tears of those accoucheurs who were responsible for transmitting disease as pernicious hand-wringing (see Chapter 2), so he implies that the insincere display of feeling associated with Willis is by the 1880s an outdated mode of masculinity. Holmes, moreover, was not alone in casting suspicion and even aspersion on a certain affective and sartorial flamboyance. The historian Janet Oppenheim quotes a nineteenth-century doctor describing his nervous patients as "'fat, pale-faced, effeminate-looking men; in the one the [nervous] affection was attributed to malaria, and he had flabby wasted testicles. . . .' Another was a 'pale and delicate' youth."[19] By midcentury, medical practitioners had begun to associate excessive feeling in men with physical pathology.

The introductory material of *A Mortal Antipathy* helps to situate questions about masculinity, the embodiment of character, and the authenticity of feeling that drive Holmes's novel. These questions are catalyzed by the figure who sets the plot in motion: a young man named Maurice Kirkwood, who inexplicably appears one day, prepared to live in the sleepy New England setting of Arrowhead Village, a location loosely based on Holmes's own summer residence of Pittsfield, Massachusetts. (The Berkshires became a popular summer destination and resort for urban New Yorkers following the opening of a rail line at midcentury.) Maurice presents a problem for the social taxonomies of the local residents, who are perplexed that an apparent gentleman would also be socially reclusive and remark that his "way of life was peculiar,—in fact, eccentric" (57). The townsfolk coalesce into an "unorganized committee of investigation" (59), employing homespun epistemologies to discover the stranger's story. The young man's landlady rifles through the personal effects in Maurice's room and concludes, "'He was a gentleman,—anybody ought to have known that; and anybody that knew about his nice ways of living and behaving, and knew the kind of wear he had for his underclothing, might have known it'" (54). Her husband concurs, pointing to slightly different evidence: "'A man that pays his bills reg'lar, in good money, and knows how to handle a hoss is three quarters of a gentleman, if he is n't a whole one,—and most likely he *is* a whole one'" (74).

Physical descriptions of Maurice, who was in possession of "fresh cheeks," "curly hair," and eyes "as blue as succory flowers" (75), sound suspiciously like Holmes's portrait of Nathaniel Willis, while the character's bookish ways mark him as "the college kind, that's brought up among books, and is handling 'em, and reading of 'em, and making of 'em, as like as not, all their lives" (75). Maurice reads voraciously, "especially all that related to electricity and magnetism" (80), but also poetry and "modern works relating to Spiritualism" (80). The townspeople's unsatisfactory diagnoses—their failed attempts to square Maurice's (lack of) professional identity with his appearance and inclinations—register the incoherence of the young stranger's character: "He was . . . a school-master without a school, a minister without a pulpit, an actor without an engagement; in short, there was no end to the perfectly senseless stories that were told about him" (55). Moreover, there is a danger that Maurice's excessive leisure, reclusive ways, and promiscuous reading might tip him into pathology, for as one French physician wrote in 1847, "the man who is feminized by some constitutive predisposition, whether innate or acquired, by his education, by some prolonged or special illness, by a languid and overtly sentimental life, by excessive sensual pleasures, and so on . . . will be liable to experience hysteria."[20] Thomas Laycock, in his study of the relations between physical and mental health, argued that "as the physical vigour decays, the instincts of astuteness and cunning are developed in its place, and therewith fraud and falsehood in the various relations of life. In these respects the man becomes literally effeminate."[21]

The emphasis in the novel on Maurice's physical culture, therefore, provides a form of inoculation against the paradigmatic female malady, hysteria. Appearing in the "battle of the sexes" crew race put together by "woman's righters" (43), Maurice Kirkwood is depicted as piloting a canoe with consummate skill and engaging in healthy girl-watching (one of Holmes's own favorite pastimes). Though Maurice spends his days in quiet study, a watchful local reports, "'at night he would be off, walking, or riding on horseback, or paddling about in the lake, sometimes till nigh morning'" (54). Maurice gains fame for mastering a wild colt and for saving a young man from drowning, who afterward opines, "'He is not an artist, as it was at one time thought he might be. He is a good-looking fellow, well developed, manly in appearance, with nothing to excite special remark unless it be a certain look of anxiety or apprehension which comes over him from time to time" (70). Far from the "fat, pale-faced, effeminate-looking men" of medical lore, Maurice is preternaturally active and physically robust.

The tenets of physiognomy affirmed that facial features offered, in the words of one physiologist, "evidence of emotions . . . written in passing on the face of man,"[22] yet the young stranger of Arrowhead Village remains an "unsolved enigma": "Egypt did not hold any hieroglyphics harder to make out than the meaning of this young man's odd way of living" (72). Holmes's narrator suggests that the "laws of physiognomy" must be supplemented by a technology that made visible "the inevitable change wrought by time": "An inscription is the same thing, whether we read it on a slate-stone, or granite, or marble. To watch the lights and shades, the reliefs and hollows, of a countenance through a lifetime, or a large part of it, by the aid of a continuous series of photographs would not only be curious; it would teach us much more about the laws of physiognomy than we could get from casual and unconnected observations" (84). While affirming a physiognomic correspondence between inner character and outward features, Holmes indicates that character does not merely emerge from within but is also shaped from without. Serial photographs help overcome what contemporary philosopher Daniel Dennett has usefully termed "timescale chauvinism": because transformations often happen at "an achingly slow pace," we have the tendency to think of entities as static, whether those entities are persons or, as Darwin argued, species.[23] Character may be embodied (the premise of physiognomy), but it is also dynamic, importantly shaped over time.

Physiology, therefore, rather than physiognomy, might provide the Rosetta stone for Maurice's corporeal hieroglyphics. In his essay on Emmanuel Swedenborg, the Victorian psychiatrist Henry Maudsley, in terms similar to Holmes, argued that one might "discover a man's autobiography" through the contemplation of his body: "When a man's deeds are discovered after death, his angels, who are inquisitors, look into his face, and extend their examination over his whole body, beginning with the fingers of each hand."[24] Maudsley explains the reason for this bodily inspection:

> The history of a man is his character, and his character is written on his organization, and might be read there had we but senses acute enough to decipher the organic letters. There is not a thought of the mind, not a feeling of the heart, not an aspiration of the soul, not a passion that finds vent, not a deed which is done, that is not graved with an unfailing art in the structure of the body; its every organ and the constituent elements of each organ grow to the fashion of their exercise, and there is nothing covered that might not be revealed, nothing hid that might not be known. (205)

In moving past the face to the body's "organization," the angel looks beyond expression to a person's deep structures and their regulating systems, which to neurologists of the day were not solely lodged in the brain, the seat of consciousness, but were dispersed in "little brains," ganglia along the spinal column, which controlled respiration, circulation, secretion, digestion, and other essential internal processes.

In Holmes's novel, it is the angelic figure of Euthymia Tower who most vividly expresses the transition from the logic of physiognomy to the logic of physiology. In her discussion of Maurice with the local physician Dr. Butts, Euthemia inquires,

> "Do you know that I met him this morning, and had a good look at him, full in the face?"
>
> "Well, to be sure! That *was* an interesting experience. And how did you like his looks?"
>
> "I thought his face a very remarkable one. But he looked very pale as he passed me, and I noticed that he put his hand to his left side as if he had a twinge of pain, or something of that sort,—spasm or neuralgia,—I don't know what. I wondered whether he had what you call *angina pectoris*." (189)

While the face held no legible clues to the mystery of the young man, the interior of the body, with its arrested flow of blood and its spasms of pain, was portentous in its significance. Charles Darwin, in *The Expression of the Emotions in Man and Animals* (1872), noted the unreliability of facial expressions as an index to character, for not only might expressions be feigned, they might be catalyzed by a purely mechanical force such as the application of electricity. Darwin cites an experiment by the French physiologist Guillaume Duchenne, who "galvanized . . . certain muscles in the face of an old man . . . and thus produced various expressions which were photographed on a large scale" and that subsequently (and deceptively) led a group that Darwin had assembled to attribute the expressions to internal feelings rather than electrical stimulation.[25] The body, to a neurologist, provides the index of character in physiological, rather than physiognomic, terms; expression alone, without attention to the involuntary systems controlling respiration, heart rate, and body temperature, might be ambiguous or deceptive.

Holmes dramatized the inadequacies of physiognomy through the nervous, hypercerebral would-be physician Lurida Vincent, who "want[s] to study up the nervous system" (126) by reading Tuke and Bucknill's study of the physiognomy of insanity. The novel comically undercuts Lurida, casting her as a case study in her own right: "Nervous system. Insanity. She had headaches, I know. . . . I wonder if any of her more remote relatives are subject to mental disorder" (126). While the principles of physiognomy meant that even an amateur medical detective could learn to read the universal, Deity-sanctioned prose "written in passing on the face of man," for both Maudsley and Holmes it was only the figure of the physician who, like inquisitorial angels, had the vision, accumulated experience, and technologies to "decipher the organic letters" that composed the body's deepest secrets.

Excess and Dissolution of the Nervous System

The problem of nervous men—of symptoms that were not just coded as feminine, such as tears and fainting spells, but were *structurally* feminized, insofar as they were in excess of generating events—was treated extensively in the discourses of medicine, and especially neurology, in the 1880s. The physician Daniel Hack Tuke reported a case from the *Lancet* in which a "gentleman" became "much excited in connection with a very trivial occurrence": he was "seized with several paroxysms of sobbing and crying, after which he again fell into a comatose condition."[26] As Tuke affirmed, "The defect in this case . . . lies in the absence of any apparent cause for the despondency" (221). As Henry Maudsley expressed it, "It is not natural to burst into tears because a fly settles on the forehead, as I have known a melancholic man to do."[27] Maurice Kirkwood, with his habit of inexplicably turning pale and fainting in the presence of women, had symptoms that similarly out-stripped their generating events.

Yet Holmes in his last novel invoked contemporary theories about the function of the nervous system, in particular the physiological basis of fear, to elucidate a narrative and etiological bridge between a catalyzing event that, despite producing only mild physical injuries, led to a persist-ent array of incapacitating, even life-threatening symptoms. The nervous system was understood to be a crucial site of amplification, whereby small external influences could produce massive somatic effects. This conceptual move distinguishes *A Mortal Antipathy* from the logic of sen-timentalism that has been well articulated by Karen Sanchez-Eppler, where the primary affect is sympathy achieved through mimesis and identification, in which the central mode of expression is tears.[28] Holmes in his narrative does not repudiate feeling, but supplants the operations of sympathy—the *imaginative* engagement with another, which entails the eradication of distinctions between self and other—with the concept of antipathy, which involves a highly particularized *bodily* response to specific stimuli. Antipathy affirms rather than disregards individual uniqueness; as Holmes's character Dr. Butts puts the operative logic, "'One man's meat is another man's poison'" (88). The primary affect of fear, expressed through cardiac symptoms, was understood by Holmes to involve the corporeal inscription of experience, operating through the sympathetic nervous system.

In the winter of 1875, the *Lancet* published a series of letters to the editor that marks the uneven shift from a reproductive to a neurologi-cal understanding of hysteria. The etymology of "hysteria," from *hys-ter,* meaning "uterus," marks its origin as a disease understood to be centered in a woman's reproductive organs, literally attributable to a womb that has vacated its normal location in the pelvis and "wan-dered" to other parts of the body. In an initial sally, a perplexed physi-cian writes to inquire, "By what figure of speech [might] an instance of deception in a man . . . appropriately be termed male hysteria[?] . . . The question here is, Where is the uterus?"[29] He urges that the term "neurosis" be employed, for "it recognizes the nervous system to be es-sentially the seat of the disorder."[30] In this way, "if a colonel of dra-goons should suffer from concussion in a railway accident, I should say that he was the subject of neurosis from physical shock; but I should never be guilty of the absurdity of saying he was the subject of male hysteria, and I should prefer to say that a strong man became emotional to saying that he became hysterical" (108). Another contributor agreed: "I carefully avoid it [the term "hysterical"] both in the wards and the lecture theatre, and am able to convey all I wish by 'emotional lesion.'"[31] This colloquy, and the seemingly oxymoronic term "emotional lesion" (where exactly might such a wound be located?) reveals the struggle to locate a physiological source for hyper-symptomatic men. Concomitant with the shift from the reproductive to the nervous system is the substitution of the concept of shock for the gender-inflected term "hysterical": "It is certainly not retrograde to say that shock, and not male hysteria, is the result of a railway accident."[32]

The repeated references to the railway accident as the exemplary shock to the masculine body are not coincidental. By midcentury, railway spine was sensationalized in lurid accounts of train wrecks featuring the figure of the traveling businessman who, though appearing physically unscathed, reaped large sums of money from insurance companies for his debilitating array of belated, mysterious symptoms. Anxiety about whether and how men might modulate the expressions of their bodies so as to maintain balance between inciting stimulus and corporeal reaction in turn raised questions about the newly discovered spinal reflex arc in the nervous system ("the power of reflection," wrote one physiologist, "is often best exhibited in the *prevention* of action prompted by feeling").[33] The spine, dislodged from its homiletic equivalence with moral character or "backbone," became instead the conduit for primitive responses that were understood to bypass volition altogether.

The anatomist Charles Bell in England and François Magendie in France had in the first decades of the nineteenth century discerned that the nerves on the front and the back of the spinal column had different functions, one sort devoted to sensation, the other sort to movement. Marshall Hall and Johannes Muller in the 1830s elaborated on this observation by describing a "reflex arc," in which sensory input might bypass the brain and directly stimulate muscular activity for example, a blink—through ganglia along the spinal column, "the twinkling of an eye being quicker than thought" (119), as Maudsley explained. An experiment described by Maudsley in *Body and Mind* made gruesomely clear the irrelevance of the brain to certain nervous responses: if "the

head of a frog, which is clinging to the female at the season of copula-
tion, be cut off, the animal still holds on to her, nay, if its paw be further
cut off, clings to her with its bloody stump" (63).

The division of the nervous system into the voluntary and involuntary systems, which were themselves further distributed into a variety of
nervous centers, meant that corporeal authority was dispersed rather
than centralized; as Peter Melville Logan has noted the "body in effect
was thought to comprise many little 'brains' dispersed throughout the
cerebrospinal axis, each with a type of regional authority."[34] Henry
Maudsley divided the nervous centers into four groups: (1) the primary
centers, located in the brain and devoted to ideation; (2) the secondary
centers, also located in the brain and devoted to sensation; (3) the tertiary
nervous centers, located in the spinal cord and directing reflex action;
and (4) the quarternary nervous centers associated with the autonomic
system, controlling vital organic processes such as circulation and digestion. In a healthy organism, the different centers are in vital equilibrium, producing concerted action and maintaining the preeminence of
volition: "the organization is such that a due independent local action is
compatible with the proper control of a superior central authority."[35] The
balance of the system, however, is delicate: if "the faculties of the spinal
cord are . . . exhausted by excesses of any kind," writes Maudsley, "the ill
effects are manifest in degenerate action; instead of definite co-ordinate action ministering to the well-being of the individual, there ensue irregular
spasmodic or convulsive movements" (71).

The neurologist John Hughlings Jackson, building on Maudsley's hierarchy of nervous centers, applied the evolutionary theories of Herbert
Spencer and Charles Darwin to posit that the most conscious and volitional actions were the most highly complex and recently evolved, while
the most automatic were primitive and foundational. Other actions were
cast along a continuum, indicating different levels of evolution and volition. Spencer schematizes these levels according to the principle of "co-
ordination" or organization: that "organisms which we rank as low, are
those which display but little co-ordination of actions; and that from
these up to man, the recognized increase in degree of life, corresponds
with an increase in the extent and complexity of the co-ordination."[36]

Holmes in his medical writings affirmed the suppleness of the gradations between voluntary and involuntary actions in human beings.
"Circulation, secretion, and nutrition," Holmes writes,

go on in health without our consent or knowledge. The heart's action is felt occasionally, but cannot be controlled by a direct act of the will. The respiration is often perceived and partially under the influence of the will, but for the most part unnoticed and involuntary. Passing to what we call the voluntary movements, we find that even when they obey our wishes the special actions which conspire to produce the effect wished for are neither ordered nor taken distinct cognizance of. Nothing shows this more clearly than the voice.[37]

In the schema of Hughlings Jackson, the highest centers located in the brain modulate the lower ones dispersed along the spinal column. Yet because of their subtle differentiation and complexity, the higher capacities on the functional hierarchy are also the most susceptible to disease and disruption.[38] Employing the analogy of the political body, in a series of lectures published in the *Lancet* in 1884, Hughlings Jackson explained, "If the governing body of this country were destroyed suddenly we should have two causes for lamentation: (1) The loss of services of eminent men; and (2) the anarchy of the now uncontrolled people."[39] Damage to the nervous system, in other words, results in what Holmes in "Mechanism in Thought and Morals" termed "the committee of the whole" (289) being, in Hughlings Jackson's words, "taken to pieces" (655). Moreover, even the nervous centers located in the brain and associated with cerebration might act independently of consciousness: as Holmes observes, "We cannot always command the feelings of disgust, pity, anger, contempt, excited in us by certain presentations to our consciousness. We cannot always arrest or change the train of thoughts which is keeping us awake" (330).

Holmes, like his neurologist colleagues, repeatedly employed the figure of the train to represent the spontaneous action of the mind, referring to a train of ideas or the train of a narrative. "When we see a distant railway-train sliding by us in the same line, day after day, we infer the existence of a track which guides it," Holmes points out; therefore, when we hear a person lose and then pick up the thread of a tale, "how can we doubt that there is a track laid down for the story in some permanent disposition of the thinking-marrow?" (297). Holmes was aware that the notion of the prelaid track, the reflex arc mediating our emotions, memories, reactions, and even thinking process, throws a wrench into standard accounts of agency and responsibility. If a drunken man causes a commotion, Holmes explains in "Crime and Automatism," "he was an automaton that did mischief, to be sure, but was no more to blame for the particular acts in question than a locomotive that runs off the track is to blame for the destruction it works" (347). Yet the idea of the track does imply a track-layer: Holmes is here applying his conception of intentionality without intention, which he first developed in his work on puerperal fever (see Chapter 2). Rather than being vitiated, agency is deflected and dispersed in his telling analogy, for while the train (the equivalent of the drunk's body) might not be blamed for its derailment, the railway companies often were.

Train disasters were unnervingly frequent in the first decades of train travel, prompting a flurry of financial settlements. The historian Ralph Harrington reports that by the early 1860s "the railways were losing almost every personal injury case that went to court and were paying out large, and increasing, sums in compensation every year."[40] The *Lancet*, in "The Costs of Railways Collisions," approved of the damage awards, given "how great the suffering, and how profound the distress, for which these sums are supposed to compensate."[41] Even railway companies generally acceded to compensation for fractures, amputations, and other severe physical injuries. But, as a *Lancet* editorial noted, there was "a class of cases in which the greatest difficulty prevails. A frequent allegation is, that the plaintiff received a concussion which caused few or no serious symptoms at the time of the accident, but that a whole train of nervous symptoms, paralysis of motion or of sensation, partial or general, and impairment of the mental powers, gradually developed themselves, reaching their acme, perhaps, only after many months."[42] Four years after the *Lancet* first began its investigation of the health effects of train travel, the British surgeon John Eric Erichsen published a full-length study entitled *On Railway and Other Injuries of the Nervous System* (1866). Doctors, he noted, were increasingly called to the witness stand in litigation involving claimants with apparently minor injuries yet terrible symptoms following a wreck. Train crashes, Erichsen asserted, were unique:

> In no ordinary accident can the shock be so great as in those that occur on Railways. The rapidity of the movement, the momentum of the person injured, the suddenness of its arrest, the helplessness of the sufferers, and the natural perturbation of mind that must disturb the bravest, are all circumstances that of a necessity greatly increase the severity of the resulting injury to the nervous system, and that justly cause these cases to be considered as somewhat exceptional from ordinary accidents.[43]

These exceptional circumstances, Erichsen reported, had prompted surgeons to coin the term "railway spine" (9) to refer to the belated symptoms associated with survivors of rail accidents.

Erichsen's study focused exclusively on injuries where there was a "disproportion . . . between the apparently trifling accident that the patient has sustained, and the real and serious mischief that has occurred" (93). Granting that "it is often difficult to establish a connecting link between . . . [the "mischief"] and the accident" (4), Erichsen sought to resolve the "discrepancies of opinion as to relations between apparent cause and alleged effect" (3). Through an analogy to physics, Erichsen argued that one could have a *functional* disorder (evident only in symptoms) without an *organic* (or lesion-based) wound: "We do not know how it is that when a magnet is struck a heavy blow with a hammer, the magnetic force is jarred, shaken, or concussed out of the horse-shoe. But we know that it is so, and that the iron has lost its magnetic power" (94–95). Similarly, "if the spine is badly jarred, shaken, or concussed by a blow or shock of any kind communicated to the body, we find that the nervous force is to a certain extent shaken out of the man, and that he has in some way lost nervous power" (95). Disruptions to the "action" of the nervous system, in other words, might or might not be accompanied by changes in the nervous "structure" (95) yet still give rise, in the words of another physician, "to an immediate and complete functional paralysis."[44]

In his early codification of the disorder, Erichsen noted that one of "the most remarkable phenomena" in these cases was that initially "the sufferer is usually quite unconscious that any serious accident has happened to him" (95), even assisting others while "congratulat[ing] himself upon his escape from immediate peril" (96). Nonetheless, while the victim's conscious mind may be cut off from his body's experience of shock, it was possible for the medical observer to "trace the train of progressive symptoms and ill-effects that often follow such injuries" (2). Usually, Erichsen observed, it was only after a survivor returned home that a "revulsion of feeling takes place. He bursts into tears, becomes unusually talkative, and is excited. He cannot sleep, or, if he does, he wakes up suddenly with a vague sense of alarm" (96). Stiffness, pain, loss of sensation, and sometimes local paralyses ensued, along with a welter of symptoms such as sleeplessness, memory loss, irritability, racing pulse, and incontinence. After a period of time ("which varies much in different cases, from a day or two to a week or more") the survivor "finds that he is unfit for exertion and unable to attend to business" (96).

"Attending to business" was a fundamental issue: produced by the rapid pace of modern commerce, railway spine transformed mobile wage earners into paralytic homebodies. Not surprisingly, narratives of lost wages and emasculation loomed large in afflicted passengers' lawsuits against railway companies. Erichsen quoted one physician who asserted, "'A more melancholy object . . . I never beheld. The patient, naturally a handsome, middle-sized, sanguine man, of a cheerful disposition and an active mind, appeared much emaciated, stooping and dejected. He walked with a cane, but with much difficulty, and in a tottering manner.' . . . His saliva dribbled away; he could only utter monosyllables, and these came out, after much struggling, in a violent expiration" (14). Even Herbert Page, an outspoken critic of Erichsen's theories, describes the "uninjured" survivor of a train wreck as a pitiable sight: "Words, in fact, fail adequately to pourtray the distressing picture which this otherwise strong and healthy man presented."[45] Far from congenitally nervous, frail, or weak, victims of railway spine were frequently described as successful professionals or burly laborers, "of very active habits," in Erichsen's words, "accustomed to field sports, and much engaged in business, habitually in the enjoyment of good health" (48). The exemplary victim of railway spine was, in short, "quite an altered man" (49) afterward, underscoring the threat to masculinity, broadly construed, that such injuries posed.

Erichsen's book quickly became the standard reference work for lawyers pursuing such cases. In the words of one neurosurgeon from Philadelphia, "Neurologists, surgeons and attorneys find so much useful information in Erichsen's book that lawsuits wherein spinal concussion is an issue are seldom undertaken without reference to this London surgeon's lectures."[46] *On Railway and Other Injuries of the Nervous System* itself had far-flung and—for the railway companies—costly consequences, which led in turn to a flurry of articles examining the question of fraud. Such inquiries focused in particular on the tendency of claimants to recover from their injuries after a case had been adjudicated in court. "The curative effect of a pecuniary settlement," one physician dryly commented, "shows itself more and more conspicuously with every case in which the facts are made known."[47] Erichsen himself cites cases in his text drawn from court records—not an auspicious source, as one commentator noted, "to escape being deceived by the voluntary and involuntary exaggeration and simulation so commonly observed in plaintiffs seeking damages."[48]

The concept of "involuntary" simulation was an important one. Herbert Page, a railway surgeon who in 1883 published an exhaustive critique of Erichsen's book, takes up this question, though his conclusions express an important ambivalence about the physical reality of spinal concussion. Page pursued two contradictory lines of argument: (1) that physical disability in the absence of an actual lesion or inflammation, "although undoubtedly a real condition to the patient himself . . . is yet unreal and the product of his disordered imagination alone" (134), and (2) that railway spine was a real but iatrogenic illness, cultivated by alarmed physicians, ill-advised activity, and the strain of legal proceedings. Litigation, Page maintained, "keeps the sufferers from nervous shock in an atmosphere of palpitating suspense or stagnant uncertainty. . . . Is recovery possible under such an influence; is there not, indeed, every likelihood that we shall find their symptoms getting worse and worse?" (181). In Page's second strain of thinking we can discern the seeds of an emotional etiology for railway spine:

> The settlement of the patient's claim for compensation has a potent influence in bringing about convalescence, not necessarily because there has been imposture or a lack of perfect genuineness in the facts and features of the case. . . . The strain removed, the anxiety lessened, there is nothing to stand in the way of a hopeful effort being made to return to a more natural and healthful mode of life, and each returning day of improved mental tone forges another link in the chain of progress toward recovery. (142)

A physician's primary therapeutic responsibility, Page concluded, was to counsel patients to abstain from lawsuits (181).

As the historian Eric Caplan has observed, Page's first account cast symptoms as fictional while the second affirmed their physical reality—not from a jarred spine but from the emotional impact of the entire experience, from accident and diagnosis to litigation and compensation. Strong emotions could themselves bring about a momentary "loss of cerebral control" (202) and lead to "excessive activity of the automatic centres" (201). Another peril, according to Page, was that overly solicitous attendants might "foster by misdirected sympathy and kindness those very symptoms whose continuance and repetition are fraught with danger to his nervous system" (205). So while indicating that railway spine should be seen as a (failed) test of a person's moral fiber rather than a physiological insult, Page nonetheless opened the door to a potent possibility: that the "incidents indeed of almost every railway collision are quite sufficient—even if no bodily injury be inflicted—to produce a very serious effect upon the mind, and to be the means of bringing about a state of collapse *from fright, and from fright only*" (148; emphasis added).

The experience of fright, Page and Hughlings Jackson concurred, might come from an accident *or* from a thought or memory: the exterior and interior experiences had no firm line distinguishing them. Herbert Spencer in *Principles of Psychology* had affirmed a similar point, applying evolutionary thinking to the empiricism of David Hume, when he urged that "psychical states" were weakened versions of actual experiences. When being physically attacked, an injured animal will engage in a range of defensive actions: cries, movements, fleeing. "To have in a slight degree those psychical states accompanying the reception of wounds"—to hear the growls of a distant predator, say—"is to be in a state of what we call fear." A "partial excitation" is "nothing else than an impulse, an emotion, a feeling, a desire" (596). The difference between a sensation and an idea was merely a matter of degree, mediated by the intensity of the emotion involved. Daniel Hack Tuke, a physician Holmes refers to in *A Mortal Antipathy*, succinctly summed up the corporeal equation: "a certain state of mind induces certain bodily sensations, without charging 'the subject' with imposture."[49] Indeed, Tuke concludes, "ideation, under certain circumstances, is, in its influence on the sensorium, as powerful as anything, in the outer world, which impresses the senses; and may be really more so, because in the states referred to, there is no disturbing element to distract the attention" (37). As the historian Anne Harrington has observed, these nineteenth-century medical men succeeded in "'neurologizing'" Hume.[50]

In the same year that Page published his comprehensive study of railway spine, the American neurologist James Jackson Putnam rehabilitated the designation "male hysteria"—while distinguishing it from its female counterpart—to explain a set of symptoms that otherwise might be cast as fraudulent. The inability to imagine that a man might suffer from a female malady had been instrumental in Erichsen's earlier formulation of railway spine; as the surgeon had explicitly stated, "In those cases in which a man advanced in life, of energetic business habits, of great mental activity and vigour, in no way subject to gusty fits of emotion of any kind . . . after the infliction of severe shock to the system, finds himself affected by a train of symptoms indicative of a serious and deep-seated injury to the nervous system—is it reasonable to say that such a man has suddenly become 'hysterical' like a love-sick girl?"[51] Putnam's account of hysteria in the male detached the disorder from its association with excessive sensitivity and "hereditary taint," instead rooting it solely in the experience of serious, externally inflicted physical injury. The two exemplary cases described by Putnam involved men of physical heft, one a laborer for the railroads, the other a fireman, "a large, powerful and robust man."[52] After separate accidents that involved being violently thrown to the ground, both men's bruises healed in a few weeks. Many months later, however, the men sought medical attention for a range of symptoms ("prostration," "wakefulness," "impairment of memory," "emotional outbreaks") that did not disappear with their physical wounds ("Concussion," 219).

Most fascinating to Putnam was the inexplicable presence, in both cases, of "a well-marked analgesia of the entire right side" (219). Putnam found that neither man was aware of this hemianaesthesia: when the neurologist suddenly and without the patient's knowledge scraped an electrified wire brush along the railroad worker's back, the man "did not wince"—something the patient "could not have feigned," since the instrument was known to be "excessively painful" (220). In this way, the doctor was able to elicit testimony directly from the body, circumventing the question of fraud—which, in the case of the fireman, was moot anyway since he was not pursuing monetary compensation.

In a crucial reformulation, Putnam suggested that apparently hysterical symptoms did not indicate that a patient was "a sick or disabled man" (220). "If occurring in a male patient," Putnam concluded, strange symptoms tell a different story: "that his nervous system has in all probability been subjected at some past time to some considerable perturbing influence, and its presence or absence might prove a welcome aid to diagnosis in other obscure cases as it did in this" (220). Mining a person's biography for etiological events could explain the existence of physical symptoms, now understood to be a corporeal record of a male patient's past. In emphasizing the patient's own lack of consciousness of his ailments, moreover, Putnam articulated the conditions for a forensics of self, in which memory might be inscribed directly on the body. In his account, formative, life-altering events could lie outside of conscious recollection yet produce bodily symptoms—a phenomenon that historian of science Henri Ellenberger, drawing on the fiction of Nathaniel Hawthorne, refers to as the "pathogenic secret."[53]

Embodied Memory and the Pathogenic Secret

In his novel *A Mortal Antipathy*, we see Holmes uniting the emotional etiology (symptoms that arise "from fright, and from fright only"—Page's account) with the corporeal etiology (symptoms attendant on a blow or concussion—Erichsen's account) to produce a conception of "impression" that translates a mental state such as fear or terror into a physical response by way of the autonomic nervous system: "A single impression, in a very early period of . . . existence . . . may establish a communication between this centre [of nervous inhibition] and the heart which will remain open ever afterwards" (236). Moreover, Holmes writes, "once the path is opened by the track of some profound impression, that same impression, if repeated, or a similar one, is likely to find the old footmarks and follow them"; this means that "the unreasoning terror of a child, of an infant, may perpetuate itself in a timidity which shames the manhood of its subject" (236). Because of the corporeal links between nervous and cardiac movements, the character Maurice is himself aware that "unexplained sudden deaths were of constant, of daily occurrence; that any emotion is liable to arrest the movements of life: terror, joy, good news or bad news,—anything that reaches the deeper nervous centres" (222). Actual events, or in some cases the memory of them, might produce mortal danger.

Maurice's diagnosis of his own precarious condition was likely informed by a *Lancet* article that appeared the year before *A Mortal Antipathy* was published. Entitled "Death of a Bridegroom," the brief medical piece described a "recent case of sudden death," occurring a few days after the victim's wedding and attributed to "the turbulence of his emotions."[54] The medical moral of the vignette is practically identical to that espoused by Holmes in his novel: "Surprise by joy, fright, or terror," the *Lancet* affirms, "will in some cases destroy life by interrupting the normal course and performance of the vital functions. . . . There is a risk of an untoward contingency when the nervous system is so agitated by strong excitation of any particular centre as to disturb the harmony of its working" (861).

Like Holmes, the writer Kate Chopin exploited this medical fact, as well as the cultural fascination with the figure of the businessman injured by train travel, in her exquisitely ironic short story "The Story of an Hour" (1894). Compressed to just over one thousand words long, the tale begins by asserting the imperative that "great care" be taken to inform Mrs. Mallard—she of a weak heart—of the terrible news, just received by telegraph, that her husband had been killed in a railway accident. Her attendants, pleased with their tact, hover about as the newly widowed woman secludes herself in her room. The reader, however, is privy to "a little whispered word [that] escaped her slightly parted lips. She said it over and over under her breath: 'free, free, free!'"[55] Mrs. Mallard's body echoed her sentiment, as the "look of terror . . . went from her eyes. They stayed keen and bright. Her pulses beat fast, and the coursing blood warmed and relaxed every inch of her body" (757). The story ends with the surprise appearance of her husband, "a little travel-stained, composedly carrying his grip-sack and umbrella. He had been far from the scene of accident, and did not even know there had been one" (758). Though the wife's reaction is left implicit and unstated, the last paragraph of the story reads, in its entirety, "When the doctors came they said she had died of heart disease—of joy that kills" (758). The story's wicked irony is predicated on the reader's realization that there are other emotions than joy that might stop the action of the heart—including, as the *Lancet* made clear, "fright or terror"—and other things that might "interrupt the vital functions," such as husbands.

The centrality of emotion to vital functioning, captured in the literary works of Holmes and Chopin, subtended a new account of memory in the nineteenth century, one that constituted a radical departure from an older, common-sense vision of the brain as a "cerebral closet" that housed mental contents. According to the physiological psychology of Alexander Bain, a memory did not simply consist in the retrieval of a mental image but instead involved the reanimation of the parts of the body that had been originally enlisted in the event being remembered. The more affecting a particular experience had originally been, the more vivid this process: "The shock remaining in the ear and the brain after the firing of artillery must pass through the same circles, and act in the same way, as during the actual sound. . . . The rush of feeling has gone on the old tracks, and seizes the same muscles, and would go the length of actually stimulating them to repetition."[56] (One thinks of a sleeping dog's occasional muffled yelps and gyrating legs: the "memory" of a lovely chase?) The distinction between experience and memory, or event in the world and representation of it, was for Bain attenuated by this conception: "recollection is merely a repetition which does not usually go quite the same length; which stops short of actual execution" ("Review," 226).

Théodule Ribot, influenced by Bain's findings, explicitly inquired into the connections among memory, representation, cognition, and the nervous system. In his *Diseases of Memory* (1882), the psychologist described an older representationalist understanding of recollection, which had two dominant metaphors for construing memory: (1) a surface or slate, involving "material imprints on the brain," and (2) a container, with "latent modifications stored up in the 'mind.'"[57] There was, Ribot asserted, a third possibility: "organic memory," which he described as "the acquired movements which constitute the memory of different organs—the eyes, hands, arm, and legs. . . . A rich and extensive memory is not a collection of impressions, but an accumulation of dynamical associations" (31). What Ribot calls "organic memory" William Carpenter termed "unconscious cerebration" and Oliver Wendell Holmes dubbed "reflex action of the brain" ("Mechanism," 277). Bringing the three thinkers together, Ribot writes:

> Unconscious cerebration does its work noiselessly, and sets obscure ideas in order. In a curious case related by Dr. Holmes and cited by Carpenter, a man had a vague knowledge of the work going on in his brain, without attaining to the state of distinct consciousness: "A business man in Boston, . . . having an important question under consideration, had given it up for the time as too much for him. But he was conscious of an action going on in his brain which was so unusual and painful as to excite his apprehensions that he was threatened with palsy, or something of that sort. After some hours of this uneasiness, his perplexity was all at once cleared up by the natural solution of his doubts coming to him—worked out, as he believed, in that obscure and troubled interval." (37–38)

The structure of the nervous system facilitated an account whereby a series of apparent oxymorons could become explicable: memory without memory, feeling without an object, and indeed thinking without consciousness.

In *A Mortal Antipathy,* the character of Dr. Butts is committed to forestalling accounts that would immediately "solve" the case of Maurice by attributing excessive symptoms to mental derangement. Upon hearing of the young man's mysterious antipathy, "he did not smile, and say to himself that this was an idle whim, a foolish fancy, which the young man had got into his head. Neither was he satisfied to set down everything to the account of insanity, plausible as that supposition might seem" (83). The physician, in fact, figures a semiology of amplification by which "oftentimes very innocent-sounding words mean very grave disorders; that . . . 'run down' may stand for a fatigue of mind or body from which a week or a month of rest will completely restore the overworked patient, or an advanced stage of mortal illness" (92). "A terrible shock," the doctor affirmed, might be produced by "apparently insignificant causes": there is "no change of taste or temper, no eccentricity, no antipathy, which such a cause may not rationally account for" (92). The doctor's role is to produce a narrative that elucidates a physiological cause for the stated effects.

James Baldwin, in his famous indictment of the sentimental mode, emphasized the equation of sentimentality and excessiveness, in which feeling outstripped the motivating event.[58] Holmes, in *A Mortal Antipathy*, repackages both feeling and excess as essential to scientific inquiry, which in turn provides explanatory narratives that translate excess into efficient causes. "The study of the natural sciences," Dr. Butts comments, "teaches those who are devoted to them that the most insignificant facts may lead the way to the discovery of the most important, all-pervading laws of the universe" (241). The sciences, like the realist novel, often do pay attention to insignificant-seeming details. The train of events that led to the invention of the electric telegraph, Dr. Butts muses, began with a frail Madame Galvani whose attentive husband prepared her some sustaining frog-broth. "From the kick of a frog's hind leg to the amazing triumphs which began with that seemingly trivial incident is a long, a very long stride. . . . A common-looking occurrence, one seemingly unimportant, which had hitherto passed unnoticed with the ordinary course of things, was the means of introducing us to a new and vast realm of closely related phenomena" (241–242). The isolation of the galvanic current in a frog's nervous system, which continued to catalyze involuntary muscle spasms even after the poor creature was beheaded, is of course not a random example of the notion that small causes might have far-flung effects. It provides the conceptual basis for the novel *A Mortal Antipathy* itself, which both thematizes and investigates the operations of the sympathetic nervous system and its susceptibility to seemingly innocuous stimuli.

This investigation reaches its climax when, lying on his sickbed, Maurice entrusts to Dr. Butts a written narrative of his "doomed and wholly exceptional life" (207)—"a story so far from the common range of experience" that the reader is temporarily "requested to suspend his judgment" (227). Maurice's autobiographical narrative recounts his falling from a woman's arms as a baby, which transformed a "pleasant,

smiling infant, with nothing to indicate any peculiar nervous susceptibility" (207) into a man who faints in the presence of the fair sex. Pieced
together from "circumstances as told me and vaguely remembered"
(207), Maurice's account echoes the "paralyzing terror" of train-wreck
survivors: "That dreadful experience is burned deep into my memory.
The sudden apparition of the girl; the sense of being torn away from the
protecting arms around me; the frantic effort to escape; the shriek that
accompanied my fall through what must have seemed unmeasurable
space; the cruel lacerations of the piercing and rending thorns,—all
these fearful impressions blended into one paralyzing terror" (209).
Maurice's "memory," corporeally registered by the terror, was nonlin-
guistic, for he "had no thought, living like other infants the life of impressions without language to connect them in a series" (224).

Here we begin to see important distinctions between Holmes and the
theorists of railway spine. In describing Maurice's "memory" as existing
in the absence of consciousness, Holmes traverses conceptual territory
familiar from his first novel. The prenatal snakebite, in that earlier narrative, provided Elsie with what Théodule Ribot termed "hereditary
memory" (65). In the physiological terms Herbert Spencer used in his
1855 *Principles of Psychology*, Elsie's "nascent intelligence"—about
how to negotiate rocky cliffs, for instance—would be understood to "belong to memory in the strictest sense." As Spencer conceived it, the past
experiences of both individuals and the species are registered in anatomical or reflex knowledge (the "reptilian brain"), though "it would be
thought a misuse of language were any one to ask another whether he *remembered* that the sun shines, that fire burns, that iron is hard, and that
ice is cold."[59] In contrast with Hawthorne's character Arthur Dimmes-
dale, cited by the medical historian Henri Ellenberger as an early instantiation of the "pathogenic secret," Holmes strips the secret of its painful
location in the consciousness of the subject, while the "memory" of it,
no longer understood to be symbolic of a prior event or the physical concomitant to a conflict of conscience, has become *commensurate with its
physical manifestations*. Memory, Ribot affirmed, is "a biological fact: it
is an impregnation" (*Diseases*, 196) of experience onto the muscles, the
tissues, the sensory organs, and—frequently but not necessarily—the
brain. Elsie had, in the words of the recent trauma theorist Babette Rothschild, a memory in the absence of memory.[60]

The operation of this new sort of memory is vividly expressed in *A
Mortal Antipathy*, when Maurice goes into a state of shock in the presence of women: "The cause of this violent and appalling seizure was but

too obvious. The approach of the young girl and the dread that she was about to lay her hand upon me had called up the same train of effects which the moment of terror and pain had already occasioned. . . . It was too evident that a chain of nervous disturbances had been set up in my system which repeated itself whenever the *original impression* gave the first impulse" (210, 211). The term *impression* could of course imply two different functions: the processing of a mental image, thereby involving something akin to conscious memory, or the physiological inscription (pressing in) of experience directly onto the nervous system. That Holmes means the latter is indicated in a scene where Maurice inexplicably experiences a "change of color, anxiety about the region of the heart, and sudden failure as if about to fall into a deadly fainting-fit" (217)—only to find that there is a woman sitting nearby but out of his line of vision. A rather silly scene, it nonetheless serves the purpose of producing a situation that cannot be explained away as a "mere" mental event, or even some odd fabrication. As such, it anticipates the double-blinding of twentieth-century control trials that are expressly structured to neutralize the influence of mental processing in order to access the "real" or purely physiological effects of drugs.

The Forensic Self

Maurice, in both inhabiting his corporeal experience and possessing a narrative of explanation, functions in an analogous manner to the Scottish physician Alexander Gordon (described in Chapter 2): "He had learned to look upon himself very much as he would upon an intimate *not* himself,—upon a different personality" (*Mortal*, 229). In this, Maurice appears to exemplify what psychiatrist Pierre Janet termed the "undoubling" *(dédoublement)* of a personality: "all the psychological phenomena that are produced in the brain are not brought together in one and the same personal perception; a portion remains independent under the form of sensations or elementary images, or else is grouped more or less completely and tends to form a new system, a personality independent of the first. These two personalities are not content merely to alternate, to succeed each other; they can coexist in a way more or less complete."[61] As the historian Ruth Leys has noted, modern theorists of trauma have discerned in Janet's writings a distinction between "'traumatic memory,' which merely and unconsciously *repeats* the past, and 'narrative memory,' which *narrates the past as past*"; Janet, moreover, "validat[ed] the idea that the goal of therapy is to convert 'traumatic memory' into 'narrative memory' by getting the patient to recount his or her history."[62] Crucially, in Holmes's novel, Maurice's inability to remember the traumatic events of his childhood does not involve what Freud would term repression; the lack of conscious memory, Holmes is at pains to assert, inheres in the fact that he was a baby when they occurred (as is not the case with Freud's theory of the dynamic unconscious, in which content found socially unacceptable is pushed out of the realm of consciousness.) Moreover, Maurice's emotional recounting of precisely what transpired when he was an infant—pieced together journalistically from eyewitnesses to the events and medical explanations—does not alleviate his symptoms.

So while Holmes in his writings is committed to exploring the corporeal substrate of double consciousness, his ideas about embodied memory are not easily subsumed to Freudian terms. Holmes focused his investigation of the operation of memory not on narratives of cases but on the anatomy of the organ of thought. "The brain proper is a double organ, like that of vision," Holmes argued in "Mechanism in Thought and Morals," his 1870 address to Harvard's Phi Beta Kappa Society; "its two halves being connected by a strong transverse band, which unites them like Siamese twins" (264). In his first novel, Holmes figured this doubleness as the battle of two creatures housed in one body: the snake, figuring the lower, automatic functions of Elsie's "reptilian brain," and the human girl, who comes to possess the higher capacities for language and for love. That these elements are inextricably associated—very much like intimately conjoined Siamese twins—is affirmed by the novel's ending, in which the extermination of Elsie's "snaky" side results in the death of the girl. The "higher" functions of cognition and representation, Holmes implied, built on "lower" capacities, also essential to human beings, of aversion, affiliation, and association: "the mystery of unconscious mental action is exemplified, as I have said, in every act of mental association. What happens when one idea brings up another? Some internal movement, of which we are wholly unconscious, and which we only know by its effect. . . . There is a Delphi and a Pythoness in every human breast" (285–286).

The "Pythoness within the breast" is for Holmes a figure for what he described as "the passive flow of thought" as opposed to "mental labor," which "implies an exercise of will" (294). Drawn from Greek sources, Holmes's Pythoness refers to the Pythia, the priestess at Delphi who, intoxicated by vapors arising from a fissure in the earth, was said to speak incomprehensible truths that then had to be interpreted by the priest. In *A Mortal Antipathy,* Maurice's account of his infantile shock is a psychophysical version of this structure. Prompted by the desire to make his strange symptoms explicable, the adult Maurice pieces together his autobiography from a variety of sources. Seeking validation, he presents his narrative to Dr. Butts, who locates a medical paper on "gynophobia" (issued as a "Report to the Royal Academy of the Biological Sciences by a Committee of that Institution"). Maurice's affliction, the medical authorities assert, is neither a "moral perversion" (223) nor "entirely exceptional and anomalous" but instead is "well known to us . . . in our common experience" (231). The link between Maurice and Holmes's own tale is here made explicit, and the structural problem of both narratives is resolved. Having prefaced *A Mortal Antipathy* with concern that he "'should have been afraid of [the novel's] subject'" due to the "improbability of the physiological or pathological occurrence on which the story is founded," Holmes's narrative succeeds in "recalling . . . a series of extraordinary but well-authenticated facts" and thereby is "rendered plausible" (v). The implausible bits of both character and novel are woven together, bringing effects into line with causes.

In a chapter suggestively entitled "An Intimate Conversation," Dr. Butts asks the bedridden Maurice about his condition while keeping his fingers on the patient's wrist, to determine whether the patient's body "tells a story" that matches the conscious tale of the teller (remember that the railway surgeon Herbert Page affirmed that "the pulse is often the only sign we have to guide us to a right estimate of the patient's condition" [*Injuries,* 159]). When under Dr. Butts's fingers Maurice's pulse indeed flutters and then fails when he speaks of a woman, the apparatus of authentication has achieved its results. The act of calibrating a person's story with the testimony of his body, modeled here by the physician, is essential for a forensics of self: first, it establishes the centrality of formal debate or argumentation, not only between the experiential subject and some outside expert but also between the individual's conscious and unconscious memory; and second, it installs the use of science and technology as essential for the elaboration and finally the integration of an individual's experience.

As the historian Paul White has discussed, one such technology, the polygraph, attended not to the body's surface but instead measured its interior motions. Holmes, in focusing his last novel on the problem of "antipathy," affirms this point by White: "Sympathy, widely regarded by Victorians as the basis for social bonds and honesty in communication, had become an obstacle to scientific observation."[63] Holmes depicts precisely such an obstacle through the character of Lurida Vincent. In one instance, she literally translates a medical case study into a sensationalized biography. After reading a "Remarkable Case of Tarantism" in an Italian medical journal, Lurida concludes that Maurice is the self-same boy described in the case study, who was bitten by a tarantula and subsequently suffered from "nervous seizures" (180): "'There, doctor! Have n't I found the true story of this strange visitor? . . . Who can this man be but the boy of that story?'" (182–183).

Lurida's solution, in other words, was to affirm that the experience of the boy in the case study and that of Maurice was one and the same. Dr. Butts, however, draws a link between boy and man that is not biographical but corporeal. The crucial transit, in the case of Maurice, is between two parts of the nervous system, one aligned with volition, the other with automatism:

> The brain, as all know, is the seat of ideas, emotions, volition. It is the great central telegraphic station with which many lesser centres are in close relations, from which they receive, and to which they transmit, their messages. The heart has its own little brains, so to speak,—small collections of nervous substance which govern its rhythmical motions under ordinary conditions. . . . There are two among the special groups of nerve-cells which produce directly opposite effects. One of these has the power of accelerating the action of the heart, while the other has the power of retarding, or arresting this action. (235)

The communication between the two systems is mediated by emotion: thus "a single impression, in a very early period" of a person's life, establishes "a communication between this centre and the heart which will remain open ever afterwards"; and, as with any repeated motion, "habit only makes the path easier to traverse" (236). Holmes's description here is a close gloss of the work of Alexander Bain when he describes memory as a "rush of feeling" that reactivates "the bodily organs engaged in the actual transaction": Recollection is construed as "repetition," while representation, no longer an image tucked away "in a separate chamber of the brain," is refashioned as corporeal expression.[64]

So while "a rush of feeling" might overload the nervous system, Daniel Hack Tuke, thinking homeopathically, hypothesized that "Fear may heal as well as cause disease" (*Body*, 333). "Fear," he wrote, "may be regarded as the digitalis of our Remedia Psychica" (351–352). The plot of *A Mortal Antipathy* produces just such a dose of therapeutic panic: a fire in the house where Maurice lies recovering from a fever. "The dread moment which had blighted his life returned in all its terror. He felt the convulsive spring in the form of a faint, impotent spasm,—the rush of air,—the thorns of the stinging and lacerating cradle into which he was precipitated. One after another those paralyzing seizures which had been like deadening blows on the naked heart seemed to repeat themselves, as real as at the moment of their occurrence" (*Mortal*, 265). Rather than a memory producing feelings, Maurice experiences the reverse: emotion catalyzes the memory. Holmes invokes the technology of the photograph to figure the corporeal inscription of memory: "The sensitive plate [the body] has taken one look at the scene, and remembers it all. Every little circumstance is there . . . but invisible; potentially present, but impalpable, inappreciable, as if not existing at all" (265). Feelings provide the "wash" to make the past, housed in the body's dynamic structures, visible: "the rush of unwonted emotion floods the undeveloped pictures of vanished years, stored away in the memory . . . and in one swift instant the past comes out as vividly as if it were again the present" (265–266). It is in this moment of terror that the past and present converge in real time, and it is Euthymia "The Wonder" (rather than Lurida, whose nickname is The Terror) who rescues Maurice from the burning building and effects "the revolution in his nervous system which would be the beginning of a new existence" (277).

By relocating the terms of the debate over railway spine from adulthood to childhood, and from biography to corporeality, Holmes established a nonpejorative account by which an individual might have an extreme reaction of fear to apparently insignificant stimuli. The connection of the boy to the man was not written in book form but rather, Holmes affirms, in the emotional record of the nervous system: "thus the unreasoning terror of a child, of an infant, may perpetuate itself in a timidity which shames the manhood of its subject" (*Mortal*, 236). The neurological track of fear—developed at an early, somatically pliable period—can become, as it were, greased through habit, catalyzing panic from increasingly insignificant events (e.g. a fly settling on the forehead). Beyond the volition or indeed consciousness of the individual, the path of transmission is corporeal and dynamic. In Holmes's terms, "consciousness is a surface; narrative is a line" (273), and emotion is that which mediates between the spatial and the temporal: it is the "wash" that coalesces the accumulations of years of experience into "one swift instant." In this, Holmes in essence repudiates the account of traumatic healing offered by twentieth- and twenty-first-century trauma theories, which focuses on integration of past traumatic memories (their translation into narrative memory). Instead, he affirms the need for *both* a narrative remembering *and* a corporeal "forgetting." Ruth Leys writes of the French psychologist Pierre Janet's insistence that "narrated recollection was insufficient for the cure. A supplementary action was required, one that involved a process of 'liquidation' that, terminologically, sounded suspiciously like 'exorcism' or forgetting" (105). As Janet wrote, in relation to one of his female patients, "To forget the past is in reality to change behavior in the present. When she achieves this new behavior, it matters little whether she still retains the verbal memory of her adventure. she is cured of her neuropathological disorders."[65]

So while Ruth Leys and other historians of trauma rightly point to the turn-of-the-century work of Pierre Janet, student of the neurologist Jean-Martin Charcot, as paving the way for a conception of traumatic memory in his studies of dissociation, the work of Oliver Wendell Holmes comprises an influential American articulation of this distinctly modern form of selfhood.[66] The idea of double consciousness that emerges in Holmes's literary and scientific writing installs narrative— more precisely, the story of an individual's life experiences—in an absolutely central yet crucially vexed position vis-à-vis the subject. For while narrative becomes the crucial technology for a forensics of selfhood, a mode of subjectivity that requires the unearthing and then uprooting of prior pathogenic experiences to produce an etiology (or explanatory "track") of bodily symptoms, it becomes construed as that which may be unavailable to the conscious mind of the person in possession of the memories, who relives rather than re-presents the past.

The legacy of this way of conceiving of the self, then, is that corporeal symptoms are increasingly understood to be inscriptions of prior experiences and therefore, unlike narrative, to provide unmediated access to a person's past. This model underwrites the role of a detached expert who, in tracing effects back to precipitating causes in a person's life, employs narrative as a crucial diagnostic tool. Narrative, in other words, is at once repudiated and installed as central to a physiological psychology. Here we encounter the enabling conditions for literary realism and its practitioners, who hover uncomfortably between fabricating events and mobilizing an apparatus of expertise to elicit the inmost secrets of persons and society. It is my contention that, in the person of Holmes, at least, the realists were indeed instrumental in helping realize (in Ian Hacking's sense of making up) a new relationship between a person and his or her past, a whole new way of conceiving of oneself as a person in the nineteenth century. Holmes succeeded in establishing a masculinity that is vexed, at best: he saved his protagonist from excessiveness at the expense of a radically refigured autonomy, produced narrative resolution at the cost of a unified self—and, as I discuss further in the next chapter, helped to establish the terror-stricken man, rather than the hysterical woman, as the elided foundational figure for modern trauma theory.

CHAPTER FOUR

Nervous Effort

Gilman, Crane, and the Psychophysical Pathologies of Everyday Life

Of course when a body begins to expand, there comes the possibility of bursting: but I nevertheless approve of a certain tension in one's being.

—HENRY JAMES, *RODERICK HUDSON* (1875)

As we have seen, the nineteenth-century ideas about mind-body continuities—enabled by the reflex arc, and resulting in somatic "memory without memory"—helped defuse the medical and cultural problem of male hysteria by reframing it as corporeal trauma. Yet it is one thing to track the neurological consequences of surviving a train wreck and quite another to measure the pathological effects of humdrum domestic routine, especially if the quotidian activities have dwindled to the minuscule proportions of, for instance, "trying to fix a small moving speck on the wall."[1] Shell-shocked men are one thing: but what of the enervated nineteenth-century woman who might be "kept awake for hours by the wallpaper in her room"?[2] Who "does no work, spends her time groaning or crying," is plagued by visualizations of moving figures and the sensation of "a disgusting odor"? And who, in spite of being "very devoted to her husband and very affectionate," has "become an insufferable wife" who can't be trusted with her beloved child?[3]

Readers of American literature will undoubtedly recognize in this description a set of symptoms familiar from Charlotte Perkins Gilman's "The Yellow Wallpaper" (1892). Cast as a series of diary entries, Gilman's story is a fictional account of a young wife and mother whose physician-husband takes her to the country to recuperate from a "temporary nervous depression."[4] At the center of the tale is the narrator's preoccupation with the hectic design of the wallpaper in her sickroom. Both the narrator and the narrative become increasingly unhinged, as the woman ultimately comes to discern not just a repulsive smell and corpse-like figures but a living woman within the wallpaper's arabesques. Despite apparently robust physical health, the narrator descends into madness, peeling off the offending paper and crawling over the body of her prostrate husband.

The tale has, in recent decades, elicited a stunning amount of critical attention from scholars who, reading it within a Freudian framework, see it as an allegorical tale of rebellion against a repressive atmosphere. Yet it is provocative to note that the initial symptoms listed earlier (tracking a speck on a wall, being kept awake by wallpaper, hallucinating smells etc.) are derived not from Gilman or Freud but rather from a novel written by Henry James and from philosophical and psychological writings of the late nineteenth century. It is James's fastidious, eminently sane character Adela Gereth who can't sleep in a room with tacky paper; while the seemingly fanatical focus on "mak[ing] out the exact form, or the nature, of a faint marking on a piece of paper a few feet off" (152) is the project of the philosopher John Dewey, drawn from his 1897 essay entitled "The Psychology of Effort." The woman plagued by fatigue and hallucinations was a patient of the psychologist Pierre Janet, who in 1894 published a study of her case in a paper entitled "History of a Fixed Idea."

This chapter argues that a range of late-nineteenth-century writers and thinkers, including S. Weir Mitchell, John Dewey, Pierre Janet, Charlotte Perkins Gilman, and Stephen Crane, were trying to make sense of the physical sensations that accompany the expenditure of cognitive effort: the way a person's body, happiness, and indeed life are caught up in what appear from the outside to be primarily imaginative or "psychical occurrences" (Dewey, 151). Yet experienced from the inside, such occurrences have sensible corporeal consequences, largely invisible from without. In the words of a 1924 psychology text, "You cannot show the observer a wallpaper pattern without by that very fact disturbing his respiration and circulation."[5] The conceptual and practical underpinnings of this notion can be traced to the late nineteenth century, in the writings of thinkers working at the nexus of philosophy, psychology, and physiology. For Pierre Janet's patient "Justine," the mere *thought* of cholera prompted a range of crippling physical symptoms. John Dewey, though focused on everyday rather than pathological acts of mind, described processes such as the attempt to recall forgotten lines of poetry in corporeal terms akin to those of Janet.

Philosopher and psychologist agreed that investigation of the psychophysical nature of things "all in the mind" required careful attention to the whole experience, not just the objective or visible bodily manifestation of thought (e.g. knitted brows) or solely its subjective or invisible mental character (e.g. the idea of cholera). Through analysis of medical and philosophical texts alongside literary ones, this chapter makes the case that the insights of the nineteenth century provide helpful instructions for engaging with realist works: with plots that not only make visible but actively enlist a range of sensory experiences, this literature calls our attention to the phenomenology of reading. As Pierre Janet wrote in his study of Justine: "To attain intelligibility, the patient's perceptions have to be grasped by entering the dream" (213).

In what follows, I propose to "enter the dream" of Gilman's celebrated short story to elucidate a context within which to understand the effects of "The Yellow Wallpaper," one that makes sense of the narrator's strange, psychophysical experience of the wall covering as well as the strange, psychophysical way nineteenth-century readers seemed to experience the story. For while Gilman's contemporary reviewers differed on the story's ultimate meaning (from a cautionary tale about the dangers of tasteless home decorating to a gothic study of psychosis), almost all commented explicitly on the story's effectiveness—and affectiveness. A typical correspondent described it as "an eerie tale of insanity that is uncommonly effective. Most attempts to work up insanity as 'material' are ineffective; but here the progress from nervous sensitiveness to illusion, and on to delusion, is put before the reader so insidiously that he feels something of that same chill alarm for his own mental soundness that accompanies actual contact with lunatics."[6]

By illuminating the psychophysical elements of perceptual effort, we can recover surprising convergences between the thought of Gilman and that of her nemesis, the neurologist S. Weir Mitchell (who had treated Gilman's own nervous prostration). As Cynthia Davis has documented, both writers vociferously repudiated Sigmund Freud's epistemology and therapeutic methods, while agreeing that the nineteenth-century home wreaked havoc on residents' minds and bodies.[7] Gilman and Mitchell agreed that "aesthetic" concerns could be assaultive, equating chaotic decorating practices with the shocks and confusion of a battlefield. Yet while both patient and doctor drew corporeal analogies between women's and men's spheres, they proposed divergent therapies for "home-shocked" wives and daughters. The neurologist, focusing his reforming strategies on the woman rather than on the home, contraindicated cerebral activity; Gilman, Mitchell's one-time patient and a budding social activist, urged home reform and promoted the salutary effects of aesthetic work.

Recently, Jennifer Fleissner has offered a provocative reading of "The Yellow Wallpaper" and *The Red Badge of Courage* that emphasizes the obsessive attempts of the protagonists as they seek to transform a "feeling of incompleteness" into "a sense of achieved completeness."[8] Fleissner draws on the work of Pierre Janet to articulate the "oscillatory thought patterns" (62) that characterize obsessive behavior; this mental oscillation, she argues, structures and indeed defines works of literary naturalism, which in their idealist drive to overcome a "stalled . . . narrative trajectory" (61) reveal the "fundamental impossibility" of "the realist ideal of narrative completion" (62). The insoluble impasse described by Fleissner, however, ignores the corporeal component of nervous effort and posits no end to obsession. It is worth remembering that Janet's case studies and even his more theoretical works, along with the writings of Gilman and Mitchell, reflect unwillingness to accept these limited options; all three generated ideas that were meant to be put into practice, to be materially transformative. Their purpose, of course, was to help mitigate the suffering associated with prolonged and vitiated nervousness. This chapter argues that a pragmatic focus on moments of realization—what in Crane is more aptly termed "fabrication"—allows us to discern how works of literary realism make palpable those full-bodied acts of engaged activity that coax the world into a livable shape and help us to situate ourselves as comfortably as possible within it. Contra Fleissner's indication, the "realist ideal" that emerges in works by Gilman and Crane tends toward exceedingly modest acts of "completion": they draw attention to therapeutic moments of dynamic equilibrium that are modeled in particular sorts of aesthetic experiences.

Gilman in fact outlined, in her fiction and sociological writings, a therapeutic encounter similar to what Pierre Janet was developing with his patients, one that was less physiologically reductive than Mitchell's yet different also from Freud's full-blown talking cure. The "artistic character" of many nervous women, Janet observed, signaled not weakness but a passionate analytical orientation. A pathological version of what John Dewey later described in *Art as Experience* (1934), the obsessive patient sought to make the agitating distraction of quotidian domestic events coalesce—in terms that were both conceptual and corporeal—into a coherent and calming experience. To cultivate these acts of realization,

Janet instituted a therapeutic regime of what he called "cerebral work" but which could be termed "art homeopathy": small doses of physically engaged patterned acts of intellection, such as playing the piano.

Janet's psychophysical treatments, moreover, help bring to light affinities between scientific discourses at the close of the nineteenth century and aesthetic ones. Both Gilman's and Janet's texts make visible the way ideas are realized in terms of the body; taken together, they provide a vocabulary for attending to modes of aesthetic realization in other nineteenth-century literary works. The chapter concludes with a reading of Stephen Crane's *The Red Badge of Courage* (1895), which in placing its protagonist in the surprising context of war affirms continuities between men and women, and between everyday and aesthetic experience. Crane's novel illuminates how readers of realist fiction, as with persons engaged in other sorts of quotidian perceptions, maintain a doubled vision that places them along a continuum of reflexive awareness of themselves as readers. Disturbed contemporary reviewers of "The Yellow Wallpaper" knew that complete absorption into one's perceptual experience—whether it pertained to wallpaper, a battle, or a short story—had the makings of pathology. Yet, as Dewey urged, complete detachment is itself undesirable and indeed untenable, for all cerebral acts, even reading and thinking, involve sensory and muscular engagement. Crane in *The Red Badge of Courage* explores these notions by following an inexperienced soldier's twinned experience of attempting to gain perspective on his own actions during a battle even as he finds himself, terrifyingly, in the midst of it.

The writings of these nineteenth-century authors affirm what the neurologist Oliver Sacks would explore a century later in his study of the man who mistook his wife for a hat: that just as the inability to detach from one's perceptual experience constitutes a form of madness, so is a complete lack of passion tantamount to a debilitating pathology, leaving one unequipped to negotiate the affective demands of a complex, potentially beautiful, but often violent world.[9] These writers help to bring us in touch with the inadequacies of a mode of criticism that is immune to the affective enlistments of literary works.

Freud, Feminist Reading, and Interrogative Criticism

Much has been written on the apparent epidemic of nervousness during the second half of the nineteenth century. "'I am nervous. I did not used to be. What can I do to overcome it?'" was, Weir Mitchell reported, a question on the lips of a vast number of Americans.[10] The historian Eric Caplan has described how "somatically inclined physicians devoted an unprecedented amount of attention to psychical symptoms of those for whom there existed no clearly discernible anatomical or organic irregularities," firm in the belief that such symptoms were "the products of certain yet-to-be determined neurophysiological processes."[11] Accordingly, neurologists like Mitchell developed treatments that focused on the physical body, using massage, electrical shocks, rich foods, rest, and isolation to coax the overtaxed body back to health.

The influence of this somatic paradigm, and indeed of Mitchell himself, is evident in the early writings of another medical man trained as a neurologist: Sigmund Freud.[12] In *Studies on Hysteria* (1895), a series of cases written with his mentor Josef Breuer, Freud used a surgical metaphor to describe his methods for locating the pathogenic objects— certain memories and ideas—troubling his nervous patients.[13] He found that hypnosis, like chloroform, placed patients in a receptive state for locating and then extracting the sources of their symptoms. So when a patient he referred to as Frau Emmy von N. entered a memory-state in which she fretted about the health of her child, Freud "interrupted her here and pointed out to her that this same child was to-day a normal girl and in the bloom of health, and [he] made it impossible for her to see any of these melancholy things again."[14] As Freud wrote of his psychic surgery: "Therapy consists in wiping away these pictures, so that she is no longer able to see them before her" (53).

Yet Freud was an admittedly poor practitioner of hypnosis; moreover, his scientific aspirations prompted him to distinguish his unconventional methods from those of faith healers, who also elicited trance states. When Emmy von N.'s symptoms reappeared, and she complained of Freud's tendency to interrupt her discourse, a resigned-sounding Freud recorded her injunction for him to be quiet and "let her tell me what she had to say" (63). Following her lead, Freud departed from the interrogative, true-or-false approach of an empiricist: "I now saw that . . . I cannot evade listening to her stories in every detail to the very end" (61). To his astonishment, Freud found that the verbal recovery of a traumatic event, when accompanied by the intense emotions adequate to the trauma, allowed the accompanying hysterical symptoms to be (in Breuer's words) "talked away" (37). A previously "strangulated affect" might "find a way out through speech" (17) rather than finding expression in disabling physical symptoms: this was the heart of the cathartic treatment developed by Breuer and Freud.

The insight that a patient's tales might provide etiological clues and even possess salutary power was, as Freud immodestly claimed in later writings, novel to psychoanalysis: "No one had ever cured an hysterical symptom by such means before, or had come so near to understanding its cause."[15] Freud, more than Breuer, devoted much of his writing in *Studies on Hysteria* to the techniques he developed "to enable [the patient] to reproduce the story of her illness" (138). Of Emmy von N. Freud writes, "Her remarkably well-stocked memory showed the most striking gaps. She herself complained that it was as though her life was chopped in pieces" (70n). Most remarkable of all was the fact that a patient's body appeared to fill the "gap" in her tale. As Freud writes of Fraulein Elisabeth von R., "Her painful legs began to 'join in the conversation' during our analysis" (148). Physiology, passed through the analyst's interpretive framework, became the discursive handmaiden of psychology: "It is difficult," he maintained, "to attribute too much sense . . . to these details" (93). As Janet Malcolm has written, "It isn't the story [the patient] tries to tell but the story he tells *in spite of himself* that the analyst listens for. What he is really after is the story behind the story."[16] Translating this imperative into the language of archaeology, Freud likened his therapeutic practice to "excavating a buried city": after "getting the patient to tell [him] what was known to her," he "would penetrate into deeper layers of her memories . . . by carrying out an investigation under hypnosis" (139). Epistemologically, Freud's method marked a dramatic shift in attention from the sometimes spectacular details of a patient's physical symptoms (apparent in Jean-Martin Charcot's use of the amphitheater to demonstrate *la grande hystèrie*) to the content of her speech. Whereas once he looked, now the doctor intent on a diagnosis *listened*.[17]

In *The Political Unconscious* (1981), Fredric Jameson provides terms for describing a mode of literary criticism that is "diagnostic" along the lines that Freud articulated and that treats a work of literature like a symptomatic body.[18] As Jameson describes it, readers operating under this paradigm seek out the telling textual moment "whose cause is of another order of phenomenon from its effects" (26). Like a psychoanalytic subject, a text is understood to harbor clues that gesture toward the "ideological system" on which the text is structured but which "remain[s] unrealized in the surface of the text" (48). This critical approach "always presupposes, if not a conception of the unconscious itself, then at least some mechanism of mystification or repression in terms of which it would make sense to seek a latent meaning behind a manifest one" (60).

Jameson's description is helpful in thinking about twentieth-century critical approaches to "The Yellow Wallpaper," for feminist readings of Gilman's story, which construe the story as a layered text demanding meticulous analytical attention in order to "listen to" its subversive subtext, tend to reprise such epistemological commitments. The tale has in fact become an important model of the "palimpsestic" literary text, "works whose surface designs conceal or obscure deeper, less accessible (and less socially acceptable) levels of meaning."[19] Just as for Freud a person's body provided a tableau on which the mind could inscribe its psychological conflicts, so "The Yellow Wallpaper" has been understood to conceal an encrypted tale of social and psychological discord. That Gilman's contemporary reviewers paid too much attention to its ostensible plot and did not appear to "listen" to its subtext was construed as lending weight to this analysis.[20] As Lisa Kasmer has noted, modern critics have construed earlier readers' (mis)interpretations as affirming their own, "align[ing] the inability of the husband to understand the wife's condition, in effect to read her text, with the difficulty Gilman's contemporaries had in understanding the work itself."[21]

Yet this approach, problematically, produces a hermeneutic circle: Freud's tendency to read the body as symbolic of the mind's conflicts is mapped onto Gilman's nineteenth-century short story, and then the story is read, in turn, as possessing a concealed significance discernible only through methods drawn from psychoanalytic theory. Moreover, to borrow Jameson's terms, this approach diverts attention away from a text's "effects" and sends readers seeking out a "cause" that is "of another order of phenomenon" altogether (26). Recasting interpretation as decryption reconfigures the experience of the reader as diagnostic rather than aesthetic. In the influential description of Elaine Showalter, "The orthodox plot recedes, and another plot, hitherto submerged . . . , stands out in bold relief like a thumbprint."[22] Showalter's terminology, which likens the critical engagement with a work of fiction to crime analysis, frames the work of the critic on a particular scientific model of expertise. The contemporary novelist Richard Powers has noted that, in recent decades, the critic has come to be an "interrogator, almost a customs guard at the border of understanding, the sites where people might be smuggling cultural work into the unsuspecting domestic conscious-ness."[23] The critic, on this model, seeks to counteract the way texts have of getting under the analyst's skin.

This sort of disciplining was something Freud, in the context of the analyst-analysand relationship, sought to put in place, for he was aware that the scientific status of his "brush-clearing" technique was uncer-tain: his case histories, which "read like short stories," also seemed to "lack the serious stamp of science" (160–161). There is, however, a par-adox at the center of a literary criticism modeled on this procedure. For even as it attributes a certain dynamism to the patient/text—which har-bors intriguing conflicts and potentially explosive challenges to social norms—such an approach defuses a text's affective engagements and renders invisible the embodied entailments of the reading experience. The method that Freud developed, after all, was explicitly committed to "curing" the object of analysis while (at least ideally) leaving the analyst essentially unmoved, unchanged, untouched. So the critic gets to think of the story as safely outside herself, an inert object that—like an actual subject of interrogation—can be "made to talk" the language that the investigator supplies. Because "The Yellow Wallpaper" has been such an important vehicle for establishing the role of critic as interrogator, to begin to enumerate the potential pitfalls of this way of conceptualizing literary works, and to locate an alternative way of thinking about the reading experience, it is useful to get a clearer sense of how thinkers prior to Freud conceived of the very state—nervousness—that has made Gilman's story seem to "cry out for analysis."[24]

A Physiological Approach to Nervousness

Although the narrator of "The Yellow Wallpaper" is Gilman's most renowned portrait of this distinctive nineteenth-century figure, nervous women and men show up repeatedly in Gilman's fiction. In "Dr. Clair's Place" (1915), for instance, a suicidal woman is advised to seek the help of a woman doctor "who is profoundly interested in neurasthenia—melancholia—all that sort of thing."[25] In this utopian vision of the perfect medical treatment, the patient travels to Dr. Clair's isolated mountain re-treat, agrees to "do anything she said" (334), is "put through an elabo-rate course of bathing, shampoo, and massage, and finally put to bed, in that quiet fragrant rosy room" (332). In slow stages the patient's body is "made as strong as might be," and her "worn-out nerves" are restored with "sleep—sleep—sleep" (334). Once the patient reclaims an increment of energy, Gilman's fictional physician then tests out a series of treatments, focusing in particular on how the patient responds to different foods and to her physical surroundings. Remarkably, Dr. Clair's approach emulates S. Weir Mitchell's (in)famous "rest cure," which placed nervous patients under the exclusive care of the physician, regulated their diets, stimulated their disused muscles, and isolated them from their domestic sphere. All physical and intellectual activity was prohibited. As Mitchell explained, "The defects of the body have to do with those of the mind, [hence] the need to begin by building up the body anew."[26]

Mitchell, however, possessed no background in women's diseases. Instead, his work with injured Civil War soldiers primed him to take seriously maladies of the nerves that were dismissed by the medical community. Hysteria in particular had presented a profound challenge for doctors, since its symptoms consisted of "strange and multiform phenomena"—including local paralysis or anesthesia, fainting, tunnel vision, and trance-like spells—that mimicked the features of other diseases while possessing no discernible organic basis.[27] As a contract surgeon for the Union army, however, Mitchell had treated equally astonishing symptoms in injured men, both direct (e.g. a gunshot wound) and indirect (such as paralyzing homesickness or "nostalgia"). Mitchell observed that a soldier with wounded nerves often became "hysterical, if we may use the only term which covers the facts. He walks carefully, carries the limb tenderly with the sound hand, is tremulous, nervous."[28] In these wartime injuries, the normal laws of physiology appeared inapplicable: a wound to the neck might produce agonizing pain in a soldier's hand; a shell exploding nearby might generate uncontrollable twitching in an otherwise uninjured combatant; and even seemingly minor injuries could leave, in the words of Stephen Crane, "bodies twisted into impossible shapes."[29] On occasion, Mitchell even had soldiers' contorted limbs molded in plaster and sent to the Army Medical Museum, to preserve their inexplicable injuries for future research.

Struggling to understand the devastating symptoms of barely wounded soldiers, Mitchell and his colleagues at the Hospital for Nervous Diseases hypothesized that a person's nervous force, analogous to an electrical circuit, could be damaged in its function without any visible lesion. "Reflecting then upon the close correlation of the electrical and neural force," Mitchell and his coauthors write, "it does not seem improbable that a violent excitement of a nerve trunk should be able to exhaust completely the power of its connected nerve centre. . . . The condition called shock is of the nature of a paralysis from exhaustion of nerve force . . . [that] may be so severe as to give rise in certain cases to permanent central nerve changes, productive of paralysis of sensation and motion, or either alone."[30] Reversing established physiological assumptions about cause and effect, they hypothesized that severe functional damage could actually produce discernible anatomical changes, thereby helping to move nerve cases from the moral realm—where sufferers were summarily accused of malingering or cowardice—to the medical.

It was this conceptual framework that authorized surgery on twisted limbs, the painful stimulation of inexplicably numbed body parts, and the use of "faradization" (electricity) and massage to cure battle exhaustion. Rather than ridicule or even imprisonment, Mitchell affirmed that shell-shocked soldiers needed medical treatments to ameliorate their suffering and to ensure that acute impairments, such as twitching or contortions, didn't become permanent disabilities. In the rare cases of malingering—the feigning of injury to evade battle—the painful and humiliating treatments themselves constituted a form of discipline. As Elaine Scarry has written of torture, "The physical pain is so incontestably real that it seems to confer its quality of 'incontestable reality' on that power that has brought it into being."[31] A solution to skepticism, Mitchell's treatment also rendered irrelevant the question of whether a soldier's debility was fabricated: reality lay in results, in the restored body ready to return to the front (though the neurologist George Beard predicted that neurasthenia—a term he coined to describe symptoms of nervous exhaustion—would also "in time be substantially confirmed by microscopical and chemical examinations of those patients who die in a neurasthenic condition").[32]

Not limited to the battlefield, nervous disease seemed a dangerously transmissible problem for nineteenth-century society. Mitchell and Beard conceived of the body's nervous system in economic terms, as being in an energetic relationship with its environment. While each individual had "a capital of vitality" to invest, Beard noted that the pressures of modern life caused individuals to use not only "the interest on these accumulations of power, but also wastefully spend . . . the capital."[33] Ironically, the very postwar changes that enhanced the nation's economic dynamism—new technologies, market growth, expanding cities—were depleting the nerve resources of individuals. "The nervous system of certain classes of Americans is being sorely overtaxed," Mitchell exhorted. "This too frequent practice of immature men going into business, especially with borrowed capital, is a serious evil."[34] The term "borrowed capital" here refers equally to matters financial and nervous, for the neurologist conceived of the body's internal economy as synecdochal to the larger economy of the nation: financial panics could be precipitated by—even as they took a corporeal toll on—enervated men.[35]

Similarly, domestic pathologies could deplete an entire family: "The [invalid] woman who wears out and destroys generations of nursing relatives ... is like a vampire, sucking slowly the blood of every healthy, helpful creature within reach of her demands."[36] Although clearly pejorative, the image of the female vampire was not exactly metaphorical. Nervous women, Mitchell observed, tended to be frail and anemic. As Mitchell ominously reported, "I have seen an hysterical, anemic girl kill in this way three generations of nurses."[37] The title of his popular tract published in 1877 supplied the remedy: *Fat and Blood,* which recommended among other things a diet of heavy cream and rare beef. This book was translated into five languages, and received favorable reviews from the young Sigmund Freud. Mitchell took seriously the exhaustion inherent in the home—as did Gilman, in her sociological writings—attributing many nervous disorders to "the daily fret and wearisomeness of lives which, passing out of maidenhood, lack those distinct purposes and aims which, in the lives of men, are like the steadying influence of the fly-wheel in an engine" (*Lectures,* 14). The neurologist also criticized bourgeois domestic arrangements, with their "furnace-warmed houses, hasty meals, bad cooking, or neglect of exercise."[38] A disorganized house, where every action requires deliberation, produces more fatigue, for (as one physician wrote), "thought exhausts the nervous substance as surely as walking exhausts the muscles."[39]

William James, in his influential text *The Principles of Psychology* (1890), urged that *habit* offered a solution to such "overdrafts" of nervous force. Thoughtful decisions, James urged, when repetitively realized in actions, became embodied in the muscles and nervous fibers, making them repeatable with less effort. Such habits might be simple and concrete, such as the daily brushing of one's hair, or more complex and abstract, such as applying logic to a problem. Just as footsteps along a frequently traveled route impress the soil to make a path, making future navigation easier and less uncertain, so the acquisition and regular pursuit of good habits become physiologically ingrained and increasingly effortless: "A simple habit, like every other nervous event . . . is, mechanically, nothing but a reflex discharge; and its anatomical substratum must be a path in the system."[40] For James, bodily organs and processes were not passive conduits for thoughtful decisions and actions; rather, a person's repeated actions and decisions become realized in the very structures and dynamic pathways of the nervous system.

So, despite the apparent passivity of so-called "couch-loving invalids," nervous exhaustion was in fact a pathology resulting from too great an expenditure of willpower rather than too little. As James wrote, "There is no more miserable human being than one in whom nothing is habitual . . . for whom the lighting of every cigar, the drinking of every cup, the time of rising and going to bed every day, and the beginning of every bit of work, are subjects of express volitional deliberation" (*Principles*, 126). Working by analogy to other physiological processes, then, Mitchell's treatment for nervous patients supplied not just rest and passive stimulation like massage but also the decisive authority of the physician. An effective doctor, Mitchell explained, cannot be "a person of feeble will," for the "man who can insure belief in his opinions and obedience to his decrees secures very often most brilliant and sometimes easy success."[41] Stripped by her illness of the habitual functions built up from infancy, a nervous patient's circumscribed capacities rendered her physiologically analogous to that earlier state. Such an unfortunate regression "necessitated," Mitchell wrote, "an entire re-education" (*Lectures*, 39).[42]

While infantilization was often a symptom of disease, Mitchell generally avoided casting it as either a moral failing or a therapeutic end. The point of the rest cure was to restore a woman to full adulthood, both in body and in mind. "The more details of our daily life we can hand over to the effortless custody of automatism," William James observed, "the more our higher powers of mind will be set free for their own proper work" (*Principles*, 126). S. Weir Mitchell, in his novel *Roland Blake* (1886), employed an explicitly evolutionary model to describe the process by which "the mind rose in the scale of soundness with the body,—slowly, of course, as when one long crouching in slavery, straightening himself, tends to walk erect."[43] "Walking erect" indicated full personhood, and involved a range of corporeal capacities, all of which were essential to human flourishing. In the case of nervous patients, the physician's orders temporarily replaced an individual's "volitional deliberation," while the desired physical habit—in the case of one woman Mitchell treated, the capacity to walk—was reinforced through repetition. Mitchell's patient, after years of immobility, was slowly trained to move up the phylogenetic ladder, from a mute, mollusk-like state, to "quadruped" (*Lectures,* 41) capable of "creeping" (*Lectures,* 42), to fully functioning woman.

Mitchell was not alone in his use of evolutionary metaphors. The idea that the bourgeois housewife was less than fully "evolved" was an essential aspect of Charlotte Perkins Gilman's feminism, undergirding her calls for social reform of the home and the professions.[44] Like the neurologist, Gilman believed that the distinctive contours of the nineteenth-century household were literally sickening: as Cynthia Davis has argued, Gilman believed that "domesticity, not anatomy, is destiny."[45] Because, as Gilman wrote, the human brain was composed of "the softest, freest, most pliable and changeful living substance," one's environment *physically* shaped one's state of mind.[46] The eclectic writer Walter Felt Evans, in his *Esoteric Christianity and Mental Therapeutics* (1886), took this notion a step further when he urged, "The influence of inanimate objects is by no means unimportant in the case of those of great nervous sensitiveness. All houses, as Longfellow has said in one of his poems, are haunted houses. . . . The walls of our dwellings, the furniture they contain, the works of art that ornament them, and the beds on which we repose at night, are charged and permanently impregnated with the material effluvia and psychical emanations of our persons and presence."[47] So when the narrator of "The Yellow Wallpaper" describes her habitation as "a colonial mansion, a hereditary estate, I would say a haunted house, and reach the height of romantic felicity" (39), she is in fact engaging with contemporary theories about the physiological influence of domestic spaces.

Not just the structure of the home but the nonroutinized efforts of the housewife, Gilman maintained, directly impinged on the pliable substance of the human brain. So while "it is true that the brain is not a sex-distinction; either of man or woman," Gilman maintained, "it is also true that as an organ developed by use it is distinctly modified by the special activities of the user."[48] Whereas a man of business tended to hone a single set of specialized skills, Gilman described the "patchwork life" (*Home,* 151) of the woman who performed multiple tasks in wearying redundancy. In *Women and Economics* (1898) Gilman in fact used terms identical to those used by doctors describing railway spine: "To the delicately differentiated modern brain the jar and shock of changing from trade to trade a dozen times a day is a distinct injury, a waste of nervous force."[49] The conditions of the housewife injured the mind, which in turn displayed its confusion in the very decorations of the house: "The bottled discord of the woman's daily occupations is quite sufficient to account for the explosions of discord on her walls and floors" (*Home,* 151). As an antidote, Gilman proposed—like James— "the power of habit."[50] She exhorted her readers, "Don't waste nerve force on foolish and unnecessary things—physical or moral; but invest it, carefully, without losing an ounce, in the gradual and easy acquisition of . . . new habits."[51] So while twentieth-century critics have almost universally read the wallpaper in Gilman's famous short story as symbolic of the narrator's psychological state, a more thorough reading of Gilman's own oeuvre sharply indicates that she conceived of the connection between environment and health—even between home furnishings and one's state of mind—in physiological terms.

Further, Gilman's reformist writings recover the history of Mitchell's own ideas about nervous disease by making explicit the connection between the bodies of soldiers and the nerves of women. If women are flighty and mercurial, it is because "the daughter of a soldier inherits her father's pride and courage, and also the centuries of . . . cowardice of her mother."[52] Because of women's submissive, domestic role, their plastic bodies and minds adapt by becoming "smaller and softer"— "and then we blame woman for extravagance indeed! We dress in their armor, their tools, their weapons of defense and offense—their battlefield, their indirect means of subsistence" ("Excessive Femininity," 30). Married life only exacerbates a woman's embattled state, plunging her into a home that, for Gilman, is itself a war zone. Martial metaphors are peppered throughout *The Home,* which describes the "tranquil" domicile as a series of breached fortifications: "First there is the bulwark aforesaid, the servant, trained to protect a place called private. . . . Back of this comes a whole series of entrenchments—the reception room, to delay the attack while the occupant hastily assumes defensive armour; the parlour or drawing room, wherein we may hold the enemy in play, [and] cover the retreat of non-combatants . . . ; the armour above mentioned . . . ; and then all the weapons crudely described in rural regions as 'company manners,' our whole system of defence and attack" (*Home,* 45). Although Gilman's tone here is irreverent, she was deadly serious in casting the wife as a domestic warrior whose strained nerves were identical to those Mitchell had encountered on the field of battle. Henry Fleming, in *The Red Badge of Courage*, realizes that war "produce[d] corpses"; Gilman, in her sociological writings, affirms that homes produced their inhabitants.[53]

The narrator of "The Yellow Wallpaper," in light of Gilman's neurological thinking, is literally correct when she sees her mental processes in the wallpaper's figures. The wallpaper's images of carnage assert the connection between the domestic sphere and the discord of war: "the pattern lolls like a broken neck, and two bulbous eyes stare at you upside down" (42). (One hears an echo of Gilman in Crane's description of soldiers awakening: "The tangled limbs unraveled. The corpse-hued faces were hidden behind fists that twisted slowly in the eye sockets" [85].) Gilman's story exposes the traces of conflict inscribed in the rented house: "The floor is scratched and gouged and splintered, the plaster itself is dug out here and there, and this great heavy bed, which is all we found in the room, looks as if it had been through the wars" (43). Figures in the paper "go waddling up and down in isolated columns of fatuity" (44), and the images appear to stage ambushes: "It slaps you in the face, knocks you down, and tramples you" (47). These distorted figures are not just metaphors but catalysts for twisted minds and deformed bodies. In a public lecture Gilman echoed "The Yellow Wallpaper" in syntax, metaphor, and meaning when she warned, "Our whole race reels to the foundation, totters and gropes and staggers blindly, because of this implied discord of our own making" ("Excessive Femininity," 22).

As Tom Lutz has pointed out, it was Gilman's exhaustion—not her husband's proscription—that prevented the aspiring author from putting pen to paper during the early years of her marriage.[54] Gilman's journal is riddled with entries describing her utter lassitude and her husband's diligent house cleaning, baby tending, and wife nursing during her malaise. "I was so weak," she recounted later in her autobiography, "that the knife and fork sank from my hands—too tired to eat. I could not read nor write nor paint nor sew nor talk nor listen to talking, nor anything. . . . To the spirit it was as if one were an armless, legless, eyeless, voiceless cripple."[55] Employing Mitchell's economic terms, she asserts, "the effects of nerve bankruptcy remain to this day" (*Living*, 97). Simply put, Gilman herself provided no evidence to indicate that "Charlotte Perkins Gilman's literary escape from S. Weir Mitchell's Fictionalization of Women" provided her with lasting good health.[56]

But if Gilman's nervous exhaustion was so dire, how then did she manage to produce such a large body of work? The way Gilman conceived of cerebral work is crucial to an understanding of how she could at once agree with Mitchell's theories about nervous depletion yet maintain her dauntingly prolific intellectual output for much of her life: "The work I have done," she later explained, "has never been 'work' in the sense of consciously applied effort" (*Living*, 98). Resembling the natural flow of a river, writing was for her "easy and swift expression, running at the rate of about a thousand words an hour for three hours" (*Living*, 103). Accordingly, the part of Mitchell's rest cure that Gilman separated out for particular reprobation was his insistence that she, in her words, limit herself to "two hours intellectual life a day. And never touch pen, brush, or pencil as long as you live" (*Living*, 96). Gilman maintained that this particular prohibition blocked a natural process that in her case was restorative rather than depleting, and therefore should be unacceptable on Mitchell's own physiological terms. (Quoting Gilman's statement that "human beings tend to produce, as a gland to secrete," Walter Benn Michaels has argued along these lines that the work of writing appears to have been for Gilman "more a matter of physiology than of psychology.")[57]

Although both Gilman and Mitchell were in a sense reformers, Gilman wished to reform social structures, while Mitchell sought to fit women to their domestic roles. Mitchell affirmed that "woman . . . is physiologically other than man," providing biological ground for the doctrine of separate spheres,[58] whereas Gilman was adamant that "we should be *human*, not feminine" ("Excessive Femininity," 34). Women's "physiological otherness" was for Gilman not the cause but the effect of domestic arrangements, akin to the contorted limbs of Mitchell's Civil War soldiers in being "produced" by civilized folly. As she expressed in "Dr. Clair's Place," the way to decouple the connection between women and nervous depletion was first to restore a woman's vitality and then— her central variation on Mitchell's rest cure—to prescribe productive, outwardly oriented work that integrated the operations of mind and body. Gilman viewed obsessive and solipsistic self-attention as "a diseased condition; most extreme in the megalomaniacs, and in those writers of intimate personal confessions" (*Brains*, 81). In "The Yellow Wallpaper," it is precisely the narrator's turning inward, away from the more detached observation of her physical environment, that forms the point of entry into the textual space designated (and indeed privileged) by some feminist critics as the "subtext." For Gilman, who denigrated in her autobiography what she saw as the "infantile delight in 'self-expression'" that characterized her age—she called it "excretion"—the narrator's intensely sub-jective self-absorption is not just morbid, but actively pathological.[59]

Dr. Clair, who turns her patient's melancholic introspection into pro-ductive work, draws on the physiological theories of Weir Mitchell and elements of Freud's "talking cure," as well. Once the invalid's energy is enhanced through massage and rich food (like Mitchell) the doctor begins to listen to her talk (like Freud)—not, however, for the story behind the story, but to determine what relieves her various symptoms. Absorbing her physician's epistemological stance, the patient's structure of self be-comes forensic: she is "more and more objective, more as if it were some-one else who was suffering, and not myself" (333). "Dr. Clair's Place" ends with the convergence of cure and denouement, but in a form that would have been unimaginable to either Mitchell *or* Freud: in Gilman's tale, the patient joins the physician's staff. No longer a professional in-valid, the former patient becomes a professional who specializes in in-valids.[60] (Indeed, many of Gilman's stories conclude with a woman in medical, financial, or marital trouble solving her difficulties by acquiring a career.) In this regard, "Dr. Clair's Place" reverses the trajectory of "The Yellow Wallpaper" by moving the nervous woman from psycho-logical self-scrutiny to physiologically focused empiricism.

"A writer can no longer expect to be received on the ground of en-tertainment only," wrote William Dean Howells; "he assumes a higher function, something like that of a physician or a priest . . . bound by laws as sacred as those of such professions."[61] The physician that Gilman's narrator emulates in "The Yellow Wallpaper" is in fact Mitchell, who employed electricity to stimulate a patient's disused muscles (and who once shocked a neurasthenic patient out of bed by offering to hop in with her). Gilman's tale was explicitly crafted as a form of shock therapy, a catalyst to social change via corporeal reform. "If I can learn to write good stories," Gilman once wrote, "it will be a powerful addi-tion to my armory."[62] She affirmed that "the story was meant to be dreadful" (*Living*, 119), and nineteenth-century readers did indeed pay "startled attention."[63] Intensely aware of the tale's somatic effects, a number viewed it as a cautionary tale that pointed up the dangers of tasteless home decorating. For Gilman, however, the descent into sick-ness was just half the story: the other half, portrayed in "Dr. Clair's Place," involved the recuperative rise through acts of creation. Such work was literally meant to re-form minds and bodies, which for Gilman was essential to lasting social change. It had an uplifting effect on the world, something Gilman claimed for "The Yellow Wallpaper": as she ecstatically declared, "My brain is to see and teach. I do this by voice and pen."[64]

Effort, Agitation, Aesthetics

"First, I am conscious of drawing myself together, my forehead contracts, my eyes and ears seem to draw themselves in and shut themselves off. There is tension of the muscles of limbs. Secondly, a feeling of movement or plunge forward occurs" (150). This is John Dewey's description of the sense of physical effort involved in trying to remember lines of poetry. Strenuous acts of mind, Dewey wrote in "The Psychology of Effort," entail a full-bodied "struggle for realization" while "these sensations report the state of things as regards effective realization" (155). Discomfort and strain index actions that are imperfectly memorized or habituated (e.g. lines of poetry) or novel circumstances that tax the body's capacity to assimilate and respond to them (e.g. a plunge into battle). Understood in Darwinian terms, effort registers, even as it seeks to correct, the imperfect alignment of an organism and the environment: as an example, Dewey cites the balancing act of learning to ride a bicycle. For human beings, *thinking* is a powerful tool of adjustment; the contemporary philosopher Daniel Dennett echoes Dewey when he refers to human beings' "prosthetically enhanced imaginations."[65] Among those physical exertions accompanying everyday thought, Dewey mentions "contracted chest and throat . . . compression of lips, clenching of fist, contraction of jaws, sensations in pit of stomach, goneness in legs, shoulders higher, head lower than usual, fogginess or mistiness in visual field, trying to see something which eludes vision, etc." (151).

John Dewey provides a conceptual frame that begins to make sense of both the agitation of nervous patients and their physicians' frustrated responses to them: he points up the ways that nervousness in the nineteenth century posed a problem that was aesthetic as well as epistemological. Not only was the behavior of a hysterical patient often baffling to physicians, its very incoherence was odious—one need only compare doctors' reactions to other inexplicable illnesses (such as puerperal fever) to see that hysterics were seen as uniquely repellent. As one historian has written, "For twenty-five centuries, hysteria had been considered a strange disease with incoherent and incomprehensible symptoms"[66]—what one medical researcher in 1867 deplored as "attacks of all kind of noisy and perverse . . . actions."[67]

We can discern, then, that for the first half of "The Yellow Wallpaper" the narrator actually emulates such a physician in her scrutiny of the wallpaper. Assaulted by its confusing design, the narrator takes on the diagnostic task of "follow[ing] that pointless pattern to some sort of conclusion" (44). She adopts both her physician-husband's empiricist outlook and his peremptory manner: "I get positively angry with the impertinence of it" (42) she sniffs, castigating the wallpaper for being "silly," "irritating," "strange," and "provoking" (43). Hysterics were notorious for impersonating the symptoms of other disease sufferers: in the case of "The Yellow Wallpaper," the object of the narrator's mimicry is her Mitchell-esque husband.[68]

According to Carroll Smith-Rosenberg, doctors' resentment of hysterical patients had two crucial factors: "the baffling and elusive nature of hysteria itself" and the fact that hysterical patients "did not function as women were expected to function."[69] The first notion indicates that hysteria was frustratingly indeterminate; the latter implies a divide between doctors' expectations (about illness and women's roles) and the disturbing actuality. Smith-Rosenberg's points, viewed through the lens of Gilman's story, provide formal terms for theorizing nervousness in terms of aesthetic experience. The feeling of uneasiness at someone's behavior (or at the design of one's wall covering) marks the difficulty of reconciling expectation and perception into a satisfying or coherent whole. Dewey explains that "certain sensory quales, usually fused, fall apart in consciousness, and there is an alternation, an oscillation, between them, accompanied by a disagreeable tone when they are apart, and an agreeable tone when they become fused again" (152). Doctors, confronted with the jarring, discordant behavior of hysterical women, had the experience (as Dewey puts it) of "two sets of sensations [that] refuse to coincide" (154). While the ideational content of the jarring perception pertained to a woman's social role and to the nature of the illness, phenomenologically it was experienced as a formal failure, which helps to explain the emotional coloring—from mild distaste to overt repugnance—of doctors' descriptions of their hysterical patients.

It is precisely to the point, then, that the narrator's explicitly aesthetic complaints in "The Yellow Wallpaper" sound like an exasperated physician faced with a refractory case of hysteria. "It is dull enough," the narrator complains, "to confuse the eye in following, pronounced enough to constantly irritate and provoke study, and when you follow the lame uncertain curves for a little distance they suddenly commit suicide—plunge off at outrageous angles, destroy themselves in unheard of contradictions" (41). Importantly, the relationship between the aesthetic and the diagnostic as elaborated in Gilman's story is not allegorical, which would affirm a distinction between the apparent story (regarding interior design) and the real story (regarding medical pathology). As we have seen, Gilman's writings about sickening home décor vitiate this distinction: hectic wallpaper can craze a sensitive soul. More important, "The Yellow Wallpaper" makes visible how corporeal responsiveness is in fact intrinsic to the stance of the empiricist. The narrator positions herself as a detached observer, yet the strong emotional language and tone point up the participatory nature of diagnosis. In noting that the wallpaper's "defiance of law . . . is a constant irritant to a normal mind" (47), she makes explicit—through the perceptual "tint" of her extreme sensitivity—the power struggle that attends a doctor's engagement with a hysterical patient: "You think you have mastered it, but . . . it turns a back somersault and . . . slaps you in the face, knocks you down and tramples on you" (47). (The "back somersault," in fact, could as easily refer to the gymnastic back-archings of Charcot's hysterical patients.) In the narrator's case study, the wallpaper becomes at once an aesthetic object and a patient: a "debased" figure "with *delirium tremens*" (44). In turning her attention to the hysterical flourishes of the wallpaper—in "studying," "watch[ing] developments" (48), "analyz[ing] it" (49), advancing "scientific hypothes[es]" (48) and "discovering something at last" (49)—the narrator is not producing a distinctly "women's discourse" (Treichler, 192) but articulating an implicit aesthetics of experience within the diagnostic approach of her physician-husband.

Objectivity, Gilman's narrator shrewdly points up, involves substituting one's own affective experience for another's under the rubric of paying attention to inert facts. "'You are gaining flesh,'" John tells the narrator. "'I feel really much easier about you'" (39). While speaking the language of objectivity, the husband explicitly takes his own affective temperature. It is the phenomenology of the *patient's* sensory experience that is thereby rendered invisible—"'[Y]ou really are better, dear, whether you can see it or not'"—while the physician's sensory experience is equated with the object world (46). The narrator's madness, then, becomes a crucial technology of visibility within the story. Its uncanny effect, in which the reader slowly realizes that the seemingly "reliable" narrator is in fact mad, and that the apparently "objective" story may be entirely a projection of the woman's mind, forces the larger realization that other seemingly dispassionate acts of witnessing are affectations of affectlessness. Indeed, indifference to the experience of nervousness from the patient's point of view characterized the medical epistemology of the so-called Napoleon of the Neuroses, Jean-Martin Charcot. In one of Charcot's famous Tuesday Lessons, in which he modeled his diagnostic technique for students and colleagues by displaying an agitated patient before a large audience, the neurologist announced, "If you want to see clearly, you must take things exactly as they are. . . . In fact all I am is a photographer. I describe what I see."[70] In Gilman's story, the narrator is a sort of "Charcot of the Wallpaper"; her scrutiny of it makes her a parodic expert in her field: "There are things in that paper," she announces, "that nobody knows but me, or ever will" (46).

Because of the first-person, journal form of Gilman's tale, readers are privy to the narrator's operations of mind. The cleverness of the story's structure is that, even as we come to realize the emphatic emotional involvement of the "investigator," we are also gaining insight into the experience of the "patient." (This observation helps to dismantle the critical divide, aptly characterized by Cynthia Davis, that has "contradictorily" cast the story "as an attempt, on the one hand, to provide a first-person account of hysteria and, on the other, to bear witness to the disease at some remove and authoritatively document its etiology.")[71] Charcot, by way of comparison, had positioned himself behind the camera, thus eliding his own involvement in the production of facts and remaining indifferent to the interior experience of the patient. Daniel Dennett, writing a century later, makes a point that is instructive: "We human beings share a subjective world—and know that we do—in a way that is entirely beyond the capacities of any other creatures on the planet, because we can talk to one another. . . . Conversation unites us" (9). Charcot, notoriously, did not listen: he once told an audience witnessing a patient's agitated vocalizations, "Again, note these screams. You could say it is a lot of noise over nothing."[72] It takes a leap of imagination—one that Charcot did not make—to conceive the distress his nervous patients must have felt as they were paraded, confused, sick, and half naked, in front of a packed auditorium.

Though Charcot neither appreciated nor sought to represent his patients' perspectives, his student Pierre Janet did, and in fact recorded his findings in his case histories. In the case of Justine, a woman suffering from an inordinate fear of cholera, Janet described the stunning physical symptoms provoked by a mere idea: "All her limbs shake, her teeth chatter and are clenched, her arms move in defensive gestures, and her body is bent backward. After several contorsions . . . her eyes stay open, fixed as if they were staring at something, her mouth is open and foaming, and in the midst of her screams she emits some intelligible words: 'Cholera, it's got hold of me, help!'" (212–213). Janet, while meticulous about cataloguing visible symptoms, also gained insight into the frenzied activity of the nervous patient by interviewing her, both during and after an episode, to elicit her own account of what transpired. He frequently quoted her directly in "History of a Fixed Idea":

> Her mind, far from being inactive during the attack, is on the contrary full of many varied images grouped in such a way as to form a unified picture. First there are visual images: two corpses, one of which is visible at the front, "a poor old naked man, green and blue"; sensations of smell, a disgusting odor of putrefaction; auditory images, "the death knell is sounded, cries of cholera, cholera, cholera," kinesthetic images in cramps, screams, vomiting, diarrhea. . . . We see in her what is currently the idea of cholera, developed, so to speak, to the utmost degree of perfection: an ensemble, a system of images taken from all the senses, each of which is clear and complete enough to turn into a reality in the form of hallucinations and movements.[73]

Janet, as investigator, sought to bring into coherence the patient's symptoms and her account of her malady, and as he did so, he came to understand that the patient herself was engaged in a very similar activity. From the "ensemble" of sensory information that she received from the world and from within her body, Justine composed "a reality" through the hallucinated images of her mind and the expressive motions of her body. Doctor and patient, in short, were busily taking bits and pieces of experience and putting them together into "unified picture[s]" that were different in effect—one potentially therapeutic, the other unmistakably pathological—but not in kind.

Accordingly, Janet's first curative attempt involved disassembling Justine's "system of images": "we must try to discompose it, to transform its elements, and it is likely that then the whole will no longer persist. This is an application to therapeutics of the well known axiom: 'divide and conquer'" (218). Janet proceeded to modify Justine's hallucinations, so when his patient described seeing dead bodies, the psychologist "devoted several sessions to dressing them" (218). Instead of ignoring

Justine's visions (along the lines of Charcot), or mining them for symbolic significance (as did Freud), Janet's "highly effective comic" cure
(which involved outfitting a phantom corpse in the "costume of a Chinese general" [218]) muted the hallucination's capacity to inspire fear
and dread, breaking up the fixed idea of cholera and transforming Justine's bouts of vomiting and diarrhea into milder symptoms: "some
screams mixed with bursts of laughter" (218).

Yet Janet quickly discovered the imperfections of this cure. Justine's
susceptibility to Janet's Chinese general also made her liable to "rein-
fection" by other suggestions. To Janet's dismay, the one overwhelming
fixed idea he had disassembled—cholera—became "a swarm of little
fixed ideas" (228). As Janet described it, "A worry, a feeling, a dream,
a word overheard by chance would, after a few days' gestation, give rise
to a thought that would grow and invade her mind anew" (227). The
psychologist theorized that, as with any bodily organ that has weath-
ered an infection, Justine's recuperating mind was vulnerable to being
"infected by some common microbe or other that had no effect on it before" (231). Justine was especially affected by works of art. Listening to
a piece of music, she became distracted by black dust before her eyes,
only to "notice with astonishment that it is the musical notes"; she read
a novel about an imperious woman, and got "so much under this character's skin that she hears people reproaching her for her behavior and
pride: an auditory hallucination" (228–229).

Nervous patients such as Justine were notorious for their artistic sensibility, which often carried the pejorative implication that they were
weak-minded, ineffectual, ethereal creatures imperfectly tied to the
"real world." Janet's work shifts the terms, revealing that hysterics were
imaginative in a stronger sense: they were, to use the terms of John
Dewey, engaged in massive "process[es] of reconstruction" (158). Such
patients tended to be overly mindful and willful, engaged in almost constant creative struggles with their environment, with few motions of
body or consciousness consigned to energy-saving habit. Effort, registered and made visible by nervousness, arises (in Dewey's words)
"whenever old habits are in process of reconstruction, or of adaptation
to new conditions; unless they are so readapted, life is given over to the
rule of conservatism, routine, and over-inertia" (158). Nervousness, in
other words, marked change and transformation: "sensations of the bodily state report to us this conflict and readjustment, . . . indicat[ing] that
the reconstruction going on is one of acts, and not mere ideas" (158). The

"imaginative power" (46) of the narrator in "The Yellow Wallpaper" accurately captures the reconstructive engine of nervousness.

Agitation, in short, both marked and effected transition. As Gilman's narrator discerned, in her urgency to "follow that pointless pattern to some sort of a conclusion" (48), agitation might therefore be "cured" by completion. Dewey writes that when all the separate elements of one's sensory experience, both within the body and without, are "co-ordinate[d] within a single whole," an action—whether it be riding a bike, remembering a poem, or comprehending a pattern—is successful. A new arrangement is achieved, registered in a feeling of ease in which the psychological, physiological, and physical are integrated—as when rider and bike, perfectly synchronized, glide along the road. Lack of resolution results in sensations of "futility, of thwartedness, or of irritation at failure": a bicycle crash, or paralyzed frustration. In an observation that has ominous significance in relation to the "couch-loving invalids" of the nineteenth century, Dewey notes that "if surrendered to," the exhaustion of irresolution "may become a delicious languor" (153)—a resigned acquiescence to "the existing activity" (156).

Yet while Gilman's enervated narrator is, at moments, practically immobilized, her fatigue is never "delicious," and she presses onward in spite of the dumb recalcitrance of her object of scrutiny and her husband's indifference to her inquiry. In the startlingly applicable words of Dewey, who writes of the immense effort it takes to scrutinize a mark on a wall, the narrator "is continually imagining the speck as having some particular form . . . as having a certain nature. . . . Then this image is as continually interfered with by the sensations of motor adjustment coming to consciousness by themselves. Each experience breaks into, and breaks up, the other before it has attained fullness" (153). The narrator remains nervous: which is to say that her "work" resists completion. It is "broken up," in two senses, one formal, the other sociocultural. In the first place, her aesthetic effort with the wallpaper never comes to fruition, simply because the intransigent design refuses to cohere into significant form. Wallpaper, to be functional, must have a pattern that is endless and therefore unframable (Henry James, writing of the preternaturally tasteful Adela Gereth, notes that in her "great wainscoted house there was not an inch of pasted paper" [19]). In the second place, and more significantly, the narrator's "work" with the wallpaper has no currency; it produces (in Dewey's terms) no "change in the existing activity" (156). She remains in the house she wishes to leave, in the room that she resisted inhabiting, with a husband committed to ignoring her perceptual experience. In her restless scrutiny, the "Charcot of the Wallpaper" remains a metaphorical investigator, not an actual one.

The fracture or lack of "realization" (Dewey's term) is not limited to Gilman's narrator but also inheres in the story's form. Journal entries—analogous to wallpaper—go on and on with no formal stopping place. Worse, for the narrator, the entries themselves end in interruption rather than resolution, cut short by the arrival of a family member or the narrator's sheer exhaustion, and finally stopping altogether at story's end as she is crawling over her prostrate husband. The once grand house that the narrator (and the narrative) inhabits is itself dilapidated, incomplete: the "riotous old-fashioned flowers" flourish in untended beds, the greenhouses "are all broken now" (42), the rearranged furniture "inharmonious" (46). Dewey writes that the "enemies of the union of form and matter" spring from "apathy, conceit, self-pity, tepidity, fear, convention, routine, from the factors that obstruct, deflect, and prevent vital interaction of the life [sic] creature with the environment in which he exists" (132). This catalogue, unfortunately, is not a bad character description of the narrator's central attendant, her husband John.

In this context, the narrator's capacity to recognize the "expression in an inanimate thing" and to derive "entertainment and terror out of blank walls and plain furniture" (46) is literally life affirming, positioning her against "tepidity, fear, convention, routine." A dynamic process, nervousness is a pathological version of what John Dewey would describe in *Art as Experience* when he equated everyday acts of perception with aesthetic experience. The obsessive patient, like an artist working overtime with intransigent materials, strives night and day to transform quotidian domestic events into meaningful, resonant wholes. In contrast to her husband's maddening calm, the narrator's nervousness is literally an animating force: "Life is very much more exciting now than it used to be," she reports. "You see I have something more to expect, to look forward to, to watch. . . . I don't want to leave now until I have found it out. There is a week more, and I think that will be enough" (53). Dewey notes that, in any act of attention, "the demand for time is simply the result of a lack of unity. The intervening process of execution . . . is the process of disintegrating acts hitherto separate and independent, and putting together the result, or fragments, into a single piece of conduct" (157). This is precisely the narrator's achievement: she succeeds in piecing together a narrative fraught with significance, featuring a woman struggling to extricate herself from the wallpaper. With the help of the narrator, who embarks on a campaign to peel the paper down and thereby complete her "project" ("I declared I would finish it today!" [51] she reports), the wallpaper unfolds: the chaotic design coalesces into a narrative trajectory.

At this point the narrator enters into the plot she has up to now purported simply to observe, as she strives to rescue the shadowy figure from the wallpaper. In a shift that articulates the larger historical and medical transformation from physiology to psychology, the patient-wallpaper loses its inertness and becomes "impatient," insistently soliciting attention from its analyst, the narrator. Just as Freud's panicky colleague Josef Breuer found himself sucked into the erotics of Anna O.'s interior drama, and just as Freud found himself anxiously entering into his patient Lucy R.'s fantasy of marrying her employer,[74] so the narrator loses her detachment and participates in the drama she sought only to report. Gilman's story, in other words, follows the narrator into the wallpaper's plot and away from the outward setting (of ancestral house, recuperating woman, etc.). In "The Psychology of Effort," Dewey observes that "we are conscious of being attentive only when our attention is divided, only when there are two centers of attention competing with each other, only when there is an oscillation from one group of ideas to another" (158). Gilman's narrator has lost the attentiveness that goes along with nervousness: her self is collapsed into the woman in the wallpaper.

Yet this is decidedly *not* the case for the reader of the story, whose attention is uncomfortably, unresolvedly divided by the story's lack of closure, and who is left to puzzle over the story's antinomies. Who is "Jane," whom the narrator inexplicably refers to in the story's notorious final scene? How can the narrator both write in her journal (now in the present tense) and also perambulate on hands and knees around her sickroom? Gilman's agitated readers recognized that the attempt to consolidate the story's unresolvable elements into a coherent narrative was impossible; many of them, appropriately, turned away frustrated from the tale's discomfiting pages. Literary critics, with our tendency to transform a fractured text into a coherent one, have tended to miss this point. Taken together, however, our accounts of Gilman's tale have in a sense produced our own, unending series of journal entries: in the delightfully apt statement of a recent scholar, "Charlotte Perkins Gilman's best-known story continues to elicit more than enough paper to decorate a fairly large room."[75] From this point of view, one can acknowledge that the cottage industry of Gilman scholarship (unlike the "work" of the poor woman in Gilman's story) has helped to translate agitation into institutional change, making a place for women and women's scholarship within the academy. It is hard to imagine Gilman quibbling with this outcome.

Gilman's tale depicted a woman's descent into pathology; Janet traced a woman's slow and uncertain rise into tolerable, if not blooming, health. Janet's conclusions echo Gilman's: "For several years we have been trying to subject a number of patients, notably Justine, to a method of treatment that consists of making them do regular brain work . . . *regard work not as a distraction but as an exercise which increases the capacity for mental synthesis* that alone is an effective counteragent to suggestibility and fixed ideas" (247; emphasis added). From his experience with these patients, Janet concluded that the best form of exercise is "work that requires judgment and the need to combine" (247), such as "little literary compositions" (248). He also discovered "a new kind of work" that "brought an astonishing result: Justine began to learn the piano, and developed a passion for music" (249). Along with these accomplishments, "the patient works constantly in her home, making herself useful, and during the hours devoted to cerebral work, seeks to *resolve* worthwhile problems, whereas previously she could not understand three lines of a newspaper" (249; emphasis added). Resolution, which is both a formal concern—the arriving at a provisional stopping place—and an affective one—the energetic impulse by which one is able to arrive—activates the cure that Janet sought for his nervous patients. As he wrote of Justine, "Thanks to cerebral work, we have been able to institute a perfectly correct and calm lifestyle" (250). Janet's emphasis on the mind does not forego the physiological: Justine's "physical health"—her wholesome appetite, muscle tone, and radiant complexion—"reflects these modifications in her mental health" (250). Janet asserts with some dignity, "One might smile at these comments and find it at least strange that this woman's hair grows again because she writes literary pieces and plays the piano. We will simply reply that we are relating facts and that a fact is never ridiculous" (250).

Justine's cure "by means of intellectual work" was admittedly imperfect, "obtained only at the cost of an enormous, continuous effort" (262). In concluding his "History of a Fixed Idea," Janet notes that "the true sign of the cure of an illness is the departure of the doctor, who is sent away with pleasure" (259). To wean herself of his visits, Justine began to converse with her doctor even in his absence; as the bemused Janet reported, "She engages in the most extraordinary conversations with me; she asks my advice, and it seems that I respond very well" (262). Although Janet remained uncertain about this habit—"even if it results in apparent health, [it] is still a peculiarly pathological fact" (262)—it seems clear that the now-internalized figure of the physician provides a means for Justine to maintain her healthy doubled vision, to prevent herself, in a sense, from collapsing into the "woman in the wallpaper."

Judging by extant reviews of Gilman's short story, its potent depiction of nervousness not only modeled but in fact elicited the nervous engagement of readers. William Dean Howells, appreciatively rereading the story decades later, confessed that he "shiver[ed] over it as much as I did when I first read it in manuscript."[76] Horace Scudder, then the editor of the *Atlantic Monthly,* refused to publish the piece, exclaiming, "I could not forgive myself if I made others as miserable as I did myself!"[77] Another letter, printed in a Boston newspaper, worried that "such literature contains deadly peril."[78] Whereas for some recent critics, readings of "The Yellow Wallpaper" take on a therapeutic cast, there is evidence that some of Gilman's contemporaries perceived that the text was likely to sicken those healthy readers unlucky enough to be exposed to its destabilizing structure.

The experience of these readers confirms and repeats the struggle of the narrator to at once vivify and make coherent her perceptual experience. In this, the agitating antiaesthetic of "The Yellow Wallpaper" succeeds in pointing up the experience of aesthetic forms. For, as Dewey argued, when an experience comes to a (necessarily transient) resolution—when effort gives way to a dynamic unity that is registered by satisfied absorption—we are precisely unaware of it: only later, "after such an absorption," does one "look back and say how attentive one was" (158). The "sense of lightness, of ease" (152) that registers the "effective realization" of an experience—for which Dewey gives the examples of "listening to a symphony" and "viewing a picture gallery" (151)—is like oxygen: tasteless, invisible, odorless, yet omnipresent and life-sustaining. What Gilman succeeded in realizing in "The Yellow Wallpaper" was a diluted version of the failure of aesthetic perception, which took on more menacing and indeed pathological form in what nineteenth-century psychologists called the "idée fixe." It is tempting to liken the readerly experience of "The Yellow Wallpaper" to inoculation with a live virus, a clever, slightly risky technology meant to promote human well-being. This is of course precisely what Gilman's readers perceived, and what Gilman herself affirmed when she wrote, "it was not intended to drive people crazy, but to save people from being crazy, and it worked."[79]

Nineteenth-century thinkers suggest an alternative to an interrogative criticism, influenced by psychoanalysis, which digs deep into what a text hides under its surface. In her work on pathogenic perception, Gilman anticipated what was nascent in John Dewey's early writings, and most fully elaborated in his great work *Art as Experience*: that everyday perception was a full-bodied event, subtly active in all mindful undertakings but most active in our profound responses to works of art—and in the crucible of the battlefield, as we will see in Stephen Crane's *The Red Badge of Courage* (1895). That there is some consanguinity between reading and skirmishing is expressed by an early commentator who wrote to Crane, "I do not confess to an unqualified liking for your work. When you hand me the book [*The Red Badge*] I am grown suddenly blind. It rather appeals to my nerves than to my reason—it gives me a thrill. Your work is of a kind so charged with electricity that it cannot be handled. It is all live wire."[80]

Fracture and Fabrication: Crane's *The Red Badge of Courage*

To return to an insight from Dewey's "Psychology of Effort": when one is unable to "fuse" the material of sensory experience with one's expectations, the full-bodied acts of perception that constitute life "fall apart in consciousness, and there is an alternation, an oscillation, between them, accompanied by a disagreeable tone when they are apart, and an agreeable tone when they become fused again" (152). This process is most apparent in basic motor activities: Dewey described riding a bike, Weir Mitchell invoked the experience of learning to walk, and the novelist Kate Chopin (examined more fully in the next chapter) portrayed a woman who, in learning to swim, was "like the little tottering, stumbling, clutching child, who of a sudden realizes its powers."[81] The gliding motion of the successful swim is marked in Chopin's novel by joy and exultation, affective concomitants to the *fabrication* of experience: the suturing of bits and pieces into seamless, smoothly unrolling, whole cloth. Dewey's physiological philosophy helps to provide a different inflection to the comment of critic Mary Esteve when, in her provocative essay on anaesthetized subjectivity in *The Red Badge of Courage*, she suggests that Crane's realism entails elements of "downright theatrical fabrication."[82]

Dewey's terms for uncoordinated, imperfectly realized experiences—which entail "an alternation, an oscillation"—are useful in thinking about the structure of Crane's novel, as well as the experience of the youthful soldier Henry Fleming. Crane's plot, with its disjointed episodes, does not so much proceed as oscillate among three modes: anticipation, figured by the soldiers waiting around in camp; action, figured by the battle scenes; and fabrication, figured by the soldiers' post-bellum rehashing of events. The experience of Henry Fleming conforms to this precise configuration, as he first tries to imagine how he'll act during an assault on the enemy, then plunges into battle, and afterward strives to justify his actions. Unlike a conventional tale of war, the novel does not build to a big climax: moments of "enlightenment" give way to mad retreat; "apparent aimlessness" (104) is followed by "furious haste" (113); and utter abjection is suddenly translated into unexpected victory. Nor does *The Red Badge* contain the standard accoutrements of the war story. Aside from the novel's subtitle, "An Episode of the American Civil War," there are no references to specific battles, places, or leaders. Although one can trace the passage of time within the novel, which takes place over the course of three days, time is detached from any external referent.

In fact, the armies are distinguishable only by the color of their uniforms, and even this tenuous distinction is troubled by the attire of the corpse Henry runs across, whose uniform "had faded to a melancholy shade of green" (126). Crane's storytelling mutes the objective, external oppositions of war—most simply stated as us versus them—and refocuses attention on divisions that are internal to the two central "bodies" of the plot: the military unit, which is likened to a massive organism, and the body of the young soldier himself. In the very first paragraph, the army is figured as a sleeping person who was "stretched out on the hills, resting"; when "awakened," the massive organism "began to tremble with eagerness at the noise of rumors. It cast its eyes upon the roads" (81). Similarly, "The youth awakened slowly. He came gradually back to a position from which he could regard himself. For moments he had been scrutinizing his person in a dazed way as if he had never before seen himself" (117). Henry's own emergence from sleep doubles the rousing of the army, and his position with respect to himself is in important ways identical to the oppositional stance toward his regiment: he is detached from "his person" and yet disturbed and alienated by his feeling of division. His inability to imagine himself standing and fighting takes on the peculiarly physical form of actually not recognizing his body as his own. These internal conflicts—Henry versus himself, Henry versus the regiment—propel the plot, rather than the external conflict on the battlefield, which is waged against an enemy who remains all but invisible throughout the novel.[83]

The "red badge of courage" (133) is Crane's most vivid manifestation of Henry's experience of fracture. The wound marks the conceptual chasm between the external appearance of heroism and the abject internal experience of detachment from the regiment, of which Henry "was a little piece" (124). It also exacerbates the division the young soldier experiences, between his aspirations for himself and his actual actions. Throughout the novel, Henry Fleming exists in a state of almost constant effort, suspended only by brief, unsustainable periods of satisfaction as he applauds his own heroism or wisdom. These fleeting moments of reprieve are explicitly aesthetic, cast as tiny hopeful portraits of courage. Yet these fabrications are always forced, effortful, with Crane's contorted syntax registering the exertion necessary to bring Henry's rabbit-like actions into alignment with a conception of soldierly valor. In one instance, Henry tries "to prove to himself that the thing with which men could charge him was in truth a symmetrical act" (142); in another, he wishes for "a tremendous force" to "throw off himself and become a better. Swift pictures of himself apart yet in himself, came to him" (143). Obviously unsustainable as a coherent whole, the portrait of himself "apart yet in himself" is echoed in his comment about his desertion: "I got separated" (155). War, with its "unspeakable jumble" and its *raison d'être* of turning men into "tatters" (150), reverses the aesthetic commitment to construction and reparation.

And indeed Henry's tenuous and unsustainable respites are quickly broken up by his own shameful recognition of his cowardice and ignorance, the affective and epistemological concomitants to his self-division and his separation from his regiment. Henry's imaginative attempts to reconcile his image of heroism with the anticipated actions of his body "were all wondrously unsatisfactory": he concludes that his groping mind had to wait for "the blaze, and then figuratively to watch his legs to discover their merits and faults" (91). In the midst of "the blaze," he finds that his "mind flew in all directions" (128), a cognitive fracture concomitant to his spatial detachment from his regiment as he fled the front line. Rather than focusing on the external enemy, Henry "fought an intense battle within his body" (149).

The critic James Dawes has attributed Henry's divided state to the structure of perception itself: "We are able to hold, indeed we *must* hold, two mutually exclusive views of the universe, like Henry Fleming from *The Red Badge of Courage*, who alternates between narcissism and abjection throughout the novel."[84] Crane does indeed, as Dawes points out, "force us to inhabit both standpoints, to feel each experience" (65), to undergo the experience of vacillation along with the protagonist. Jennifer Fleissner has analyzed Crane's novel in terms that are more structural, less phenomenological: she argues that *The Red Badge of Courage* extends two subject positions, one involving endless vacillation and resulting in formal and identic "incompleteness," the other entailing "a gothically grotesque stuckness in place" and marked by closure and "perfect completeness."[85] I am arguing, however, that Crane is interested in identifying those respites, ever so brief, that punctuate and make bearable the oscillations of existence yet also eschew the finality of what Fleissner aptly terms "stuckness": Crane directs our attention to those moments of successful fabrication that collect the fragments of experience into a coherent whole—or, to use a phrase of John Dewey, into a "single piece of conduct" (157).

Dewey provides, in terms pertinent to Henry's actions in the novel, a description of the transformation of a structure of oscillation into a reparative process of fracture and fabrication. Dewey writes that "the sense of effort arises, not because there is an activity struggling against resistance, or a self which is endeavoring to overcome obstacles outside of it; but it arises within activity, marking the attempt to co-ordinate separate factors within a single whole" (157). This effort takes form as "the process of disintegrating acts hitherto separate and independent, and putting together the result, or fragments" (157) into a coherent *action*. The report of one's bodily state merely alerts one to the status of the process, with aversive feelings such as strain, fear, and anxiety marking the experience of fracture, and compelling feelings of calm, comfort, and elation registering completion, wholeness, and connectedness. The turning point of Crane's novel, from this perspective, is not the moment that Henry is wounded by a retreating soldier. Instead, it takes place after Henry returns to his regiment and experiences the first effortless moment of the narrative: "An exquisite drowsiness had spread through him. The warm comfort of the blanket enveloped him and made a gentle languor. . . . He gave a long sigh, snuggled down into his blanket, and in a moment was like his comrades" (158). In slumber, as Walt Whitman famously observed in "The Sleepers," all human beings are alike; moreover, sleep embodies a state of repose in which self-division is muted. The mind and the body are, at least momentarily, at peace.

Having tasted this moment of calm, Henry is eager to repeat it in a wakeful state: "he felt that he had earned opportunities for contemplative repose. . . . He had received his fill of all exertions, and he wished to rest" (172). He finds repose in an encounter that—in the absence of Dewey's theory of effort—appears the ultimate inversion of peace: the charge to battle. In the "furious rush" (which certainly describes both the internal and the external experience of a colossal assault on an enemy) the young soldier experiences "the delirium that . . . is a temporary but sublime absence of selfishness" (183). This moment of coordinated effort—what might be termed harmony—takes place in the penultimate chapter, when Henry, joining his regiment in an attack, "felt the daring spirit of a savage, religion-mad": "He had not time for dissections, but he knew that he thought of the bullets only as things that could prevent him from reaching the place of his endeavor. There were subtle flashings of joy within him that thus should be his mind. He strained all his strength. His eyesight was shaken and dazzled by the tension of thought and muscle" (204–205).

The onslaught in the final pages of Crane's novel expressly, and strangely, takes shape as an aesthetic struggle, a competition over who has control over the colors, with Henry assaulting "the rival color bearer" and inhabiting the role himself. The scene itself unfolds in great blotches of primary color: the "desperate bleach of death" on the color bearer's face, "the dark and hard lines of desperate purpose" as he resisted Henry's attack, "the scampering blue men," the "blood upon the grass blades," and the "red brilliancy" of the flag that Henry succeeds in wrenching from his rival's hands (206–207). The novel's notorious final pages bring into stunning convergence the (usually distinguishable!) activities of painting and battling, as Henry reflects on the events of the day—"those performances"—and sees them "now in wide purple and gold, having various deflections. They went gaily with music. It was pleasure to watch these things. He spent delightful minutes viewing the gilded images of memory" (210).

From one perspective, this moment is a shockingly irresponsible aestheticizing of a scene of carnage. Yet, as Dewey, Janet, and Gilman help to elucidate, human effort—which takes its most monumental, ambitious, and ultimately ironic form in war, but which also silently and often invisibly attends the most mundane domestic ritual—entails the full-bodied transformation of a world broken apart into a world made coherent and, in the best of circumstances, harmonious. The "sensational character of this experience," Dewey writes, affirms that the "tension of adjustment is not merely ideal, but is actual (i.e. practical); it is one which goes on in a struggle for existence" (154). As Dewey theorized, and as Gilman and Crane made explicit in their writings, effort itself is a "war" of sorts, waged against the habits of the body and the ingrained codes of culture: against, in short, "the rule of conservatism, routine, and over-inertia" (158). It is worth revisiting Dewey's summary of the transformative possibilities of effort:

> To make a new co-ordination the old co-ordination must, to some extent, be broken up, and the only way of breaking it up is for it to come into conflict with some other co-ordination; that is, a conflict of two acts, each representing a habit, or end, is the necessary condition of reaching a new act which shall have a more comprehensive end. That sensations of the bodily state report to us this conflict and readjustment, merely indicates that the reconstruction going on is one of acts, and not mere ideas. (158)

Reconstruction is, then, the animating principle of effort; this transforming energy is realized in actions that reconcile mind and body, self and world. While potentially revolutionary, the impulse toward transformation and reconciliation can take a variety of sociopolitical forms, some reformist, others reactionary. S. Weir Mitchell, novelist and nerve doctor, built a career around the reconstruction of middle-class women, equipping them to return to their domestic roles after pathological nervousness had broken apart their lives. Charlotte Perkins Gilman extended Mitchell's more limited agenda to agitate, in both her fiction and her sociological writings, for the reconstruction of the American household and of gender relations within it. Stephen Crane, writing tales of embattlement in post-Reconstruction America and later reporting on the Spanish-American war in Cuba, made disturbingly visible the violence that attends the translation of an aesthetics of effort into the geopolitical scale entailed by major military acts of consolidation. Crane also recognized—and recognized as importantly aesthetic—the powerful sense of purpose and "oneness" that soldiers could gain from their profound affective engagement, both with their fellow soldiers and (in the heat of battle) with themselves. *The Red Badge of Courage* suggests a redirection of the misguided effort of war, with its horribly costly affective potency and often brutal form of unification, pointing us toward the reconstructive power of literary works committed to piecing together—on a more limited scale, but surely a less catastrophic one—a fractured world.

Coda: Reconstruction and "The Yellow Wallpaper"

As discussed earlier, contemporary readers of "The Yellow Wallpaper" seem to have valued (or reviled) the story for its meticulous portrayal of nervousness verging on insanity. Readers, that is, praised or critiqued the narrative's ability to make the reader experience directly the unhinging of a mind from the inside. For twentieth-century critics, however, the plotline that engaged nineteenth-century readers—the concern, for instance, with the somatic effects of home furnishings—was simply an overlay for the real story that lay submerged beneath it. Returned to the non-Freudian, nineteenth-century context of John Dewey's philosophy, Pierre Janet's psychology, and Weir Mitchell's neurology, the reactions of Gilman's contemporary readers become much more explicable. Rather than seeing them as duped by the patriarchal script when they avoided the hermeneutic entanglements of the text, we can begin to understand that they reacted to "The Yellow Wallpaper" in culturally defined, physiological terms.

Yet this does not mean that it was unreasonable for feminist critics, beginning in the 1970s, to interpret the story so tenaciously. As Freud explained in *Studies on Hysteria,* whereas a physiologist would trace innocuous-seeming symptoms, such as a facial tic or the convulsive wiggling of toes, to the "stimulation of cortical centres" (94), the radical semiotics of psychoanalysis presumed that "it is difficult to attribute too much sense to them" (93). Gilman's story has elicited in post-Freudian readers an almost irresistible will-to-interpret: to in fact "doctor" the text, assembling its fractured narrative, and the narrator's fractured mind, into a coherent story. Not surprisingly, and despite many indicators to the contrary, this critical doctoring has included an account of someone "getting better": whether the narrator (who, last seen on all fours, purportedly triumphs over her husband and patriarchy) or Gilman (whose biography, which involved a lifelong struggle with nervous illness, is dramatically reshaped to model an archetypal feminist success story) or even the text itself (which has, in recent decades, quite literally been canonized).

Unlike the critic Julia Dock, however, who suggests that twentieth-century feminist scholars engaged in sloppy scholarship in producing the "dramatic story of Saint Charlotte and the evil Doctor Mitchell,"[86] I am suggesting that post-Freudian critics have "doctored" the story in a much less disreputable sense: by recasting what one contemporary reviewer termed its "un-narration"[87] into a recognizable ur-feminist tale and then—as did Freud—by conceiving of their readings as a form of therapy as well as a form of criticism. And while the unhappy plight of the narrator at story's end suggests the dangers inherent in solitary, unproductive acts of reading, the sort of collaborative effort that women scholars have engaged in as we read and reread the text marks the difference between solipsism and what Gilman referred to as reformist "organizing," or what contemporary thinkers, drawing on Hannah Arendt, have termed "world making." As Michael Warner explains, "The idea is that the activity we undertake with each other, in a kind of agonistic performance in which what we become depends on the perspectives and interactions of others, brings into being the space of our world, which is then the background against which we understand ourselves and our belonging."[88] Dewey would surely recognize in this description the sort of reconstruction he saw as emerging from the "struggle for realization in the world of concrete quales and values"; in Warner's comment we hear an echo of Dewey's case for "the tremendous importance of effort" (158).

Though Gilman may have puzzled over the meanings that twentieth-century scholars discerned in "The Yellow Wallpaper," and would likely have disapproved of its being used to establish a textual paradigm for gender difference, she would certainly be enthusiastic about its effects: the founding of a vibrant, contentious field of study and myriad institutional venues that have helped propel women into the academy in startling numbers since the 1970s.[89] These women, like Gilman herself, have found productive, specialized "work [that] lies mainly in public speaking, in writing for a purpose, and in organizing."[90] I think it is not irrelevant that these women, like the character in Gilman's story "Turned" (1911), are in fact Doctors of Philosophy.[91] What Dock somewhat disparagingly terms "invested scholarship" is in fact an apt phrase for Gilman's own reconstructive goals: that middle-class women would stop dissipating their precious energies in unpaid housework and barely disguised sexual labor and instead invest their "capital of nervous force" by joining the ranks of the professions. With this in mind, I suggest that we read feminist critic Jean Kennard's purposefully shocking comment about "The Yellow Wallpaper"—that "the value of our rereadings lies not in their 'correctness' [read *meanings*] . . . but in their ability to enrich our present [read *effects*]" (185)—not as an abdication of the work of a critic but the reverse: as an invitation to engage in scholarship that is affectively attuned, as well as theoretically sound, and that is aesthetically oriented as well as historically situated.

CHAPTER FIVE

"Mindless" Pleasure

Embodied Music in *The Awakening* and *Theron Ware*

When words leave off, music begins.

—ATTRIBUTED TO HEINRICH HEINE (1797–1856)

We saw in the previous chapter how a range of writers and thinkers worked to realize the intense bodily effort of activities so banal as to seem not just mindless but practically bodiless: contemplating one's wallpaper, waiting to receive marching orders, thinking about cholera. Yet for John Dewey, these invisible feats of exertion entailed "an amount of stress and strain relevant to the most serious problems of the universe."[1] Nervousness at the end of the nineteenth century took on not just medical but also philosophical significance, as both medium and physiological marker of the complex, full-bodied harmonizing of person and environment. This active coming into relation, as Dewey described it, was essential to aesthetic experience: "The moments when the creature is both most alive and most composed and concentrated are those of fullest intercourse with the environment."[2] If, however, the material of the world proves too intransigent, or the pressure of the effort too unrelenting, a person and her surroundings remain unreconciled, a conflict embodied in the "aimlessness of a mere succession of excitations" (*Art*, 56–57). The dissociation of the mad housewife, like the shell shock of the tattered soldier, marked the failed "struggle for realization" ("Effort," 155) of the self in relation to a hostile world.

Yet Dewey also gestured toward a sensation of equilibrium—and those activities that sponsored it—that offered a respite from nervous exertion: "Compare, for example, the psychophysical energy put forth in listening to a symphony, or in viewing a picture gallery, with that exercised in trying to fix a small moving speck on the wall. . . . In the former case, the whole being may be intensely active, and yet there may be, at the time, absolutely no consciousness of effort or strain" ("Effort," 152). This chapter examines how attention, when focused on certain evocative objects or forms, enlisted a corporeal experience blessedly different from that generated by a field of battle or hectic home. Whereas Charlotte Perkins Gilman and S. Weir Mitchell charted the rough psychophysical terrain of an urbanizing, industrializing world that taxed and thereby made visible the adaptive, aesthetic powers of the human organism, Kate Chopin and Harold Frederic depicted a range of culturally significant anodynes for the modern soul: music, novels, religion, meditation, and sex. These, as we shall see, are the resonant activities that, in the words of Dewey, provoked "a sense of lightness" ("Effort," 152), easing the jolted nineteenth-century self into an experience of sensuous rapture. The provocative oscillation between the pleasures of the body and the elevation of the spirit is thematized, in the writings of both Chopin and Frederic, as the tension between "damnation" and "illumination."

Critics referring to Harold Frederic's best known novel, *The Damnation of Theron Ware* (1896), often fail to include its title for publication in England: *Illumination*. Yet the conflict indicated by the two titles establishes the problematic that structures the novel: whether the eponymous protagonist, a young Methodist minister who becomes entranced with the music of Frédéric Chopin and a freethinking, flame-haired Catholic pianist, is embarked on a sexually suspect moral decline *or* an aesthetically inspired spiritual awakening. According to Levi Gorringe, a successful businessman with his eye on Reverend Ware's wife, people often mistake temptation for illumination by misconstruing a fundamentally physiological sensation such as sexual ardor for a transcendent emotion. Of his own past feelings of "sacred" passion Gorringe remarks, "'I felt myself full of all sorts of awakenings of the soul and so forth. But it was really that girl . . . what I took for experiencing religion was really a girl.'"[3] In the brusque words of Dr. Ledsmar, another character who helps to advance Reverend Ware's un-sentimental education, "what you regard as religion is especially calculated to attract women" (209). In Frederic's novel, religious feeling is revealed to have a twofold sexual trajectory: its proximate object is a pretty woman, while its ultimate purpose is the propagation of the species.

Kate Chopin's *The Awakening* (1899), in which a young Protestant woman, married to a Catholic Creole, is aroused by piano playing and eventually sleeps with a New Orleans rake, bears a striking resemblance to Frederic's novel—down to the composer whose music enraptures both Theron Ware and Edna Pontellier (and who knits together the two authors' surnames): Frédéric Chopin. Indeed, in a statement that, in its Darwinian impulse, would be right at home in the mouth of *Theron Ware*'s Dr. Ledsmar, *The Awakening*'s Dr. Mandelet wonders if the sublime stirrings of young love are merely "decoy[s] to secure mothers for the race."[4] Though Chopin's novel avoids the explicit doctrinal politics of *Theron Ware*, the tension between a Protestant and a Catholic sensibility is nonetheless central, as the Calvinist-raised Edna is captivated by the sumptuous Creole culture during a languid summer spent by the Gulf of Mexico. Chopin expresses the damnation/awakening dichotomy when she writes of Edna, "There was with her a feeling of having descended in the social scale, with a corresponding sense of having risen in the spiritual" (629). Contemporary readers of the novel translated the rhythm of rising and falling in *The Awakening* into terms of religious censure: Edna Pontellier's awakening was an "unholy passion" that might promote "unholy imaginations" in young readers.[5]

This chapter argues that *The Damnation of Theron Ware, or Illumination* and *The Awakening*, published four years apart, explicitly inquire into the relations among religion, embodied feelings, music, and books: a set of concerns that preoccupied a range of thinkers during the late nineteenth century. William James, for one, in *The Varieties of Religious Experience* (1902), tried to identify and describe the centrality of religion, and its attendant emotions, in the lives of individuals. As Pericles Lewis has cogently noted, "The problem confronting William James . . . was how to explain religious experience without explaining it away."[6] Acutely aware of this difficulty, James sought to realize religion as it was experienced, thereby setting aside the question (which preoccupied Harold Frederic) of whether a person's sense of God was the intuition of an ultimate truth or mere delusion. James detached religion from its doctrinal and institutional manifestations, inquiring instead into the corporeal texture of the experience that accompanies—or indeed constitutes—an individual's profound belief in the divine: "the feeling of reality," James concluded, "may be something more like a sensation than an intellectual operation properly so-called."[7] Religious experience, James observed, inhered in the sensuous rhythms of feeling: "Stated in the completest possible terms, a man's religion involves both *moods of contraction and moods of expansion* of his being" (*Varieties*, 75; emphasis added).

Situated within this context, these late-century novels become recognizable as innovative examinations of the transporting effects of music on the susceptible mind and body. Moreover, Chopin's and Frederic's attention to how states of somnolence and receptivity are linked to natural rhythms (e.g. waves, breathing) and to humanly constructed ones (e.g. poetry, chanting) was pertinent to late-nineteenth-century mind-cure practices, in particular the "New Thought" espoused by such popularizers as Horatio Dresser, Walter Felt Evans, and Annie Payson Call. Reading *The Awakening* in light of philosophies and practices contemporary with the novel steers us away from the moralistic register that was established by early critics—"it is not a healthy book," wrote one, while another fumed at its promotion of "unclean desires"—and also from the moralism that tends to persist, though in different form, in the work of some more recent critics.[8] Both novels, as we shall see, engaged with turn-of-the-century theories about the "power of sound" and the special connection between musical form and human emotion. Once considered mere accompaniment to other activities such as dancing or singing, music in the nineteenth century was elevated to the status of exemplary art—by thinkers and composers such as Arthur Schopenhauer, Eduard Hanslick, Franz Liszt, and Richard Wagner—and granted physiological preeminence by the likes of Charles Darwin, Edmund Gurney, and William James, who argued for music's privileged access to the innermost drives and even the evolutionary history of the species.

While it is music's connection to sexual reproduction that preoccupies Frederic in *Theron Ware*, Chopin, by contrast, works to achieve a rapprochement between the aesthetic and the physiological in her work. She employs music thematically, through the portrayal of individuals responding to sensuous sounds and primal rhythms, and also formally, through the narrative use of repetition, rhythm, lyrical language, and melodic plots that echo the poetry of Walt Whitman. Chopin's exploration of corporeality and sound and her association of music, sensual expansion, and literary production found their fullest expression in her last, most controversial works, *The Awakening* and "The Storm," a short story unpublished during her life. Just as the popular mind-cure practitioner Annie Payson Call in her best-selling manual *Power through Repose* (1891) urged Americans to surrender to Nature's "law of rhythm: action, re-action; action, re-action; action, re-action,"[9] so Chopin worked to elicit an aesthetically pleasurable experience through the emulation of musical structures.[10]

This inquiry into the musical in the writings of Frederic and Chopin reveals an intense engagement on the part of cultural actors from many disciplines with questions of aesthetic form and its power to elicit bodily response. Chopin's novel in particular solicits yet reshapes the sort of cultural analysis that scholars of New Historicism and cultural studies have brought to bear on literary works. The tools of historicism are mustered here against historicism's antiformalism, suggesting a new direction for a historically engaged criticism that, under more cognitive models of subjectivity, has tended to neglect the affective and corporeal elements of the experience of literary works.

New Varieties of Religious Experience

By explaining feelings of joy and sublimity in utilitarian terms attributed to Darwinian theory, Harold Frederic's novel reframes religion in terms of natural history. Whereas Reverend Ware, from his naïve perspective as ministerial ingénue, has pictured biblical figures with a holy reverence that has bathed them in "a poetic light," after spending time under the cultural tutelage of an atheistic priest and a materialistic physician, he begins to see them "instead as untutored and unwashed barbarians, filled with animal lusts and ferocities, struggling by violence and foul chicanery to secure a foothold" (57). Human institutions, religious and commercial, are depicted as tapping into religious feeling in order to perpetuate themselves; the successful ones manipulate these "animal lusts" to sell their product, be it a particular denomination (such as Methodism), whose congregants' good standing is proportionate to their annual donation, or more tangible commodities, such as pianos and books. The liturgical forms of the Catholic Church, in the hands of the novel's Father Forbes, are revealed as so much "machinery," employing seductions of sound and incense in order to attract susceptible converts like the hapless Reverend Ware, who finds himself "drawn against his will—like fascinated bird to python" (88). Buffeted from one set of seductions to another, the minister advances the novel's case that religion, divested of its sacred purpose, nonetheless leaves a host of substitutes—department stores, secular art forms, politics—that, under the guise of spiritual uplift, capitalize on individuals' most primitive emotions. Frederic's realism involves an elaborate act of demystification, in which a seemingly sublime sensation—Gorringe's "awakening of the soul"—is reattached to its decidedly material object: "a girl."

In response to negative reviews of *The Awakening*, Kate Chopin published a rejoinder in *Book News* that echoed the religious terminology of her critics: "I never dreamed of Mrs. Pontellier making such a mess of things and working out her own damnation as she did. If I had had the slightest intimation of such a thing I would have excluded her from the company."[11] This passage raises three distinct rhetorical registers that shed light on Chopin's fictional practice. With "damnation," Chopin invokes her critics' language of religious censure (and, perhaps, subtly references Frederic's novel). Yet the description of Edna "*working out* her own damnation" (emphasis added) undermines the language of predestination, introducing a second rhetorical register of volition, agency, and human design. The third rhetorical register is that of creative passivity, embodied in Chopin's peculiar comment that, despite being the author, she had not the "slightest intimation" of her character's actions.[12]

Chopin's description of her writing process as "the spontaneous expression of impressions gathered goodness knows where" helps to situate these comments. "Completely at the mercy of unconscious selection" (*Chopin,* 365), Chopin maintained that "the story must 'write itself' without any perceptible effort on my part, or it remains unwritten."[13] Readerly concomitants to this strangely passive authorial figure abound in Chopin's writing, where reading is associated with states of pleasure and relaxation. In the short story "At *Chênière Caminada*" (a tale that later would be partly integrated into *The Awakening*), a young woman becomes so absorbed in her surroundings that "with the breath of the sea stinging her . . . she laid the book down in her lap, and let her soft eyes sweep dreamily along the line of the horizon where sky and water met."[14] In a tale entitled "A Mental Suggestion," reading and lovemaking are linked as activities that replace cognitive and prosaic pursuits ("wordy discussion") with sensuous rapture: two young lovers read "soft lines whose beauty had melted and entered into their souls like an ointment, soothing them to inward contemplation rather than moving them to speech and wordy discussion."[15] Chopin writes in her journal of her friend, the journalist Charles Deyo, who "spoke of the ecstatic pleasure which he finds in reading Plato. . . . He feels that there is nothing for him beyond that poetic height" (*Papers,* 186–187).

In emphasizing the transporting pleasures of writing and reading, Chopin echoes the philosopher Arthur Schopenhauer in his description of the composer's art: "The invention of melody, the disclosure in it of all the deepest secrets of human willing and feeling, is the work of genius, whose effect is more apparent here than anywhere else, is far removed from all reflection and conscious intention, and might be called an inspiration."[16] For Schopenhauer, the motions of melody "inspire" in the spiritual sense yet also literally emulate the rhythms, the in-and-out, rise-and-fall, of breathing. Ralph Waldo Emerson approximates Schopenhauer when he writes that, for the "active soul," books "are for nothing but to inspire": this is their proper "use."[17] Chopin, for her part, provided an immanent critique of both philosophers, whom she suggested were unable to fully attend to the complex and pleasurable aspects of "inspiration"—an evocative experience that Chopin believed could be provoked by both music and books. Eschewing the utilitarian terminology that framed Emerson's comment, and Schopenhauer's legendary pessimism ("existence itself," he wrote, "is a constant suffering" [*World*, 267]), Chopin in her first novel *At Fault* (1890) gently mocked the notion that books were to be either "used" *or* "abused" through her portrayal of a customshouse official who "remained at his post during the various changes of administration" due to his "many-sided usefulness." In contrast to Hawthorne's more famous civil servant of "The Custom-House," the "small unobtrusive, narrow-chested person" in *At Fault* keeps his prosaic job and remains a collector rather than a composer of books.[18] He is dismayed by his wife's utilitarian employment of his weighty philosophical tomes: he found that "a volume of Schopenhauer, which he had been at much difficulty and expense to procure, Emerson's Essays, and two other volumes much prized, . . . had served that lady as weights to hold down a piece of dry goods which she had sponged and spread to dry on an available section of roof top" (*Fault*, 52). (The woman had earlier put the books in a closet, for their drab bindings "spoilt the looks of any room.") The disgruntled public-servant-cum-scholar consoles himself by remembering that women are themselves useful objects, providing "an interesting study to a man of speculative habit" and providing a necessary function "as propagators of the species" (*Fault*, 52).

Chopin here raises the question of whether volumes of Schopenhauer and Emerson are better "used" for their intellectual heft—as blunt instruments in the intellectual armory of a petty misogynist—or for their more material weightiness, as useful appliances in one's domestic economy. The conjugal squabbling over the volumes represents the controversy over religious feeling writ small: meant to gesture toward a "higher" realm of inspiration, the books are debased to a purely terrestrial use. But clearly Chopin has little sympathy for the veneration that the less-than-loving husband ("of speculative habits") has for books; and just as clearly, Chopin harbors a certain fondness for the practical wife's sensible recognition that the volumes might stabilize some laundry or prop open a door. So while the low-key humor appears to center on the characters' "abuse" of the books, I would suggest that the anecdote directs us instead to the inadequacies of a disembodied philosophy and the quotidian callousness it sponsors.

Chopin's fiction, in contrast to philosophy's tendency to privilege the mind, is unusually attentive to the dynamics of the body, especially of the breath. In her stories Chopin explicitly links the rhythmical physical activity of taking in and expelling air—inspiration—with an expansion that is not solely intellectual but also corporeal. "'To love him is like breathing,'" an aging spinster tells her priest in "A Sentimental Soul"; "'I do not know how to help it.'"[19] Breathing in this instance bears the mark of authenticity, of both bodily impulse and transcendent feeling. In "A Respectable Woman," a woman conversing with a compelling visitor and in dire need of "a little whiff of genuine life, such as he was breathing now," finds that "her mind only vaguely grasped what he was saying," while "her physical being was for the moment predominant."[20] Another female character, assertively single and nonmaternal, learns to "sleep comfortably with [a child's] hot, plump body pressed close against her, and the little one's warm breath beating her cheek like the fanning of a bird's wing."[21] Breathing is an action that plays with the mind/body divide, suggesting a continuum that is constantly traversed, from mindful and regulated (as when the body is engaged in swimming, or playing an instrument, or singing) to embodied and unconscious (as when the mind is engaged in thinking, reading, or sleeping). In Chopin's stories, breathing also resituates the social isolation of a lonely widow, an alienated wife, or a grouchy spinster (with its implied opposite, a state of marriage) along a continuum of emotional and physical closeness.

Chopin's reworking—or better, *expansion*—of Emerson receives its most precise expression in *The Awakening*, in the well-known scene in which Edna spends a postprandial evening reading his work. This moment has crystallized a trend in critical approaches to Chopin's work: scholars have tended to juxtapose the scene's central activities (reading philosophy and falling asleep), thereby construing the moment as critique, either of Emerson, who "shapes and reflects the sexual chauvinism against which women have to defend and define themselves,"[22] or of Edna, whose "'narrow vision' . . . cannot encompass Emerson's breadth."[23] As in her first novel *At Fault,* Chopin does indeed invest this scene of reading with philosophical importance. Yet rather than contrasting philosophy and drowsiness, Chopin radicalizes Emerson's notion that books are for nothing but to inspire, by resituating the cerebral process of reading—and of philosophizing—within the diurnal vicissitudes of the physical body.

It is worth quoting the scene at length to revisit its details: "Then Edna sat in the library after dinner and read Emerson until she grew sleepy. She realized that she had neglected her reading, and determined to start anew upon a course of improving studies, now that her time was completely her own to do with as she liked. After a refreshing bath, Edna went to bed. And as she snuggled comfortably beneath the eiderdown a sense of restfulness invaded her, such as she had not known before" (*Awakening,* 605). The scene depicts transition: a woman moving from activities linked to cerebration (reading, determining, improving) to those increasingly tuned to processes of the body (comfort, relaxation, sleep). Since books are "for nothing but to inspire," and, as a nun in Chopin's short story "Lilacs" murmurs to a friend, "'your own respiration . . . [is an] inducement to sleep [that] seldom fails,'" Edna's experience with Emerson suggests the precise opposite of failed reading.[24] What is it, Chopin inquires in her writings, that stimulates the "soul"— her term for what we could call the nexus of body and mind—to sensations of somnolence, sensuality, and sublimity?

This is precisely the question that compelled William James in his inquiry into religious experience. While James secularized the term "soul," he did not simply psychologize it by construing it as analogous to mind: "When I say 'Soul,'" he writes, "you need not take me in the ontological sense unless you prefer to; for although ontological language is instinctive in such matters, yet Buddhists or Humians can perfectly well describe the facts in the phenomenal terms which are their favorites" (*Varieties,* 164). In James's terms, soul was not a thing but a "succession of fields of consciousness" each having a focal point or "centre of our dynamic energy" (164, 165). Emotional excitement was for James a central component of the motions of soul, transforming a person's field of consciousness: "The sudden and explosive ways in which love, jealousy, guilt, fear, remorse, or anger can seize upon one are known to everybody. Hope, happiness, security, resolve, emotional characteristics of conversion, can be equally explosive. And emotions that come in this explosive way seldom leave things as they found them" (166–167). James himself acknowledged that his association of religious experience with feelings (or "mysticism") rather than intellect (or "rationalism") was not new, noting that "the ancient saying that the first maker of the Gods was *fear* receives voluminous corroboration from every age of religious history" (75; emphasis added). James, however, shifted the emphasis from fear to the delightful self-surrender that distinguished religious experience, the sense that "the time for tension in our soul is over, and that of happy relaxation, of calm deep breathing, of an eternal present, with no discordant future to be anxious about, has arrived" (54).

Even in an increasingly secular culture obsessed with forward momentum, James observed that religiously tinged renunciations of effort occurred with surprising frequency in everyday life. James gives the simple example of bootlessly trying to remember a forgotten name: "Give up the effort entirely; think of something altogether different, and in half an hour the lost name comes sauntering into your mind, as Emerson says, as carelessly as if it had never been invited" (172). The same is true for more sophisticated acts: "A certain music teacher . . . says to her pupils after the thing to be done has been clearly pointed out, and unsuccessfully attempted: 'Stop trying and it will do itself!'" (172). The musical example is especially pertinent to James's discussion, which he concludes by quoting the opinion of J. R. Seeley, author of *Natural Religion* (1886), that any "'habitual and regulated admiration . . . is worthy to be called a religion'"—including "our Music" (77).

Along with instrumental music, the late nineteenth century witnessed the emergence of a number of "habitual and regulated" practices that promised to stimulate spiritual health. James was the first analyst to give these "living system[s] of mental hygiene" (99) systematic attention, grouping them together as "the 'Mind-cure movement'" (89)—also known as "New Thought." James isolated "the 'Gospel of Relaxation'" (91) as one of the movement's central tenets. Paradoxically, this practice entailed the willful suspension of effort: one avenue James considered was yoga, suggesting that "postures, breathings, fastings, and the like" worked by "breaking through the barriers which life's routine had concreted round the deeper strata of the will, and gradually bringing its unused energies into action."[25] James was not alone in finding the healing, energizing, spirit-expanding practices of the "New Thoughters" illuminating. The psychiatrist Richard Dewey wrote in 1900, "The phenomena of mental healing are worthy of more attention than they have received. Those of Eddyism (which is the proper name for so-called Christian Science), of osteopathy, or 'divine healing,' whether by saints' relics or waters of Lourdes . . . have in them lessons for our profession."[26] The practice of mind cure found its cultural place at the provocative nexus of religion, philosophy, and medicine. Although the historian Eric Caplan has recently argued for mind cure's importance to the history of American psychotherapeutics, historians have tended to view mind cure as a "local color" or debased theology. One historian has opined that it "was a woman's kind of religion": "New Thought," he writes, "did not discriminate against the ladies, but offered them responsible positions of leadership."[27]

Similarly, Chopin's writing—especially her first collection of stories, *Bayou Folk* (1894)—has been celebrated for its vivid local color, its nuanced portrayal of Catholic Creole culture.[28] Yet Chopin, in expressly linking practices of corporeal passivity and spiritual expansion in her writing, was pursuing questions about the mind's relationship to the body that were being investigated by a range of practitioners from the medical researcher Hippolyte Bernheim in France to Mary Baker Eddy and James in the United States. "It is quite obvious," James asserted, "that a wave of religious activity, analogous in some respects to the spread of early Christianity, Buddhism, and Mohammedism, is sweeping over our American world."[29] In beginning to articulate a secular language to describe the centrality of physiological states and practices to what James termed "mental hygiene," Chopin makes an indigenous contribution to the turn-of-the-century nexus of ideas about psychospiritual healing. Rather than advocating a muscular theology, mind cure—as a forerunner to Transcendental Meditation—urged Americans to pursue the healthy pleasures of letting themselves go.

It is within this expanded (and expansion-oriented) context, then, that we can assess the cultural "work"—a term that begins to seem slightly problematic—of Kate Chopin's fiction.[30] Harold Frederic also considers the corporeal effects of music, and examines the significance of the pleasures it instills, in his portrayal of Reverend Ware, whose "longing for [music] raised on occasion such mutiny in his soul that more than once he had specifically prayed against it as a temptation. Dangerous though some of its tendencies might be, there was no gainsaying the fact that a love of music was in the main an uplifting influence—an attribute of cultivation" (47). These novels, when placed in relation to Edmund Gurney's work on aesthetic experience, suggest a way of historicizing the links among reader, form, and pleasure. A correspondent of William James, Gurney was an eclectic nineteenth-century thinker who wrote on topics from music theory to spiritualism. Citing in particular Gurney's "vindication of the unreasonable, magical, or purely physiological character of the charm of poetry," the notoriously discriminating James called Gurney's book *The Power of Sound* (1880) "the best book on aesthetics ever written."[31] Gurney's great innovation was to emphasize the way music's essential form engages not just the mind but also the body. "*Physical movement*," Gurney writes, "is continually suggested by melody. . . . it is a thing which we realise as directly agreeable in our own bodies; . . . there is perpetually involved something more even than a suggestion of movement, namely, a direct impulse to move; which is not only felt but constantly yielded to in varying degrees."[32] James's own contribution to psychology and aesthetics, his account of the stream of consciousness, owes a debt to Gurney's attentiveness to the moment-by-moment physiological effects of musical rhythm on listeners.

Theron Ware and the Ironic Rhythm of the Sick Soul

Frederic's 1896 novel, which predated *The Awakening* by four years, takes Gurney's notion of "yielding to impulse" and explores its effects in the life of the naïve minister Theron Ware. The novel also provides a glimpse of those characters—primarily women—who exercise their worldly power by manipulating religious feeling. The thrust of the novel is toward the demystification of not just religious institutions but religious sensibility itself. Theron's own powerful preaching is portrayed as the result not of piety or inspiration but of studied practice: "He set to work now, with resolute purpose, to puzzle out and master all the principles which underlie this art, and all the tricks that adorn its superstructure. . . . He practised effects now by piecemeal, with an alert ear, and calculation in every tone" (21). Frederic, in his cynical portrayal of the power of religious rhetoric and ritual, literalizes the idea expressed by Edmund Gurney that "the impassioned orator, bard, or musician, when with his varied tones and cadences he excites the strongest emotions in his hearers, little suspects that he uses the same means by which, at an extremely remote period, his half-human ancestors aroused each other's ardent passions during their mutual courtship and rivalry" (119). Gurney was working from the theories of Charles Darwin, who in *The Expression of the Emotions in Man and Animals* (1872) observed, "When male animals utter sounds in order to please the females, they would naturally employ those which are sweet to the ears of the species; and it appears that the same sounds are often pleasing to widely different animals, owing to the similarity of their nervous systems, as we ourselves perceive in the singing of birds and even in the chirping of certain tree-frogs giving us pleasure."[33] Gurney, like Darwin, was interested in tracing the continuities, enabled by neurological similarities, between rudimentary sounds and more exalted human expression. Harold Frederic, by contrast, discerns in the affective potency of preaching a structure not of continuity but of diametrical opposition, expressed as the tension between spiritual and carnal stimulation. Frederic suggests that the former is merely a cover story for the latter: that under the guise of religious ecstasy, congregants are in fact moved through the arousal of sexual instincts.

The allure of Catholicism, as portrayed by Frederic, lies in its more established rituals for cultivating these primal reactions. When Theron happens upon a silent procession of Irish Catholics carrying a mortally wounded worker, the minister falls in line, mesmerized by the sounds of the "whimpering children," the "low-murmured minor . . . wail" (37) of the grieving women, the "muttered conversation"(38) around the dying man's litter, the "low buzz of prayer" and the "click of beads on their rosaries" (40). Theron is so "moved by the rich, novel sound of the Latin as the priest rolled it forth in the *Asperges me, Domine,* and *Misereatur vestri omnipotens Deus,* with its soft Continental vowels and liquid *r*'s" (40), that he finds himself kneeling before the priest, who sprinkles the Methodist minister with holy water. Later, Theron muses over the experience, paring down the Latin phrases to their essential sounds and rhythm: The "recital—*beatum Michaelem Archangelum, beatum Joannem Baptistam, Petrum et Paulum*—*em!*—*am!*—*um!*—[were] like strokes on a great resonant alarm-bell, attuned for the hearing of heaven. He caught himself on the very verge of feeling that heaven must have heard" (47). Doctrinal antagonisms fall away in the passion of the moment, and Theron later confides to the priest, "'What I have just seen in there *did* make a very powerful impression upon me'" (43).

The novel downplays the difference between the two faiths by suggesting that, while Catholics openly ascribe to the sensory stimulus of liturgical ritual, even the Methodists, with their avoidance of ceremony and their unmelodic singing, manage to import the power of sound through the back door. When the board of trustees of Theron's congregation wish to enrich church coffers, they hire a "debt-raiser" who "took possession of the pulpit as if it were an auctioneer's block, and pursued the task of exciting liberality in the bosoms of the congregation by alternating prayer, anecdote, song, and cheap buffoonery in a manner truly sickening" (29). Ironically named Sister Soulsby, the debt-raiser turns out to be a former fortuneteller and professional clairvoyant who first provides a "tranquillizing overture" (166) and then kindles the group of Methodists to a fervor of enthusiasm by singing sacred verses set to seductive secular tunes. Sister Soulsby describes the "'machinery'" (168) of the "revival business" (164) to Theron: "'I simply took Chopin—he is full of sixths, you know—and I got all sorts of melodies out of his waltzes and mazurkas and nocturnes and so on . . . and there you are. . . . We take these tunes, written by a devil-may-care Pole who was living with George Sand openly at the time, and we pass 'em off on the brethren for hymns. It's a fraud—yes: but it's a good fraud'" (168). Like the liquor-laced hot toddy passed off to a strict teetotaler as "medicinal," the secular melodies (born of sexual passion and continuing to bear its traces) are repackaged as reverential hymns. Sister Soulsby's approach is thus "two-storied," both in the sense of being *layered* (words arbitrarily laminated onto melodies) and of being *divided,* with the audience privy only to the official story of the spirit while the debt-raiser boldly manipulates the unstated story of the flesh. This two-storied structure, which installs hypocrisy on the part of the performers and false consciousness on the part of the listeners, is aptly encapsulated in Soulsby's term "fraud."

A touchstone for sensory manipulation, the composer Frédéric Chopin is at the center of Theron's sorry bid to achieve cultural capital and to win entry into the worldly coterie of Catholic freethinkers. The group includes Dr. Ledsmar, a sexually suspect physician who breeds orchids and tests the effects of opium on his Chinese "house-boy"; Celia Madden, a wealthy young woman who pounds out piano tunes and drinks Benedictine in her velvet-curtained chamber; and Father Forbes, the urbane priest who manipulates liturgical forms and carries on a barely clandestine affair with Celia. Under their tutelage, Theron comes to believe that he sees the second story underlying his (formerly) naïve perceptions, causing him to disdain his own congregation, with "the miserable combination of hypocrisy and hysterics which they called their spiritual life" (263). Theron instead cultivates an interest in music: "'I am interested in Shopang,'" he confides to Celia. "'He lived with—what's his name?—George something. We were speaking about him only this afternoon'" (185). She mockingly plays a Chopin mazurka, while the ignorant minister, "in a ferment of awakened consciousness . . . surrendered his senses to the mere unthinking charm of it all" (185). When Theron gushes over the "'revelation'" (191) of her playing, Celia yawns and excuses herself with the comment, "'You forgive me, don't you? . . . Chopin always first excites me, then sends me to sleep'" (193).

In portraying what he takes to be the "machinery" behind organized religion and the business of secular culture, Frederic produces the textual machinery for the reader to inhabit this two-storied universe. As Theron learns to condescend to his former self and the people he once held dear, the reader is placed in a similarly worldly position vis-à-vis the minister and smiles along with Frederic and Celia Madden at Theron's mistaking George Sand, Chopin's mistress, for a man. The minister's social missteps intensify in the course of the novel from the innocent *faux pas* to actual vulgarity. Theron courts the company of Celia by asking her to accompany him on a "Shopang" expedition, for his transports upon hearing her play have made him itch to purchase a piano for himself. Having seen a sign in what can best be described as an early version of Walmart announcing "Pianos on the Instalment [*sic*] Plan" (52), Theron goes on a buying spree. He tries to insinuate himself into the wealthy young woman's cultural milieu by "studying up" on the composer: his "study" takes the form of purchasing a titillating book: "'It is a life of George Sand,' whispered Theron. 'I've been reading it this morning—all the Chopin part—while I was waiting for you'" (202). What Theron takes to be his worldly "illumination" is a form of social and moral "damnation."

Under the tutelage of Sister Soulsby, the minister becomes aware of the two-storied structure of his life. At each plot juncture Theron feels he suddenly "gets" it: he realizes that Christianity is, in the bland words of Father Forbes, merely "'this Christ myth of ours'" (68); that his own theological erudition is vaporous and he is in fact "'the most ignorant man alive!'" (122); that the avuncular relationship between the priest and the church piano-player is actually a sexual one; and so on. The pattern of the novel's plot reinforces the thematic of disillusionment, tracing as it does Theron's rises and falls, from heights of passion to sloughs of despond. This is precisely the rhythm of what William James termed the Sick Soul, the modern individual afflicted with feelings of anomie and dissociation. These feelings of utter detachment register a tenuous relationship to reality: the Sick Soul secretly suspects that behind the façade of appearances lies an emptiness. As one Sick Soul in James's *Varieties of Religious Experience* describes it, "'It is as if I could not see any reality, as if I were in a theatre; as if people were actors, and everywhere were scenery; I can no longer find myself'" (132). James explains that, to the Sick Soul, "the world is a *double-storied mystery*. . . . There are two lives, the natural and the spiritual" (143; emphasis added). Theron's oscillations are the emotional concomitant of the Sick Soul's perception of the doubleness of existence. Pericles Lewis has commented that this doubleness entails "the recognition of a radical difference between this world and the next and an accompanying sense of division within the sick soul between noble aspirations and base desires."[34] Theron's description of his new perspective is almost identical: "there was a time, I dare say, when I should have believed in [the Soulsbys'] sincerity. But of course I saw them and their performance from the inside—like one on the stage of a theatre, you know, instead of in the audience. . . . I can use no word for my new state short of illumination" (207).

By the novel's end, this "illumination" or detached, godlike sense of seeing behind the façade of life—a position that is extended to the reader, who sees behind the façade of Theron's continued self-deception—has become a form of sick-souled damnation. Indeed Theron's final outburst of despair sounds identical to one of James's case studies: "'Was I really rotten to the core all the time, years ago, when I seemed to everybody, myself and the rest, to be good and straight and sincere? . . . It isn't worth while to discuss me at all as if I had a soul. I'm just one more mongrel cur that's gone mad, and must be put out of the way—that's all'" (318). Such feelings of disenchantment are stronger than mere doubt or disbelief. In the crisis of the Sick Soul, one's very nature appears "'duplex'" (144): the facts of existence, and one's emotional reaction to it, suffer from "a certain discordancy" (144). The Sick Soul's affective attachment to the world is eradicated, and the negative emotions of nausea and self-loathing fill in the space, an experience James describes as commensurate with the sudden silencing of music: "The buzz of life ceases at their touch as a piano-string stops sounding when the damper falls on it. Of course the music can commence again;—and again and again—at intervals" (120).

As James described it, and as Frederic choreographed it, the rhythm of the Sick Soul is equivalent to a game of musical chairs. This is precisely the rhythm of *The Damnation of Theron Ware*, in which the minister is either passionately "illuminated"—his whole body aroused by stirring music, an intimate conversation, or a religious ritual—or desperately divided from the world and immobilized by thoughts of self-disgust: "Now that he thought of it, he was a sick man" (149). The novel, in other words, replicates this monotonous rhythm with its binary tones of either/or: either the music is "on"—and one waltzes on through a life of illusion—or it is "off," and one remains frozen, conscious of but cut off from the world, in what James called a state of "psychical neuralgia" (129). James also offers the term *"anhedonia"* (drawn from the physiologist Théodule Ribot) to describe the "passive joylessness and dreariness, discouragement, dejection, lack of taste and zest and spring" that marks this "'complete absence of emotional reaction'" (127). For without music, which James aligns first with "sentiments" (130) and then with "excited interest" and "passions," "the sense that life had any meaning whatever [is] for a time wholly withdrawn" (130–131).

While Theron is allowed to pass through this passionless state and conclude the novel on the upbeat—"he smiled, shook himself with a little delighted tremor, and turned on the stoop to the open door" (326)—the reader is left in a place that approximates the Sick Soul, who sees everything double and lives in what James called "a universe two stories deep" (158). For even at novel's end, the chronicle of Theron Ware continues to extend two diametrically opposed possibilities, with no way to adjudicate between them.[35] The reader, primed by Theron Ware's unrelenting rhythm of rising and falling, knows that what looks like Theron's "illumination" at the narrative's conclusion (his humbled, fresh start out west) merely promises a different form of damnation, this time in the guise of a politician rather than a minister. (On the novel's final page Theron has a strikingly auditory daydream: poised before a huge crowd, "strain[ing] their ears to miss no cadence of his voice," the audience lets loose "a mighty roar of applause, in volume like an ocean tempest" [326].) The inability of critics to determine the site of value in the novel is eloquent testimony to the text's sick-souled effect: it is finally impossible to work up any feeling—in the sense of both caring and of intuitive knowledge—for this character and his outcome.[36] Theron, it turns out, is strangely prescient when he observes,

"'I *can* speak, you know, if I can't do anything else. Talk is what tells, these days'" (326). For, in the absence of music in the thematic, formal, or affective sense, what Frederic leaves us with is a prosaic world of talk. As Nietzsche might respond to this version of realism, "Without music, life would be a mistake."[37]

Kate Chopin's Lyrical "Gospel of Relaxation"

Unlike Frederic's characters, who frequently discuss theological questions and who often cite contemporary sources such as Schopenhauer and Darwin, characters in Chopin's tales do not attend religious revivals, and rarely do they refer to specific intellectual movements. What they *do* do is willfully pursue such rhythmical, embodied activities as breathing, rocking, swimming, singing, and sex. So whereas the historian Gail Parker has dismissed mind cure practitioners with the comment "It is hard to find anything in the New Thought creed which Emerson did not say first" (*Mind Cure*, 58), Chopin for one confronts and radicalizes the disembodied idealism of Emerson through the palpable materiality of the sensuous, breathing, reproductive human body. The challenge that she sets for herself is to reconnect the mind with the body through writing, a medium that would appear intransigent in its abstraction and immateriality. For this she turns to Whitman, and to a Darwin who (unlike Frederic's) is tempered by the full-body aesthetics of Edmund Gurney.

Whereas Frederic portrays characters who are pathologically wakeful—Celia suffers from insomnia, and Theron asserts "'I don't want to sleep at all'" (193)—Chopin in her fiction explores most deeply that which precedes any awakening, actual or metaphorical: the state of somnolence or sleep. Chopin's fiction is riddled with moments of lassitude and incantatory rhythm: whispering waves, dreamy reveries, rocking babies, crooning voices, languid walks, and the sensuous strokes of arms through water, bristles through hair, fingers on flesh. Just as Edmund Gurney observes, "In the country or by the sea . . . the prolonged and gentle sounds of Nature have a markedly soothing, and even a soporific, effect on most organisms. . . . The lulling effect of a gentle voice reading aloud is well known" (36), so *The Awakening*'s Edna Pontellier, in a rare moment of maternal intimacy, takes her child "in her arms, and seating herself in the rocker, began to coddle and caress him, calling him all manner of tender names, soothing him to sleep" (565). In Chopin's tale "A Matter of Prejudice," even a fussy old lady engages in the pleasures of rhythm and in so doing transforms from a disagreeable shrew into a nurturing presence: "The child's breathing was quick and irregular. Madame was not long in detecting these signs of disturbance. . . . She rocked very gently to and fro. She fanned the child softly with her palm leaf fan, and sang 'Partant pour la Syrie' in a low and agreeable tone."[38] Chopin's innovative fictional practice inheres in her willingness to examine how a state of physical receptivity—the dampening of consciousness, the blurring of boundaries between self and other, thought and action, mind and body—need not entail sexual manipulation; it can also be a humanizing force, transpiring every day between friends, or between mother and child. Part of what sets Chopin apart from Gustave Flaubert (Willa Cather once dubbed *The Awakening* a "Creole *Bovary*")[39] is her willingness to portray the sensuality of women who take pleasure not just in fantasies of courtship but also in simple actions such as humming, swimming, walking, eating, and napping.

Two key moments depicting drowsiness in *The Awakening* situate the novel at the suggestive borderland between organized religion, medicine, and philosophy. The first takes place during Edna and Robert's trip to the little island in the Gulf of Mexico, where Edna is overcome with a deep physical weariness while attending services in a little gothic church named Our Lady of Lourdes (a church that also figures in Chopin's story "At *Chênière Caminada*"). The name invokes the tales of miraculous healing associated with the spring at Lourdes in France. The holy site comes up a few times in Chopin's writing, as when a woman in the short story "*Nég Créol*" considers sipping from "a bottle of *eau de Lourdes*" to soothe her insomnia.[40] Although the Catholic Church did finally canonize Bernadette Soubiros, the French peasant famous for her angel-inspired discovery of healing waters gushing from a secret grotto, controversies over the spring's healing powers also place Chopin's reference to Lourdes and its waters within a secular context. Since the nineteenth century, the Catholic Church has in fact collaborated with scientists to distinguish truly miraculous cures effected by contact with *eau de Lourdes*—remarkably few, the Church has decided— from those brought about by the suggestive power of visitors' *belief* that the waters would heal their ills—thousands and counting. As the former cleric turned mind-cure practitioner Walter Felt Evans wrote, "If only the ministers (and their congregations) really understood how mind could influence mind, they might accomplish the same results without having to rely on supernatural intervention" (*Mind Cure*, 51). "Even the least religious man," William James declared, "must have felt with Walt Whitman, when loafing on the grass on some transparent summer morning, that 'swiftly arose and spread round him the peace and knowledge that pass all the argument of the earth.'"[41] Chopin's reference to Lourdes even as she has her protagonist flee church services places Edna's experience on the island within the cultural context of spirituality and health.

Indeed, medical wisdom frequently replaces clerical authority in Chopin's writings. Despite the decidedly Catholic Creole culture portrayed by Chopin, there is no priest present in her major novel, *The Awakening;* instead, a bemused Léonce Pontellier turns to Dr. Mandelet for marital advice. In Chopin's short stories, priests tend to be hardhearted, like the bored prelate in "A Sentimental Soul" who bridles at having to listen to an elderly spinster's "little babblings" and then scolds her "roundly, unpityingly" (459) for admitting her secret love for the local locksmith. By contrast, the local physician who compassionately tends the dying locksmith is given the author's own name (spelled, perhaps, to give a tip on pronunciation): Choppin. In another story, "Dr. Chevalier's Lie," a kindhearted doctor pays for the burial of a young "woman of doubtful repute" and then tactfully tells the family she died of a lingering sickness rather than a tawdry murder.[42] Biographer Emily Toth reads this tale as an implicit homage to the doctor who attended Kate Chopin at her first childbirth. That physician had been awarded the "Chevalier of the Legion of Honor" for discovering the telltale sign distinguishing between (potentially curable) malaria and yellow fever, the deadly disease that sent wealthy New Orleans families to the Gulf of Mexico every summer. In yellow fever, Chopin's doctor had observed, the rhythm of the pulse falls rather than escalates, as it does in the case of malaria.[43]

Pulses might be affected by influences other than disease, and Chopin was interested in pursuing—and expanding on—these sources of physical stimulation and relaxation. The historian Gail Parker reports that the New Thought publicist Henry Wood, "at the end of his influential [book] *Ideal Suggestion through Mental Photography*"—published the same year as Chopin's *Awakening*—"appended a workbook to encourage the methodical practice of autosuggestion" (66) to soothe wearied nerves. As Walter Felt Evans described his theory of "undulation or vibration," there was a physiological conduit between the mind and the rest of the body that could be exploited either by mental healers or individuals themselves: "The nerves are the appointed and natural conductors of the peculiar force, that is generated in the brain and spinal column, to the various parts and organs of the body. . . . [The] vibratory force that is transmitted by the nerves to the organs [operates] in the same or similar way in which an undulatory wave is transmitted through the telegraphic wire."[44] Learning to relax required the careful calibration of body and mind, of conscious and unconscious activity. Chopin herself wrote in her 1894 diary that if she could "take back a little wisdom with me; it would be the spirit of a perfect acquiescence" (*Papers*, 183).

The popular writer Annie Payson Call, whose books were a blend of physiology manual and mental-health guide, earned praise from William James, who advocated "'the gospel of relaxation' as preached by Miss Annie Payson Call, of Boston, in her admirable little volume called *Power through Repose*, a book that ought to be in the hands of every teacher and student in America of either sex."[45] For Call, even jarring rail travel became the occasion for relaxation: "Much, indeed most of the fatigue from a long journey by rail is quite unnecessary, and comes from an unconscious officious effort of trying to carry the train, instead of allowing the train to carry us, or of resisting the motion, instead of relaxing and yielding to it. There is a pleasant rhythm in the motion of the rapidly moving cars which is often restful rather than fatiguing, if we will only let go and abandon ourselves to it."[46] Call also suggested that for many people, music provides a model of willful abandon "so that the moment they hear a fine strain they are one with it." Another avenue is the "rhythm of a perfect walk," and Nature itself provides dynamic patterns for human beings to emulate: "We have the rhythm of the seasons, of day and night, of the tides, and of vegetable and animal life,—as the various rhythmic motions in the flying of birds" (32). The child—"the babe in its bath"—might also be emulated, as it "yields to the soft pressure of the water with a repose which is deeply expressive of gratitude" (33). The paradox of New Thought is that repose must be achieved through consciously "training for rest" (35), while the ultimate telos of relaxation is progress and achievement. As Call concludes, "No matter what our work in life, whether scientific, artistic, or domestic, it is the same body through which the power is transmitted; and the same freedom in the conductors [i.e. nerves] for impression and expression is needed, to whatever end the power may be moved, from the most simple action to the highest scientific or artistic attainment" (72).

In its motifs (birds, tides, rest) and its rhythms (walking, swimming, rocking), *The Awakening* echoes Call's *Power through Repose* and, more famously, the poetry of Walt Whitman. The celebrated clinician William Osler, a friend and medical attendant to Whitman, had admired the poet's "faculty of 'rhyming and rolling'" in his undulating lines of free verse.[47] Another contemporary described the "singular resemblance in the great measured yet irregular roll of Whitman's lines to the onset of waves along the shore—now creeping white and low in long successive array, now madly surging and towering spray, now lipping sunlit and blue upon the land."[48] The cadences of the pulse, the waves, and the voice provide the metronome for Whitman's poetic birth announcement "Out of the Cradle Endlessly Rocking," inspired by a bird's song of sorrow over the loss of his mate:

> Soothe! soothe! soothe!
> Close on its wave soothes the wave behind,
> And again another behind embracing and lapping, every one
>   close . . .
> O throat! O throbbing heart!
> And I sing uselessly, uselessly all the night.

Chopin's own hypnotic, onomatopoetic prose, threaded together through participles and alliteration, is resonant of Whitman's verse: "The voice of the sea is seductive, never ceasing, whispering, clamoring, murmuring, inviting the soul to wander in abysses of solitude" (*Awakening*, 654).

Horatio Dresser, the most prominent spokesperson for New Thought, merely echoes the poet and the novelist when he writes, "There is a universal tide, throbbing, pulsing, ever flowing forward, and on and on. . . . A man may rage and tear and buffet it. He may idly float with its silent rhythms. Or his strong arms may carry him onward with its harmonious motion."[49] It's tempting to think that Chopin in her description of Edna's experience in the ocean was expressly playing with this image. Another advocate of "the New Thought" wrote in 1897: "The strong swimmer is fearless. If he is wearied he will float. . . . And what a glorious life electrifies him! What a sense of power over the new element, gained simply through his fearlessness! . . . Many of us venture into spiritual thought with something of the same anxiety we feel in taking our first surf bath. . . . But what do we know of the confident swimmer in the deep seas beyond the breakers? . . . We are only wading yet in the new thought" (*Mind Cure*, 166). Edna's "first surf bath" also expresses the connection between spiritual searching and swimming "beyond the breakers": "A feeling of exultation overtook her, as if some power of significant import had been given her to control the working of her body and her soul. . . . As she swam she seemed to be reaching out for the unlimited in which to lose herself" (551, 552). William James, similarly, was attentive to the bodily experience of transition and transformation essential to transporting experiences (such as Edna's swimming, or her perambulations around New Orleans). Moreover, the "sense of deeper significance" that emerges from such moments is not, James observed, "confined to rational propositions. Single words, and conjunctions of words, effects of light on land and sea, odors and musical sounds, all bring it when the mind is tuned aright" (*Varieties*, 301–302).

The idea of "significance" without "rational propositions," when theorized in light of key scenes in *The Awakening* (Edna's reading of Emerson, mothers rocking their children), gestures toward an important question about the relationship of activity to idea. For it is clearly not accurate to say that reading or bathing or rhythmic breathing *represented* sleep, or that a mother's crooning words (or, for that matter, reading Emerson) *conveyed the idea of* sleep; indeed, by appealing to the sensory, both reading and rocking often dampen the activity of consciousness and *bring about* sleep. Taken together, Edna's evening rituals of reading and bathing bring about a "sense of restfulness . . . such as she had not known before" (605).

This dampening of consciousness and heightening of the corporeal is not just described in Chopin's stories: it is also intrinsic to the reading experience. When *The Awakening* was first published, reviewers commented on the novel's seduction: Emily Toth quotes a series of reviewers who were "charmed," "deeply stirred and strangely fascinated," "completely engrossed, . . . absorbed," brought under "the spell of the book" (*Chopin*, 356, 337, 339). Some rebelled against its effects, asserting it was "not a healthy story," "unwholesome in its influence." Detractors were nonetheless perceptive: as one wrote, "This unhappy Edna's awakening seems to have been confined entirely to the senses, while reason, judgment, and all the higher faculties and perceptions, whose office it is to weigh and criticise impulse and govern conduct, fell into slumber deep as that of the seven sleepers. It gives one a distinct shock to see Edna's crude mental operations" (*Chopin*, 347–348). Edna willfully gives herself over to music, to love, and finally to the sea; Chopin's readers find themselves sensually affected by not just the story, but the rhythms of the plot and the prose. Even the otherwise critical Willa Cather commented of Chopin, "hers is a genuinely literary style; of not great elegance or solidity; but light, flexible, subtle, and capable of producing telling effects directly and simply" (*Chopin*, 352). In Chopin's fiction, readers' attention is directed away from the referential function of language toward literature's "telling effects" through an appeal to music, or more precisely, to an important nineteenth-century debate over the status of music as representation.

Music and the Sounding Board of the Body

Chopin's engagement with music dated from her childhood, in which she had an extensive musical education. In her youthful diary Kate O'Flaherty recorded the extremity of her attempts to entertain a young man who came to call: "I immediately took to the piano as the most pleasing way both to himself and me of fulling [*sic*] my mission of entertainer. . . . I played pieces of every variety: Operas—Sonatas—Meditations—Galops—Nocturnes—Waltzes & Jigs . . . when to my utmost dismay, he coolly informed me that there was nothing on earth he disliked more than music" (*Papers*, 17). Her first published work, which appeared in 1888, was actually a polka that she named for her daughter.

A concern with music structured Chopin's first published story, "Wiser Than a God," which appeared in the *Philadelphia Musical Journal*. In it, she treats a young woman's decision to pursue a musical career rather than marry, a tale that climaxes with the woman's speech to her admirer: "'Is music anything more to you than the pleasing distraction of an idle moment? Can't you feel that with me, it courses with the blood through my veins?'"[50] In a gesture suggesting the influence of the German philosopher Arthur Schopenhauer, whose magnum opus *The World as Will and Representation* argues for music as the ultimate art form, Chopin's story concludes with the protagonist emigrating to Schopenhauer's home town of Leipsig, followed by her music teacher, Max Kuntzler, he of "the ever persistent will" (*Complete*, 669). Fluent in German, Chopin conducted her own literary and cultural salon, and her own home town, St. Louis, was the nerve center of a philosophical movement known as the Young Hegelians. Active after the Civil War, St. Louis's Philosophical Society published the secular *Journal of Speculative Society* from 1867 to 1893, and Emerson spoke to the group on three separate occasions in 1867. Within this cultural context, Chopin was doubtless aware of lively debates about what precisely wordless music conveyed to the listener.

The character of Theron Ware provides a study in what the nineteenth-century music critic Eduard Hanslick termed "pathological listening," or listening for the story beneath the music.[51] Theron treats melody as essentially referential, an encrypted language of sex that one might "translate" into biography by reading of the amorous exploits of the composer. The minister buys a piano to hear the gorgeous Celia "'make it speak'" (*Damnation*, 197); he listens for the "impulsive yet very earnest words" embedded in her piano playing, which "appeal[ed] to him in strenuous argument and persuasion" (189). Nietzsche in *The Birth of Tragedy from the Spirit of Music* (1872) had noted the implicit dualism in such an approach to music, in which "the words, it is argued, are as much nobler than the accompanying harmonic system as the soul is nobler than the body."[52]

Chopin resists the notion that music might simply be translated into words—to extend Nietzsche's metaphor, she opposed severing the soul from the body. The very opening scene of *The Awakening*, in fact, pursues the question of how words and sounds are linked. In it, a parrot hanging in a cage "kept repeating over and over: '*Allez vous-en! Allez vous-en! Sapristi!* That's all right!'" (521). The narrator asserts that "he could speak a little Spanish, and also a language which nobody understood, unless it was the mocking-bird that hung on the other side of the door, whistling his fluty notes out upon the breeze with maddening persistence" (521). Critical attention to this scene has tended to focus on the caged bird as trope of female confinement, with the bird's "language that nobody understood" referencing the pathos of Edna Pontellier's "world of limited linguistic possibilities."[53] Yet this point begs a prior question: in what sense should the bird's sounds count as language at all?

In framing her novel with the juxtaposed soundings of the two birds, the parrot's composed of mimed words, the mockingbird's of "fluty notes," Kate Chopin references an influential debate of the late nineteenth century over the representational status of "absolute" music, that is, music detached from any dramatic or functional context and unaccompanied by the human voice. As philosopher Peter Kivy has observed, "Most of the music in the world is now, and always has been, music sung to words. As an art form in its own right, absolute music did not become a subject of philosophical inquiry until late in the eighteenth century."[54] Even music that served as a backdrop for other activ-

ities (such as marching or marrying) was understood—like the parrot—
to imitate the tones and accents of the human voice under the influence
of emotion. The French cleric Abbe du Bos, one of the first commentators on modern music aesthetics, urged that "just as a painter imitates
the forms and colours of Nature, so the musician imitates the tones, the
accents, the sighs, the inflexions of voice."[55] Martial music, therefore,
was thought to replicate the shouts and intonations of courageous war-
riors, and religious music to copy the murmured supplications of a be-
liever deep in prayer.[56]

Eduard Hanslick, in his formalist manifesto *The Beautiful in Music*
(published in English in 1891), challenged the mimetic theory, affirming
that "music consists of successions and forms of sound, and these alone
constitute the subject" (119). Any associations one may have with a
particular piece of music had, to use Hanslick's words, "only a subjective existence": "Now, whatever be the effect of a piece of music on the
individual mind, and howsoever it be interpreted, it has no subject beyond the combinations of notes we hear, for music speaks not only by
means of sounds, it speaks nothing but sound" (21, 119). Musical compositions, Gurney asserted, "imply no external fact at all. The function
is to *present*, not to represent, and their message has no direct reference
to the world outside them" (*Sound*, 60).

Much nineteenth-century thinking about aesthetic form focused on
the relationship between music and the other arts: in particular, whether
instrumental music was representational. Kate Chopin invokes this debate in *The Awakening* when she writes of Edna's tendency to translate
music into images of persons: "Musical strains, well rendered, had a
way of evoking pictures in her mind. . . . When she heard it ['a short,
plaintive, minor strain'] there came before her imagination the figure of
a man standing beside a desolate rock on the seashore. . . . Another
piece called to her mind a dainty young woman clad in an Empire
gown" (549). The idea that music conjures pictures in the minds of listeners was in fact a controversial one. Hanslick, in particular, railed
against the ekphrastic notion that music "dosed the listener with a sort
of vision-promoting medicine" (*Beautiful*, 6). Here is the poet and music
critic Heinrich Heine on the same phenomenon: "however much I love
Liszt, his music does not have a pleasant effect on my state of mind, all
the more so because I see ghosts which others only hear; and that, as you
know, with every sound the hand strikes on the piano, the corresponding
figure [*Klangfigur*] rises up in my mind—in short, the music becomes vis-

ible to my eye."[57] The passage's emphasis on visibility, coupled with the terms *ghost* and *figure,* suggests that what "rises up" in Heine's mind is a vision—albeit an attenuated one—of the human form. This experience is disturbing to Heine partly because of its privacy and idiosyncrasy—"I see ghosts which others only hear"—and partly because of its repudiation of the philosophical consensus since Aristotle, that music, unlike poetry, sculpture and painting, does not "produce some concrete image" (*Beautiful,* 23).

The pictures that music conjures in a person's mind can only, Hanslick believed, be private and idiosyncratic. This observation was, at the time, by no means controversial. But the use to which Hanslick put this observation *was* actually highly significant. For he maintained that music's nonrepresentational nature actually repudiated any important link between music and emotion: "Music, we are told, cannot, like poetry, entertain the mind with definite conceptions; nor yet the eye, like sculpture and painting, with visible forms. Hence, it is argued, its object must be to work on the feelings. 'Music has to do with feelings' [we are told]" (*Beautiful,* 9). But, Hanslick insisted, emotions can only be catalyzed by a representation. If a listener "discover[s] in a piece of music the idea of *youthful contentedness* or that of *transitoriness,*" it is only, he believed, because of a prior image aroused by the music: a "picture of a flower girl" or a "picture of a snow-covered churchyard" (*Beautiful,* 23; emphasis added).

The visualizations that music prompts in the fictional Edna Pontellier are strikingly parallel to those described by Hanslick: the naked man "standing beside a desolate rock" as a bird disappears on the horizon is a reasonable facsimile of "transitoriness,"[58] while the "dainty young woman" dancing along a hedged avenue could serve as a conventional portrait of "youthful contentedness." Indeed, one hears an echo of Hanslick's repudiation of musical visualizations, which he finds irrational and solipsistic, in some readers' critique of Edna Pontellier as increasingly moody, isolated, and narcissistic. Bert Bender gestures toward such a position when he writes that Chopin's fiction depicts characters "tragically cut off from their social surroundings."[59]

Yet it is worthwhile to return to Heine's troubled comment "with every sound the hand strikes on the piano, the corresponding figure [*Klangfigur*] rises up in my mind." We need to pay closer attention to the notion of "corresponding figure," the English phrase offered for Heine's German term *Klangfigur.* The critic Susan Bernstein has pointed out a more precise translation would be "Chladni figure," which has a very specific designation: it is the pattern produced when sand deposited on tempered glass is made to vibrate by the touch of a bow to the plate. The mechanism for producing these figures was first created by the scientist and music lover Ernst Florens Friedrich Chladni in 1797. Once set to vibrating, the sand on the smooth surface is distributed into different shapes depending on the tone and velocity of the disturbance. As one historian of acoustics writes, "These 'tone figures,' as Chladni explained in *Die Akustik* (1802), were not arbitrary but rather in some sort of a 'necessary'—indexical—relation to the sounds. In the graphic traces of these *'script-like ur-images of sound'* one could see, what another German physicist, Johann Wilhelm Ritter, called 'the notation of that tone *which it has written by itself.*'"[60] The Chladni figure, Bernstein argues, provides an "epistemological model" that "guarantees an accurate recording or translation of music into textual images."[61] I would modify her claim slightly to emphasize the indexical rather than mimetic nature of the relationship: the Chladni figure does not so much guarantee the "textualization" of music as it registers music's physical effects. A quick reminder of the work of C. S. Peirce helps to clarify the significance of the index.

A nineteenth-century semiologist and irascible colleague of William James, Peirce articulated three semiotic categories: the icon, the symbol, and the index. Whereas an icon has a direct visual relationship to the object being represented (e.g. a picture of a person, a model of a house) and a symbol has a purely conventional relationship (e.g. a country's flag), the index indicates a relationship of cause and effect. In Peirce's words, an index is "a sign which refers to the Object that it denotes by virtue of being *really affected* by that Object."[62] Peirce's examples include entities that "point to" another: smoke and fire, weathervane and wind, wound and bullet, symptom and disease. The indexical relation is thus distinct from a mimetic relation: the latter implies an equivalence, as in "X sounds like Y" or "A looks like B." The indexical relationship is also different from a "symbolical" relation based on convention or stipulation. If, as Eduard Hanslick wrote, "yellow is the emblem of jealousy, the key of G major that of gaiety, the cypress that of mourning" (26), it is simply because we have arbitrarily attached these meanings to them. A Chladni figure, by contrast, neither "looks like" nor "sounds like" nor "symbolizes" the tones that produced it. Philosopher Thomas A. Sebeok explains indexicality in these terms: "Temporal succession, rela-

tions of a cause to its effect, or vice versa, of an effect to its cause . . .
lurks . . . between an index and its dynamic object."[63] The product of
reverberation, the Chladni figure provides for music a material form
that is tactile, visual, and dynamic.

Dilating on his distinction between music (which for Hanslick never
involves emotion) and representational art forms (which can evoke
emotion) Hanslick maintains that music cannot be "reduced to ideas"
(20). Essential to his argument is the notion that *emotion* is itself essentially bound to identifiable objects: "only by virtue of ideas and judgments," he maintained, "can an indefinite state of mind pass into a
definite feeling" (21). In Hanslick's account, a feeling is always generated by, and therefore secondary to, a *thought*. The feeling, in turn, produces a motion within the body: "The feeling of love cannot be
conceived apart from the image of the beloved being, or apart from the
desire and the longing for the possession of the object of our affections"
(22). While we may *think* that we hear in music "the whispering of love,
or the clamor of ardent combatants," Hanslick insisted we are mistaken: "The *whispering* may be expressed, true, but not the whispering
of love; the *clamor* may be reproduced, undoubtedly, but not the clamor
of ardent combatants. Music may reproduce phenomena such as whispering, storming, roaring, *but the feelings of love or anger have only a
subjective existence*" (21; emphasis added). Ideas and actions may be
public, objective; but feelings are merely private, subjective: in this idea
we can discern the conceptual roots of the Affective Fallacy identified
by W. K. Wimsatt and Monroe Beardsley (discussed in detail in the Introduction). "Music," Hanslick concluded, "ought to deal with the *motion* accompanying a feeling" (37).

But what is the relationship between *motion* and *emotion*? Chopin
explicitly engages Hanslick's writing through *The Awakening*'s now famous refrain, "The voice of the sea is seductive; never ceasing, *whispering, clamoring*, murmuring, inviting the soul to wander for a spell in
abysses of solitude" (535; emphasis added). With as yet no reference to
ideas such as love or combat (that association is reserved for Heine,
who famously wrote, "The Wedding March always reminds me of the
music played when soldiers go into battle"—a sentiment affirmed by
the character of Edna), Chopin uses Hanslick's words, and her sentence
echoes the sense: alliteration provides the sussura sounds of the ocean
while stringing together the onomatopoetic words "whispering" and
"murmuring," and the series of anapestic gerunds emulates the repeti-

tive, wavelike motion of the sea. In doing so, the sentence conforms to Hanslick's prescription that "music can undertake to imitate objective phenomena only, and never the specific feeling they arouse. . . . The fluttering of birds . . . can be painted musically only by producing auditory impressions which are *dynamically related* to those phenomena" (36; emphasis added). The crucial question, then, pertains to whether "the *motion* accompanying a feeling" is indeed, as Hanslick asserts, secondary to the really important stuff, the mental content of a feeling, which Hanslick considers to be contingent on "objective phenomena" in the world.

We can now perceive Kate Chopin's invocation of the Chladni figure (a mechanism for translating insubstantial vibration into material form) and what is at stake in this appeal (the possibility of bypassing the mental image). Listen to the oddly clinical description of the music's effect on Edna one evening by the Gulf of Mexico: "the very first chords which Mademoiselle Reisz struck upon the piano sent a keen tremor down Mrs. Pontellier's spinal column" (549). Max Nordau, in his 1895 screed against "decadent aesthetics," described the "degenerate" in just such terms: the decadent listener "weeps copiously without adequate occasion; a commonplace line of poetry [Nordau mentions Whitman] or of prose sends a shudder down his back; . . . and music especially, even the most insipid and least commendable [Nordau mentions Frédéric Chopin] arouses in him the most vehement emotions."[64] Yet for Kate Chopin, such a corporeal response is explicitly offered as an alternative to the pictorial consciousness, for although Edna "waited for the material pictures which she thought would gather and blaze before her imagination," we are told "she waited in vain": "She saw no pictures of solitude, of hope, of longing, or of despair. But the very passions themselves were aroused within her soul, swaying it, lashing it, as the waves daily beat upon her splendid body" (549–550). Chopin's sentence echoes Richard Wagner's famous statement that music "speaks not of the passion, love and longing of this or that individual in this or that situation, but of passion, love and longing in themselves."[65]

The motion of the music, received by and reverberating through the human body, does not mimic feeling, nor does it arbitrarily prompt an image that in turn evokes a feeling. Returned to the context of nineteenth-century music theory and physiology, Chopin's text makes clear that the music *was* waves beating upon Edna's body: from the chords "struck upon the piano" to the "keen tremor down . . . [the] spinal column" to the release of "the very passions" of hope, longing, and despair. In his 1884 essay "What Is an Emotion?" William James remarks, "Hardly a sensation comes to us without sending waves of alternate constriction and dilation down the arteries of our arms. . . . No shade of emotion, however slight, should be without a bodily reverberation."[66] The line of transmission is therefore not representational, but vibrational: "'Bon Dieu! It shakes a man!'" (*Awakening*, 550) gasps one listener after the last chord is played. Like Chladni's tempered glass plate, Edna's "being was tempered" (549) to respond to the music by the heat of the day, the blaze of the lights, the throb of the dancing, the warmth of Adele's and Robert's attention. After Mademoiselle Reisz's recital, Edna expresses her thanks not with words but by "press[ing] the hand of the pianist convulsively" (550). Far from an epiphenomenon or mistranslation of musical experience, the play of emotion is precisely the index—the patterned sand—of musical expression.

Chopin's text, in short, repudiates the idea that emotion is the subjective aftereffect of cognition: that one needs to have a concept of a thing before one can have a feeling. Instead, *The Awakening* conforms to Schopenhauer's argument that music "does not express this or that particular and definite pleasure, this or that affliction, pain, sorrow, horror, gaiety, merriment, or piece of mind, but joy, sorrow, horror, merriment, peace of mind *themselves* . . . without any accessories, and so also without the motives for them" (*World*, 261). It does this, precisely, through melody, which emulates the essentially rhythmical structure of willing, or of human desire: in Schopenhauer's words, music "portrays every agitation, every effort, every movement of the will, everything which the faculty of reason summarizes under the wide and negative concept of feeling, and which cannot be further taken up into the abstractions of reason. Hence it has always been said that music is the language of feeling and of passion, just as words are the language of reason" (259). It is not the *content* of the music that in some way represents joy or sorrow but the motion of the music—its tones, coloring, pace, and so on—that follows the rhythm of the emotions as experienced by the human body. Schopenhauer writes, "As rapid transition from wish to satisfaction and from this to a new wish are happiness and well-being, so rapid melodies without great deviations are cheerful" (260).

For Edmund Gurney, influenced by the writings of Charles Darwin, the capacity of music to affect listeners led him to meditate on the dynamics of pleasure as such. He begins his monumental work on the philosophy and physiology of music, *The Power of Sound* (1880), with the observation that the organs of sense—"the channels by which we keep up our constant and various intercourse with what we call the external world" (*Sound,* 1)—are responsible, at the simplest level, for the undifferentiated feelings of pleasure and pain. And while pain, he concludes, has an indisputable "force and reality" (2), pleasure is always differential, in dynamic tension with discomfort: "The *pleasure* which is obtainable by this latter class seems to depend almost wholly on some pre-existing distress or craving, or, at the very least, desire. It is delightful to eat and drink when one is hungry and thirsty, and to plunge into cold water when the skin is hot or irritated" (2). Since "relief and contrast then seem necessary factors" (2), the experience of pleasure implies an essential rhythmical structure. Music, then, is not simply one delight among many: insofar as it is determined by a "group of sounds or movements to be repeated," which provoke listeners "to feel a vivid longing for its recurrence at a particular instant," it *is* pleasure distilled, abstracted, detached from material objects (pastry for hunger, water for thirst) and yet condensing the most elemental tempos of respiration, pulse, and tide.[67] As Schopenhauer put it, musical tones "make the aesthetic impression as effect, and this without our going back to their causes, as in the case of perception" (266).

Hanslick's commitment to music as nonrepresentational ("it speaks nothing but sound"), which excises the emotive from aesthetic experience, had a number of stakes. One was to elevate music to the status of art, while it had long been seen as mere accompaniment to other aesthetic forms such as poetry or dance. Second, the imperative of "keeping ourselves free from all subjective feeling" countered one "of the oldest attacks on music, grounded on the reproach that it enervates, effeminates, and benumbs its votaries" (*Beautiful,* 93). Hanslick—like the New Critics writing almost a century later—wished to secure music for "science": "I only protest against the intrusion of the feelings upon the province of science; in other words, that I take up the cudgels against those aesthetic enthusiasts who, though presuming to teach the musician, in reality only dilate upon their tinkling opium dreams" (*Beautiful,* 4). (Theron Ware fits the description of one of Hanslick's "enthusiasts" who, "reclining in their seats and only half-awake, suffer themselves to be rocked and lulled by the mere flow of sound" [*Beautiful,* 90].) Finally, Hanslick's desire to excise emotion from aesthetic experience arises from the commitment to distinguishing music from other emotionally resonant activities: to listen to a musical composition for other than "the aesthetic criterion of intelligent gratification" was implicitly to acknowledge that "a good cigar, some exquisite dainty, or a warm bath yields" the same enjoyment and thus to "drag [music] . . . down to the level of mere physical stimulant" (*Beautiful*, 91).

Recently, the philosopher of music Carl Dahlhaus has distinguished between representational and expressive music, with the former enlisting images and the latter eliciting feeling. Theron Ware, to use Dahlhaus's description of representational music, quite literally remains in the world of "*aped* feeling," the debased and purely sensory realm of primitive life.[68] As one pseudo-Darwinian character asserts in Frederic's novel, "'the only animals who make the noises we call music are of the bird family—a debased offshoot of the reptilian creation—the very lowest types of the Vertebrata now in existence. . . . Musicians stand on the very bottom rung of the ladder in the sub-cellar of human intelligence—even lower than painters and actors'" (*Damnation*, 75). Chopin in her fiction disrupts both versions of the "chain of being"—Hanslick's, which limits music to rarified, disembodied heights, and Frederic's, which places it at the nadir of human carnality—by recasting rhythm and melody as essential to the ebb and flow of quotidian experience.

The Rhythm of Desire in *The Awakening*

It is the pared-down structure of sensory experience, divided into pain and pleasure, that Kate Chopin explores in the first chapters of *The Awakening*. Edna's tears in the opening encounter with her husband Léonce initiate the simple rhythm of longing and gratification. For prior to her encounter with (to use Gurney's terms) "distress or craving, or, at the very least, desire," Edna has existed in a state of plenitude, plied with bonbons and supplied with every creature comfort, including Robert's devoted attendance, soft linens, diaphanous garments, plumped cushions, "freshly befurbelowed" (533) children, and "the finest of fruits, *patés*, a rare bottle or two, delicious syrups" (528). Edna's newfound ability to savor her food depends on an initial sensation of emptiness, a state almost unknown in the midst of Creole largess, available at first only in the fairy-tale moment on the little island of Chênière Caminada. (Adele Ratignolle's state of eternal pregnancy emblemizes the near impossibility of being physically "empty," as does Edna's own difficult eluding her husband's bounty: the narrator states explicitly that Léonce left nothing to be desired, a comment we should take literally.) After quitting the "stifling atmosphere of the church" (561) Edna naps in a tiny cottage, awaking to find "she was very hungry. . . . Edna bit a piece from the brown loaf, tearing it with her strong, white teeth. She poured some of the wine into the glass and drank it down" (563). This experience initiates her to the rhythm of appetite and satisfaction that, as Gurney declared, is precisely constitutive of pleasure. Edna, having been afflicted with satiety, seeks out the experience of incompleteness.

Gurney discerned in even the most modest bodily motions—"such as is sometimes experienced in tapping the table with perfectly regular up and down movements of the hand, or in swinging a foot to and fro" (*Sound*, 110)—the same structure of tension and release that obtained in more overtly aesthetic experiences. He observed that the capacity of music to influence and delight listeners is crucially directed toward the body: "Any one who watches himself or other people as they listen to Music," he notes, "will perceive that the pleasure is often enhanced by the actual rhythmical movements, by the actual series of tactual and muscular sensations, which accompany the sounds" (110). The psychiatrist Adolf Meyer concurred with this formulation, taking it a step further: "Our body is not merely so many pounds of flesh and bone figuring as a machine, with an abstract mind or soul added to it. It is throughout a live organism pulsating with its rhythm of rest and activity, beating time (as we might say) in ever so many ways. . . . The whole of human organization has its shape in a kind of rhythm . . . *larger rhythms* of night and day, of sleep and waking hours, of hunger and its gratification, and finally the big four—work and play and rest and sleep."[69] Meyer's "big four"—work/play, rest/sleep—quite succinctly sum up the central events of Chopin's novel.

It is significant, then, that the tears Edna sheds in the beginning pages of the novel are accompanied by just such rhythmical movements: "She began to cry a little . . . and began to rock gently to and fro" (526). Crying, as Chopin emphasizes, involves elements of shuddering, moaning, and singing: "There was no sound abroad except the hooting of an old owl . . . and the everlasting voice of the sea that was not uplifted at that soft hour. It broke like a mournful lullaby upon the night" (526). Chopin's literary excursion into the venue of rhythm is clinched as the scene concludes with Léonce's return to the city the next day ("they would not see him again at the Island till the coming Saturday" [527]), a departure that underscores the gendered ebb and flow of the summer

resort, where husbands arrive as with the tide each weekend only to re-
cede come Sunday in the rush back to the city. To sum up the multiple
rhythmic motifs of the novel's opening scenes, Léonce's mode of transportation as he bids goodbye to his family is repeatedly specified: a
rockaway.

The writings of Schopenhauer, Gurney, and Meyer allow us to perceive how Chopin's plot itself follows a melodic structure as it tracks
the central character's diurnal longings. Robert, in this formal analysis,
is not so much the *object* of desire (a notion explored by Hanslick and
Frederic) but rather an "interval" or rest that is productive of desire—
which of course is why the Creole husbands happily tolerate his presence. Think of Robert's mischievous separation of the clinging lovers
after the soirée musicale: walking between them, he necessitates slowing
downs and speeding ups, dips and feints and maneuvers, as the two
parts try to reunite. This is precisely his role in the community of
Grande Isle. If in Creole culture marriage provides the "keynote"—two
parts blended into one—Schopenhauer offers terms to describe the motion that Robert initiates: "the nature of melody is a constant digression
and deviation from the keynote in a thousand ways . . . yet there always
follows a final return to the keynote. In all these ways, melody expresses
the many different forms of the will's efforts, but also its satisfaction by
ultimately finding again a harmonious interval, and still more the
keynote" (260). Far from disruptive in any essential way, Robert's role
in distracting the women at Madame Lebrun's is all about preserving
marital harmony.

Robert, in short, formally provokes desire. It is telling that at the
moment he trails behind to conduct the lovers, Edna, walking ahead,
wonders at his withdrawal: "Of late he had sometimes held away from
her for an entire day, redoubling his devotion upon the next and the
next" (550–551). His absence prompts Edna to sing a song he had sung,
with the words "Ah! *Si tu savais*" (567). Chopin points away from the
meaning of the words with a double gesture: the phrase is French (a language Edna does not speak) and cast in the conditional tense—"if you
knew"—emphasizing the noncommunication of the unstated object
(i.e. "knew what?"). Instead the passage calls attention to the sound of
the words and their sensuous reception: "Robert's voice . . . was musical and true. The voice, the notes, the whole refrain haunted her memory" (567). William James affirms this sentiment when he writes, "Music
gives us ontological messages which non-musical criticism is unable to

contradict, though it may laugh at our foolishness in minding them. There is a verge of the mind which these things haunt; and whispers therefrom mingle with the operations of our understanding, even as the waters of the infinite ocean send their waves to break among the pebbles that lie upon our shores" (*Varieties,* 330). "Minding" for James not only involved the notion of caring but also implied a state of sensuous attunement. A central navigator of these mystical waters was, for James, the poet Walt Whitman, who grasped the "deliciousness of some of these states . . . beyond anything known in ordinary consciousness" (*Varieties,* 323).[70]

As with a musical rest, Edna's moments away from Robert are productive of a simple rhythmic line: "She missed him . . . just as one misses the sun on a cloudy day without having thought much about the sun when it was shining" (551). Learning to "miss" is the first step in an education in the melody that is desire. Here is Schopenhauer: "Now the nature of man consists in the fact that his will strives, is satisfied, strives anew, and so on and on; in fact his happiness and well-being consist only in the transition from desire to satisfaction, and from this to a fresh desire, such transition going forward rapidly. For the non-appearance of satisfaction is suffering; the empty longing for a new desire is languor, boredom" (260). It is precisely the state of "languor, boredom" that Edna experiences in the unrelenting domestic serenity of the Ratignolles, which "gave her no regret, no longing. . . . she could see in it but an appalling and hopeless ennui" (585). The Ratignolles had perfected the "fusion of two human beings into one"—a contrast with the give-and-take of the enigmatic lovers whom Robert teases. As an exemplary Creole couple, the Ratignolles monotonously chimed together to tell the same quotidian story at the dinner table. The keynote, as Schopenhauer described it, "expresses the satisfaction and composure of the will, but with which nothing more can then be done, and the continuation of which would be only a wearisome and meaningless monotony corresponding to boredom" (321).

The significance of music, for Schopenhauer, is that it emulates the rhythm of the will's strivings, the imperative to go "on and on." Chopin structures the plot of her novel accordingly, so that it begins with Edna's transformation from a "listless woman" (601) to one who hungers, misses, seeks, achieves, and desires afresh a variety of objects: food, children, the pigeon house, music, men. What is significant is not the content of her wishes but their form, and the melody is crucially tied to emotion and mood. Yet lurking forever in the back of desire is, perversely, satisfaction. Schopenhauer writes, "Now absolutely every human life continues to flow on between willing and attainment. Of its nature the wish is pain; attainment quickly begets satiety. The goal was only apparent; possession takes away its charm" (313–314). The imperatives of harmony, from this perspective, require dissonance.

The arrival of Edna's father, to whom "she was not very warmly or deeply attached," provides just such a complicating element, something made explicit by the comment "His coming was in the nature of a welcome disturbance; it seemed to furnish a new direction for her emotions" (598). The requirement of discord also helps to explain why Edna seeks the presence of Mademoiselle Reisz, "the most disagreeable and unpopular woman who had ever lived in Bienville Street" (588). In her grumpy presence Edna "was now beginning to feel hungry" (593). After reading a letter from the absent Robert, and listening to the pianist play Chopin and Wagner, Edna finds herself sobbing. Having completed her business of achieving a painful state, she "arose in some agitation to take her departure" (595). The men in Edna's life, from Robert and Léonce to her sons and her father, gratifyingly absent themselves one after another, thereby initiating the rhythm of desire that constitutes the plot. The dinner party scene, the novel's most vivid depiction of sumptuous opulence, is crucially concluded with the "voices of Edna's disbanding guests," which "jarred like a discordant note upon the quiet harmony of the night" (626). So when critics note the "problem" of Edna's fickle moods, they miss the point: prior to the summer at Grande Isle, we presume, the emotionally somnolent Mrs. Pontellier likely had no moods at all.

Edna's physical intimacy with Arobin ("a flaming torch that kindled desire") is thus not unique but only the most complicating of "disturbances": "Edna cried a little that night after Arobin left her. It was only one phase of the multitudinous emotions which had assailed her" (617). The short chapter that follows this encounter amounts to an itemization of the feelings it catalyzed and the melodic lines that accompany them. The major or "vehement passions" (to borrow Philip Fisher's phrase) attendant on her action include "shock" and an "overwhelming feeling of irresponsibility" as she defies convention and her husband. This timpanic opening is followed by "a quicker, fiercer, more overpowering love" as Edna considers Robert's response to her action. The minor strain is "a dull pang of regret because it was not the kiss of love which

192 · "Mindless" Pleasure

had inflamed her" (618). These are precisely the plot lines that constitute the rest of the novel, as Edna concludes the "*'coup d'état'*" (619) against her husband by moving out of the house (irresponsibility, shock), playing the reviving prince to Robert's sleeping beauty (love), and sleeping with Arobin (passion, pang of regret).

Chopin explicitly reverses the "normal" course of events, in which music is understood to appeal first to the mind, producing an image, which is subsequently colored by emotion. Instead, what comes first is the tremor down the spinal column, the interior turmoil (the "swaying" and "lashing"), the wash of tears, and the convulsive squeezing of the hand. The visual sense, with its link to what James referred to as the brain's "cognitive and volitional performances," tends to mask the corporeal experience. Chopin's youthful effusions after hearing a famous violinist register this insight: "To describe the effect whis [*sic*] his music had upon me would be impossible. It seemed the very perfection of the art,—and while listening to him, I for the first time longed to be blind, that I might drink it all in undisturbed and undistracted by surrounding objects."[71]

Charles Darwin, in his book *The Expression of the Emotions in Man and Animals,* had earlier observed, "Most of our emotions are so closely connected with their expression that they hardly exist if the body remains passive" (237–238). What Darwin couched in somewhat cautious terms William James expressed more boldly in what came to be known as the James-Lange Theory of Emotion: "Our natural way of thinking about these standard emotions is that the mental perception of some fact excites the mental affection called the emotion, and that this latter state of mind gives rise to the bodily expression. My thesis on the contrary is that *the bodily changes follow directly the* PERCEPTION *of the exciting fact, and that our feeling of the same changes as they occur* IS *the emotion*" ("Emotion," 247). The distinction, for James, turns on the difference between cognition (understood as primarily an activity of the mind and aligned with the capacity to produce mental images) and feeling (which is concomitant with bodily changes and only later is expressed as the *idea* of longing and sadness). Most important, he argues for the temporal priority of feeling in the experience of an "exciting fact": "Without the bodily states following on the perception, the latter would be purely cognitive in form, pale, colourless, destitute of emotional warmth. We might then see the bear, and judge it best to run, receive the insult and deem it right to strike, but we could not actually *feel* afraid or angry" (248). Following James's assertion that one must "distinguish between the idea of an emotion and the emotion itself" (256), Kate Chopin portrays a woman who no longer pictures a conventional image of a feeling when she listens to music but rather experiences the emotion itself. "The entire difference," James concludes, "lies in the fact that the bodily sounding-board, vibrating in the one case, is in the other mute" (269).

The figure of "the bodily sounding-board" expresses the association between music and emotion that Kate Chopin pursues in her fiction. The contemporary neurologist Antonio Damasio describes emotions as "the continuous musical line of our minds, the unstoppable humming of the most universal of melodies that only dies down when we go to sleep, a humming that turns into all-out singing when we are occupied by joy, or a mournful requiem when sorrow takes over."[72] Upon meeting someone, Damasio points out, one attends to the person's movements, coloring, posture, and facial expression—those physical expressions that constitute the "background emotions" of the person: "If words do get uttered," Damasio writes, "you do not just listen to the words and picture their dictionary meanings, you listen to the music in the voice, to the prosody" (*Spinoza,* 43). In the words of the Schopenhauer scholar Bryan Magee, "wishes, emotions, feelings, decisions, thoughts, and so on" are crucially embodied processes: "not only are they always accompanied by microphysical changes—changes in our brains and our central nervous systems, and so on—but . . . they *are* those microphysical changes" (*Schopenhauer,* 13). As portrayed by Chopin and theorized by James, the neurologically networked body is analogous to the well-tempered plate of Ernst Chladni.

The Pleasures of "The Storm"

While the tone of moral outrage has largely vanished from critical analyses of Chopin's writings, the same cannot be said of scholarly work that treats "mind cure" or New Thought. Twentieth-century commentators have described this loosely knit set of beliefs with a truculence reminiscent of Ann Douglas's scathing critique of sentimentalism. Here is H. L. Mencken, writing in 1924: "What remains of Emerson . . . is . . . a debased Transcendentalism rolled into pills for fat women with vague pains and inattentive husbands—in brief, the New Thought—in brief, imbecility. This New Thought, a decadent end-product of American superficiality, now almost monopolizes him."[73] The historian Gail Thain Parker describes Mary Baker Eddy, the founder of Christian Science, in pejorative terms: "Unable to cope with her infant son, she left him to the care of a neighbor and sought to recapture her own infancy, ordering her father to build a large cradle and provide an attendant who would rock her on demand. . . . Mrs. Eddy . . . hoped never to leave the cradle, endlessly rocking" (116). More recently, William Leach in *Land of Desire* (1993) wrote that, at the turn of the century, "a cult of swamis began to attract hundreds of disaffected, affluent women" (230).

Parker's *Mind Cure in New England* (1973) was one of the first historical studies to document—and to take seriously—the tenets and influences of the loosely aligned persons, pamphlets, and practices consolidated by James under the rubric of "mind cure." In her introduction, Parker establishes the central problematic of her book, which is to try to explain James's "mistake" in seeing "consistencies in the mind cure ideology where there were only unresolved contradictions" (18). Though critical of what she saw as New Thought advocates' and Christian Scientists' "timidity and inarticulateness" (critical notions often lodged against the character of Edna Pontellier), Parker does herself imbibe some of the spirit of William James in acknowledging that "anyone who read their books attentively . . . in the end had a *genuine experience*—perhaps not a distinctively spiritual experience, but a real one nonetheless" (21; emphasis added). Her language to describe the nature of that "genuine experience" provides an important clue to reading Chopin:

> The publicists and practitioners of mind cure were testing their spontaneous powers of recovery by seeing how it might feel to float in mother seas. And, in the end, they were invigorated not by their moral holidays so much as by the fact that they found themselves eager to get back to work. What seems timidity and philosophical confusion to us was health to their bones. They had immersed themselves in the fatal element, had let go for long minutes at a time, and had then returned to the business of living. (19–20)

The "business of living" is almost precisely the focus of "occupational therapy," which was first developed by the Johns Hopkins psychiatrist Adolf Meyer. Human beings tend, Meyer noted, to have "dreams of timeless eternity," but he insisted that individuals cultivate an "equally religious valuation of *actual time* and its meaning in wholesome rhythms": this would constitute "awakening" to the tangible fruits of *work and occupation,*" all that is accomplished "between eating, drinking, . . . and the flights of fancy and aspiration."[74] Combining Parker's comment with Meyer's, we can of course recognize the experience of Edna Pontellier, who indeed dreams of timeless eternity and tests out how it feels to float in mother seas. The question then is, in *The Awakening*'s notorious last chapter, why doesn't Chopin see to it that her heroine is "returned to the business of living"?

A cultural analysis might lead us to conclude that a pampered rich woman during Chopin's time had no "work and occupation" to return to. Yet Chopin's own rich and varied life militates against this conclusion, as does the fact that, within the novel, Edna is beginning to sell her paintings. A feminist analysis might instead read the final pages of the novel as Edna's suicide, the final act of resistance of a Sick Soul. In Schopenhauer's terms: "The suicide wills life, and is dissatisfied merely with the conditions on which it has come to him. Therefore *he gives up by no means the will-to-live, but merely life*" (398; emphasis added). This sounds as persuasive a gloss as any on Edna's enigmatic refrain to Adele Ratignolle: "'I would give up the unessential; I would give my money, I would give my life for my children; but I wouldn't give myself'" (575). Yet the notion that Edna is acting on a calculated plan—"the will's strong affirmation" (398) as Schopenhauer puts it—is in fact explicitly disallowed by the narrative: Edna is precisely "not thinking of these things [her dissatisfactions] when she walked down to the beach" (654).

Moreover, not all Sick Souls commit suicide, despite the "logic" of the outcome. William James, commenting on Schopenhauer's influence on Leo Tolstoy, notes that an "absolute disenchantment with ordinary life" leads the Sick Soul to view "the whole range of habitual values" as a "ghastly . . . mockery": "Suicide was naturally the consistent course dictated by the logical intellect" (*Varieties*, 135). This is precisely what the "logical intellects" of most readers indeed "dictate" with respect to Chopin's text: that "suicide was naturally the consistent course." Yet the narrative, tellingly, neither mentions nor depicts suicide; and much earlier in the narrative, when Edna (then a novice swimmer) strayed from shore and experienced a "quick vision of death," she nonetheless "managed to regain the land" (552). In terms of precedent, Tolstoy himself was a Sick Soul who experienced a "second birth": after a "blood-freezing, heart-palsying sensation," the Russian writer went through a "deliverance," revealing (James writes) that a "man must die to an unreal life before he can be born into the real life" (*Varieties,* 142, 139, 141–142). In this statement is a clue: Adolf Meyer insists that a "regime of *pleasurable ease,*" while it may begin with the rhythms of "hunger and its gratification" had another crucial dyad: "Performance and completion form also the backbone and essence of what Pierre Janet has so well described as the *'fonction du real'*—the *realization* of reality, bringing the very soul of man out of dreams of eternity to the full sense and appreciation of actuality."[75] These comments provide a framework for thinking about the end of Chopin's novel in terms of "completion": of "deliverance" to an "appreciation of actuality."

Reading *The Awakening* in the larger context of nineteenth-century discussions about the capacity for music both to enlist and express a range of human feelings helps to situate the novel's ending not in logical or indeed psychological terms but in formal and affective ones. Bryan Magee, writing of Schopenhauer's influence on Richard Wagner, argues that "Wagner came to regard himself as doing *in concreto* what Schopenhauer as a philosopher was doing *in abstracto*" (350). Thus Wagner's opera *Tristan and Isolde* was not so much a love story as the formal expression of the operations of desire. Magee argues that "throughout the work the perpetual longing of the ear for the resolution of dischord is at every moment partially satisfied and partially not" (355). In *The Awakening,* this experience is surely indexed by the character of Edna who, listening to Mademoiselle Reisz play "the quivering love-notes of Isolde's song," felt the music as it "grew strange and fantastic—turbulent, insistent, plaintive and soft with entreaty," an experience that leaves her sobbing (594). It is this sort of experience, Magee asserts, that attunes one to the fact that "existence is an inherently unsatisfiable web of longings, willings and strivings from which the only permanent liberation is the cessation of being" (355).

This is of course Chopin's point when she writes that Edna "had said over and over to herself: 'To-day it is Arobin; to-morrow it will be some one else'" (653). The repetition—that she "had said over and over"—is crucial; it is less an affirmation of an idea than a refrain, a mantra. In the novel's final scene, as a naked Edna approaches the water and begins to swim, the text emphasizes repetition: she had been here before ("she remembered the night she swam far out"), and now "she went on and on. . . . She . . . went on and on" (654). What Magee referred to as a "permanent liberation" is, in the case of Edna Pontellier, less a suicide than a "cessation of being." The novel's end marks not a mimetic death but a formal "stopping point," to use a term from Henry James's preface to *Roderick Hudson*: the fate of any character in a novel when the last page is turned.

The reader, by contrast, lives on, tingling from the aftereffects of a lyrical novel, puzzling over an ending that is thematically enigmatic yet formally exquisite, pulling together as it does all of the novel's threads: its images (the birds, the water, the nakedness), its characters (each central figure is named in the final pages), and its rhythms ("on and on," "whispering, clamoring, murmuring"). The reader, I submit, has had precisely the temporary respite of having been absorbed in the lyrical novel, the sort of "cessation of willing" or freedom from "the world of representation" that Schopenhauer believed listening to music could provide (and that suicide, he maintained, could *not*). To music, that most philosophically and spiritually rich of "mindless pleasures," Kate Chopin in *The Awakening* adds other delightfully rhythmical, corporeally poetic activities: walking, swimming, drinking, making love— and reading. The *"realization of reality"* (to quote Meyer and Janet), when it comes to works of realist fiction, transpires at the level of the reader.

Despite its relative brevity (*The Awakening* is usually printed at a scant 130 pages) and myriad pleasures, Chopin's readers were decidedly ambivalent about the temporary "liberation" it extended. The (continued) insistence on reading the ending as a suicide (on the part of both scholars and lay readers) indicates that the "logical intellect" wins out over other possible and more "healthy-minded" responses (*Varieties*, 143). Chopin's tale "The Storm," by contrast, written shortly after the controversial novel and unpublished before Chopin's death, might be read as a more successful companion to *The Awakening*—though technically it is a sequel to Chopin's short story "At the 'Cadian Ball." In "The Storm," two former lovers, now married to other people, are suddenly thrown together, alone, in the woman's house while a storm rages outside. Calixta and Alcée both remember the moment in their past when "he had kissed her and kissed her and kissed her" (*Complete*, 929)—an echo of Edna's solitary swim "on and on . . . on and on" (654). This time, as thunder crashes outside, "he possessed her," and "they seemed to swoon together at the very borderland of life's mystery" (929). Chopin describes the two lovers' postcoital rhythms in language that could equally describe the corporeal harmony of a mother rocking her child: "He stayed cushioned upon her, breathless, dazed, enervated, with his heart beating like a hammer upon her. With one hand she clasped his head, her lips lightly touching his forehead. The other hand stroked with a soothing rhythm his muscular shoulders" (929). In contrast to *The Awakening*, in "The Storm" Chopin also depicts Alcée's departure and with it, the passing of the turbulence (which was clearly both internal and external to the characters' bodies): "He turned and smiled at her with a beaming face; and she lifted her pretty chin in the air and laughed aloud" (929). The lovers had, to quote historian Gail Parker again, "let go for long minutes at a time, and had then returned to the business of living."

The pleasures of "The Storm," however, do not reside only in the couple's almost gleeful happiness following their temporary tryst. They also inhere in Chopin's comedic depiction of the reverberations of "the storm" within the married lives of the two couples. Rather than rending the fabric of the two marriages, the "temporary liberation" strengthens it, making for an ending that merges the potentially explosive disruption of expectations one associates with a good joke (or a violent storm) with the continuity demanded by comedic convention. For when Calixta's husband and child return home, expecting a scolding for mussing their clothes in the downpour, she "express[ed] nothing but satisfaction at their safe return . . . and when the three seated themselves at table they laughed much and so loud that anyone might have heard them as far away as Laballiére's" (930). As for the lover Alcée, he writes his vacationing wife and babies (stand-ins for Edna and her children) "a loving letter, full of tender solicitude. . . . Though he missed them, he was willing to bear the separation a while longer—realizing that their health and pleasure were the first things to be considered" (930). (One suddenly thinks of Léonce Pontellier's extended stays away from Edna in a new light.) Alcée's wife, "charmed upon receiving her husband's letter," enjoyed "the first free breath since her marriage," experiencing again "the pleasant liberty of her maiden days" (931). In the wife's demure delight, we receive a tiny glimpse of the point of view occupied by Edna throughout *The Awakening*. Far from feeling neglected or rejected, Alcée's young wife clearly nestles into the pleasures of a husband-free sojourn at the beach.

The final paragraph of the story draws together the various couplings and recouplings in a wonderful comedic line. The paragraph reads, in its entirety, "So the storm passed and every one was happy" (931). Knowing absolutely nothing about each other's deep intentions or for that matter their amorous activities, all the characters experience a renewed connection and reinvigorated capacity for the "business of living," predicated on the rather undisciplined and somewhat indiscriminate circulation of loving. Far from being antagonistic toward the form of marriage as such, Kate Chopin appears to have understood the need for a "storm" now and then precisely to counteract monotony and to open space for moments of domestic harmony. As a writer, she intimates that such commotion might be the province of art rather than (or, given the suggestive details of Chopin's biography, in addition to) other more risky satisfying interludes.[76]

If Harold Frederic dramatized the problem of the Sick Soul in *The Damnation of Theron Ware or Illumination*, Chopin sketched a (temporary) solution in her writing. As did practitioners of mind cure, Chopin sought a melodic mode of realization that could offer readerly transport, a close-to-home embodied vacation from the world of will and representation. In his *Land of Desire*, William Leach grumbles that "in mind cure, there was no darkness, no Melville or Hawthorne, no secrets, no sin or evil, nothing grim or untidy" (225). Indeed: in mind-cure, there were more women than men, more breathing than thinking, more practice than philosophizing—more Chopin than Hawthorne. William James, with his firsthand experience with the "anhedonia" of the Sick Soul, was perhaps uniquely situated to comment on the hazards attendant on the summary rejection of "mindless" pleasures.[77] James's response to moralistic critics of mind cure might be extended to more recent commentators:

> How far the mind cure movement is destined to extend its influence, or what intellectual modifications it may yet undergo, no one can foretell. It is essentially a religious movement, and to academically nurtured minds its utterances are tasteless and often grotesque enough. . . . Yet many of us are well aware of how much freer and abler our lives would be, were such important forms of energizing not sealed up by the critical atmosphere in which we have been reared. . . . One part of our mind dams up—even *damns* up!—the other parts. (*Varieties*, 99)

James, that is, sees the "academically nurtured mind" and its "critical atmosphere" as a potential curse, implicitly concurring with Annie Payson Call, who suggests, "So prone are mortals to their own damnation, it seems as though a devil's use were gone" (*Power,* 11). We certainly might escape "damnation" by suppressing or ignoring our affective responses to works of fiction, but we also risk—as Chopin, James, and others make explicit—forgoing the "illumination" such moments provide in sick-souled times.

CHAPTER SIX

Corporeal Wonder

The Occult Entrancements of
The Wings of the Dove

A person's psychic influence . . . will be tinged with the
quality of his ruling loves. He infects his patients with
his own habitual mental states. He impregnates the
subject with the sphere of his own life,—his modes of
thought and feeling.

—WALTER FELT EVANS, *MENTAL MEDICINE* (1873)

The last chapter examined the array of resonant activities that intro-
duced *The Awakening*'s protagonist—and Kate Chopin's readers—to
the corporeal rhythms of pleasure. Yet while Edna Pontellier plumbed
the dynamic possibilities of swimming, listening, eating, painting, and
loving, her husband Léonce took delight in *things:* "he greatly valued
his possessions, chiefly because they were his, and derived genuine pleasure from contemplating a painting, a statuette, a rare lace curtain—no
matter what—after he had bought it and placed it among his household
gods."[1] From a Marxist perspective, Léonce Pontellier is on the winning
side of commodity fetishism: the money he earns from his financial
transactions is materialized in the objects he purchases, which in turn reflect back to him his sense of himself. In a modern update on traditional
fetishistic practices, where sacred objects were understood to lodge different *loas,* or gods, Léonce's goods—his "household gods"—could be
said to accommodate his self. In caressing his objects (including his wife,
whom he viewed as "a valuable piece of personal property" [522]),
Léonce's "civilized" fetishism makes him feel connected with the world
around him even as he engages in the solitary satisfaction of auto-
arousal.

The collector Henry James portrays in *The Spoils of Poynton* (1897)
has things in common with Léonce Pontellier. Adela Gereth, also in possession of a house filled with beloved objects, has patiently composed
the estate at Poynton as "the record of a life."[2] But despite the apparent

similarity in their affection for their belongings, the approach of James's Mrs. Gereth crucially diverges from that of Mr. Pontellier; these differences, in fact, align her interest in things with Edna's rapturous response to music. As Chopin's narrator makes clear in a dry aside, Léonce's goods take value from their fungibility: he is equally aroused by a window curtain or a work of art—"no matter what"—as long as he purchased it. Léonce's "record of a life," it seems, might as easily be written in the form of double-entry bookkeeping. Mrs. Gereth's, by contrast, "was written in great syllables of color and form, the tongues of other countries and the hands of rare artists" (18–19). Though Adela Gereth's "taste was her life," this did not signify a diminishment: her "life was somehow the larger for it" (20). And while James's devoted collector acknowledged (as does any wise mother with a marriageable son) that *she* might be replaceable—"'*You* would replace me,'" she whispered to the sensitive young woman she wishes to inherit Poynton—the things in the house, which she "had cared for . . . as a happy whole" (57), were not. Divorced from a mercantile sensibility, Mrs. Gereth's collection at Poynton constituted not an investment but an experience: Bill Brown has aptly observed that "the 'things' at Poynton are not so much objects as they are congealed actions, passionate acts of seeking, selecting, and situating."[3] In the words of James's narrator, "the beauty of the place throbbed out like music" (21)—and, in contrast to Léonce's solipsistic throbs, the experience of Poynton was not limited to its owner's pleasure. This expansive and sharable experience is testified to by the sensitive visitor who bursts into appreciative tears upon entering the house. Poynton, in short, conforms to John Dewey's imperative for aesthetic works, that the "*material* out of which a work of art is composed belongs to the common world rather than to the self."[4]

The divergent approaches to household aesthetics, as exemplified in the figures of Chopin's Mr. Pontellier and James's Mrs. Gereth, help to situate a central concern of this chapter: what, precisely, is the relationship of the self to emotionally resonant things in the world? Is one diminished by one's association with objects, as it appears with fetishistic Léonce, whose identity is lodged in his stuff like a genie squeezed into a bottle? Or is one expanded, as with Mrs. Gereth, whose feelings are embodied in her things and yet somehow broadcast through the experiences of those who also appreciate them? This inquiry, insofar as it is focused on the work of Henry James, might seem somewhat rarified, likely centered on hushed drawing rooms and musty museums. There is an element of truth to this: James's great novel *The Wings of the Dove* takes place inside refined interiors, within cities that loom large in the European cultural imagination. Yet I wish to argue that James's literary practice recovers experiences that are more elemental, even primal, within spaces that are almost parodically "civilized." John Dewey argued in *Art as Experience* (1934) that in order to "grasp the sources of esthetic experience it is . . . necessary to have recourse to animal life below the human scale" (18). In the vigilant attentiveness of unschooled creatures—not just animals, but also Americans—one can discern "active and alert commerce with the world" and become aware of the "complete interpenetration of self and the world of objects and events" (19).

To begin to elaborate these more elemental aspects of aesthetic experience, this chapter examines what William James called the "unclassified residuum" of modern culture: practices such as trance, hypnosis, fetish worship, shamanistic rituals, and voodoo.[5] As Dewey put it, "Art throws off the covers that hide the expressiveness of things; it quickens us from the slackness of routine and enables us to forget ourselves by finding ourselves in the delight of experiencing the world about us in its varied qualities and forms" (104). When it comes to aesthetic experience, there are deep affective continuities that belie the distinction of "primitive" and "civilized": all human beings have the capacity, Dewey suggests, to become rapt in wondering attention at the marvels of the world. Elaine Scarry in *The Body in Pain* (1985) alerts us to this commonality, elegantly observing that "poets and ancient dreamers" share a commitment to "project[ing] their own aliveness onto nonalive things," suggesting "that *it is* the basic work of creation to bring about this very projection of aliveness."[6] Howard Kerr's wide-ranging cultural study of the influence of spiritualism in the nineteenth century provides a literary-historical precedent for an inquiry into the kinship between certain "occult" (and occulted) practices and spheres of "civilized" appreciation.[7] More recently, Pamela Thurschwell has investigated the links between magical thinking, new technologies such as the telegraph, and the power of human consciousness in the work of James and British writers of the period. Her study, *Literature, Technology, and Magical Thinking, 1880–1920* (2001), establishes that certain realms of belief and experience—what modern culture might disparage as "occult"—were a matter of serious inquiry at the turn of the century, not just a source of metaphors for the operations of mind.[8] Susan Gillman's book *Blood Talk: American Race Melodrama and the Culture of the Occult* (2003) persuasively examines how *"oc-cultist"* conceptions of consciousness in the late nineteenth century fertilized a quasi-mystical understanding of racial identity—though her study treats only William, and not Henry, James.[9]

While a few critics have begun to think through the links between Henry James and magical thinking, other recent accounts of James—one biographical, one novelistic—make the connection in a stranger, more encrypted fashion. One such example is Lyndall Gordon's biography, *A Private Life of Henry James: Two Women and His Art* (1998). Gordon begins her account with what she terms "A Biographic Mystery" but which she casts as the fishy actions of a fetishist:

> In April 1894, a middle-aged gentleman, bearing a load of dresses, was rowed to the deepest part of the Venetian lagoon. A strange scene followed: he began to drown the dresses, one by one. There were a good many, well-made, tasteful, and all dark, suggesting a lady of quiet habits and some reserve. The gondolier's pole would have been useful for pushing them under the still water. But the dresses refused to drown. One by one they rose to the surface, their busts and sleeves swelling like black balloons. Purposefully, the gentleman pushed them under, but silent, reproachful, they rose before his eyes.[10]

The dresses, we learn, had belonged to the author Constance Fenimore Woolson, a good friend of Henry James; the gentleman was James himself. Gordon begins her biography of James with this tale not just for its sensationalistic possibilities but also to advance an argument about the occult relationship among people and things in James's life and in his writing.

One could certainly interpret James's gondola ride, and his disposal of Woolson's clothes, as the action of a grieving friend. Gordon, instead, uses the scene to establish a metonymic logic: James's attempt to submerge the dresses, Gordon insinuates, entailed the substitution of inanimate objects for the woman herself, who three months earlier had plunged to her death from her window. Gordon's biography suggests that this sort of fetishism was a persistent, even defining habit of Henry James. Not only, in Gordon's terms, did he "drown" the dresses; the biographer also discerns ominous significance in the novelist's actions toward objects associated with his beloved yet short-lived cousin Minny Temple, whose picture he kept in a drawer and whose letters he later burned. Again, casting what might be seen as understandable (if somewhat deplorable, in the case of the letters) behavior—preserving the image of a loved one, protecting the privacy of one's relationship—as nefarious acts of eradication, Gordon argues that James was a "destroyer" who "was fading out the ghostly companions of his art" (8).

Strange as Gordon's case appears, she is not alone in attributing to Henry James occult thinking (or even occult practices). Of James's postmortem connection to his young cousin, Colm Tóibín in his novel *The Master* (2004) writes, "It was not true to say that Minny Temple haunted him in the years that followed [her death]; rather, he haunted her. He conjured up her presence everywhere. . . . He wondered . . . if Hawthorne or George Eliot had written to make the dead come back to life, had worked all day and all night, like a magician or an alchemist, defying fate and time and all the implacable elements to re-create a sacred life."[11] Tóibín, in casting "The Master" as a sort of literary shaman, conceives of James's "alchemy" in a more positive light than does Gordon. Yet Tóibín's depiction of James's manipulation of the memory of Woolson, as well as her personal effects, echoes the vaguely necrophiliac overtones of Gordon's indignation at James's "possession" of the dead women's things. Tóibín, describing James's preparations to leave for Venice after receiving word of Woolson's death, writes, "She came to him forcefully, palpably, in the days before he traveled. The woman he had kept at arm's length was replaced by a woman of possibilities, a phantom he dreamed about" (242). Tóibín also dwells, in an extended scene, on the Venetian gondola ride to dispose of Woolson's wardrobe: "The smell had brought her so close to him [James] that he would not have been surprised if, at that moment, he had found her standing in the bare room. He almost felt free to speak to her, and . . . he sensed that she was there, an *absolute presence*" (253; emphasis added). In *The Master,* the gondolier, after first blessing himself, sinks the garments. Tóibín portrays James as too squeamish: "They might as well have been carrying her body, he thought, to lift her and drop her from the boat" (254).

Why do both chroniclers pay such weird attention to the actions of an aging, grieving man? On its face, Gordon's biography seems to possess an unremarkable thesis: that James was a man with peculiar habits, and that two important women in his life influenced and inspired his fiction. Gordon is by no means the first to point out James's eccentricities, or to note that the personal qualities of Temple and Woolson may be glimpsed in his great female portraits: Isabel Archer, Maria Gostrey, May Bartram, Milly Theale. It is an old conceit that artists confer a form of immortality on their muses through their work (the aphorism

Ars longa, vita brevis is here suggestive). Even Gordon's notion that James was at times an ambiguous friend to these women, if friend at all, has been treated by earlier commentators such as Leon Edel and Richard Poirier.[12] One critic has written at length on what he terms the "emotional cannibalism" in James's fiction, and this would seem to be a governing trope in Gordon's assessment of James's relationship to these women in his life.[13]

What raises the stakes of Gordon's otherwise conventional claim is her sense that James, far from a benevolent admirer, was in some way responsible for the deaths of Temple and Woolson: "Feeling, breathing women who provided the original *matter* for Milly and Miss Gostrey were disappointed in untold ways not unconnected with their deaths" (328; emphasis added). In employing the term "matter" rather than "material," Gordon suggests that these fictions came at the corporeal expense of the persons on whom they were modeled. The significance with which the biographer treats these events—such as her notion that James "drowned" Woolson's dresses—obeys the metonymic logic of fetishism, in which an object is understood to house, rather than merely refer to or represent, a thing (or in this case, a person). At the time that James was writing, Freud had not yet elaborated his theory of the fetish; fetishism was, however, an active concept in anthropology and associated with non-European religious practices.[14] W. B. Seabrook, writing of Haitian voodoo rituals early in the twentieth century, described the operation of the fetish in these terms: "Articles intimately connected with the individual to be affected, a part of his own body such as hair or nail-paring if it can be procured, or a piece of clothing saturated with his perspiration or grease, are used variously as a substitution for himself."[15] Such practices, Seabrook reports, pertained not just to matters religious but also influenced Haiti's penal code, which in the nineteenth century had prohibitions against murder by charms and fetishes as well as by more conventional means.[16]

Gordon in her biography suggests that James's renderings of the lives of these two women were also obliquely homicidal. Of Minny Temple Gordon writes, "In some way her death and his act of writing were linked, as though her vitality had passed to him" (124). What Elaine Scarry suggests is part of the creative act—"to bring about this projection of aliveness"—in Gordon's hands takes on alchemical overtones when she asserts that "a writer will transmute actuality into something else" (126). Gordon implies that this "something else," the aesthetic object, contains or even *replaces* the referent. What fiction took away, Gordon indicates, biography might restore: "It is on behalf of these women that biography must redress the record James controlled" (328). Laying siege to the citadel of James's oeuvre, Gordon intends "to draw out these two women on their own terms" (5), even to "bring her back from the dead" (354). Gordon in fact speaks of her own feelings for Henry James in mediumistic terms: "Women were drawn to him— Minny and Fenimore were not alone. I feel this attraction a century on. . . . A century on, it is easy to meet James, easy to enjoy his extraordinary intimacy with our far-out selves" (363). Gordon concludes her book with an oracular pronouncement, "But see, they return, and bring him with them" (372).

I focus on these details from *A Private Life of Henry James* at some length because the theory of language implicit in Gordon's account is precisely that of a small but influential strain of current trauma theory. Traumatic stress has in recent years received much needed attention by therapists, physicians, and psychologists, such as Judith Herman and Bessel van der Kolk, committed to meliorating the suffering it instills.[17] Likewise, historians such as Alan Young and Mark Micale have sought to understand the emergence of trauma as an important therapeutic concept in the nineteenth and twentieth centuries.[18] The strain I refer to here consists primarily of critical theorists, who draw parallels between a certain conception of trauma and a poststructuralist theory of language. Drawing on the linguistic theories of Jacques Lacan and Paul deMan, the literary critic Cathy Caruth has argued that trauma enacts a "confrontation with death"; as such, the traumatic event resists representation and is "passed on" in a "revelationlike" manner conceived as unmediated and direct: "What is passed on, finally, is not the meaning of the words but their performance."[19] This notion is affirmed by Colm Tóibín, who describes the Woolson of James's memory as an "absolute presence" (253). It is, as the historian of trauma Ruth Leys has commented in *Trauma: A Genealogy*, "as if the ghosts of the past could speak to those living in the present, contagiously contaminating them in turn."[20]

Ann Cvetkovich, who approaches trauma through the lens of affect theory, has aptly noted that Caruth's conception of "unclaimed experience" is itself "quite portable," "circulat[ing] within a milieu that includes work by Geoffrey Hartman, Dominick LaCapra, Shoshana Felman, and Dori Laub."[21] In *An Archive of Feeling* (2003), Cvetkovich distinguishes her work from Caruth's, with its emphasis on "questions of epistemology"

(19) and "trauma's paradoxes" (18): by contrast, Cvetkovich is "compelled by historical understandings of trauma as a way of describing how we live, and especially how we live affectively" (19). Through a reading of James's novel *The Wings of the Dove,* this chapter also inquires into the limitations of Caruth's strain of trauma theory. In terms similar to Cvetkovich, I examine how, if one has no account of the full-bodied, affective experience prompted by resonant objects, their corporeal enlistments, unsubsumable to our conventional ideas about how cognition and representation work, can begin to look like trauma. The inability to speak cogently about human beings' profound bodily responses to memories and to representations leads, I argue, to the strangeness of Lyndall Gordon's implicit thesis, that representations possess the occult power to kill the living or reanimate the dead. Yet, as we shall see, Gordon's formulation points to its own solution: subtended by a Caruthian account of trauma, her biography provides a twisted but revealing assessment of Henry James's own sense of the potency of aesthetic objects, in particular their capacity to engage us not just mentally but also on and through the physical body. As extensions of human passion and sentience, works of literature do, James affirmed, provide experiences that both embody and stimulate our capacity for wonder.

For James, certain resonant experiences (not limited to the arts) are world-transforming; as John Dewey has noted, "The painter and poet like the scientific inquirer know the delights of discovery" (*Art,* 139). The affective concomitant to discovery, Philip Fisher has urged, is wonder: the first among the passions for René Descartes, wonder "amounts to the energy by which we are interested in something new and attentive to it. Not to feel this pleasurable interest is not to be aware of something as new or surprising . . . since wonder is the means by which we single out, so to speak, the figure from the ground. Without wonder and attention, we have neither figure nor ground."[22] Attentiveness to strangeness consolidates the first motion of wonder; the second inheres in the process by which the extraordinary is absorbed by the wondering mind. James's focus was on precisely this: the affective transit by which things apparently exterior to the self are moved inward, assimilated to one's psychophysical architecture, repositioning one with respect to the world. This process does not, however, amount to a form of possession, as imagined by Gordon or Caruth. What for James existed at the occulted center of experience were not ghostly presences but a zone of human feeling that calibrated one to the richness of one's surroundings. Most vivid and distilled in relation to aesthetic objects, this receptiveness has appeared under different rubrics: in literary studies as "sympathy" and "identification," in anthropology as "trance," in psychology as "transference," and in biomedicine as "the placebo effect." The notion that special occurrences or objects might enlist the deepest human capacities for feeling and belief has of course deep religious roots, and this is not to suggest that religion (in its many forms, and as practiced in American, Haitian, and other cultures) was supplanted by these new fields. Rather, I am interested in how a range of disciplines were, by the end of the nineteenth century, supplementing religion's preeminence to claim wondrous phenomena as its own.

The argument of this chapter proceeds in five sections. The first analyzes how Henry James in *The Wings of the Dove* (1902) links words and violence in gestures that insist on the body's permeability to the thoughts and images of others.[23] It is not just Milly Theale's stunning wealth but her wonderful receptiveness that makes her the "mark" of an intriguing pair of lovers and the poor but titled Englishman Lord Mark. The second section situates ethnographical accounts of voodoo rituals, contemporary with James's writing, within a longer history of suggestion. Beginning with Franz Anton Mesmer, who provided a materialist explanation for miraculous cures, and proceeding through Sigmund Freud, this section focuses on the central problematic of the mind's relationship to the physical body. The third section turns to William James's investigations into psychical research, the nether zone of nineteenth-century materialism. In his work with the Boston medium Leonora Piper, James troubled a positivistic insistence on objectivity—and its concomitant, the dualistic distinction between products of the imagination and the material of the world—when he explored how affective attunement was essential to the manifestation of spiritual presences. We return to Henry James in the fourth section, which explores how in *The Wings of the Dove* he created not only a "new *genre littéraire*"[24] (William's comment) but also an account of the centrality of affect to consciousness alternate to that of Freud.

In the chapter's fifth and final section, I conclude that the wonder enlisted by aesthetic objects, most fully theorized and practiced by Henry James in his late novels and prefaces, points us toward a recognition: that a crucial filament of the emotive—William James's "unclassified Residuum"[25]—is woven into the very fabric of post-nineteenth-century materialism. The Jamesian power of the feeling mind in constituting the very matter of experience threads its way into such stubbornly positivistic fields as physiology, via the early works of the scientist Walter Cannon; as well as into a poststructuralist strain of trauma theory. Moreover, elucidating this historical and conceptual story helps to illuminate how, in literary study, the compulsion to avoid the Affective Fallacy has led some theorists to repudiate the importance of feeling while nonetheless importing it "through the back door," as it were. We can discern this importation in the implicit logic—which Lyndall Gordon makes weirdly but helpfully visible—that objects might house persons, like the "household gods" of Léonce Pontellier. The chapter concludes with a reading of Cathy Caruth's particular form of trauma theory, which echoes Gordon's sense that a mediumistic biographer/theorist might provide not just moving stories but, to again borrow Tóibín's phrase, "absolute presence[s]" (253). Acknowledging, along with Henry James (and Elaine Scarry's "ancient dreamers"), that resonant aesthetic objects are meaningful extensions of the human life of feeling may give us a way to talk about their "haunting" qualities without recourse to the occult (and frankly mistaken) notion that they encrypt actual persons.

Charming Milly

The physiologist Théodule Ribot, writing of "the religious sentiment," notes that "the history of ritual is a chapter of the expression of the emotions."[26] He goes on to qualify this assertion: "The only difference is this: emotional expression, in the sense given to the words by . . . Darwin . . . and the world in general, has an individualist character, showing fear, anger, love, etc.; while ritual expression has a *social* character; being the spontaneous product of a collectivity, of a group" (321). In its earliest forms, Ribot writes, ritual is "the *immediate and direct* expression of the religious sentiment" (321), often involving some sort of sacrifice; only later, when "we have the passage from the literal to the figurative; [does] ritual becomes *symbolism*" (322). The trace of the anthropological move away from literal to symbolic sacrifice, according to Ribot, remains active in the form of "metaphor in spoken language. Thus the offering of a lock of hair, or a figure made of dough, becomes a substitute for human sacrifice" (322). In its final stage, the religious sentiment is expressed in "rites which are simply survivals, analogous to a frown when we are perplexed, vestiges of certain ways of feeling and acting which have been, but have long ago disappeared" (322). Ribot's Darwin-inspired reflections on the evolutionary link between emotion and religious ritual, and between the literal and the metaphorical, offer a framework for considering Henry James's late-career novel *The Wings of the Dove*.

Millicent Bell provides a concise and apt directive for thinking about the religious images that cluster around Milly Theale: "there is no need to see allegory in the novel."[27] Despite all the seemingly metaphorical talk of sacrifice in James's novel, the telos of the plot leads inexorably toward what looks suspiciously like an actual human sacrifice. James's novel is not a murder mystery: the question is never *whether* Milly Theale, the incandescent American heiress, will be killed. "'What sort of a use for me is it,'" the young woman inquires of Lord Mark, "'. . . to kill me?'" (269). The lingering uncertainties are merely those of time, place, and person, which the implicated characters spend an inordinate amount of time discussing: "'Do you mean we should kill you in England?'" (269) Lord Mark inquires directly. Equally blunt, the plotting Kate Croy queries her lover Merton Densher, "'Do you want to kill her?'" (293). Densher, in turn, realizes, "It was in the cards for him that he might kill her" (321). The deed is finally done by proxy. Lord Mark pays the young heiress a visit in Venice, and "it was what then took place that simply killed her" (357): ostensibly, Mark told Milly of the lovers' plot to have Densher marry her for her money and, after her death, wed the impoverished Kate. But, as the crucial term "simply" indicates, Densher for one does not confuse the proximate or "simple" cause of her death with the efficient cause.

What, one might ask, actually *does* kill Milly Theale? Though the novel bristles with explicit death threats and admissions of guilt, critics usually focus on Milly's nebulous illness. Perhaps most refreshing in this regard is F. O. Matthiessen, who complained of James's "tedious mystification" and gives a summary diagnosis: "as Milly behaves, she can hardly be dying of anything except tuberculosis, as Minnie Temple died."[28] Even James in his notebooks refers to Milly's illness in dismissive-seeming terms: "Isn't perhaps something to be made of the idea . . . of some young creature . . . who, at 20, on the threshold of a life that has seemed boundless, is suddenly condemned to death (by consumption, heart-disease, or whatever) by the voice of the physician?"[29] I would like to propose, however, that while James initially conceived for *The Wings of the Dove* an unproblematic melodramatic scenario (doctor informs rich beautiful patient of hitherto unknown mortal illness), what finally occupied his attention was the idea literally suggested by the notebook entry: that a person might be "condemned to death" purely "by the voice" of another. In the novel, that is, a psychologically coherent narrative, in which two lovers conspire to benefit from the trust and generosity of a dying heiress, is supplanted by a plotline that troubles realistic conventions of cause and effect. In this new plot, Milly's eventual death appears to be the product of, rather than the enabling condition for, the couple's perfidy.

On its surface, this latter account, with its hints of romance, appears uncontroversial. Numerous readers have concluded that Milly's illness is a metaphor, and that she actually dies of a broken heart in her Venetian palace, melodramatically killed by the knowledge that the man she loves is engaged to her best friend.[30] But thirty years after the death of Minny Temple, James in *The Wings of the Dove* is at pains to forestall this reading, which he disparages in the novel as a "fool's paradise, from which the specified had been chased like a dangerous animal" (347). What better way to discredit the romantic vision than to place these sanitizing words in the mouth of the compromised Kate Croy: "'She won't smell, as it were, of drugs. She won't taste, as it were, of medicine'" (215)? When he wrote the novel, James was no stranger to physical suffering. Close to his sister Alice in England, Henry was a crucial presence during her final illness, as he watched breast cancer reduce her to "a mere anatomy." Alice James in her journal, punning on "Henry the patient," wrote of her brother, "He comes at my slightest sign and hangs on to whatever organ may be in eruption and gives me calm and solace by assuring me that my nerves are his nerves and my stomach is his stomach."[31] When, after Alice died, William telegraphed Henry from the United States to caution that her apparent demise might be a "trance-trick," Henry responded dryly, "You wouldn't have thought your warning necessary if you had been with us."[32] Plagued with gout and intestinal troubles for many years, Henry consulted with the most important medical lights of his time, from Johns Hopkins's William Osler to the eminent neurologist Sir Henry Head in England. Henry and William James corresponded about their most intimate physical disabilities, and the often diffident older brother once wrote, "I blush to say that detailed bulletins of your bowels, stomach & back are of the most enthralling interest to me"; he also urged Henry to try localized shock therapy to cure his constipation.[33] Like William, Henry James was aware of the methods of mind-cure practitioners, having witnessed the soothing effects of hypnotism in easing his dying sister's anguish and sleeplessness.

Writing of Milly Theale, then, James prods the reader to realize the brute facts of human decay. This knowledge is registered not as Milly's own suffering but through the affective responses of those around her. In the case of Merton Densher, "the facts of physical suffering of incurable pain, of the chance grimly narrowed, had been made, at a stroke, intense, and this was to be the way he was now to feel them" (347). Densher's perception of his own role in the girl's pain—like so many intensely felt visions in James's most linguistically violent novel—is received as "the touch of the lash" (339) and then "cut[s] like a knife" (349). James's writing exemplifies a point made by the anthropologist Catherine Lutz, that "emotion words have force. . . . To speak of one's feelings of 'compassion,' for example, is to attempt to portray an event as having an actor who is suffering rather than comfortable, and perhaps to suggest that actions ought to be taken to alleviate that condition. It is to attempt to characterize and *to move events,* not merely or even mainly to map them."[34] Not isolated to the interiors of individual bodies, emotions involve events that enter language and are negotiated in the social world of relations.

Moreover, the idea that linguistic figures had corporeal concomitants, propagated by Théodule Ribot and Henry James, also occupied the young Sigmund Freud. In *Studies on Hysteria,* published a few years before James's novel, Freud inquired,

> How has it come that we speak of someone who has been slighted as being "stabbed to the heart" unless the slight had in fact been accompanied by a precordial sensation . . . ? . . . These [originally intense physical sensations] may now for the most part have become so much weakened that the expression of them in words seems to us only to be a figurative picture of them, whereas in all probability the description was once meant literally.[35]

As Freud describes it, the distinction between the figurative and the literal is commensurate to the divide between the linguistic and the corporeal. Obscured in modern usage, Freud suggests, this lost connection reasserts itself in indigenous cultures (and, in pathological form, in the expressive symptomology of the hysteric).

Freud, in fact, was elaborating an idea developed by Charles Darwin, in *The Expression of the Emotions in Man and Animals* (1872). Darwin discerned that the expression of strong emotions in human beings across cultures involved not just the face but the entire body, especially respiration, cardiac activity, muscle tension, and visceral movements. Emotions, Darwin argued, were crucially both actions and the preparation for action. A "man with his back up," he noted, resembles the physical presence of an angry cat whose body is poised to lash out at the object of its ire; while someone "fuming with anger" is often engaged in short, violent respirations that are the body's preparation for a fight.[36] "Most of our emotions," Darwin concluded, "are so closely connected with their expression that they hardly exist if the body remains passive—the nature of the expression depending in chief part on the nature of the actions which have been habitually performed under this particular state of mind" (237–238). For Darwin, the link between the metaphor (e.g. fuming with anger) and the literal (hyperventilation) was not merely analogical or linguistic but also evolutionary, with the body's emotional expressiveness providing the corporeal link between the two registers.

Milly Theale herself, at the outset, embodies the conceptual polarity evident in critical interpretations of novel: the more romantic version (Yeazell: she died of a broken heart) and the more positivistic one (Matthiessen: she died of TB). James renders Milly's romantic tendencies suspect by making her the parodic princess of a fairy tale. During her first dinner at Lancaster Gate, Milly herself adopts this perspective, casting Mrs. Stringham "in the character of a fairy godmother" who "had only to wave a neat little wand for the fairy-tale to begin at once" (97). Milly, having descended from the timeless ether of the possible (figured by her trip up an Alpine slope, and fueled by her inexhaustible wealth), lights on the intermediate realm of the romance. Yet she also craves the firm turf of actual lived experience, and she is determined to wrest from her physician Sir Luke Strett an unadulterated diagnosis: "'I like you to see me just as I am'" (148), she tells Sir Luke at her first appointment. In the course of the novel, imagination and diagnosis, or the flights of the mind and the knowledge of the body, come to be absolutely intertwined, rather than opposed, stances toward the world.[37]

When Milly arrives in England, "seeing things as they are" is for her an uncomplicated project. James offers her as a strikingly pared-down figure, disburdened of family ties (her relations have all died, one by one), dislocated from any tangible home town, and set adrift on a tour of foreign lands. Her wealth not only provides the motivation for others' designs; it also unhinges Milly from the normal limitations of material life. "'I *don't* know where I am,'" she says repeatedly, ironically underscoring the detachment that is associated with the positivist ideal of objective vision. Milly enters the plot and the sphere of the indomitable Maud Lowder at the same moment, approaching the "florid, alien, exotic" (96) culture of Lancaster Gate with the discriminating eye of the anthropologist.

In a twist on the Jamesian tendency to cast Americans as naïve or primitive, James in this novel aligns English society and "some island of the south" (127): in Milly's and her chaperone Sally Stringham's European tour, which James terms an "education in the occult" (76); in the formidable Aunt Maud, who "taboos" (125) Densher as an undesirable suitor for her niece; in Lord Mark's estate, "the court of a native ruler" (132), populated with "native princes"; and in Lord Mark himself, who reveals "the obscure depths of a society constituted from far back" by "showing [Milly] visions" (104). (The critic Quentin Anderson aptly refers to Matcham, Lord Mark's estate, as "the house of death.")[38] Densher picks up on this strain of imagery in his reaction to Maud Lowder's furniture: surprised that such "heavy horrors . . . could still flourish . . . in an age so proud of its short way with false gods," he nonetheless "felt it less easy to laugh at the heavy horrors than to quail before them" (63). Surrounded by the fetishized artifacts of English culture, Milly's detachment proves untenable; ripe with the imperative "truly to live," surprised and delighted by the exotic people, places, and objects she encounters, she becomes absorbed by what she observes, in the dual sense of *intrigued* and *digested* (Lord Mark, for one, gazes on her "[as] if she and her like were the chief of his diet" [101]). Further compromising her disconnection, Milly's great talent turns out to be her felt ability to perceive the world—and herself—through the eyes of those who surround her: "it was quite as if she saw in people's eyes the reflexion of her appearance and place" (153).

The visions, representations, and plots that circulate in the novel, in other words, do not stay safely external for Milly; they are instead figured as media in which she might float, swim, or drown. When Milly visits her doctor, "she was in fact launched in some current that would lose itself in the sea of science" (143); while Merton Densher, in conversation, "simply drenched [Milly] with his sociable story" (181). James's prose captures this effect of watery dissolve most vividly when he depicts Milly's experience of being in Maud Lowder's house. At first preoccupied by the weightiness of the things in the house—by "halls of armour, of pictures, of cabinets, of tapestry, of tea-tables" (130)—Milly recognizes that these particulars are suspended in a more capacious medium: "The largeness of style was the great containing vessel, while everything else . . . became but this or that element of the infusion" (130). Objects, that is, blur and become indistinct in the wash of Maud Lowder's controlling aesthetic.

The shift away from the solidity of objects to the solution of style is echoed by James's prose. His depiction of Milly's new environment touches only briefly on the concrete details of interior decorating—that mode that Frank Norris criticized as the drama of the broken teacup—and expands instead into a richly metaphorical depiction of Milly's suspension in the world of Lancaster Gate. Maud Lowder's social medium not only surrounds and buoys Milly up, it appears to condense into the stimulating drink she holds in her hands: "The elements melted together and seasoned the draught, the essence of which might have struck the girl as distilled into the small cup of iced coffee she had vaguely accepted from somebody, while a fuller flood somehow kept bearing her up" (130). In the course of the passage, the persons and objects of the household are distilled into the image of the magic potion, leaving Milly with the impression that she both ingests and floats in their society. She is "charmed" (132) by everyone and everything that surrounds her, but not in the sense of "pleased." The entire scene suggests that Milly, an American Alice in the wonderland of an exotic culture, is "charmed" in a more literal sense: entranced or subdued, as by magic or an occult power.

James's prose takes a metaphorical notion—that Milly was "awash in impressions"—and makes it weird, even hallucinogenic, by literalizing it. Milly, trance-like, appears to float in her own consciousness, then to imbibe of it. Marking the hypnotic nature of the scene, as well as suggesting that actual hypnosis or suggestion might be occurring, the following unattributed words urge Milly with incantatory insistence: "'You must stay among us—you must stay; anything else is impossible and ridiculous'" (131). An oblique reference, toward the end of the scene, suggests that not just these quoted words but everything that has transpired might be "part of Aunt Maud's own spiritual ebriety" (131). That is, not just the words that float with impersonal, coercive authority over the scene—"you must stay"—but the increasingly surreal perceptions attributed to Milly herself might have originated in Maud Lowder's own intoxicated sense of Milly's brilliant possibilities. Milly (and the reader) have been coaxed into mistaking the older woman's impressions for her own.

Not just anyone possesses the great talent of Maud Lowder (or *The Spoils of Poynton*'s Adela Gereth) for creating a compelling, even enrapturing environment: think of Léonce's tasteful yet ultimately banal home in *The Awakening*, a setting that fuels his wife's disaffection. Not everyone is a capable collector, especially not—as is Maud Lowder—of *persons*. She shrewdly lights on the possibilities of Milly Theale, despite her being accompanied by the inconsequential Sally Stringham, whose brief childhood friendship with the English dowager prompted the Americans' visit. Maud had expected the reunion to be tiresome and brief; but like all clever collectors, she has an eye for treasures tucked away next to dingy companions. Maud Lowder, in short, has the potency of style. William James, writing of possession in *The Principles of Psychology* (1890), mentions style as a critical element of the trance-like activity of automatic writing: "'It seems reasonable to me—upon the hypothesis that it is a person using another's mind or brain—that there must be more or less of that other's style or tone incorporated in the message.'"[39] Only a person with a forceful style can have such an influence; as Henry James's novels make clear, such talent is rare, especially in the American cultural landscape. No wonder, then, that the scene of virtual intoxication at Maud Lowder's house "served to Milly, then and afterwards, as a high-water mark of the imagination" (131). James is, of course, performing his own style in this passage, in which objects of the world are dissolved, reconstituted, and made strange by the power of a controlling narrative consciousness.

If Milly is "possessed" by the redoubtable Maud Lowder, who hopes to add her to her collection of rarities at Lancaster Gate, it is not simply in the debased sense: that position is occupied by Kate Croy, who as her father points out is an "'asset'" (29) to whoever is empowered to dispose of her. (In this sense, Kate is in a long line of Jamesian heroines, beginning with *Roderick Hudson*'s Christina Light, who is "caressed and manipulated" by her mother "as a sort of fetish.")[40] Milly, in the scene just discussed, is "possessed" by Maud Lowder in the mediumistic sense: Milly has entered into the temple of Mrs. Lowder's vision. The danger, of course, is that in the world of Maud Lowder, persons once entranced and rendered susceptible may also be reduced to possessions.

When Milly first visits Sir Luke Strett's doctor's office ("the brown old temple of truth" 149), possession is again the operative term, but with a twist. James distills their encounter to a mere ten minutes, giving the barest *form* of the diagnostic ritual between doctor and patient. Whereas Maud Lowder seeks additions to her exclusive circle, the physician appears to offer himself—or more precisely, their relation—as a prized addition to *Milly's* "whole collection" (143) of acquaintances. In contrast to Lancaster Gate's "heavy horrors," there is no description of Sir Luke's office, nor any dialogue between the two: the narrative simply traces Milly's impressions of the encounter. Instead of receiving a diagnosis or prescription, Milly finds herself in relation with the doctor, something that James renders as a precious object: "It was like an absolute possession, a new resource altogether, something done up in the softest silk and tucked away under the arm of memory. She hadn't had it when she went in, and she had it when she came out; she had it there under her cloak, but dissimulated, invisibly carried" (143). The "great, grave, charming man" (146) indeed charms Milly, in the sense of "equips her with a charm." Whereas her hostess had plied the young woman with a draught filled with her, Maud Lowder's, vision, Sir Luke's offering is an empty vessel: "so clean the great empty cup of attention he set between them on the table" (142).

Sir Luke, in other words, tenders a stance of ritualized openness, the doctor-patient relation in its purest form. (William James had written in 1864, "A doctor does more by the moral effect of his presence on the patient and family than anything else.")[41] After this content-free consultation, Milly is convinced that Sir Luke "had found out simply by his genius—and found out, she meant, literally everything" (145) about her condition. This *genius*, of course, is not of the Western medical mode; the word draws on other, primary meanings: "With reference to classic pagan belief: The tutelary god or attendant spirit allotted to every person at his birth, to govern his fortunes and determine his character, and finally to conduct him out of the world" *(Oxford English Dictionary)*. By outfitting his patient with the charm of his presence, and by allowing her to glimpse and feel on the right side of Medicine's ritualistic power over life and death, Sir Luke establishes himself as Milly's shaman.[42]

From Trance to Transference—and Back Again

Whence the power of the shaman? James wrote *The Wings of the Dove* at the turn of the nineteenth century, when Europeans' sensationalized and moralistic travel accounts of native cultures were beginning to give way to the nascent discipline of cultural anthropology. To an earlier set of jingoistic explorers, fetishistic practices exemplified a depraved otherness rather than a religious ritual: popular works such as Sir Spencer St. John's *Hayti: Or, the Black Republic* (1884) had claimed to document "a country in a state of rapid decadence" in which human sacrifice is rampant and "midwives [slay] children for the purpose of eating them."[43] St. John's offensive account rationalized healings and hexings as trickery and fraud, casting "the fetish sect of Vaudoux" (208) as primitive in the most pejorative of terms. W. B. Seabrook's book *The Magic Island* (1929), while still construing Haitian religious practices as "other," took a more anthropological approach. For Seabrook, the rituals he observed served as a reminder that, despite the disenchantments of modernity, there existed "another world invisible"—at least to European eyes—"a world of marvels, miracles, and wonders" (12).

St. John's and Seabrook's ways of thinking about the practices of another culture differed bluntly in tone. St. John detached the power of the Haitian shaman from any religious context and placed it within a secular political framework: "These people endure every possible oppression from the Papaloi . . . it may be inferred that they tolerate this conduct because they fear" (212). He portrayed Papaloi (and Mamaloi) as canny manipulators who used poisons and drugs to establish their social authority. A chapter ostensibly focused on religious rituals, pejoratively titled "Vaudoux Worship and Cannibalism," turns out to be devoted to legal cases brought against Papaloi for fraud and homicide. Seabrook, by contrast, gropes—albeit crudely—for terms to take seriously other systems of belief: "White men have died in London—and the records are in Scotland Yard—because some monk in the mountains of Thibet marked them to die, and sat droning in his far-off cell among the Himalayas. A subtle poison leaving no trace? Who knows? How can one be ever sure?" (49). Seabrook seeks to conceptualize Haitian religious practices in terms that are more sociological than theological, and he entertains the possibility that protective fetishes—or their opposite, "the black death-*ouanga*"—at once represent and compel the active consensus of the community. When residing in Haiti, Seabrook was offered a protective *ouanga,* of which he writes, "Had I not accepted it seriously I should have been wrong, for into its making went something more than aromatic leaves and powders; into it went also the imponderable will-to-protect of a community, so that whatever it was or was not magically, it not only deserved respect but had an actual potency-value as the sacred symbol and earnest of their protection" (49). In Seabrook's account, accepting the charm sealed a pact in which the people in the village affirmed their communal decision to safeguard its recipient. So while the source of the shaman's power is somewhat different as described by the indignant St. John and the proto-anthropological Seabrook—poisons and drugs versus the ability to direct communal goodwill—they describe the potency of voodoo rituals within a rationalist framework of material causes and effects. There are no *loas,* both imply, living in fetishes.

But Seabrook wishes, finally, to make a stronger claim (though one that is admittedly still Eurocentric) about the power of the fetish to protect the bearer: "There is a queer point involved here which I find difficulty in putting into words. It will doubtless seem to many readers superstitious when I aver that I actually believe the protective virtue would have been destroyed in this charm unless I myself had faith in it. . . . *I tell you my believing gave it power.* And connected with this truth are many deep collateral truths concerning the power of all magic, miracles, and prayer" (52, emphasis added). Here the efficacy of the fetish, a matter of neither *loas* nor communal goodwill, emanates instead from the authority attributed to it by the belief of the recipient. Seabrook credits his experience in Haiti with revealing a truth pertinent to all religions. The source of a fetish's potency is far from fictional: Seabrook argues that tapping into the internal energy of belief realizes the very state of affairs (such as protection) that a materialist account would say the fetish simply represented. In this, Seabrook refers to a special category of fact that William James outlined in his essay "The Will to Believe": that sort *"where faith in a fact can help create the fact."*[44]

The centrality of faith in shaping the material world has a long history, though Henri Ellenberger in his *Discovery of the Unconscious* (1970) emphasizes in particular the end of the eighteenth century as a period when secular accounts claimed a share of seemingly supernatural phenomena. The crucial register in this history is the human body: its susceptibility to disease, and its capacity for both remarkable cures and dispiriting declines. Marking the emergence of a medical epistemology alongside a theological one was the Austrian priest Johann Joseph Gassner, who performed miraculous healings across Europe. "In all of these cases," Ellenberger explains,

Gassner first told the patient that faith in the name of Jesus was an essential prerequisite to being healed and asked his consent for the use of *exorcismus probativus* (trial exorcism). He then solemnly entreated the demon to make manifest the symptoms of the disease; if the symptoms were produced, Gassner considered it proven that the disease was caused by the devil and proceeded to exorcise him. But if no symptoms appeared, he sent the patient to a doctor. In that manner he felt his position to be unimpeachable, both from the viewpoint of Catholic orthodoxy and from that of medicine.[45]

Gassner, that is, distinguished between supernatural and natural phenomena, urging that the patient's faith only obtained in the former. This faith made the sufferer receptive to the will of God, which could then exorcise the intruding demon; faith, in such cases, acted as a therapeutic agent.

Franz Anton Mesmer, however, attributed Gassner's remarkable cures to a physical rather than a metaphysical source. Mesmer developed the theory that a real, measurable, magnetic "fluid" emanated from the healer and alleviated symptoms; by establishing a "rapport" with his subject, Mesmer believed he could direct this fluid at a patient and elicit a "crisis" or fit of symptoms. Whereas Gassner had believed such outbursts to be evidence of demonic possession, Mesmer took them to be at once proof of the organic illness and the means of assuaging it. Describing Mesmer in 1897, a contemporary of William James wrote that the healer "first took the whole subject of these abnormal or supranormal conditions out of the domain of the supernatural, and in attempting to show their relation to natural forces he placed them in the domain of nature as proper subjects of rational study and investigation."[46] Such an investigation was launched to inquire into Mesmer himself, and in 1784 a commission of eminent scientists, including Benjamin Franklin, issued a report denying the existence of a magnetic fluid and discrediting the practitioner. Mesmer's cures were not contested, merely "ascribed to 'imagination'" (Ellenberger, 65). So by the beginning of the nineteenth century, positivism came down hard on the distinction between real substances and fictional ideas. The beliefs and bodily experience of the patient, first sidelined by Mesmer, were ignored completely by the physicists and physicians who were committed to ending his career.

Almost one hundred years later, the neurologist Jean-Martin Charcot in France resurrected the notion of mesmeric "rapport" from the auspices of the sideshow, placing it under the rubric of hysteria when he found that his nervous patients at the Salpêtrière hospital could be stripped of their symptoms by dramatically acting them out while hypnotized. Convinced that hysteria was a pathology of the body and not a product of the imagination, Charcot attributed hysterics' suggestibility to the disease itself. His detractors, however, pointed out that the hysterical symptoms of Charcot's patients bore a suspicious resemblance to the stages of the grand-mal seizures of epileptics—who, in the Salpêtrière, happened to be housed in the ward next to Charcot's hysterics. Charcot had attempted to keep hypnosis, along with hysteria, in the sphere of the material, while challengers to his theories asserted that the imagination played a central, even defining, role.[47] The most influential challenge to Charcot's notion that hypnosis itself was a pathological state came from the researcher Hippolyte Bernheim, who argued that healthy persons could also be hypnotized: "it is a psychical and not a physical or fluid influence," Bernheim wrote in *Suggestive Therapeutics: A Treatise on the Nature and Uses of Hypnotism*.[48] Further, Bernheim argued that most doctors "made use of suggestion without knowing it" (206), thereby aligning the instruments of modern medicine with "the therapeutic virtue of talismans and amulets" (192).

This account alone, of course, begs the question of *how* the human mind effects such miracles. Frederic Myers, writing of the hypnotic trance in 1902, noted that a patient suffering from a skin infection "already fruitlessly wishes [the affected cells] to stop their inflammation; the mere fact of my expressing the same wish can hardly alter the cellular tissue."[49] Bernheim located the operative principle in the hypnotic state of mind, which neutralized "the faculties of reason, attention and judgment" (x). Normal cognition, he noted, worked by abstraction, by organizing experience into categories and applying rules of logic and evidence to the material of the senses. These faculties, during trance or hypnosis, were "dull and weakened; imagination rules supreme; impressions are accepted without verification, and the brain transforms them into actions, sensations, movements and images" (x). The hypnotic experience, Bernheim observed, was crucially interpersonal and ritualized, dependent on the subject's "psychical receptivity" and "cerebral docility," which allowed the hypnotist "to persuade the brain to do what it can to transform the accepted idea into reality" (207).

In William James's terms, the suggestions of the operator are palpitat-

ingly *alive* to the hypnotized subject, disabling the usual distinctions between truth and falsity, or between the literal and the metaphorical use of
language. Hypotheses, James wrote in "The Will to Believe," might fruitfully be categorized as "either *live* or *dead* . . . deadness and liveness in an
hypothesis are not intrinsic properties, but relations to the individual
thinker. They are measured by his willingness to act" (2–3). In hypnosis,
the "willingness to act" is amplified; indeed, the subject receives ideas as
experiences, as themselves actions. It was this translation of a representation (or memory) into a physical (or physiological) action that under-
girded the early cathartic treatments of Freud and Breuer. They found that
a patient's dispassionate recounting of a past trauma possessed no therapeutic value, whereas "symptoms of the disease would disappear when in
hypnosis the patient could be made to remember the situation and the as-
sociative connections under which they first appeared, *provided free vent
was given to the emotions which they aroused.*"[50]

In establishing the cathartic treatment, Freud drew on Pierre Janet's researches into the dissociation of personality. Rather than consciousness being singular, Janet's studies of persons with multiple personalities suggested
that trauma could result in the splitting of the self into parts, each inacces-
sible to the other.[51] Frederick Myers, a longtime colleague of William
James through their mutual involvement in the Society for Psychical Research (SPR), also elaborated on Janet's theories. Myers's psychical topography distinguished everyday or "supraliminal" consciousness from the
"subliminal" consciousness; the latter, he maintained, was visible in the
many instances of occult phenomena investigated by the SPR. James
wrote that Myers's great work, *Human Personality and Its Survival of
Bodily Death* (1902, 1907), was the "first attempt in any language to
consider the phenomena of hallucination, hypnotism, automatism,
double personality, and mediumship as connected parts of one whole
subject."[52] According to Myers, much of the time, the supraliminal consciousness is in charge, and life proceeds according to rational rules.
Like Freud, however, Myers mined everyday phenomena for evidence of
the subliminal at work, pointing up such common occurrences as sleep,
performing a habitual act without thinking, or forgetting and later re-
trieving a bit of information. The more the subliminal encroaches on
the supraliminal consciousness, the more unusual the phenomena: from
sleep and mild automatisms to hypnotism, telepathy, and possession.

It was possession that Myers delineated most fully in his chapter entitled "Trance, Possession, and Ecstacy." In terms similar to Bernheim's,

Myers outlined how the supraliminal consciousness might become muted under special circumstances, opening the receptive subject to one of three possibilities. First, the subject's own subliminal consciousness could manifest itself, "a kind of possession" (301) seen in cases of double consciousness. Second, the consciousness of another person could take over: Myers gives the examples of telepathy and hypnosis. Third, the entranced subject could become inhabited by the wandering consciousness of someone who has passed away, "reproducing, in speech or writing, facts which belong to *his* memory and not to the automatist's memory" (298). "So Mr. Myers," William James wrote, "starting from the most ordinary facts of inattentive consciousness, follows this clue through a long series which terminates in ghosts" ("Psychical," 695).

In this last possibility the history of the trance has come full circle. Myers acknowledged, "Now this seems a strange doctrine to have reached after so much disputation. For it simply brings us back to the creeds of the Stone Age. We have come round again to the primitive practices of the shaman and the medicine-man;—to a doctrine of spiritual intercourse which was once oecumenical, but has now taken refuge in African swamps" and other pockets of traditional cultures (299). Rather than symptoms of an imbalanced (or mendacious) mind, occult phenomena—"things recorded under the name of divinations, inspirations, demoniacal possessions, apparitions, trances, ecstasies, miraculous healings and productions of disease" ("Psychical," 681)—became in the hands of Myers serious evidence of the mind's power to impinge on the material world.

Freud, aware of the similarities between trance and transference, was determined to discipline the nascent occultism of the psychoanalytic cure.[53] William James noted Freud's reluctance to inquire into the efficacy of mind-cure therapies; after attending Freud's Clark University lectures in 1907, an annoyed James wrote to Theodore Flournoy, "I can make nothing in my own case with his dream theories, and obviously 'symbolism' is a most dangerous method. A newspaper report of the congress said that Freud had condemned the American religious therapy (which has such extensive results) as very 'dangerous,' because so 'unscientific.' Bah!"[54] More recently, the psychoanalyst Mikkel Borch-Jacobsen has reexamined the links among psychoanalysis, hypnosis, exorcism, and shamanism. Psychoanalysis, Borch-Jacobsen has urged, "is nothing more than . . . a chapter in the history of the trance" (114); both trance and transference entail the "overturn[ing] of the ordinarily accepted borders between 'self' and 'other'" (100) and "constitutes an incommunicable *lived experience*" (101). The twentieth-century physiologist William Sargant also points out that psychoanalytic treatment—in which a traumatic event is "relived in the *present tense*"—is "markedly similar to techniques which men have employed for thousands of years all over the world in their dealings with the abnormal: not only in terms of mental illness, but in relation to 'supernormal' or 'supernatural' agencies—gods, spirits, and demons."[55]

In the final decades of the nineteenth century, the battle was still being waged within the scientific and medical communities about the centrality of phenomena discernible only, in William James's words, "in the shrubbery beyond the parapet."[56] James himself fought against a coterie of Boston physicians who sought to regularize medical practice by requiring that all healers obtain licenses from the state. In *The Varieties of Religious Experience* (1902), James documented case after case of successful mind cures, all of which employed trance or "surrender."[57] To achieve this state, "something must give way, a native hardness must break down and liquefy; . . . leav[ing] on the Subject an impression that he has been wrought on by an external power" (101). Borch-Jacobsen has described psychoanalytic transference as a therapeutic trance-*manqué*: not limited to ancient religious practices, the blurring of boundaries between self and other offered a homeopathic prescription for sicknesses that, in involving a crisis of identity or dispossession of self, themselves took on the contours of trance. In what Borch-Jacobsen terms the "paradoxical operation of the trance" (111), the cure looks like the illness. It is a form of possession, but one that requires the ritualized placing of oneself in an absolute way in the hands of the shaman—or the modern figure endowed with the social capital to accomplish miraculous cures, the physician.

William James and Mrs. Piper: The Medium Is the Message

In 1890 Frederick Myers asked William James to record his observations of the spiritualist medium Leonora Piper for a special issue of the Proceedings of the SPR devoted to papers on "Certain Phenomena of Trance." James complied, and Myers then invited Henry James, who was living in England, to present his brother's paper to the London-based SPR. Henry wrote to William of the plan ("imagine me at 4 P.M. on that day, performing in your name"); his elder brother responded, "I think your reading of my Piper letter . . . is the most comical thing I ever heard. I will *think of you* on the 31st at about 11 A.M. to make up for the difference of longitude." In a footnote to his letter, William James added, "Alice [William's wife] says I have not *melted* enough over your reading of my paper. I *do* melt to liquefaction. 'Tis the most beautiful and devoted brotherly act I ever knew, and I hope it may be the beginning of a new career, on your part, of psychic apostolicism. Heaven bless you for it!"[58] William James's playful reference to his "liquefaction" points up the amusing blurring of brotherly boundaries and the aptness of Henry's adopting the role of medium to relate William's report on the mediumship of Mrs. Piper. The brothers agreed that it was shrewd of Myers to transform dry prose into living words, and Henry's performance was by all accounts a great success.[59]

There was a serious aspect to the brothers' good-humored interchange, for both men were committed on a more philosophical level to the dialogical aspect of speech.[60] "All life," Henry James asserted in a speech at Bryn Mawr College, ". . . comes back to the question of our speech, the medium through which we communicate with each other; for all life comes back to the question of our relations with each other. These relations are made possible, are registered, are verily constituted, by our speech."[61] William Dean Howells, in his column entitled the "Editor's Study," had described the project of realist writers as the attempt to "represent and *body forth* human experience."[62] In his study of spirit mediumship, William James found that bodily participation in the relational exchange of the séance was a vital prerequisite to belief. "One who takes part in a good sitting," James explained, "has usually a far livelier sense, both of the reality and of the importance of the communication, than one who merely reads the record. Active relations with a thing are required to bring the reality of it home to us, and in a trance talk the sitter actively cooperates. . . . The whole talk gets warmed with your own warmth, and takes on the reality of your own part in it."[63] The transcripts of séances, James found, were notoriously unpersuasive, enlisting only the reader's intellect. Quoting Walter Bagehot's article "The Emotion of Conviction," James commented, "Probably, when the subject is thoroughly examined, *conviction* will be found to be one of the intensest of human emotions, and one most closely connected with the bodily state."[64] Belief, James argued, involved a person's body as well as her mind; participation in a sitting was an essential aspect of its realization.

❊   ❊   ❊

The American Society for Psychical Research (ASPR) was founded in 1884, two years after its English counterpart, and included some of the country's leading scientific lights: Simon Newcomb, an astronomer from Johns Hopkins; Henry Bowditch, the dean of Harvard's medical school; Alexander Graham Bell, inventor; G. Stanley Hall, chair of psychology at Johns Hopkins; and William James.[65] As the historian Eugene Taylor reports, "almost everyone of any consequence in Cambridge and Boston held a séance with Piper"—including Harvard's president, Charles Eliot, the neurologist James Jackson Putnam, the philosopher Charles Sanders Peirce, and the Philadelphia-based S. Weir Mitchell.[66] In 1887, an initially skeptical Australian named Richard Hodgson became secretary of the ASPR and investigated Leonora Piper, the wife of a Boston physician. Though Hodgson over time became convinced that departed spirits indeed spoke through the medium, he couldn't persuade William James, and Hodgson vowed to return after he died to palliate his friend's skepticism.

In 1905, after a fatal heart attack, Hodgson got his chance, and James reported that eight days later "a message purporting to come from him was delivered in a trance of Mrs. Piper's, and she has hardly held a sitting since then without some manifestation of what professed to be Hodgson's spirit taking place" (2). The year after Hodgson's death, James began to investigate Piper himself, pursuing in particular the spiritual presence of his old ASPR colleague. In James's remarkable transcripts, published in 1909 as the "Report on Mrs. Piper's Hodgson-Control," the debate between the two colleagues over the truth of Mrs. Piper's mediumship continues beyond the grave. James was himself sensitive to how rare this situation was. Sifting through the mass of material that he collected from sixty-nine sittings, James commented, "Hodgson was extraordinarily expert in this sense, and one of the weirdest feelings I have had, in dealing with this business lately, has been to find the wish so frequently surging up in me that he were alive beside me to give critical counsel as to how best to treat certain of the communications of his own professed spirit" (20–21). During Hodgson's life, an agnostic James had also envied his colleague's sense of utter conviction; if through these séances he were able to feel deeply Hodgson's presence, the argument would finally be settled, for the dead man's belief would quite literally become his own.

The document that James finally published consisted of two parts, each framed by James's introductory and summary narratives. Both parts contain an amalgam of genres and voices. At the center of both are mininarratives consisting of dialogues between the "control" (the personality purportedly occupying the medium) and a "sitter," often James himself. These dialogues begin and conclude with James's remarks, with his running editorial comments and relevant background material inserted parenthetically into the dialogue or placed in footnotes. Brief commentaries by the sitters are also included in these mininarratives, either inserted in brackets or quoted from letters later solicited by James. Part 1 of the report includes one brief dialogue between James and the Hodgson control; there are several extensive ones in part 2. Part 1 is largely devoted to tracing whether the particulars related by the medium in the person of Hodgson were veridical—whether, that is, they contained information known only to Hodgson. James, at the end of part 1, remains skeptical: "The phenomena [that the case] presents furnish no knock-down proof of the return of Hodgson's spirit" (28). While still committed to writing part 2 and including a more complete report of various transcripts, James predicted that "the conclusions I shall then draw will probably not be different from those which I now draw" (28).

In part 2, however, James's tone changes from skepticism to belief, a transformation that James himself is at pains to probe. Having immersed himself in the material, he finds that he is now persuaded by the "quantitative massiveness of the phenomenon" (36): "If one sticks to the detail, one may draw an anti-spiritist conclusion; if one thinks more of what the whole mass may signify, one may well incline to spiritist interpretations" (33). If he allows his own sense of "dramatic probability" free play, he finds himself "shar[ing] the feeling with which Hodgson came at last to regard it after his many years of familiarity" (36). Aware that empirical evidence was a small part of what finally held sway with him, James in part 2 concentrates on giving "as candid an account of my own personal equation as I can give. . . . [The reader] must draw his conclusions for himself; I can only arrange the material" (36). Given his sense of the unpersuasiveness of written depictions of séances, James faced a daunting task; "I confess that I should at this moment much like to know (although I have no means of knowing) just how all the documents I am exhibiting in this report will strike readers who are either novices in the field, or who consider the subject in general to be pure 'rot' or 'bosh'" (115). In the report itself, he yearns for a way to communicate with his absent and future readers, much as he had hoped to speak with his departed friend. One hears this imperative in another essay written by James entitled "What Makes a Life Significant": "I tried to make you feel how soaked and shot-through life is with values and meanings which we fail to realize because of our external and insensible point of view. . . . I wish that I could convince you of it as I feel it myself."[67] Feeling is, in this passage, both the medium and the message of James's text.

In the conversations conducted "through" Mrs. Piper, James explicitly searches out veridical information—for instance, urging "the R. H. control" (as James refers to it) to retrieve details from an obscure article by his ASPR colleague, to which the Boston matron would have had no access. James also beseeches the R. H. control to be more persuasive: to use proper grammar, to stick with one topic, to desist with offering obscure passwords that are impossible to decode. Over the course of the sittings, the R. H. control comfortably adopts the persuasive role familiar to James from actual conversations he'd had with Richard Hodgson. Further, the control takes an active interest in the representations of himself that were beginning to circulate within the ASPR membership, including the very report in which the dialogues would later appear. It is in this sort of prompting discussion that James's divergent roles—as sitter, friend of Hodgson, member of the ASPR, and investigator—condense into a single figure: the verbal interchange works to realize James's belief in the face of inconclusive empirical evidence. What is extraordinary about William James is that, as investigator, he both analyzes and experiences his belief: "Your 'personality,'" he tells the Hodgson control, "is beginning to make me feel as you felt" (83). Enacting a forensics of self reminiscent of the Scottish physician Alexander Gordon (discussed in chapter 2), James remains intellectually aware of what is happening, even as he is emotionally drawn into the dialogue.

James, in short, experiences a revealing disconnect between his rational and emotive self, something he had described in general terms in his psychological writings of the 1880s and 1890s. In *Psychology: The Briefer Course* (1892), James referred to the work of the theater critic William Archer (discussed in chapter 1), whose extensive and systematic surveying of actors revealed that "the emotion of the part masters them whenever they play it well."[68] Archer in 1888 had argued against Denis Diderot's famous "antiemotionalist" position on acting, in which the Frenchman had maintained that actors do not actually feel but merely "render so exactly the outward signs of feeling, that you fall into the trap."[69] The actor could, in Diderot's account, produce all the bodily manifestations of a given feeling without "having" it. By contrast, Archer adopted an "emotionalist" position: his empirical study led him to conclude, along with one of the actors who filled out his questionnaire, that "if you do not weep in the agony of grief, . . . if you do not blush with shame, if you do not glow with love, if you do not tremble with terror, if your eyes do not become bloodshot with rage, if, in short, you yourself do not intimately experience whatever befits the diverse characters and passions you represent, you can never thoroughly transfuse into the hearts of your audience the sentiment of the situation" (112). The actor, in short, must "body forth" (to use William Dean Howells's phrase) the emotion if he is to enlist the affective engagement of the audience. Yet, Archer affirmed, "there is no absolute illusion on either side"—there is no "absolute transmigration of soul from Richard to Garrick" (94). Though one of his respondents did indeed use "transmigration" in depicting the communication of emotion from actor to audience, Archer hastens to add that "he uses it in a figurative, not in a literal and, so to speak, supernatural sense" (94).

In his report on Mrs. Piper, however, William James does not shy away as Archer does from imagining that the "bodying forth" of another's emotion is equivalent to something like "transmigration." The following conversation exemplifies how James is brought into relation through a dialogical process that works to realize the "other," in this case the R. H. control. (The conversation is presented as James did, with the control's speech unattributed, and with James's comments inserted in brackets. "W. J." refers to William James, and "Mrs. J." to his wife, Alice.)

> I wanted to recall,—Alice, perhaps you can help me to recall,—what was that balcony where we used to go and smoke?
>
> *Mrs. J.:* Why, yes, it was up-stairs, the upper story of the piazza.
>
> [*If Chocurua were meant, Mrs. Piper had seen this "balcony."*— W. J.]
>
> That is all right. That is perfectly clear. She always did have a clear head. . . . Now I want,—William, I want one thing. I want you to get hold of the spiritual side of this thing and not only the physical side. I want you to feel intuitively and instinctively the spiritual

truth, and when you do that you will be happy, and you will find that I was not idling and was not spending my time on nonsense; and as I thought over all, as it came to me after I entered this life, I thought "What folly! If I could only get hold of him!"

W. J.:   I wish that what you say could grow more continuous. That would convince me. You are very much like your old self, but you are curiously fragmentary.

Yes, but you must not expect too much from me, that I could talk over the lines and talk as coherently as in the body. You must not expect too much, but take things little by little as they come and make the best of it, and then you must put the pieces together and make a whole out of it. Before I lose my breath, is there any other question you want to ask me? What do you think of that bust, William? I don't quite approve of it. I think it is all nonsense. [On March 12th Mr. Dorr had told the R.H. control that Mr. Biela Pratt had begun to model a bust of him for the Tavern Club.]

W. J.:   I do not know anything about it. I have not seen it. But it is a natural thing for the Tavern Club to want of you, they were so fond of you, all of them.

I want to know, William, what is that you are writing about me?

W. J.:   I am not writing about you at present.

Aren't you going to?

W. J.:   Perhaps so.

Can I help you out any?

W. J.:   Yes, I want you to help me out very much. I am going to write about these communications of yours. I want to study them out very carefully, everything that you say to any sitter.

Well, that is splendid. You could not have said anything to please me more than that.

The dialogue reads like a play, and it is almost impossible for the reader to keep in her mind's eye the image of William James speaking *with Leonora Piper,* a middle-aged woman. One without thinking follows the control's instructions and "put[s] the pieces together and make[s] a whole out of it," or treats the talk as if it emanated from a coherent personality. In extending consciousness to both parts, one imaginatively vivifies the absent (or for the modern reader, *dead*) James during the act of reading, in a fashion akin to James's own vivification of Hodgson. And James in turn constitutes his own readers when he threads his own awareness of them throughout the text, particularly in his despair at actually conveying the "reality-feeling" (33) of the sittings. Each voice in the written dialogue prompts the other to behave in a particular way, and thus demands acknowledgement as a coherent consciousness. James in his report gives ample "air time" to a variety of other voices, both living and dead, and his own tentative, skeptical, confused, and above all personal voice seems to speak off of the page. The sitting quoted above, like James's dialogical text, becomes a mutual performance: the control is queried and scripted by the sitter, who is himself roped in by the questions and demands coming from the mouth of Mrs. Piper.

James's dawning belief that Hodgson's spirit spoke through Mrs. Piper prompts him to theorize that one's actions during life leave vestiges in the material world, centrally in one's own body, where they are stored as memory, though also in the works that one has produced and in the precious objects one leaves behind. After death a person's friends, offspring, and creations embody traces of her actions during life. James offers a musical example, quoting Samuel Butler: "It is Handel's work, not the body with which he did the work, that pulls us half over London. There is not an action of a muscle in a horse's leg upon a winter's night as it drags a carriage to the Albert Hall but what is in connection with, and part outcome of, the force generated when Handel sat in his room at Gopsall and wrote the Messiah" (119n). Works of art, James suggests, give consciousness extension, producing prodigious and wide-ranging physical effects.[70] This is true of human beings, as well: "The bodies (including of course the brains) of Hodgson's friends who come as sitters, are naturally parts of the material universe which carry some of the traces of his ancient acts" (120). As Uriah Clarke had urged sitters and mediums in the *Plain Guide to Spiritualism* (1863), "seek to put yourself in sympathy with those with whom you would communicate; elevate your thoughts and emotions to the plane they occupy."[71] As James describes it, the interested sitters who visited the medium threw the traces of Hodgson's acts "into gear" and caused them "to vibrate all at once," thereby igniting "a Hodgson-system" and making it "active in the cosmos again" (120). The combined bodies and consciousnesses of all the participants formed a sort of "Marconi-station" or telegraph office: "The sitter, with his desire to receive, forms, so to speak, a drainage opening or sink; the medium, with her desire to personate, yields the nearest lying material to be drained off; while the spirit desiring to communicate is shown the way by the current set up, and swells the latter by its own contributions" (120).

So for William James spirit mediumship catalyzed the embodied memories and beliefs of participants. Spirits were realized through what he termed "ontological wonder": "Existence," he concludes, ". . . is a brute fact to which as a whole the emotion of ontological wonder shall rightfully cleave."[72] The centrality of feeling to human existence, James concludes, is most visible in those instances "*where faith creates its own verification. Believe, and you shall be right. . . . Doubt, and you shall again be right.*"[73] Skepticism and detachment—those essential tools of positivism—are, as James describes them, active positions that can translate "living" into "dead" hypotheses. James's formulation withdraws the modern wedge driven between the subjective and the objective, the phantoms of the mind and the real matter of life. Because "belief and doubt are living attitudes" ("Is Life Worth Living?" 54), they entailed living consequences: "God himself, in short, may draw vital strength and increase of very being from our fidelity" (61).

Possession, for William James, was neither purely physiological (possession in the ancient sense) nor precisely psychological (possession in the modern sense). Rather, it resulted from collaborative acts of consciousnesses brought into vital correspondence.[74] Henry James, contemplating the persistence of consciousness in his essay "Is There a Life after Death?" adopted terms—*vibration, experience*—that resonate with William's: "The mere acquired momentum of intelligence, of perception, of vibration, of experience in a word, would have carried them [spirits] on."[75] William James died the year after he published his findings on Mrs. Piper's Hodgson control. The biographer Linda Simon reports that, after his brother's death, Henry stayed with William's widow, Alice, "partly because she hoped, and he encouraged her in the hope, that William would succeed in communicating with them from

the spiritual realm in which she knew he was now, profoundly, alive"
(387–388). There is no record that William James's spirit made the appearance that Alice James desired; his voluminous writings and correspondence, however, have preserved his thought for future generations.

"Tremendous Rites of Nullification"

In *The Wings of the Dove,* the great talent of Milly's medical shaman,
Sir Luke Strett, "was the way he carried off, as one might fairly call it,
the business of making odd things natural" (351). In his introduction to
his book *Voodoo in Haiti,* the anthropologist Alfred Metraux explains
that anthropology, at its best, reverses this procedure, exposing "the
process by which the apparently bizarre becomes ordinary. Therein the
matter-of-factness of modern life finds its other nature, in the view of
strangers: for is there doubt that the character of modern life is as
bizarre and exotic as any other man has invented[?]" (6). Metraux's
comment applies nicely to James's novel, and to Milly Theale in particular. A stranger to English culture, Milly is in tune with the wonder and
weirdness of all that surrounds her. Reified social systems, ossified domestic relations, deadened works of art—all become vividly, dangerously alive for the American heiress.

Milly's mediumistic qualities make her the incarnation of William
James's "social self," whose identity depends on "the recognition which
[a person] gets from his mates" (*Principles,* 281).[76] In the circulating
images of Milly, Henry James affirms William's point, that "*a man has
as many social selves as there are individuals who recognize him* and
carry an image of him in their mind. To wound any one of these images
is to wound him" (281–282). Enmeshed in the social web of Lancaster
Gate, Milly increasingly begins "to borrow from the handsome girl
[Kate] a sort of view of her [own] state" (113). Lord Mark's attempts to
enchant Milly partake of Freud's posthypnotic mode for eliciting free
association: "He had administered the touch that, under light analysis,
made the difference" (130). Although she doesn't *like* Lord Mark, Milly
is entranced: "Everything, anything, was charming when one was so
justly charmed" (132). Drawn into the "mystic circle" (135) of her new
companions, Milly tours Matcham, Lord Mark's estate, and her host
tells her that he possesses an image of her. As "once more things melted
together" (137), Milly suddenly finds herself standing before a Bronzino painting, beautiful but lifeless, of a young woman. She receives the

image—which "was dead, dead, dead" (137)—on a corporeal level, "looking at the mysterious portrait through tears" (137). As a hypnotized subject translates the operator's words into embodied actions, so Milly "realizes" the painting: first in the spontaneous flow of tears, in which she mimes the joylessness of the portrait's subject; and then in her willingness to act on what she takes to be the painting's message—that she is mortally ill.

Directly after assimilating the dead image as of herself, Milly visits Sir Luke. In the suggestively literal realm of James's prose, one must take the following exchange between patient and physician at face value: "'So you don't think I'm out of my mind?'" Milly enquires; "'Perhaps that *is*,' he smiled, 'all that's the matter'" (151). (Sir Luke's smile here is certainly James's as well: the sophisticate's apologetic acknowledgment of a humble pun.) Milly is not "out of her mind" in the psychological sense of being insane; rather, she is "out of her mind" in something approaching a physiological sense: she is too much "in the mind" of Lord Mark. Sir Luke, sensing his patient's capacity for somatizing images, prescribes for Milly what could be termed a social cure, urging her to diversify herself into many different people: "'I'm only, after all, one element in fifty. We must gather in plenty of others'" (149). Such a remedy-by-diversification would dilute the morbid power of the Bronzino portrait over Milly, giving her many facets, ensuring that she remain the dazzling kaleidoscope that figures her presence for Sir Luke: "All her little pieces had now then fallen together for him like the morsels of coloured glass that one used to make combinations, under the hand, in the depths of one of the polygonal peepshows of childhood" (150). As the novel progresses, however, the images of Milly supplied by others condense, with her help, into a single, unchanging image. Milly translates her physician's lack of a diagnosis, and repeated assurances that she is well, into an ominous realization: "What indeed she was really confronted with was the consciousness that he hadn't after all pronounced her anything" (154). In the absence of a diagnosis, Milly takes the vacancy as itself a positive content equivalent to nothingness, the void—or death. (Millicent Bell helpfully refers to such moments in James's novels as "blanks" that "invite the writing in of what has been left out.")[77] In this instance, Milly takes the form itself as the content, then in turn communicates this dynamic emptiness to Kate: "[Milly] believed herself nevertheless—and Kate couldn't help believing her—seriously menaced" (213).

Kate Croy, after glimpsing Milly's tendency to make others' visions her own, notes the girl's susceptibility to the charms of Merton Densher; as he himself later admits, "'I can be "charming" to her'" (198). Kate embarks on an intricate campaign to suggest to Densher what the Bronzino had suggested to Milly: that the young heiress is ill. On the one hand, Kate is perfectly "straight" with Densher when she tells him "'The girl has nothing'" (214). Readers over the years have supplied possible contents for the "nothing": Milly has no family, no one to protect her, no deviousness, no sexual experience. Cannily, Kate is aware—as was William James, in his account of the deadly nature of skepticism—that "nothing" could be animated into a "live" and potentially toxic proposition. Kate Croy's and Merton Densher's elaborate dialogues, which circle around the unstated content of Milly's illness (and which drove William James and later F. O. Matthiessen to distraction) are absolutely to the point: they are Kate's way of drawing her lover into a deadly collaborative creation. This presumptive illness, conjured by Kate—who claims as one of her skills the ability to "'conjure trouble away'" (307)—becomes embodied in Densher's actions, first through the imperative to be "kind" to a sick girl, and eventually in his inability to leave her, or for that matter stay with her, without causing her great pain. That which is suggested and never represented, then, becomes the animating vortex of the plot: it takes on extension and becomes active in the world, realigning relationships, moving persons from England to Venice, informing every move Densher does, and does not, make.

William James, in his essay "The Psychology of Belief," noted that persuasive notions can, like certain resonant artifacts, take on a potency for those emotionally attuned to them that belies their status as representation. "To many persons among us," he notes, "photographs of lost ones seem to be fetishes" (1041). This is not a matter of mimetic reference: "that the mere materiality of the reminder is almost as important as its resemblance is shown by the popularity a hundred years ago of the black taffeta 'silhouettes'" (1041), black cutout figures that, lacking all detail, depict merely the form of the departed loved one. James goes on to describe how heady thoughts "tend invincibly to attach themselves to something sensible so as to gain in corporeity and life. Words serve this purpose, gestures serve it, stones, straws, chalk-marks, anything will do. As soon as any one of these things stands for the idea, the latter seems to be more real . . . [and] rouse[s] the believing reaction and give[s] to the ideas a more living reality" (1042). The minimal materiality was necessary, James argued, for a fetish. Even a word: a stroke of ink on a page, a mere sound emanating from the lips. Or, in the virtuoso hands of Henry James, even a palpable silence.

Merton Densher, Kate's instrument, learns in the practicum of the novel how ideas might become realized in the world. By profession a man of words rather than a man of action, Densher is portrayed as doomed to an impotent impoverishment, and he quails before the heavy functionalism of Maud Lowder. In this context, his sexual proposition to Kate might seem a pathetic attempt to regain his manhood. But Densher's delight is less in the exercise of sexual power over another human being—something explicable in conventional psychological terms—and more in the superhuman capacity to make the word flesh: "It had simply *worked*, his idea, the idea that he had made her accept. . . . It was, otherwise, but the fact of the idea as directly applied, as converted from luminous conception into an historic truth" (312). In coercing his lover to participate in the action that realized the idea of sex, condensing it into an actual intimate encounter, Densher reverses the sublime logic that Henry James had articulated decades prior upon the death of Minny Temple: "The more I think of [Minny]," he had written to William, "the more perfectly satisfied I am to have her translated from this changing realm of fact to the steady realm of thought."[78] In *The Wings of the Dove*, Densher succeeds in translating his wish from "the steady realm of thought" into "this changing realm of fact." Densher becomes a fetishist, in the anthropological sense that underlies Freud's narrower sexual usage: he condenses an immaterial conception into a material entity.

For not only does Densher's idea of sleeping with Kate become an actuality when she visits him in his rooms, it lingers on as a tangible thing, a precious addition to the contents of his flat: "It played for him—certainly in this prime afterglow—the part of a treasure kept at home in safety and sanctity, something he was sure of finding in its place when, with each return, he worked his heavy old key in the lock. The door had but to open for him to be with it again and for it to be all there; so intensely there that, as we say, no other act was possible to him than the renewed act, almost the hallucination, of intimacy" (313). While the passage is suggestive of masturbation, James's prose makes it irrelevant whether Densher actually engages in sex, merely thinks about it, or just recalls his erotic encounter with Kate. Doing, thinking, and remembering have, in this case, become similarly delightful, identically orgasmic—and therefore, equally real in their capacity to make Densher vibrate with pleasure.[79] (Unlike someone with a shoe fetish, whose pleasure is contingent on his getting his hands on a stiletto, Densher has fetishized his own thinking, which is of course profoundly portable.) Densher's idea, which "he couldn't have banished if he had wished," takes possession of its creator, who finds himself under "the spell of what he conceived himself" (313).

In *The Wings of the Dove* visions, thoughts, and representations take form in the "changing realm of fact." In this Maud Lowder is instructive but, as we have seen with both Kate Croy and Merton Densher, not unique: "when she adopts a view she . . . really brings the thing about, fairly terrorises with her view any other, any opposite view" (287).[80] The eminent Harvard physiologist Walter Cannon, describing what he termed "voodoo death" in 1942, explained the phenomenon in succinct terms: "It is the fatal power of the imagination working through unmitigated terror."[81] A research physiologist, Cannon published his first paper on the bodily effects of the emotions in 1898; his study of fatal terror, which expanded on this early work (and William James's theory of emotion), examines the essentially social and ritualistic nature of the phenomenon. Cannon describes how a person, purposefully excluded from his social milieu, becomes "alone and isolated. The doomed man is in a situation from which the only escape is by death. During the death illness which ensues, the group acts with all the outreachings and complexities of its organization and with countless stimuli to suggest death positively to the victim, who is in a highly suggestible state. . . . He becomes what the attitude of his fellow tribesmen wills him to be. Thus he assists in committing a kind of suicide" (174).

What distinguishes voodoo death from common murder is the deep cooperation between the victim and his community, which "subject[s] him to the fateful ritual of mourning. The purpose of the community now, as a social unit with its ceremonial leader, who is a person of very near kind to the victim, is at last to cut him off entirely from the ordinary world and ultimately to place him in his proper position in the sacred totemic world of the dead. The victim, on his part, reciprocates this feeling" (174). This feeling, as Emile Durkheim notes in *The Elementary Forms of the Religious Life* (1915), is neither private nor idiosyncratic: "mourning is not a natural movement of private feelings wounded by a cruel loss; it is a duty imposed by the group. . . . It is a ritual attitude, which [a person] is forced to adopt out of a respect for custom, but which is, in a large measure, independent of his affective state."[82]

In *The Wings of the Dove,* the case can be made that each character serves, in Cannon's terms, as the "ceremonial leader": Sir Luke Strett, who offers Milly that empty cup she so inexorably fills; Susan Stringham, who in Venice opens the door to both Densher and Lord Mark; Kate Croy, who works with others to conjure the illness into existence; Lord Mark, who first charms Milly and then delivers the fateful news in Venice; Merton Densher, whose power to beguile Milly turns out to be far from benign; or Maud Lowder, whose "hard smooth sheen" (164) and "onyx eyes" (165) make her a harsh little fetish "ineffaceably stamped by inscrutable nature and dreadful art" (169). The process of moving Milly from life to death is a cooperative venture. The anthropologist A. G. Leonard wrote in 1906 of witnessing men in Africa succumb to community hexing; they expired, he explains, because they believed "they were bound to die."[83] The ceremonial leader at Lancaster Gate is finally Milly herself, who makes her last public appearance (at that "sacred" Anglo ritual so familiar to James, the dinner party) dressed all in white. In the role of high hostess, Milly makes herself equal to the image—the dove, the girl in the shroud, the blank page— that everyone in the room already possesses.

Cannon describes the social ritual of voodoo death, in which a victim's consciousness realizes fatal suggestions through the complete failure of the autonomic nervous system, a process that challenges dualistic pairings of self and other, mind and body, voluntary and involuntary, and imaginary and real. Writing of the epistemological questions raised by placebos—inert materials or "nothings" that nonetheless elicit the body's healing processes—historian Anne Harrington employs a trope that is particularly apt in the Jamesian context: "Placebos are the ghosts that haunt our house of biomedical objectivity, the creatures that . . . expose the paradoxes and fissures in our own self-created definitions of the real and active factors in treatment."[84] Voodoo death as described by Cannon is the ultimate "nocebo" effect, the imaginative marshalling and subsequent realization of the body's capacity for sickness.

The placebo can be understood as a particular and biomedical distillate of trance. "'Suggestion,'" William James explained in *The Principles of Psychology* (1890), "is only another name for the power of ideas, *so far as they prove efficacious over belief and conduct*" (103): "An idea, to be suggestive, must come to the individual with the force of a revelation" (104). Unlike the other characters in *The Wings of the Dove,* Sir Luke has no particular social use to which he would like to put Milly; the physician's prescription is at once content-free and ultimate: that she must simply live, "by option, by volition." William James identifies the myriad states loosely consolidated under the rubric of *trance* as "a perfectly definite class of experiences . . . which certain persons may live by in a deeper sense than they live by anything else with which they have acquaintance" (107). It is precisely this state that Milly seeks, and that Sir Luke tautologically prescribes. But this capacity comes at a cost: Milly realizes that "if it were in her power to live," the flip side of the equation must also be true: that "one might die" (152).

Having absorbed Milly into their occult intrigues, the tribe at Lancaster Gate slowly withdraws its attention, a paring down that occupies the last quarter of the novel. Just as William James, in his psychical researches, hypothesized that the willing presence of a dead person's friends could form a "vibrating system" that might conjure the dead consciousness back into activity, so the "wonderful system" (354, 355) of Kate and Densher, which ends with Densher committed to "being still . . . to create the minimum of vibration" (322), succeeds in performing the opposite office. Densher "had taken with himself on leaving Venice the resolution to regard Milly as already dead to him" (368). Like a hesitant assassin steeling himself for a hit, the journalist tells himself, "'Let me assume the thing actually over.' . . . He consequently tried, so far as shutting his eyes and stalking grimly about" (368). Densher and the others "spoke of the dying girl in the past tense" (368); using tones of hushed reverence, they encase her in the sanctity of the transcendent image of the dove. "We begin," Henry James wrote in "Is There Life after Death?" "by pitying the remembered dead even for the very danger of our indifference to them . . . 'they must be dead as 'science' affirms,' for this consecration of it on such a scale, and with these *tremendous rites of nullification,* to take place" (473; emphasis added). Milly plays her part, entering into the ritual by dressing in the white clothes that constitute her winding sheet: "Milly herself did everything . . . still more than anything else, Milly's 'imagination'" (314).

Producing his own stages of grief, James in "Life after Death" warned that mourners, first pitying the deceased, may "end by pitying ourselves for the final demonstration, as it were, of their indifference to us" (473). After her ritualized ending, Milly "turns her face to the wall," away from the London coterie. The character exits the novel in book 9, immured behind the thick walls of her Venetian palazzo. But the young American's "course of disintegration," as James put it in the

New York preface, rather than the ostensible source of her isolation, is instead its uncanny effect—which helps to explain the nagging, communal, free-floating sense that each character is guilty. Densher can only momentarily reassure himself "it wasn't a bit he who, that day, had touched her, and if she was upset it wasn't a bit his act," for it is precisely in this apparently exculpatory detachment that guilt resides. Agatha Christie's *Murder on the Orient Express,* in which each character plunges the knife into the victim, would offer a later, more tangible rendering of the sort of collaborative death Milly dies. Paradoxically, Milly dies *at the hands of everyone,* precisely because she is not in the hands of anyone; and *by her own hand,* precisely because she has placed herself so completely in the hands of those around her. The immuring of Milly is, of course, a prelude to the final crucial chapters of the novel in which Merton Densher and Kate Croy assimilate her death.

Conclusion: Burning Issues

"Who does not 'realise,'" William James asks in the essay "The Psychology of Belief," "more the fact of a dead or distant friend's existence, at the moment when a portrait, letter, garment, or other material reminder of him is found?" (1040). James's telling use of quotation marks around the verb *realise* (spelled according to British convention) indicates that he is not using the term in the ordinary, psychological sense, but in a stranger, more occult, more physiological sense. We see the elements of just such realizing in the final pages of Henry James's *The Wings of the Dove,* where the logic of the verbal fetish is taken to its logical conclusion. After Milly's death, Merton Densher receives a letter from her, timed to arrive on Christmas Eve. In standard plot terms, Densher realizes that Milly's post-mortem correspondence will communicate the vast sums she has left him in her will, indicating not just her forgiveness of his perfidy (and in so doing expressing her love for him) but also giving him the means finally to wed Kate Croy. As Kate herself aptly puts it, the letter was to convey Milly's peace and satisfaction "of having . . . realized her passion," of not just loving but "having *been* loved" (364). Milly's passion, in other words, had achieved material form in the letter, the "undisclosed work of her hand" (394), which Densher recognizes as a "sacred script" (393). What the letter communicates for Densher is not Milly's intention to include him in her will but her passion, which resides in the object not as meaning but as presence.

So while the "intention announced in it he should but too probably know" (398)—the public meaning would be conveyed by lawyers and official documents and London gossips—Densher resolves that "he would never never know what had been in Milly's letter" (398). The emphasis, here, is on the verb "know," in its carnal as well as its cognitive meaning. He would never violate Milly's corporeal integrity by sleeping with her or by reducing her letter—the vehicle of her sacred "passion"—to a vulgar public meaning.

The notion that a life might be literally, rather than metaphorically, distilled into a written record was, as nineteenth-century anthropologists recorded, not unusual in traditional cultures. In a long footnote to his "Psychology of Belief," William James cites H. M. Stanley's *Through the Dark Continent* (1878), in which the American journalist recounts his attempt to record in his notebook some of the words of the inhabitants of the island of Mowa. After watching him jot down notes, Stanley reports, the Mowans hastily departed. Appearing the next day in full warrior regalia, one of the islanders replied to Stanley's anxious inquiries, "'Our people saw you yesterday make marks on some tara-tara [paper]. This is very bad. Our country will waste, our goats will die, our bananas will rot, and our women will dry up. What have we done to you that you should wish to kill us? . . . If you burn it we will go away, and shall be your friends as heretofore'" (1047n). Stanley thus found himself in a serious predicament. Unwilling, in his words, to "sacrifice" the text filled with "valuable notes" to what he (in shamelessly pejorative terms) considered "the childish caprice of savages," Stanley lit on an intermediate solution: rather than sacrifice his irreplaceable work to the fire, he instead produced a well-worn edition of Shakespeare, which resembled his notebook. The "poor deluded natives" refused to touch it—"'It is fetish. You must burn it'"—and Stanley "gravely consigned the innocent *Shakespeare* to the flames" (1047–1048n).

So when Kate Croy, speaking with Densher at Christmastime and holding Milly's unopened letter, "with a quick gesture . . . jerked the thing into the flame" (394), the question arises: is she making a grand gesture that indicates she will marry Densher no matter what the letter says, no matter how much money Milly has left to him? Such an action would be a real sacrifice, the equivalent of Stanley tossing his irreplaceable notebook into the flames to appease the Mowans. Or is Kate making an empty gesture, the equivalent of immolating the printed Shakespeare text or some other reproducible substitute? Kate's comment to Merton as they watch the letter burn confirms that she understands herself to have done the latter: "'You'll have it all,' Kate said, 'from New York'" (394). That is, Densher will hear from the law offices charged with executing Milly's will. Kate's action is warranted by her conception of representation, in which a document conveys a person's meaning, her public intentions, such that another document or person might just as easily pass along the significance. The material entity (e.g. the letter written in Milly's hand) is mere medium. The meaning, whatever package it comes in, is everything.

How does Merton Densher view Kate's "jerking" of the letter into the flames? If he ascribed to the perspective of the Mowans, if he understood the material object to be a fetish that enclosed Milly's irreplaceable spirit, he would be as distraught as the natives were relieved by the burning text. If he ascribed to Kate's view, if he understood the material object to be an insignificant medium for a meaning that could as easily be conveyed by lawyers, he would be essentially unconcerned about the consequences of the burning. Instead, Kate's lover pursues a third course, in which the absent letter, like the absent woman, provides the endless opportunity for "thought," though this term must be understood in a specifically Jamesian light as something that centrally involves the mind yet enlists the entire body. Merton, like James's child protagonist in the earlier novel *What Maisie Knew,* "embalmed in his wonder" Milly's passion. By endlessly "wondering about" the letter, "his imagination had [become] extraordinarily filled and refined" (398). Milly's passion kindles his own.

Of James's novel *The Spoils of Poynton,* published after *Maisie* and before *Wings,* Bill Brown has observed that "the novel's chief narratological device—withholding things" establishes the climactic conflagration that burns down Mrs. Gereth's precious Poynton "as an act (or a mark) of purification."[85] In a novel that is predicated on the absolute centrality of things but avoids the mimetic representation of them, Brown concludes that "the fire marks this strength" and "should be understood as the conflagration in which realism as such is consumed" (228). The final scenes of *The Wings of the Dove,* which come after Kate's burning of the letter, allow us to cast Brown's persuasive analysis in slightly different terms. While the fires concluding both novels may indeed mark the immolation of a certain mimetic, objectivist understanding of realism (Brown quotes Willa Cather's description of the "popular superstition that 'realism' asserts itself in the cataloguing of a great number of material objects" [228]), it has been my contention throughout this study that such accounts are deeply inadequate to the novels, philosophy, and sciences of the late nineteenth century. Only with the absolute annihilation of the *apparent* vehicle of realism—not just inert-seeming "things" but indeed words on a page—are we brought fully to accept as irrefutable the centrality of the feeling, thinking, breathing human being to the realization of aesthetic experience. The burning that concludes James's great novel of obliquity is, I argue, not the event in which "realism as such is consumed" but the moment at which it achieves its consummation. The final realization of Merton Densher and indeed the reader of *The Wings of the Dove* is, to use a term of John Dewey, a "consummatory experience." Such an experience, Dewey writes, "involves reconstruction which may be painful"; for this reason intense aesthetic experiences "are certainly not to be characterized as amusing, and as they bear down upon us they involve a suffering that is none the less consistent with, indeed a part of, the complete perception that is enjoyed" (*Art*, 41).

To return to Merton Densher's wonderment at the burning of Milly Theale's letter: in this we see a glimmer of William James's ideas about human immortality: "It is not as if there were a bounded room where the minds in possession had to move up or make place and crowd together to accommodate new occupants. . . . The space of my imagination, for example, in no way interferes with yours" (1125). A strictly materialist fetishism requires that a particular object, such as a letter or a photograph, house a single spirit; William James notes that "for our ancestors, the world was a small, and—compared with our modern sense of it—a comparatively snug affair" (1121). For the Jameses, however, the aesthetic imagination has no similar space shortage: there is no "bounded room." Henry James speaks of the extensions of human feeling as "thought"; William James refers to the "power of sympathetic vibration with other lives" (1125). The beauty of the notion is that, in William's words, it "seems to be governed by no law analogous to that of the so-called conservation of energy in the material world. When one man wakes up, or one is born, another does not have to go to sleep, or die, in order to keep the consciousness of the universe a constant quantity" (1125). Corporeal wonder is expansive, productive, vital—it is not a zero-sum game.

In *The Wings of the Dove,* the manner of transmission works in this fashion: Densher's receipt of Milly's letter provokes in him a "thought precisely of such freshness and such delicacy" (400). This *thought,* rather than the letter itself, becomes Densher's fetish, something that he might fondle and caress. In a description reminiscent of Léonce Pontellier's tender custody of his "household gods," Merton Densher when alone "took it out of its sacred corner and its soft wrappings; he undid them one by one, handling them, handling *it*, as a father, baffled and tender, might handle a maimed child" (398). (The psychoanalyst Serge Leclaire, writing of dream interpretation, has asserted that "the representation of a mangled child, even if it is veiled, disguised, or displaced is to be taken as a clue not to be overlooked.")[86] Merton Densher's wonder is the afterlife of Milly's passion: as Kate puts it, "Her memory's your love" (403). Memory in this account is not mimetic but passional. The neurologist Antonio Damasio casts this Jamesian insight into neurobiological terms when he writes, "The very prospect of suffering and death breaks down the homeostatic process of the beholder. The natural endeavor for self-preservation and well-being responds to the breakdown with a struggle to prevent the inevitable and redress the balance, . . . [seeking] ways to resist the anguish conjured up by suffering and death, cancel it, and substitute joy instead" (269, 271). Which is why Densher is so sickened by Kate Croy, for she imagines that, when speaking of the death of Milly, one could have knowledge without feeling, isolated facts without bodily responsiveness, recognition of beauty without joy: "He had brought her there to be moved, and she was only immoveable—which was not, moreover, because she didn't understand. She understood everything" (373). In Kate we can discern a commitment to the Affective Fallacy: to meaning without movement, to gifts of passion that don't transform. In the important missives of human connection, it is *not* just the thought that counts: the material embodiment of the thought, along with its sensuous reception, are essential to its significance.

In contrast to the immovable Kate, Densher's reception of Milly's gift brings together creation, intention, and feeling. Here Henry James produces a more nuanced version of his brother's notion that, in the context of a spiritualist sitting, a "willingness to receive" can bring the dead to life. William James's passion for knowledge, shared with his colleague Richard Hodgson, moved him to pursue the inquiry that had obsessed them both while Hodgson lived. Yet even Densher, in his stillness, harbors a "wasted passion" (373), the hushed memory of Milly that he is as much possessed by as in possession of (and that is perfectly analogous to Mrs. Gereth's memory of her beloved things at Poynton). Henry James is moved to do as Howells had urged and "body forth" in his novel his theory of corporeal wonder, putting into circulation the feelings kindled in his relation to what he calls his "sources." As an artist, Henry James writes, "I deal with being, I invoke and evoke, I figure and represent, I seize and fix, as many phases and aspects and conceptions of it as my infirm hand allows me strength for; and in so doing I find myself—I can't express it otherwise,—in communication with *sources;* sources to which I owe the apprehension of far more and far other combinations than observation and experience, in their ordinary sense, have given me the pattern of" (476). Art expresses and broadcasts human feeling; James, in the philosopher Suzanne Langer's terms, aligns as well as theorizes form and feeling.

Which suggests the way the biographer Lyndall Gordon, and a certain strain of trauma theory, gets it *almost* right in imagining that traumatic experience is not a matter of pure cognition. As Cathy Caruth writes, "The story of dreams and of dying children, cannot be reduced . . . to a simple mastery of facts and cannot be located in a simple knowledge or cognition."[87] One can even grant the notion that trauma resists representation traditionally understood and is instead passed along as a "haunting," as long as the term is limited neither to possession in the physiological sense (e.g. a fetish) nor in the psychological sense (e.g. an idea). The work of the Jameses and those who fertilized their thinking—passionate believers, along with the researchers who sought to understand their beliefs—helps us to explain the strangeness of Caruth's theory of trauma. In her unwillingness to address directly the realm of affect, Caruth draws, in unacknowledged form, on occult ideas about transmission (couched in terms of "the performative") in order to avoid the limited sense of "mere" psychological possession, of being metaphorically "haunted by the memory" of something or someone. As Joan Didion has recently described in *The Year of Magical Thinking* (and as any brokenhearted person can attest), human beings frequently animate, in ways that are physical and tactile as well as "mental," a lost love. The notion that such magical thinking is "mistaken" is deeply inadequate to the painful rhythm of bereavement, where one might turn to share a joke or solicit the opinion of a companion who has died, only to be caught up short, again and again, by the sickening jolt of their irreversible absence.

Because of our tendency to engage in magical thinking, it is, in one sense, understandable that human beings would seek to supplement or correct the inadequate-feeling position that ideas and representations enlist just our minds. One can see this impulse underlying Lyndall Gordon's approach to biography, which is predicated on a theory of language in which words fail to signify and instead are treated as fetishes that house the person being represented—a ghostly haunting that is not imagined as metaphorical. "Things" in such accounts—texts, stories, paintings, objects—are, in the strong sense, personified: which is why, as Amy Hungerford has written of Holocaust memoirs, critics sometimes treat texts with the reverence normally reserved for actual persons.[88] This is precisely Caruth's understanding of traumatic speech, which can never represent a harrowing event, but instead conveys it as by contagion. As Caruth states in *Unclaimed Experience: Trauma, Narrative, History,* "What is passed on, finally, is not the meaning of the words but their performance."[89]

Gordon imagines that biography might reanimate the dead: Caruth indicates that for her, critical theory has a similar conjuring power. In *Unclaimed Experience,* she ends her discussion of trauma with a reading of Freud's and then Lacan's treatment of a grieving father's dream. Caruth traces how a child's posthumous words, which came to the father as he slept by his son's body, migrate from Freud's *Interpretations of Dreams,* through the work of Lacan, into Caruth's own text. As reported by Freud, a father known to one of his colleagues was awakened while dreaming that his dead child spoke the words "Father, can't you see I am burning?"—only to find that the child's actual corpse, lying in state, had in fact been burned by the sacramental candles that surrounded it. How to express the horror of a father's anguish? For Caruth, the child's impossible words, conveying an impossible request, can only haunt the living with their own failure. What is conveyed in this account is endless repetition in the form of theory: the child's words are recounted by the father to a friend, who tells Freud, who "tells" Lacan, who "tells" Caruth . . . ad infinitum. What is puzzling about this idea is that nothing is ever understood to change: nobody is moved, no project is advanced, no one's suffering is relieved. Like Densher, theory in this account only seems to be in motion: in actuality, it is content to remain in an oddly sacral stillness.

Kenneth Kidd has pointed out that psychoanalysis itself has produced the problem that it needs to solve in these extraordinary feats of quasi-supernatural connection. Kidd helpfully references the work of Janet Malcolm to explain the impasse at the heart of Freud's theories: "The concept of transference at once destroys faith in personal relations and explains why they are tragic: we cannot know each other. We must grope around for each other through a dense thicket of absent others. We cannot see each other plain. A horrible kind of predestination hovers over each new attachment we form. 'Only connect,' E. M. Forster proposed. 'Only we can't,' the psychoanalyst knows."[90] This structure of impassible disconnection is "solved" by Caruthian trauma theory, which, Kidd has argued, keeps "trauma unconscious and always moving"(127). Kidd observes that transference is no longer the "ultimate downer" isolating us each in our own "dense thicket": instead, "for Caruth it is what makes intellectual life worthwhile" (127). Amy Hungerford has persuasively traced the logic of Caruth's (and Shoshana Felman's and Dori Laub's) theories, in which readers are understood to "experience trauma by listening to testimony about trauma," to argue that the mechanism of transmission implies that "those who bear witness to suffering reverse death."[91] This suggests one sort of intimacy, to be sure, but an oddly necrophiliac one. (It also does not acknowledge directly the pleasures of intellectual life, indeed the pleasures of theory itself: for a fantastic discussion of the question "What emotions become the theorist?" see Rei Terada's *Feeling in Theory* [128].) In the terms of William James, such repetitions cast critical theorists not as agents but as mediums along the lines of Mrs. Piper, possessed in the quasi-physiological sense of being inhabited by the voice or experience of another—one might think of Freud, Lacan, and Caruth repeating the dream words of the burned child.

Yet finally, for Merton Densher, there is movement, which transpires on the final pages of James's novel. To be sure, Merton Densher's experience with Milly's letter entails what looks like a repetition, for after receiving Milly's personal missive—which Kate Croy burned—he receives official notice of her bequest: her intention comes through, after all. Yet James, in pairing these scenes at the end of the novel, indicates that for Densher "the intention announced in it"—an actual sum of money— was "the least part of it": in forgoing knowing for "wondering," Densher's "imagination had [become] extraordinarily filled out and refined" (398). James in his repetitions-with-a-difference mutes the cognitive, object-oriented relation to meaning and affirms the essential form of human relation, realized as the communication of feeling. The letters, Densher realizes, were intended to prompt a collaborative act of loving; in this, Densher moves beyond his fetishistic husbanding of Milly's passion, his hiding it away and keeping it to himself, and recognizes the imperative to amplify it. So while Kate breaks the seal of the official document to harvest its monetary message, her lover "'saw' nothing, and it was only into her eyes that her remark made him look, declining any approach to the object indicated" (399). James in this moment works to prevent readers from reading like Kate, who lifts out the message lodged in a letter—in this case, a sum of money—and consigns the rest to the flames. In the practicum of his novels, James enlists the sort of expansive affective engagement modeled finally by Merton Densher's relationship to Milly's letter.

In "Is There Life after Death?" Henry James hypothesized that his "thought" might live on after the death of his physical body. In a footnote to her chapter on *Wings,* Sharon Cameron notes that "James's magical thinking about life after death is also inevitably magical thinking about writing. The immortality he will get will exist in books, which are not only the objects of thought, but also, as much to the point, are thoughts made into objects" (159). Though Cameron isn't explicit here, she indicates that "thought" in the hands of Henry James is not reducible to a mere idea lodged in the brain. The objects of love and beauty become, for James, the occasion for an extension and amplification not of particular egos but of human feeling: wonder, joy, and finally, something like peace or rapture. Such objects are not the primitive fetishes imagined by trauma theorists for the transmission of meaning understood to operate as a *loa* (or its modern equivalent, a virus), inhabiting and replicating itself in the "host."[92] The humanities-trained trauma theorist who has no account of the biological human body, with its astonishing abilities to connect with the rich world beyond the skin, in essence casts everything exterior to the body as (to quote William James's *Human Immortality* [1898]) "swarms of alien kinsmen" who appear as "merely grotesque or even repulsive aliens."[93] William James had a warning for the holders of such an untenable, constricted position: "'Tis you who are dead, stone-dead, and blind and senseless, in your way of looking on" (1124).

The ability to come into relation is to be, in William James's terms, "a Marconi-station" that is importantly *affective:* active, sentient, efficacious—both moved and moving. Human beings, he believed, had the capacity to extend through and beyond the seemingly isolate individual body and to recognize that every living thing "is animated," in James's words, "by an inner joy of living as hot or hotter than that which you feel beating in your private breast" (1125). As the contemporary novelist Richard Powers has written, aesthetic objects can be understood as "technologies" that facilitate these recognitions: the novel, in his words, is a "supreme connection machine—the most complex artifact of networking that we've ever developed."[94] Antonio Damasio traces the essential and shared capacity to realize this sort of commonality to the human organism itself. People are uniquely equipped, through nerves and brain and body (what William James called *soul*),

> to intuit the essences of the human condition. That intuition is commingled with a serene feeling whose ingredients include pleasure, joy, delight, but for which the words "blessedness" and "beatitude" seem the most appropriate given the transparent texture of the feeling. . . . Goethe noted that this process offers love without asking for love back [the perfect description of Milly's final offering], . . . a joy that is perhaps best conceived as pure feeling almost liberated for once, from its obligate body twin. (*Spinoza*, 276)

The brothers Henry and William James realized a hundred years earlier—one in the context of literature, the other in the context of science—that aesthetic objects were more than telegraphs of meaning that either are received as a form of penetration or possession ("sink[ing] right into your brainstem," as Walter Michaels writes) or remain forever unread, unreceived, and unrecognized ("we cannot know each other," as Janet Malcolm puts this position). There is, as the Jameses show us, another option, one that is mind- and world-expanding and that puts us in touch with our common embodiment. "To miss the joy," as William wrote, quoting Robert Louis Stevenson, "is to miss all" (847, 1125).

Notes

Introduction

1. W. K. Wimsatt, Jr., "The Affective Fallacy" (written in collaboration with Monroe C. Beardsley), in *The Verbal Icon: Studies in the Meaning of Poetry* (Lexington: University of Kentucky Press, 1954), 30. Subsequent references to this essay appear in parentheses in the text.
2. Catherine Lutz, *Unnatural Emotions: Everyday Sentiments on a Micronesian Atoll and Their Challenge to Western Theory* (Chicago: University of Chicago Press, 1988), 3. Subsequent references to this work appear in parentheses in the text.
3. Even the attempt to think of emotion in more objective terms, in Wimsatt's and Beardsley's account, is repellent, necessitating equally distasteful acts of translation and distillation, such as the production of "statistically countable reports about a poem" through "tabulat[ion] of the subject's responses to it" (34).
4. Walter Benn Michaels, *The Shape of the Signifier: 1967 to the End of History* (Princeton, N.J.: Princeton University Press, 2004), 73. Though his work in the 1980s and 1990s was instrumental in modeling and elaborating the New Historicism, a mode of criticism that was established in opposition to the formalism of New Critics such as Wimsatt and Beardsley, Michaels and the New Critics find common ground in their vehement opposition to the Affective Fallacy.
5. My thanks to Walter Michaels for clarifying his point for me.
6. See for instance Judith Butler, *Bodies that Matter: On the Discursive Limits of "Sex"* (New York: Routledge, 1993); Thomas Lacqueur, *Making Sex: Body and Gender from the Greeks to Freud* (Cambridge, Mass.: Harvard University Press, 1990); and Elaine Showalter, *Hystories: Hysterical Epidemics and Modern Culture* (New York: Columbia University Press, 1997).
7. Julia Kristeva, "Women's Time," trans. Alice Jardine and Harry Blake, *Signs*, 7, no. 1 (Autumn 1981): 35.

8. C. P. Snow, *Two Cultures* (Cambridge: Cambridge University Press, 1998).

9. A response to a book by Paul R. Gross and Norman Levitt, *Higher Superstition: The Academic Left and Its Quarrels with Science*, this issue of *Social Text* prompted myriad articles and books on the topic. It was quickly followed by Alan Sokal's *Fashionable Nonsense: Postmodern Intellectuals' Abuse of Science* (New York: Picador, 1998); *The Sokal Hoax: The Sham That Shook the Academy*, ed. editors of *Lingua Franca* (Lincoln: University of Nebraska Press, 2000); and a slew of inflammatory titles such as Keith Windschuttle, *The Killing of History: How Literary Critics and Social Theorists Are Murdering Our Past* (New York: Free Press, 1997).

10. Wai Chee Dimock and Priscilla Wald, "Literature and Science: Cultural Forms, Conceptual Exchanges," special issue, *American Literature* 74, no. 4 (December 2002): 705. Subsequent references to this article appear in parentheses in the text.

11. Antonio Damasio, for instance, draws on William Styron's *Darkness Visible*, his memoir of depression, in developing his neurological account of feeling states in *Descartes' Error: Emotion, Reason, and the Human Brain* (New York: HarperCollins, 1994), 147; and critical work in the new field of medical humanities, such as Kathleen Montgomery Hunter, *Doctors' Stories: The Narrative Structure of Medical Knowledge* (Princeton: Princeton University Press, 1991), is increasingly finding its way into medical school curricula.

12. Donna Haraway, *Simians, Cyborgs, and Women: The Reinvention of Nature* (New York: Routledge, 1991), 187.

13. Thomas Laycock, *Mind and Brain: Or, The Correlations of Consciousness and Organisation; With Their Applications to Philosophy, Physiology, Mental Pathology, and the Practice of Medicine* (Edinburgh: Sutherland and Knox, 1860).

14. William James, "What Is an Emotion?" (1884), in *Collected Essays and Reviews* (New York: Longmans, Green, 1920), 244–245.

15. I. A. Richards, *Principles of Literary Criticism* (New York: Routledge and Kegan Paul, 1924), 75, 82.

16. Jeffrey Williams, "The Last Generalist: An Interview with Richard Powers," *Cultural Logic* 2, no. 2 (spring 1999), electronic publication.

17. Antonio Damasio, *Looking for Spinoza: Joy, Sorrow, and the Feeling Brain* (Orlando, Fla.: Harcourt, 2003), 28.

18. William James, *The Varieties of Religious Experience: A Study in Human Nature, Being the Gifford Lectures on Natural Religion Delivered at Edinburgh in 1901–1902*, in *Writings, 1902–1910*, ed. Bruce Kuklick (New York: Library of America, 1987), 72.

19. Théodule Ribot, *The Psychology of the Emotions* (London: Walter Scott), 1911, 8. For a helpful discussion of contemporary taxonomies of emotions, see Paul E. Griffiths, *What Emotions Really Are: The Problem of Psychological Categories* (Chicago: University of Chicago Press, 1997), esp. 44–55.

20. Ribot, preface to *Psychology of the Emotions*, vii–viii; emphasis added.

21. Marianne Noble, *The Masochistic Pleasures of Sentimental Literature* (Princeton, N.J.: Princeton University Press, 2000).

22. For an account of the "new regimes of self-knowledge" that Hacking associate with modernity, see "Truthfulness," *Common Knowledge* 11, no. 1 (2005), 171.

23. Quoted in Ribot, *Psychology of Emotions*, 29.

24. "Bain on the Senses and Intellect," *Fraser's Magazine for Town and Country* 53, no. 316 (February 1856): 217, 226.

25. John Dewey, "The Psychology of Effort" (1897), in *The Philosophy of John Dewey* (Chicago: University of Chicago Press, 1973), 154. Subsequent references to this work appear in parentheses in the text.

26. Edmund Gurney, *The Power of Sound* (New York: Basic Books, 1966), 60.

27. Philip Fisher, *The Vehement Passions* (Princeton, N.J.: Princeton University Press, 2003), 2.

28. Walter Cannon, "Voodoo Death," *American Anthropologist* 44, no. 2 (April/June 1942): 170.

29. Daniel Dennett, *Kinds of Minds: Toward an Understanding of Consciousness* (New York: Basic Books, 1996), 33.

30. George Beard, the neurologist who coined the term "neurasthenia" to describe nervous exhaustion, maintained that "where there is no civilization there is no nervousness"; *American Nervousness: It's Causes and Consequences* (New York: Putnam, 1881), 175.

31. Recent theorists of emotion, in fact, often explicitly draw on the nineteenth-century evolutionary neurology of John Hughlings Jackson (1835–1911) to describe the shared human capacity for feeling (as well as those capacities that human beings share with animals): see, for instance, Don M. Tucker, Douglas Derryberry, and Phan Luu, "Anatomy and Physiology of Human Emotion," in *The Neurophysiology of Emotion*, ed. Joan C. Borod (Oxford: Oxford University Press, 2000): 56–79. For an influential account of emotional expression in terms of both physiological mechanisms and cultural conventions modulating their display, see Paul Ekman, "Biological and Cultural Contributions to Body and Facial Movement in the Expression of Emotions," in *Explaining Emotions*, ed. Amélie O. Rorty (Berkeley: University of California Press, 1980): 73–102.

32. For an evenhanded overview of recent debates over the status of emotions, see anthropologist William M. Reddy's book *The Navigation of Feeling: A Framework for the History of Emotions* (Cambridge: Cambridge University Press, 2001), esp. 31–33.

33. Dennett, *Kinds of Minds*, 128.

1. "The Zest, the Tingle, the Excitement of Reality"

1. The epigraph is from Diane Ackerman, *An Alchemy of Mind: The Marvel and the Mystery of the Brain* (New York: Scribner, 2004), 27. Subsequent references to this work appear in parentheses in the text. See Henry James, *Roderick Hudson* (New York: Penguin, 1986), 42. Subsequent references to this work appear in parentheses in the text.

2. Ibid.

3. John Dewey, *Art as Experience* (1934) (New York: Perigee Books, 1980), 42; emphasis added. Subsequent references to this work appear in parentheses in the text.

4. For a very helpful discussion of what Daniel Mark Fogel calls "James's role as a founder of modernism" (*Covert Relations: James Joyce, Virginia Woolf, and Henry James* [Charlottesville: University of Virginia Press, 1990], 2) see David McWhirter, "Henry James, (Post)Modernist?" *Henry James Review* 25, no. 2 (spring 2004): 168–194, esp. 170–171.

5. Millicent Bell has described (and critiqued) Edel's Freudian biographical perspective in pithy terms: "In search of the inner man . . . Edel sought revelations in the novelist's fiction which he tended to read, simplistically, as a transposition of life, thereby making a fiction of his own. And laying James on the psychoanalytic couch, he hypothesized buried tensions" ("The Divine, the Unique," *Times Literary Supplement*, December 6, 1996, 3–4.) See, for instance, Edel, *Henry James: The Treacherous Years*, (Philadelphia: Lippincott, 1969), vol. 4. The importance of Shoshana Felman's psychoanalytic reading of "The Turn of the Screw" for James criticism can't be overestimated; see "Turning the Screw of Interpretation," *Yale French Studies* 55/56 (1977): 94–207. For a more recent reading of James in terms of a "psychoanalytic paradigm" (16), see Kaja Silverman, *Male Subjectivity at the Margins* (New York: Routledge, 1992).

6. Elizabeth Wilson, *Psychosomatic: Feminism and the Neurological Body* (Durham, N.C.: Duke University Press, 2004), 82.

7. William James, "What Is an Emotion?" (1884), in *Collected Essays and Reviews* (New York: Longmans, Green, 1920), 252. Subsequent references to this work appear in parentheses in the text.

8. John Dewey, "Psychology as Philosophic Method" (1886), in *The Philosophy of John Dewey*, ed. John J. McDermott (Chicago: University of Chicago Press, 1973), 119.

9. I wish to credit Nicholas Gaskill with formulating the link between being moved and being repositioned.

10. John Dewey, "The Reflex Arc Concept in Psychology" (1896), in *The Philosophy of John Dewey*, 139.

11. W. K. Wimsatt and Monroe Beardsley, *The Verbal Icon: Studies in the Meaning of Poetry* (Lexington: University of Kentucky Press, 1954), 34.

12. Scholars of early and antebellum American literature have written persuasively on the centrality of sympathy to democratic nation-building: see, for instance, Julia A. Stern, *The Plight of Feeling: Sympathy and Dissent in the Early American Novel* (Chicago: University of Chicago Press, 1997); Elizabeth Barnes, *States of Sympathy: Seduction and Democracy in the American Novel* (New York: Columbia University Press, 1997); Caleb Crain, *American Sympathy: Men, Friendship, and Literature in the New Nation* (New Haven, Conn.: Yale University Press, 2001); and Elizabeth Maddock Dillon, "Sentimental Aesthetics," *American Literature* 76, no. 3 (September 2004): 495–523.

13. Lawrence Rothfield, *Vital Signs: Medical Realism in Nineteenth-Century*

Fiction (Princeton, N.J.: Princeton University Press, 1992), 85. Rothfield's description of the "new, absolute gap" between the subject and object of investigation (e.g. doctor and patient) draws on Michel Foucault's conception of the silent, unemotive, "clinical gaze"; see *The Birth of the Clinic; an Archaeology of Medical Perception*, trans. A. M. Sheridan Smith (New York: Pantheon Books, 1973).

14. George Levine, *Dying to Know: Scientific Epistemology and Narrative in Victorian England* (Chicago: University of Chicago Press, 2002), 14.

15. Nancy Glazener, *Reading for Realism: The History of a U.S. Institution, 1850–1910* (Durham, N.C.: Duke University Press, 1997), 113.

16. Caroline Levine, in *The Serious Pleasures of Suspense: Victorian Realism and Narrative Doubt* (Charlottesville: University of Virginia Press, 2003), modulates this equation of realism and science and the concomitant suppression of affect. Drawing a more supple alignment between the methods of science and the operations of narrative suspense, Levine urges that both share an epistemological skepticism as well as a rich sense of the pleasures of investigation. Yet even in Levine's nuanced account, literary realists and scientists are said to share the commitment to seeking facts and objects in the world that are understood to exist independent of human knowledge, values, and activity.

17. Amy Kaplan associated the critical retrenchment of the late 1970s and 1980s with "the perceived failure or impossibility of mimesis"; *The Social Construction of American Literary Realism* (Chicago: University of Chicago Press, 1981), 6. Eric Sundquist, in his influential introduction to *American Realism: New Essays*, ed. Sundquist (Baltimore: Johns Hopkins University Press, 1982), set the terms for a criticism focused on realism's inevitable failure when he wrote, "The period between the Civil War and World War I is one in which American writers felt most compelled, and tried hardest, to become 'realists'—and failed"; "Introduction: The Country of the Blue," 7. The verdict of failure is sounded in the titles of some academic studies, as with Brook Thomas, *American Literary Realism and the Failed Promise of Contract* (1997), and Michael Davitt Bell, *The Problem of American Literary Realism* (1994). Jennifer Fleissner, in *Women, Compulsion, Modernity: The Moment of American Naturalism* (Chicago: Chicago University Press, 2004), has recently added a turn to the screw of realism's failure: she suggests that a key difference between realism and naturalism is that naturalist fiction demonstrates the inevitable failure of certain obsessive aspirations ("the subject's failure to escape," "the failure of the individual developmental story," "a failure to develop into a woman or a man," 52), while realism fails to acknowledge its own affinity with naturalism's (admittedly failed) commitments to agency, narrative plenitude, and gender stability.

18. Sundquist, "Introduction," 23; Louis Budd, quoted in Donald Pizer, "Introduction: The Problem of Definition," in *The Cambridge Companion to American Realism and Naturalism, Howells to London*, ed. Pizer (Cambridge: Cambridge University Press, 1995), 16.

19. Glazener, for example, argues that writers such as William Dean Howells were legislating taste and "reproduc[ing] relations of class, gender, and race

dominance" (*Reading for Realism*, 96). See also Phillip Barrish, *American Literary Realism, Critical Theory, and Intellectual Prestige, 1880–1995* (Cambridge: Cambridge University Press, 2001); Kenneth Warren, *Black and White Strangers: Race and American Literary Realism* (Chicago: University of Chicago Press, 1993); and Joan Burbick, *Healing the Republic: The Language of Health and the Culture of Nationalism in Nineteenth-Century America* (Cambridge: Cambridge University Press, 1994).

20. Studies by Eve Kosofsky Sedgwick and Philip Fisher constitute partial exceptions to this assertion. Sedgwick, in *Touching Feeling: Affect, Pedagogy, Performativity* (Durham, N.C.: Duke University Press, 2003), does treat the nineteenth-century writers Charles Dickens (but not Darwin) and Henry James (but not William). However, Sedgwick's work on the affect theories of Sylvan Tompkins, done with Adam Frank, attends more directly to the history of the body in its biological form; see Sedgwick and Frank, eds., *Shame and Its Sisters: A Silvan Tompkins Reader* (Durham, N.C.: Duke University Press, 1995). Fisher, though beginning *The Vehement Passions* (Princeton, N.J.: Princeton University Press, 2002) with a discussion of Charles Darwin and William James, is finally more interested in a particular literary-philosophical tradition than historical accounts of embodiment. Subsequent references to this work appear in parentheses in the text.

21. R. W. B. Lewis, *The American Adam: Innocence, Tragedy and Tradition in the Nineteenth Century* (Chicago: University of Chicago Press, 1955), 35.

22. Martha Nussbaum has written extensively on the cognitive nature of emotion, in works such as *Love's Knowledge: Essays on Philosophy and Literature* (New York: Oxford University Press, 1990) and more recently in *Upheavals of Thought: The Intelligence of Emotions* (New York: Cambridge University Press, 2001). Rei Terada, in her *Feeling in Theory: Emotion after the "Death of the Subject"* (Cambridge, Mass.: Harvard University Press, 2001), argues for the relevance of feeling to poststructuralist theory, claiming that emotions "are less sensations that happen to one than thoughts that one pursues" (19). (Subsequent references to this work appear in parentheses in the text.) Charles Altieri, in his desire to avoid the cognitivist recuperation of feeling evident in Nussbaum and Terada, urges that critics should not "overread for 'meaning'" and should instead attend to the mystical "attunements" that aesthetic objects make possible; see *The Particulars of Rapture: An Aesthetics of the Affects* (Ithaca, N.Y.: Cornell University Press, 2003), 2, 3.

23. Wilson, *Psychosomatic*, 7.

24. Bill Brown, "Thing Theory," in *Things* (Chicago: University of Chicago Press, 2004): 1–21, 7.

25. An important exception to this tendency toward disciplinary division is Steven Meyer's immensely intriguing work on Gertrude Stein. In *Irresistible Dictation: Gertrude Stein and the Correlations of Writing and Science* (Palo Alto, CA: Stanford University Press, 2001), Meyer argues that Stein's work exemplifies how "writing . . . is a function of neurology" and "the life sciences are a function of writing."

26. Quoted in "Bain on the Senses and the Intellect" (anonymous review), *Anthropological Review* 2, no. 7 (November 1864), 252.

27. Bill Brown, *A Sense of Things: The Object Matter of American Literature* (Chicago: University of Chicago Press, 2003), 64.

28. Elaine Scarry, *The Body in Pain: The Making and Unmaking of the World* (New York: Oxford University Press, 1985), 280. Subsequent references to this work appear in parentheses in the text.

29. Daniel Dennett, *Kinds of Minds: Toward an Understanding of Consciousness* (New York: Basic Books, 1996), 33.

30. Lori Merish, *Sentimental Materialism: Gender, Commodity Culture, and Nineteenth-Century American Literature* (Durham, N.C.: Duke University Press, 2000), 151.

31. William James, *A World of Pure Experience* (1904), in *Writings, 1902–1910*, ed. Bruce Kuklick (New York: Library of America, 1987), 1180, 1177.

32. Kaplan, *Social Construction,* 13. See, for instance, Marianne Noble, *The Masochistic Pleasures of Sentimental Literature* (Princeton, N.J.: Princeton University Press, 2000), and Fleissner, *Women, Compulsion, Modernity.*

33. George Lakoff and Mark Johnson, *Philosophy in the Flesh: The Embodied Mind and Its Challenge to Western Thought* (New York: Basic Books, 1999), 4. Subsequent references to this work are included in parentheses in the text.

34. Dennett, *Kinds of Minds,* 24.

35. See Babette Rothschild, *The Body Remembers: The Psychophysiology of Trauma and Trauma Treatment* (New York: Norton, 2000), 44; and Bessel van der Kolk, "The Body Keeps the Score," *Harvard Review of Psychiatry* 1 (1994): 253–265.

36. Quoted in Dennett, *Kinds of Minds,* 79.

37. Charles Darwin, *The Expression of the Emotions in Man and Animals* (1872), 2nd ed., ed. Francis Darwin, in *The Works of Charles Darwin,* ed. Paul H. Barrett and R. B. Freeman, vol. 23 (New York: New York University Press, 1989).

38. Ronald de Sousa, *The Rationality of Emotion* (Cambridge, Mass.: MIT Press, 1987), xv.

39. Philip Fisher, *Hard Facts: Setting and Form in the American Novel* (New York: Oxford University Press, 1987), 98.

40. See Karen Sanchez-Eppler, *Touching Liberty: Feminism, Abolition, and the Politics of the Body* (Berkeley: University of California Press, 1993).

41. Michael Bell, *Sentimentalism, Ethics, and the Culture of Feeling* (New York: Palgrave, 2000), 65.

42. Joseph LeDoux, *The Emotional Brain: The Mysterious Underpinnings of Emotional Life* (New York: Touchstone, 1996), 69.

43. James Dawes, "Fictional Feeling," *American Literature* 76, no. 3 (September 2004): 462. This issue of *American Literature* is devoted to the topic of aesthetics, especially as it is currently being reenergized as a relevant category by literary and cultural critics.

44. Immanuel Kant, *The Critique of Judgment* (1790), trans. James Creed Meredith (Oxford: Clarendon Press, 1964), 145.

45. Elizabeth Dillon, "Sentimental Aesthetics," *American Literature* 76, no. 3 (2004): 501.

46. Suzanne Langer, *Feeling and Form: A Theory of Art* (New York: Scribner, 1953), 17. Subsequent references to this work appear in parentheses in the text.

47. Paul Gilmore, "Romantic Electricity, or the Materiality of Aesthetics," *American Literature* 76, no. 3 (September 2004), 472.

48. Isobel Armstrong, *The Radical Aesthetic* (Oxford: Blackwell, 2000), 2–3; emphasis added.

49. Antonio Damasio, *Looking for Spinoza: Joy, Sorrow, and the Feeling Brain* (New York: Harcourt 2003), 91. Subsequent references to this work appear in parentheses in the text.

50. Dewey, *Art as Experience*, 133.

51. Adam Frank, "Some Avenues for Feeling" (review essay), *Criticism* 46, no. 3 (2004): 522.

52. Pamela Thurschwell, *Literature, Technology, and Magical Thinking, 1880–1920* (Cambridge: Cambridge University Press, 2001), 11. Subsequent references to this work appear in parentheses in the text.

53. William James, *The Varieties of Religious Experience: A Study in Human Nature* (New York: MacMillan, 1961), 67.

54. Rockwell, "Some Causes and Characteristics of Neurasthenia," *New York Medical Journal* 58 (1893): 590, quoted in F. G. Gosling, *Before Freud: Neurasthenia and the American Medical Community, 1870–1910* (Urbana-Champagne: University of Illinois Press, 1987), 13.

55. Henry James, *A Small Boy and Others* (New York: Scribner, 1913), 104.

56. S. Weir Mitchell, *Wear and Tear, or Hints for the Overworked* (1871) (Philadelphia: Lippincott, 1887), 28–29.

57. Louis Menand, *The Metaphysical Club: A Story of Ideas in America* (New York: Farrar, Straus, and Giroux, 2001), 123.

58. James Hutton, *Theory of the Earth with Proofs and Illustrations* (London: Cadell, Junior, and Davies; Edinburgh: William Creech, 1795). *Historiae Naturalis Classica*, ed. J. Cramer and H. K. Swann, 2 vols. (Weinheim, Germany: H. R. Engelmann, 1960), 1:200.

59. Nathaniel Hawthorne, *The House of the Seven Gables* (1851) (New York: Signet Classics, 1990), 279.

60. William James, *The Principles of Psychology* (1890) (Cambridge, Mass.: Harvard University Press, 1983).

61. Gerald E. Myers, *William James: His Life and Thought* (New Haven, Conn.: Yale University Press, 1986), 61.

62. William James, "Does Consciousness Exist?" (1904), in *Essays in Radical Empiricism* (New York: Longmans, Green, 1920), 9.

63. Quoted in Myers, *William James*, 61.

64. Quoted in ibid., 62.

65. William James, *Psychology: The Briefer Course* (1892), in *Writings: 1878–1899* (New York: Library of America, 1992), 169.

66. "The Case of George Dedlow," *Atlantic Monthly*, July 1866, 1–11. Subsequent references to this story appear in parentheses in the text.

67. William James, "Remarks on Spencer's Definition of Mind as Correspondence" (1878), in James, *Writings: 1878–1879*, 908. James was pointed in his critique of Herbert Spencer, whose 1855 *Principles of Psychology* was explicitly replaced by James's own 1890 work of the same title. James was dismissive of Spencer's lack of both appropriate scientific knowledge and appropriate passion: "His dry schoolmaster temperament, the hurdy-gurdy monotony of him, his preference for cheap makeshifts in argument, his lack of education even in mechanical principles, and in general the vagueness of all his fundamental ideas, his whole system wooden, as if knocked together out of cracked hemlock boards—and yet the half of England wants to bury him in Westminster Abbey"; *Pragmatism: A New Name for Some Old Ways of Thinking* (1907), in *Writings, 1902–1910*, 503.

68. James, "The Sentiment of Rationality," in *Writings 1878–1899*, 950.

69. See Randall Knoper, "American Literary Realism and Nervous 'Reflexion,'" *American Literature* 74, no. 4 (2002): 715–745, for an excellent précis of the reflex arc; also Peter Melville Logan, *Nerves and Narratives: A Cultural History of Hysteria in Nineteenth-Century British Prose* (Berkeley: University of California Press, 1997).

70. There have been a number of first-rate studies that examine nervousness as a discursive index to nineteenth-century culture. See Tom Lutz, *American Nervousness, 1903: An Anecdotal History* (Ithaca, N.Y: Cornell University Press, 1991); and George Rousseau, *Nervous Acts: Essays on Literature, Culture, Sensibility* (Houndmills, England: Palgrave Macmillan, 2004). Historical studies of nervousness and neurasthenia include Sander L. Gilman et al., *Hysteria beyond Freud* (Berkeley: University of California Press, 1993); Janet Oppenheim, *"Shattered Nerves": Doctors, Patients, and Depression in Victorian England* (New York: Oxford University Press, 1991); and Marijke Gijswijt-Hofstra and Roy Porter, eds., *Cultures of Neurasthenia: From Beard to the First World War* (Amsterdam: Rodopi, 2001).

71. The year after Oliver Wendell Holmes's *Elsie Venner* appeared in serialized form, 1860, also saw the publication of *The Life and Labours of Sir Charles Bell*, followed by the *Memoirs of Marshal Hall, M.D., F.R.S*, in 1861.

72. Thomas Laycock, *Mind and Brain: Or, The Correlations of Consciousness and Organisation; With Their Applications to Philosophy, Physiology, Mental Pathology, and the Practice of Medicine* (Edinburgh: Sutherland and Knox, 1860), 55; emphasis added.

73. Oliver Wendell Holmes, *Elsie Venner: A Romance of Destiny* (1861) (Boston: Houghton, Mifflin, 1892), 111–112.

74. The term *proprioception* was coined by Charles Sherrington (1857–1952), a British neurophysiologist, who was educated in medicine at Cambridge and was later a professor of physiology at Oxford.

75. Myers, *William James*, 36.

76. Alexander Bain, *The Emotions and the Will* (London: John W. Parker, 1859), 9–10. Subsequent references are included in parentheses in the text.

77. Henry Maudsley, *Pathology of Mind* (1879), 222, quoted in Théodule Ribot, *The Psychology of the Emotions* (1897) (New York: Scribner's, 1914), 111.

78. James, "The Psychology of Belief" (1888), 1035n; "On a Certain Blindness in Human Beings" (1899), in *Writings: 1878–1899.*

79. Charles Darwin, *On the Origin of Species* (1859), ed. Gillian Beer (Oxford: Oxford University Press, [UK], 1996), 37.

80. Claude Bernard, *An Introduction to the Study of Experimental Medicine,* trans. Henry Copley Greene (New York: Macmillan, 1927).

81. John Hughlings Jackson, "Remarks on Evolution and Dissolution of the Nervous System," *Journal of Mental Science* 33 (1887–1888): 25–48, 29–30, quoted in Anne Harrington, *Medicine, Mind, and the Double Brain: A Study in Nineteenth-Century Thought* (Princeton, N.J.: Princeton University Press, 1987), 211.

82. The twentieth-century researcher Paul D. MacLean adapts Hughlings Jackson's model of the evolutionary-based tripartite structure of the nervous system in his (MacLean's) conception of the "triune brain"; "Sensory and Perceptive Facts in Emotional Functions of the Triune Brain," in *Explaining Emotions,* ed. Amélie Rorty (Berkeley: University of California Press, 1980), 9–36. MacLean writes, "In evolution the human brain expands in hierarchic fashion along the lines of three basic patterns," which he terms "reptilian, paleomammalian, and neomammalian" (14).

83. Wilson, *Psychosomatic,* 82. Wilson is similarly interested in the theories of Paul MacLean, arguing for their recuperation for feminism. She writes, "Without jettisoning hierarchy entirely (for it remains a powerful conceptual device), MacLean and [Oliver] Sacks amplify the relations that exist across evolutionary branches" (87).

84. James, *Psychology: The Briefer Course,* 146.

85. Ibid., 151.

86. James, "On a Certain Blindness," 842.

87. Sämi Ludwig, *Pragmatist Realism: The Cognitive Paradigm in American Realist Texts* (Madison: University of Wisconsin Press, 2002), has initiated a helpful reconsideration of the connections, historical and philosophical, between pragmatism and literary realism. He argues that a focus on how texts are experienced "implies agency and cognitive construction that go beyond mimesis in a simple, positivist sense" (213). Grounded in cybernetic and cognitive theory, Ludwig's analysis centers on the "'practical,' operational qualities" of literary representations; this orientation, however, leads him to overlook the affective textures of aesthetic experience.

88. Quoted in David L. Hildebrand, *Beyond Realism and Antirealism: John Dewey and the Neo-Pragmatists* (Nashville, Tenn.: Vanderbilt University Press, 2003), 36–37.

89. William James, "The Gospel of Relaxation" (1899), in *Writings: 1878–1899,* 843.

90. Quoted in Hildebrand, *Beyond Realism,* 64.

91. Quoted in ibid., 65.

92. For a range of approaches to the question of Mark Twain's realism, see Gregg Camfield, *Sentimental Twain: Samuel Clemens in the Maze of Moral Philosophy* (Philadelphia: University of Pennsylvania Press, 1994);

Randall Knoper, *Acting Naturally Mark Twain in the Culture of Performance* (Berkeley: University of California Press, 1995); and Susan Gillman, *Dark Twins: Imposture and Identity in Mark Twain's America* (Chicago: University of Chicago Press, 1989).

93. Mark Twain, *Adventures of Huckleberry Finn* (New York: Bantam, 1981), 150. Subsequent references to this work appear in parentheses in the text.

94. Sacvan Bercovitch, "Deadpan Huck: Or, What's Funny about Interpretation," *Kenyon Review* 24, nos. 3/4 (summer/fall 2002): 90–134.

95. Thomas Hobbes, *The Elements of Law Natural and Politic* (1650), chap. 9, "Of the Passions of the Mind," electronic text center, University of Virginia Library, [http://etext.lib.virginia.edu/toc/moderng/public/Hob2Ele.html].

96. William Archer, *Masks or Faces?* (1888), reprinted in *The Paradox of Acting and Masks or Faces* (New York: Hill and Wang, 1957), 157. Subsequent references to this work appear in parentheses in the text. For a provocative reading of Mark Twain's affinity for Archer's theories, in terms of the novelist's *anxieties* about "connections between the body surface and its interior, gesture and emotion, sign and referent," see Knoper, 97.

97. Bell, *Sentimentalism, Ethics, and the Culture of Feeling*, 64.

98. Janice Radway, *Reading the Romance: Women, Patriarchy, and Popular Literature* (Chapel Hill: University of North Carolina Press, 1991), 197.

99. John Dewey, "The Theory of Emotion" (1895), reprinted in *What Is an Emotion? Classic and Contemporary Readings*, ed. Robert C. Solomon (Oxford: Oxford University Press, 2003), 86, 87.

100. Henry James, *Hawthorne* (New York: AMS Press, 1968), 55, 56.

101. Charles Darwin, *The Works of Charles Darwin*, 23:151.

2. Statistical Pity

1. Charles J. Cullingworth estimates that "during the fifty-seven years (1847–1903), for which the statistics for England and Wales are available, there were registered no fewer than 93,243 mothers as having died from puerperal septicemia"; *Oliver Wendell Holmes and the Contagiousness of Puerperal Fever* (London: Henry J. Glaisher, 1906), 25.

2. This passage from Charles D. Meigs, *Females and Their Diseases* (Philadelphia: Lea and Blanchard, 1848) is quoted in *Childbed Fever: A Documentary History*, ed. Irvine Loudon (New York: Garland, 1995), 61.

3. Charles D. Meigs, *On the Nature, Signs, and Treatments of Childbed Fevers; In a Series of Letters Addressed to the Students of His Class* (Philadelphia: Lea and Blanchard, 1854), 215. Further quotations from this work are cited parenthetically in the text. Meegan Kennedy, in *Case Fictions: Medical Narrative and the British Novel* (unpublished manuscript), examines case histories of British women stricken with puerperal fever and the sentimental rhetoric and tropes employed by the writer/physician.

4. Ian Watt, *The Rise of the Novel: Studies in Defoe, Richardson, and Fielding* (Berkeley: University of California Press, 1957). Watt makes this point

succinctly: "Philosophically the particularising approach to character resolves itself into the problem of defining the individual person" (18). For studies that treat the links between the history of the novel and the rise of individualism, see also Michael McKeon, *The Origins of the English Novel, 1600–1740* (Baltimore: Johns Hopkins University Press, 1987); Nancy Armstrong's *Desire and Domestic Fiction: A Political History of the Novel* (New York: Oxford University Press, 1987); Gillian Brown, *Domestic Individualism: Imagining Self in Nineteenth-Century America* (Berkeley: University of California Press, 1990); and Catherine Gallagher, *Nobody's Story: The Vanishing Acts of Women Writers in the Marketplace* (Berkeley: University of California Press, 1994).

5. Adam Zachary Newton, *Narrative Ethics* (Cambridge, Mass.: Harvard University Press, 1995), provides an excellent introduction to this strain of criticism. See also Lawrence Buell, "Introduction: In Pursuit of Ethics," *Proceedings of the Modern Language Association* 114, no. 1 (January 1999): 7–19, esp. 13.

6. The phrase "epistemological violence" is drawn from Wai Chee Dimock, *Residues of Justice: Law, Philosophy, Literature*, a provocative study of nineteenth-century literature and culture (Berkeley: University of California Press, 1996), 7.

7. Mary Poovey, "Figures of Arithmetic, Figures of Speech: The Discourse of Statistics in the 1830s," in *Questions of Evidence: Proof, Practice, and Persuasion across the Disciplines*, ed. James Chandler, Arnold I. Davidson, and Harry Harootunian (Chicago: University of Chicago Press, 1994), 414; Dimock, *Residues of Justice*, 10, 7. In a sustained critique of numerical representation, Poovey provides an illuminating historical account of the rise of statistics in England and its uncertain status as a science in early nineteenth-century England. In "Sex in America," *Critical Inquiry* 24 (winter 1998): 366–392, Poovey urges that narrative, in the form of the ethnographic interview, may be a way of producing knowledge that serves as a remedy for the noxious effects of statistics.

8. Martha Nussbaum, *Poetic Justice: The Literary Imagination and Public Life* (Boston: Beacon Press, 1995), 26–27.

9. Elaine Scarry, introduction to *Literature and the Body: Essays on Populations and Persons*, ed. Scarry (Baltimore: Johns Hopkins University Press, 1988), xxiv. Scarry anatomizes what she terms the "materialist conception of language" (xi) that links the essays in her volume, noting that this critical stance extends the ethical purview of literature to the role of the critic, leading some essayists to conceive of their scholarly work as directly ameliorative with respect to past events, a critical project she finds "quite astonishing and immodest" (xxii).

10. Literary critics are not alone in disparaging systematic modes of understanding. The medical anthropologist Arthur Kleinman, for instance, has written an impassioned critique of the diagnostic techniques of modern medicine in his influential book *The Illness Narratives: Suffering, Healing, and the Human Condition* (New York: Basic Books, 1988).

11. Martha Nussbaum, *Love's Knowledge: Essays on Philosophy and Literature* (New York: Oxford University Press, 1990), 22.

12. Charles E. Rosenberg, *Explaining Epidemics and Other Studies in the History of Medicine* (Cambridge: Cambridge University Press, 1992), 92; emphasis added.

13. Charles D. Meigs makes a notorious appearance as a bitter opponent of administering anesthesia during childbirth in Mary Poovey, "Scenes of an Indelicate Character: The Medical Treatment of Victorian Women," in Poovey, *Uneven Developments: The Ideological Work of Gender in Mid-Victorian England* (Chicago: University of Chicago Press, 1988).

14. Holmes was part of a rising coterie of American physicians—including influential men such as Jacob Bigelow, Henry Bowditch, James Jackson Putnam, and Elisha Bartlett—who were trained in Paris by a talented group of French clinicians attempting to infuse the observational techniques of modern science into the study and practice of medicine. As Holmes later wrote of his Parisian mentor, "[The pathologist Pierre] Louis taught us who followed him the love of truth, the habit of passionless listening to the teachings of nature, the most careful and searching methods of observation, and the sure means of getting at the results to be obtained from them in the constant employment of accurate tabulation"; "Some of My Early Teachers," in *Medical Essays*, in *The Works of Oliver Wendell Holmes*, 13 vols. (Boston: Houghton Mifflin, 1892), 9:436. All subsequent citations from Holmes's writings are from this edition of his *Works*.) Michel Foucault calls this detached, observational approach "the medical gaze" in *The Birth of the Clinic: An Archaeology of Medical Perception*, trans. A. M. Sheridan Smith (New York: Vintage Books, 1973); see especially 107–122. For Holmes's assessment of the move from traditional therapeutics to scientific medicine, see "Currents and Counter-currents in Medical Science," *Works*, 9:173–208, esp. 180–186, 195.

15. In referring to the morally integrated world of traditional therapeutics, I am drawing on the historian Charles E. Rosenberg's examination of early nineteenth-century medicine as a practice predicated on a "model of the body, and of health and disease . . . [that] was all-inclusive, antireductionist, and capable of incorporating every aspect of man's life in explaining his physical condition" (*Explaining Epidemics*, 18).

16. In *Kinds of Minds: Toward an Understanding of Consciousness* (New York: Basic Books, 1996), Dennett distinguishes between an everyday understanding of intention and *intentionality* in "the philosophical sense": "In ordinary parlance, we often discuss whether someone's action was intentional or not. . . . Intentionality in the philosophical sense is just *aboutness*. Something exhibits intentionality if its competence is in some way *about* something else. An alternative would be to say that something that exhibits intentionality contains a *representation* of something else—but I find that less revealing and more problematic. Does a lock contain a representation of the key that opens it? A lock and key exhibit the crudest form of intentionality; so do the opioid receptors in brain cells" (35). (Sub-

sequent references to this work appear in parentheses in the text.) In my discussion of Holmes's *Elsie Venner* I argue that the idea of intention in the psychological sense—e.g. did the doctors *intend* to kill their patients?—is supplemented by intention in the philosophical sense, which allowed Holmes to discern "intentionality" in the pattern of deaths in the absence of murderous intent on the part of the doctors. In this sense, intentionality needn't be about specific aims, beliefs, or desires—it doesn't require a particular mental content on the part of the (inadvertently homicidal) physician, and strikingly, it doesn't require a particular mental content on the part of the person "tracking" the entity in question. Holmes, crucially, had absolutely no sense of the ultimate cause of maternal mortality (an invisible particle? a miasma? the evil eye?), only the proximate cause: the physicians. Because Holmes himself worked in medicine, he was uninterested in legalistic questions about culpability for "unintentional" actions, something his son Oliver Wendell Holmes Jr. would take up later in the century in the context of tort law. Holmes Sr. focused solely on the pragmatics of the situation: how to mitigate suffering and prevent future deaths.

This new way of thinking about intentionality, in turn, provided a way of thinking about bodies as themselves harboring intentions, in a Darwinian sense. Mindfulness, in other words, is not a state limited to cerebration and higher consciousness; the character Elsie Venner's orientation toward cliffs, for instance, exhibits a rudimentary "aboutness," as does her affinity for her nurse Sophy, even though Elsie does not cast it into language (e.g. "Gee, I'd like to climb up those rocks" or "Sophy's the greatest—I really love her."). Darwin's insight, which Holmes extends in his work, was to discern in these "lower" capacities not just the distant evolutionary origin of cognition classically understood (and the "higher" feelings such as love) but the everyday substrate of both. Holmes's assertion that "there is a Pythoness in every breast" is not merely metaphorical: there is, as Paul MacLean would put it, a "reptilian brain" in every human being.

17. Charles Darwin, *The Origin of Species by Natural Selection*, ed. Gillian Beer (Oxford: Oxford University Press, 1996), 154.

18. William James, "What Is an Emotion?" (1884), in *Collected Essays and Reviews* (New York: Longmans, Green, 1920), 68.

19. Théodule Ribot, *Diseases of Memory* (1882), trans. William Huntington Smith (Washington D.C.: University Publications of America, 1977), 31.

20. Eric Sundquist has succinctly summed up this approach to literary naturalism in his introduction to *American Realism: New Essays*: "Revelling in the extraordinary, the excessive, and the grotesque in order to reveal the immutable bestiality of Man in Nature, naturalism dramatizes the loss of individuality at a physiological level by making a Calvinism without God its determining order and violent death its utopia"; (Baltimore: Johns Hopkins University Press, 1982), 13.

21. In trauma, to borrow a chapter title from the book *Traumatic Stress*, "The Body Keeps the Score"; in *Traumatic Stress: The Effects of Overwhelming Experience on Mind, Body, and Society*, ed. Bessel A. van der Kolk, Alexan-

der C. McFarlane, and Lars Weisaeth (New York: Guilford Press, 1996). As theorized by the literary critic Cathy Caruth in *Unclaimed Experience: Trauma, Narrative, and History* (Baltimore: Johns Hopkins University Press, 1996), a traumatic event is associated with the horribly, irrefutably real insofar as it shuts down the human capacity to express it; elusive to cognition or memory understood as a function of consciousness, traumatic events are (in the words of Ruth Leys) "permanently 'etched' or 'engraved' in a way that is theorized as standing outside all ordinary cognition"; *Trauma: A Genealogy* (Chicago: University of Chicago Press, 2000), 250.

22. Elizabeth Wilson's recent work, *Psychosomatic: Feminism and the Neurological Body* (Durham, N.C.: Duke University Press, 2004), wittily refers to the tendency of some cultural and feminist critics to declare the "neurophysiological body" "soma non grata to a sophisticated account of hysteria" (8).

23. Henry James, *Roderick Hudson* (London: Penguin, 1986), 37.

24. Oliver Wendell Holmes, *Elsie Venner: A Romance of Destiny*, in *Works*, 3:429. Subsequent references to this novel appear in parentheses in the text.

25. Charles D. Meigs, *On the Nature, Signs, and Treatments of Childbed Fevers; In a Series of Letters Addressed to the Students of His Class* (Philadelphia: Lea and Blanchard, 1854), 88. Further quotations from this work are cited parenthetically in the text.

26. James Dawes, *The Language of War* (Cambridge, Mass.: Harvard University Press, 2002), 48. Dawes's pithy analysis of writing by Holmes's contemporaries encapsulates the dangers of a sentimental epistemology: "Because sympathy is a form of transferential narrative, it risks superimposing a simplifying and possibly alien structure upon concrete others" (48).

27. The historian of medicine John Cassedy elaborates the historical connection between nineteenth-century medicine and the theories of Benjamin Rush in his *American Medicine and Statistical Thinking* (Cambridge, Mass.: Harvard University Press, 1984), 52–56.

28. Benjamin Rush, *Medical Inquiries and Observations*, 4 vols. (Philadelphia: Carey, 1818), 3:6.

29. Rosenberg, *Explaining Epidemics*, 92. For other accounts of how doctors of traditional therapeutics conceived of disease, see John S. Haller, *American Medicine in Transition, 1840–1910* (Urbana: University of Illinois Press, 1981), esp. 17–29; and James H. Cassedy, *Medicine in America: A Short History* (Baltimore: Johns Hopkins University Press, 1991), 25–33.

30. Charles D. Meigs, *Woman: Her Diseases and Remedies. A Series of Letters to His Class*, 4th ed. (Philadelphia: Lea and Blanchard, 1859), 39. Subsequent references to this work appear (abbreviated *Woman*) in parentheses in the text.

31. Meigs, *On the Nature, Signs, and Treatments of Childbed Fevers*, 147. Subsequent references to this work appear (abbreviated *Childbed Fevers*) in parentheses in the text.

32. Hugh L. Hodge, *On the Non-contagious Character of Puerperal Fever: An Introductory Lecture* (Philadelphia: T. K. and P. G. Collins, 1852), 18. See also Meigs, *Childbed Fevers*, 102, 114.

33. Owsei Temkin draws on this term when he refers to the "'ontological' and the 'physiological'" conceptions of disease, in "The Scientific Approach to Disease: Specific Entity and Individual Sickness," in Temkin, *The Double Face of Janus and Other Essays in the History of Medicine* (Baltimore: Johns Hopkins University Press, 1977). Temkin points out that "ontologists have . . . been suspected of clinging to a demoniac aetiology of disease, even if the demon was replaced by a bacterium" (442–443).

34. Hodge, *On the Non-contagious Character*, 11.

35. Sharon Marcus, "Anne Frank and Hannah Arendt, Universalism and Pathos," in *Cosmopolitan Geographics (Essays from the English Institute)*, ed. Vinay Dharwadker (New York: Routledge, 2001): 89–132.

36. Holmes, "The Contagiousness of Puerperal Fever," in *Works*, 9:103–172; 128, 126. Further references to this essay appear parenthetically in the text.

37. Meigs, *Females and Their Diseases*, in Loudon, *Childbed Fever*, 59–60.

38. For a solid historical account that provides superb documentation of the prostatistical rhetoric in American medicine, see Cassedy, *American Medicine and Statistical Thinking*.

39. Holmes, "Some of My Early Teachers," 9:432.

40. Loudon, *Childbed Fever*, 20.

41. Holmes, "Currents and Counter-currents in Medical Science" (1861), in *Works*, 9:173–208, 195.

42. The type of personal knowledge that bolstered physicians' authority in traditional therapeutics is here overshadowed by the technique of numerical analysis; as Holmes's Harvard colleague Henry Bowditch put it, "The adherents to the numerical school . . . want something more definite. Give us your numbers"; *Remarks Relative to Dr. Paine's Commentaries upon the Writings of M. Louis* (Boston: D. Clapp Jr., 1840), 7. Regularization of technique and centralization of knowledge signaled the possibility of an American medicine that was, in the words of Worthington Hooker, a "rational therapeutics"; *Rational Therapeutics* (Boston: John Wilson, 1857).

43. The "microbe en chapelet" that Pasteur isolated was what we now term *streptococcus pyogenes*. Under normal circumstances, a woman's reproductive tract is relatively impermeable to such bacteria, but following the wounds of parturition and the detachment of the placenta, the vagina and uterus are highly susceptible to infection by contaminated instruments or hands. Physicians would often attend (or even dissect) a patient infected with strep bacteria before delivering another patient's baby. In the extreme case of Meigs's infamous student Dr. Rutter, who took great pains in washing himself, it is probable that the physician was an asymptomatic carrier, harboring the bacteria in his nasal passages. See Irvine Loudon, introduction to *Death in Childbirth: An International Study of Maternal Care and Maternal Mortality 1800–1950* (Oxford: Clarendon Press, 1992), xxix–xxxi.

44. While my analysis investigates the tensions between the novel's two plots—one treating medical/scientific concerns, the other treating affective or "human" issues—critics of the novel have tended to emphasize one plot

at the expense of the other. For science-focused analyses, see Charles Boewe, "Reflex Action in the Novels of Oliver Wendell Holmes," *American Literature* 26 (June 1954): 309; and Joan Burbick, *Healing the Republic: The Language of Health and the Culture of Nationalism in Nineteenth-Century America* (Cambridge: Cambridge University Press, 1994). For analysis of the marriage plot, see Margaret Hallisey, "Poisonous Creature: Holmes's *Elsie Venner*," *Studies in the Novel* 17 (winter 1985): 406–419.

45. Holmes, *The Professor at the Breakfast-Table* (1860), in Works 2: 119. Subsequent references to this work appear in parentheses in the text.

46. William Dean Howells, "Editor's Study," *Harper's*, November 1889, 966.

47. Oliver Wendell Holmes, "The Stereoscope and the Stereograph," *Atlantic Monthly*, June 1859, 744. Subsequent references to this piece appear in parentheses in the text.

48. Charles Darwin, *The Expression of the Emotions in Man and Animals* (1872), in *The Works of Charles Darwin*, vol. 23, ed. Paul H. Barrett and R. B. Freeman (New York: New York University Press, 1989).

49. Herbert Spencer, *The Principles of Psychology* (London: Longman, Brown, Green, and Longmans, 1855), 606, 548.

50. Paul MacLean, *The Triune Brain: Role in Paleocerebral Functions* (New York: Plenum, 1990); Neil Greenberg and Paul D. MacLean, eds., *Behavior and Neurology of Lizards: An Interdisciplinary Colloquium* (Rockville, Md.: Department of Health, Education, and Welfare, Public Health Service, Alcohol, Drug Abuse, and Mental Health Administration, National Institute of Mental Health, 1978).

51. An example of this approach to the character of Elsie may be found in Jenny Franchot, *Roads to Rome: The Antebellum Protestant Encounter with Catholicism* (Berkeley: University of California Press, 1994), in which Franchot characterizes Holmes's novel as a "romance of hybridity" (243).

52. Holmes, "Mechanism in Thought and Morals" (1871), in *Pages from an Old Volume of Life: A Collection of Essays, 1857–1881*, in *Works*, 13:286.

53. Irvine Loudon, *Death in Childbirth*, 1–2. Further references to this work appear parenthetically in the text.

54. In *Doctor's Stories: The Narrative Structure of Medical Knowledge* (Princeton, N.J.: Princeton University Press, 1991), Kathleen Montgomery Hunter echoes Holmes's work when she writes, "Impersonality is a virtue of medicine that these days, given the perceived diminution of medical caring, fails to receive its due. Intrinsic to the permission we grant physicians to touch our bodies, impersonality is not only a part of the scientific stance, it is also understood as an open and charitable, even egalitarian disinterestedness" (132).

3. Fear and Epistemology

1. Nathaniel Hawthorne, *House of the Seven Gables* (1851) (New York: Oxford University Press, 1991), 287.

2. Holmes, "Mechanism in Thought and Morals" (1871), in *Pages from an*

Old Volume of Life: A Collection of Essays, 1857–1881, in *The Works of Oliver Wendell Holmes* (Boston: Houghton Mifflin, 1892), 8:282. The quotation that serves as the epigraph to this chapter is on pp. 300–301.

3. "The Influence of Railway Travelling on Public Health: Report of the Commission," *Lancet*, January 4, 1862, 15–19, 15.

4. Oliver Wendell Holmes, "Bread and the Newspaper," in *Works* 8:7.

5. Oliver Wendell Holmes, *A Mortal Antipathy*, in *Works*, 7:20, 149. Subsequent references to this work are included in parentheses in the text.

6. Though we concur about the equation of emotional and physical shock in Holmes's last novel and in the discourse of railway spine, Randall Knoper emphasizes Holmes's linkage of neurological damage and sexual "inversion." In his compelling essay "Trauma and Sexual Inversion, circa 1885: Dr. Holmes's *A Mortal Antipathy* and Maladies of Representation," in *Neurology and Literature at the Fin de Siècle*, ed. Anne Stiles (forthcoming), Knoper positions Holmes's novel within "a history of the medicalization of homosexuality" (14, in ms.). For a useful contextualization of scientific themes in *Elsie Venner, The Guardian Angel*, and *A Mortal Antipathy*, see Charles Boewe, "Reflex Action in the Novels of Oliver Wendell Holmes," *American Literature* 26, no. 3 (November 1954): 303–319. More recently, Peter Gibian, in *Oliver Wendell Holmes and the Culture of Conversation* (Cambridge: Cambridge University Press, 2001) has framed Holmes's self-titled "'medicated novels'" in the context of discourse and dialogue, casting the narrative voice as that of the "doctor-confessor-psychoanalyst hero" (71).

7. Quoted in Anne Harrington, *Medicine, Mind, and the Double Brain: A Study in Nineteenth-Century Thought* (Princeton, N.J.: Princeton University Press, 1989), 10, 8.

8. Herbert Page, *Injuries of the Spine and Spinal Cord without Apparent Mechanical Lesion and Nervous Shock in Their Surgical and Medico-Legal Aspect* (London: J. and A. Churchill, 1883), 159.

9. While the work of Michel Foucault has been most influential among critical theorists, Barbara Ehrenreich's and Deirdre English's more popular account of the damage wrought by the rise of the (male-dominated) medical profession has also made an important contribution to work in this area. See *For Her Own Good: 150 Years of the Experts' Advice to Women* (Garden City, N.Y.: Doubleday, 1978). Stephanie P. Browner, *Profound Science and Elegant Literature: Imagining Doctors in Nineteenth-Century America* (Philadelphia: University of Pennsylvania Press, 2004), traces how the physician replaced the minister as the figure with the knowledge, expertise, and virtue to usher individuals through life's profound transitions of birth, sickness, and death. Browner's account, however, perpetuates what might be termed a doctrine of separate spheres when it comes to the encounters between science (and its emissaries) and the individual, especially in the emphasis on authorial resistance to the "medicalized body" and on the sorts of losses entailed by the encroachment of public science into the private zone of intimate suffering and joy.

10. Michel Foucault, *The Birth of the Clinic: An Archeology of Medical Per-*

ception (1963), trans. A. M. Sheridan Smith (New York: Vintage Books, 1973), xvii, xix. Subsequent references to this work appear in parentheses in the text.

11. Foucault, *Discipline and Punish: The Birth of the Prison* (1975), trans. A. M. Sheridan Smith (New York: Pantheon Books, 1977).

12. Mark Seltzer, *Serial Killers: Death and Life in America's Wound Culture* (New York: Routledge, 1998), 37.

13. John Skoyles, *Edge* (www.edge.org), "The World Question Center" (2005), www.edge.org/q2005/q05_6.html.

14. This reformulation of the doctor's role has been taken up, in more practical form, by contemporary medical writers such as Atul Gawande. Gawande proposes a model in which the physician does not merely tend an inert body (sociologist Talcott Parson's "sick role" model) or relinquish all responsibility for medical decisions to the patient (the model first theorized in 1984 by Jay Katz in his influential book *The Silent World of Doctor and Patient*). Instead, in his article "Whose Body Is It Anyway?" Gawande suggests something like a collaborative autonomy. Patients, he notes, are "glad to have their autonomy respected, but the exercise of that autonomy means being able to relinquish it"; *Complications: A Surgeon's Notes on an Imperfect Science* (New York: Holt, 2002), 220. "Where many ethicists go wrong," he concludes, "is in promoting patient autonomy as a kind of ultimate value in medicine rather than recognizing it as one value among others. . . . What patients want most from doctors isn't autonomy per se; it's competence and kindness" (223–224).

15. For a terrifically cogent discussion of the nervous system and its connection to the realism of William Dean Howells see Randall Knoper, "American Literary Realism and Nervous 'Reflexion,'" *American Literature* 74 no. 4 (December 2002): 715–745.

16. Glenn Hendler, *Public Sentiments: Structures of Feeling in Nineteenth-Century American Literature* (Chapel Hill: University of North Carolina Press, 2001), 167.

17. Paul White, "Of Scientific Character: The Physiology of Emotions and Emotions of Physiology in Victorian Britain," paper presented at the annual meeting of The History of Science Society, Milwaukee, Wisconsin, November 7–10, 2002, 2–3.

18. Christopher J. Lukasik, in his fascinating account of early American portraiture, argues that theorists of physiognomy sought to overcome this difficulty, focusing on "unalterable and involuntary facial features" to discern "a person's permanent moral character despite their social masks"; see "The Face of the Public," *Early American Literature* 39, no. 3 (2004): 426.

19. Thomas Laycock, *A Treatise on the Nervous Diseases of Women* (London: Longman, Orme, Brown, Green, and Longmans, 1840), 8, 82, quoted in Janet Oppenheim, *"Shattered Nerves": Doctors, Patients, and Depression in Victorian England* (New York: Oxford University Press, 1991), 143–144.

20. Jean-Louis Brachet, *Traité clinique et thérapeutique de l'hystérie* (Paris: Balliere, 1847), quoted in Evelyne Ender, *Sexing the Mind: Nineteenth-*

Century Fictions of Hysteria (Ithaca, N.Y.: Cornell University Press, 1995), 37–38.

21. Thomas Laycock, *Mind and Brain: Or, The Correlations of Consciousness and Organisation; With Their Applications to Philosophy, Physiology, Mental Pathology, and the Practice of Medicine* (Edinburgh: Sutherland and Knox, 1860), 31.

22. Guillaume Duchenne, quoted in Charles Darwin, *The Expression of the Emotions in Man and Animals*, 3rd ed. (New York: Oxford University Press, 1998), 18–19; introduction to first edition.

23. Daniel Dennett, *Kinds of Minds: Toward an Understanding of Consciousness* (New York: Basic Books, 1996), 60–61.

24. Henry Maudsley, "Emmanuel Swedenborg," in *Body and Mind: An Inquiry into Their Connection and Mutual Influence, Specially in Reference to Mental Disorders* (New York: Appleton, 1874), 205. Subsequent references to this work appear in parentheses in the text.

25. Charles Darwin, *The Expression of the Emotions in Man and Animals* (New York: Appleton, 1899), 22, 21. Paul White includes an excellent discussion of Darwin's departure from the physiognomists Bell and Duchenne in his unpublished paper "The Physiology of Feelings."

26. Daniel Hack Tuke, *Illustrations of the Influence of the Mind upon the Body in Health and Disease, Designed to Elucidate the Action of the Imagination* (Philadelphia: Henry C. Lea, 1873), 221. Subsequent references to this work appear in parentheses in the text.

27. Henry Maudsley, "Suicide in Simple Melancholy," *Medical Magazine* 1 (1892–1893): 46, quoted in Oppenheim, *Shattered Nerves*, 5.

28. See Karen Sanchez-Eppler, *Touching Liberty: Feminism, Abolition, and the Politics of the Body* (Berkeley: University of California Press, 1993).

29. D. De Berdt Hovell, "Male Hysteria (?)," letter to the editor, *Lancet* January 2, 1875, 37.

30. Hovell, "Not Hysteria, but Neurosis," letter to the editor, *Lancet*, June 16, 1875, 108.

31. J. Langdon Down, letter to the editor, *Lancet*, June 16, 1875, 108.

32. Hovell, "Not Hysteria, but Neurosis," letter to the editor, *Lancet*, February 27, 1875, 323.

33. Henry Maudsley, *Physiology and Pathology of the Mind* (1867) (Washington, D.C.: University Publications of America, 1977), 162; emphasis added.

34. Peter Melville Logan, *Nerves and Narrative: A Cultural History of Hysteria in Nineteenth-Century British Prose* (Berkeley: University of California Press, 1997), 166–167. Logan argues that the division of the nervous system into two functions, one voluntary and one involuntary, produced a body that might have two narratives, which in turn led to a new epistemological quandary centering not on what the story of the body was but whether the body had a coherent story to tell at all. I wish to argue that the notion that the body might have a story unavailable to the person leads to a conception of self that was predicated not on incoherence or meaninglessness but rather on a deep logic of corporeal significance that enhanced the interpretive authority of physicians and realist novelists. Moreover,

while Logan perceives English realism to be committed to the thick mustering of detail, a reading of Holmes (an anatomist) indicates that instead diagnosis involves the paring away of insignificant detail to reveal the underlying structure.

35. Maudsley, *Physiology and Pathology of the Mind*, 54. Subsequent references to this work appear in parentheses in the text.

36. Herbert Spencer, *The Principles of Psychology* (London: Longman, Brown, Green, and Longmans, 1855), 355. Subsequent references to this work appear in parentheses in the text.

37. Oliver Wendell Holmes, "Crime and Automatism" *Atlantic Monthly,* April 1875, 469. Subsequent references to this work (abbreviated "Crime") are included in parentheses in the text.

38. For a detailed examination of Jackson's evolutionary understanding of the nervous system, see Anne Harrington, *Medicine, Mind, and the Double Brain* (Princeton, N.J.: Princeton University Press, 1987), esp. chap. 7.

39. John Hughlings Jackson, "Evolution and Dissolution of the Nervous System," *Lancet*, April 12, 1884, 651.

40. Ralph Harrington, "The Railway Accident: Trains, Trauma, and Technological Crises in Nineteenth-Century Britain," in *Traumatic Pasts: History, Psychiatry, and Trauma in the Modern Age, 1870–1930*, ed. Mark S. Micale and Paul Lerner (Cambridge: Cambridge University Press, 2001), 37.

41. "The Costs of Railway Collisions," *Lancet*, August 25, 1860, 195.

42. *Lancet*, editorial, September 14, 1861, 255.

43. John Eric Erichsen, *On Railway and Other Injuries of the Nervous System* (London: Walton and Maberly, 1866), 9. Subsequent references to this work are included in parentheses in the text.

44. Philip Coombs Knapp, "Nervous Affections Following Injury ('Concussion of the Spine,' 'Railway Spine,' and 'Railway Brain')," *Boston Medical and Surgical Journal*, November 1, 1888, 422.

45. Herbert Page, *Injuries of the Spine*, 152. Subsequent references to this work appear in parentheses in the text. I am grateful to Karen M. Odden for bringing to my attention the British literature on railway spine, in her essay "Problems with Railways, Problems with Stories: A Narrative History of the Origins of Trauma, 1840–1890" (unpublished paper).

46. S. V. Clevenger, *Spinal Concussion* (Philadelphia: F. A. Davis, 1889), 3, quoted in Ralph Harrington, "The Railway Accident," 44.

47. R. M. Hodges, "So-Called Concussion of the Spinal Cord," *Boston Medical and Surgical Journal*, April 28, 1881, 387.

48. Ibid.

49. Tuke, *Illustrations of the Influence of the Mind upon the Body*, 23.

50. Harrington, *Medicine, Mind, and the Double Brain*, 220n1.

51. Quoted in Ralph Harrington, "The Railway Accident," 52.

52. James J. Putnam, "Recent Investigations into the Pathology of So-Called Concussion of the Spine," *Boston Medical and Surgical Journal*, Septem-

ber 6, 1883, 219. Subsequent references to this work appear in parentheses in the text.

53. Henri Ellenberger, *The Discovery of the Unconscious: The History and Evolution of Dynamic Psychiatry* (New York: Basic Books, 1970), 45. Though Ellenberger notes that since the time of St. Augustine, the Catholic Church was aware of the importance of confession in effecting the "cure of souls" (43), he focuses on the nineteenth century as the period when the concept of the pathogenic secret gained wide public currency. "In 1850," the French historian writes, "Nathaniel Hawthorne described, in his masterpiece *The Scarlet Letter*, how a pathogenic secret can be discovered by a wicked man and exploited in order to torture his victim to death" (45).

54. "Death of a Bridegroom," *Lancet*, May 10, 1884, 861.

55. Kate Chopin, "The Story of an Hour," in *Kate Chopin: The Complete Novels and Stories* (New York: Library of America, 2002), 757. Subsequent references to this work appear in parentheses in the text.

56. Quoted in "Review of Alexander Bain on the Senses and the Intellect" (1855), *Fraser's Magazine for Town and Country* 53, no. 316 (February 1856): 225.

57. Théodule Ribot, *Diseases of Memory: An Essay in the Positive Psychology*, trans. William Huntington Smith (New York: D. Appleton, 1882), 39. Subsequent references to this work appear in parentheses in the text.

58. For Baldwin, this discrepancy provides the space not just of artifice but of cruelty: "Sentimentality, the ostentatious parading of excessive and spurious emotion, is the mark of dishonesty, the inability to feel; . . . it is always, therefore, the signal of secret and violent inhumanity, the mask of cruelty" ("Everybody's Protest Novel," *Partisan Review* 16 (1949): 578–585).

59. Théodule Ribot quoted these passages from Spencer in his *Diseases of Memory*, 64.

60. Babette Rothschild, *The Body Remembers: The Psychophysiology of Trauma and Trauma Treatment* (New York: Norton, 2000). A psychotherapist, Rothschild develops a concept of "stored cellular memories" and then develops ways to help her patients elicit and integrate them.

61. Pierre Janet, *The Mental State of Hystericals: A Study of Mental Stigmata and Mental Accidents*, trans. Caroline Rollin Corson (New York: Putnam, 1901); reprint, Washington, D.C.: University Publications of America, 1977), 492–493.

62. Ruth Leys, *Trauma: A Genealogy* (Chicago: University of Chicago Press, 2000), 105.

63. White, "Of Scientific Character," 11.

64. Quoted in "Review of Alexander Bain on the Senses and Intellect," 225.

65. Janet, *La medicine psychologique* (1923; reprint, Paris, 1980), 126, quoted in Leys, *Trauma*, 115.

66. See also Alan Young, *The Harmony of Illusions: Inventing Post-traumatic Stress Disorder* (Princeton, N.J.: Princeton University Press, 1995); Paul Antze and Michael Lambek, eds., *Tense Past: Cultural Essays in Trauma and Memory* (New York: Routledge, 1996); Ian Hacking, *Rewriting the*

Soul: Multiple Personality and the Sciences of Memory (Princeton, N.J.: Princeton University Press, 1995).

4. Nervous Effort

1. John Dewey, "The Psychology of Effort," in *The Philosophy of John Dewey*, ed. John J. McDermott (Chicago: University of Chicago Press, 1973), 151. Subsequent references to this work appear in parentheses in the text.
2. Henry James, *The Spoils of Poynton* (1897) (New York: Penguin, 1985), 5.
3. Pierre Janet, "History of a Fixed Idea" (1894), ed. and trans. Lilian Furst, in *Before Freud: An Anthology of Late Nineteenth Century Psychiatric Cases* (unpublished manuscript), 212, 227, 228.
4. Charlotte Perkins Gilman, *The Yellow Wallpaper*, ed. Dale M. Bauer (New York: Bedford, 1998), 42. Subsequent references to this work appear in parentheses in the text. Completed in 1890, Gilman's short story was first published in *New England Magazine* in 1892. In 1920 William Dean Howells, a longtime booster of "The Yellow Wallpaper," included the story in his collection entitled *The Great American Short Stories*. The Bedford edition reprints the text from the original 1892 publication, which included the inconsistent hyphenation of the word "wallpaper," although the editor follows critical convention (as do I) in omitting the hyphen from the story's title.
5. This quotation is drawn from I. A. Richards, *Principles of Literary Criticism* (New York: Routledge, 1924), 85; he was quoting Tichener, *Textbook of Psychology* (1924), 248.
6. Anon., "Book Notes," *Criterion* (New York), July 22, 1899, 25; folder 301, Charlotte Perkins Gilman Papers, Schlesinger Library, Radcliffe College, Cambridge, Massachusetts.
7. Cynthia Davis, *Bodily and Narrative Forms: The Influence of Medicine on American Literature, 1845–1915* (Stanford, Calif.: Stanford University Press, 2000), 136–137.
8. Jennifer Fleissner, *Women, Compulsion, Modernity: The Moment of American Naturalism* (Chicago: University of Chicago Press, 2004), 61. Subsequent references to this work appear in parentheses in the text.
9. Oliver Sacks, *The Man Who Mistook His Wife for a Hat and Other Clinical Tales* (New York: Touchstone, 1985). Sacks recounts the case of Dr. P, an artist who, after a brain injury, suffered from from "absurd abstractness of attitude" (19): he could perceive things only in objective terms, drained of all "emotional reality" (16), which led him to mistake persons for things. Sacks notes that Dr. P. provides an object lesson for cognitive science (and, I would add, literary studies): "if we delete feeling and judging, the personal, from the cognitive sciences, we reduce *them* to something as defective as Dr P.—and we reduce *our* apprehension of the concrete and real" (20).
10. S. Weir Mitchell, "Nervousness and Its Influence on Character," in *Doctor and Patient* (Philadelphia: Lippincott, 1889): 116. Important studies of the rise of nervousness in the nineteenth century include Tom Lutz, *American Nervousness, 1903: An Anecdotal History* (Ithaca, N.Y.: Cornell Univer-

sity Press, 1991); Sander L. Gilman et al., *Hysteria beyond Freud* (Berkeley: University of California Press, 1993); Carroll Smith-Rosenberg's *Disorderly Conduct: Visions of Gender in Victorian America* (New York: Knopf, 1985).

11. Eric Caplan, *Mind Games: American Culture and the Birth of Psychotherapy* (Berkeley: University of California Press, 1998), 7.

12. Frank J. Sulloway, in his biography *Freud: Biologist of the Mind* (New York: Basic Books, 1979), analyzes Freud's ideas as the outgrowth of his training as a neurologist in the nineteenth century, arguing that psychoanalysis "owe[s] many of its most fundamental *theoretical inspirations* to biological sources" (5). For a genealogy of psychoanalysis as a discursive science, see Dianne F. Sadoff, *Sciences of the Flesh: Representing Body and Subject in Psychoanalysis* (Palo Alto, Calif.: Stanford University Press, 1998), especially her analysis of Freud's hesitant move away from the somatic paradigm to a psychoanalytic understanding of the modern subject (152–165). For her account of S. Weir Mitchell's rest cure, which conceives of "the reflex body" as embedded in "an economy of exchanges with the nurturing or depleting social world" (125), see 124–127.

13. Sigmund Freud, *The Origin and Development of Psychoanalysis* (New York: Henry Regnery, 1965), 65. On his first trip to the United States, Freud gave a series of lectures at Clark University in Worcester, Massachusetts, which were originally published in *American Journal of Psychology* 21 (April 1910).

14. Josef Breuer and Sigmund Freud, *Studies on Hysteria*, trans. and ed. James Strachey (New York: Basic Books, 1957), 60–61. Subsequent references to this work appear in parentheses in the text.

15. Sigmund Freud, *The Origin and Development of Psychoanalysis*, 7.

16. Janet Malcolm, "*Six Roses ou Cirrhose?*" in *The Purloined Clinic: Selected Writings* (New York: Random House, 1992): 31–47, 46.

17. For terrific analyses of the visual epistemology of modern medicine, see Lisa Cartwright, *Screening the Body: Tracing Medicine's Visual Culture* (Minneapolis: University of Minnesota Press, 1995); and Sander L. Gilman, *Seeing the Insane* (Lincoln: University of Nebraska Press, 1985).

18. Fredric Jameson, *The Political Unconscious: Narrative as a Socially Symbolic Act* (Ithaca, N.Y.: Cornell University Press, 1981), 48. Subsequent references to this work appear in parentheses in the text.

19. Sandra Gilbert and Susan Gubar, *The Madwoman in the Attic: The Writer and the Nineteenth Century Literary Imagination* (New Haven: Yale University Press, 1979), 73. See Annette Kolodny, "A Map for Rereading: Or Gender and the Interpretation of Literary Texts," *New Literary History* 11, no. 3 (spring 1980): 451–467; and Jean E. Kennard, "Convention Coverage or How to Read Your Own Life," in *The Captive Imagination: A Casebook on 'The Yellow Wallpaper'* (New York: Feminist Press, 1992), 168–190. In addition to the groundbreaking articles of Kolodny, Kennard, and Gilbert and Gubar, there is an expanding critical oeuvre that discerns

some form of *écriture féminine* in "The Yellow Wallpaper." Among these, exemplary essays include Mary Jacobus, "An Unnecessary Maze of Sign-Reading," in *Reading Woman: Essays in Feminist Criticism* (New York: Columbia University Press, 1986); Diane Price Herndl, "The Writing Cure: Charlotte Perkins Gilman, Anna O., and 'Hysterical' Writing," *National Women's Studies Association Journal* 1, no. 1 (1988): 52–74; and Paula A. Treichler, "Escaping the Sentence: Diagnosis and Discourse in 'The Yellow Wallpaper,'" in *The Captive Imagination: A Casebook on "The Yellow Wallpaper"* (New York: Feminist Press, 1992): 191–210.

20. Rather than comment on the story's feminist theme, contemporary reviewers paid inordinate attention to the story as a tale of deadly interior design. One review called the story "a strange study of physical environment" (Anon., "A Study of Physical Environment," *Times* [Boston, Mass.], July 9, 1899 (?), folder 301, Gilman Papers) while another praised Gilman for "warning of the quite frightful consequences which might follow disregard of discretion in such permanent furnishings of a sick chamber"; Anon., "Colors in Hygiene," (n.d.), folder 301, Gilman Papers. "Every householder," one reviewer emphatically wrote, "ought to be *made* to read that story" to prevent his "inflict[ing] a 'Yellow wallpaper' on a defenceless prospective tenant"; Charles Bainbridge, "Choosing Wallpaper," *National Food Magazine* 53 (April/May 1916): 9–10, 9.

21. Lisa Kasmer, "Charlotte Perkins Gilman's 'The Yellow Wallpaper': A Symptomatic Reading," *Literature and Psychology* 36, no. 3 (1990):1–15.

22. Elaine Showalter, "Review Essay," *Signs* 1, no. 2 (winter 1975), 435.

23. Jeffrey Williams, "The Last Generalist: An Interview with Richard Powers," *Cultural Logic* 2, no. 2 (spring 1999): 1–16, 6.

24. William Veeder, "Who Is Jane? The Intricate Feminism of Charlotte Perkins Gilman," *Arizona Quarterly* 44, no. 3 (1988): 40–79, 48.

25. Charlotte Perkins Gilman, "Dr. Clair's Place," in *The Yellow Wallpaper*, 328. Subsequent references to this work appear in parentheses in the text.

26. S. Weir Mitchell, *Lectures on Diseases of the Nervous System, Especially in Women* (Philadelphia: Henry C. Lea's Son, 1881), 31. Subsequent references to this work appear in parentheses in the text.

27. S. Weir Mitchell, *Fat and Blood: An Essay on the Treatment of Certain Forms of Neurasthenia and Hysteria* (Philadelphia: Lippincott, 1877), 141.

28. S. Weir Mitchell, *Gunshot Wounds and Other Injuries of the Nerves* (Philadelphia: Lippincott, 1864), 103.

29. Stephen Crane, *The Red Badge of Courage* (1895) (New York: Norton, 1994), 91.

30. Mitchell, *Gunshot Wounds*, 22, 23.

31. Elaine Scarry, *The Body in Pain: The Making and Unmaking of the World* (New York: Oxford University Press, 1985) 27.

32. George Beard, "Neurasthenia or Nervous Exhaustion," *Boston Medical and Surgical Journal* 80 (1869): 218. As late as 1895, an article on neurasthenia in the *Medical Record* argued, "To understand this [condition] more

fully we have only to study closely the anatomy of the brain"; W. A. Mc-Clain, "The Psychology of Neurasthenia," *Medical Record* 48 (1895): 82.

33. S. Weir Mitchell, *Wear and Tear, or Hints for the Overworked* (Philadelphia: Lippincott, 1871), 6. Mitchell believed that a person's class status provided a crucial predisposition to nervous disease (a position Beard also held). Some neurologists, however, were adamant that these maladies struck all sorts of persons: "It does not make any difference whether it is a mechanic or the man who has the whole responsibilities of the country upon his shoulders, it is an overaction of the brain . . . that produces the result"; B. W. James, "Report of the Section in Neurology and Electro Therapeutics," *Transactions of the American Institute of Homeopathy* 57 (1901): 592. One thing was certain: only well-to-do patients could afford Mitchell's rest cure.

34. Mitchell, *Wear and Tear*, 47.

35. For an excellent account of Beard's neurological theories, which contain "no hint" of "a psychological etiology" for neurasthenia (104), see Charles E. Rosenberg, *No Other Gods: On Science and American Social Thought* (Baltimore: Johns Hopkins University Press, 1997), chap. 5.

36. Mitchell, *Wear and Tear*, 30.

37. Mitchell, *Fat and Blood*, 41.

38. Mitchell, *Wear and Tear*, 43.

39. McClain, "Psychology of Neurasthenia," 82.

40. William James, *The Principles of Psychology* (Cambridge, Mass.: Harvard University Press, 1983), 112.

41. Mitchell, *Wear and Tear*, 58, 55.

42. This physical reeducation was grueling; in a passage that warrants the analogy between a nervous patient's path to recovery and infant development, William James quotes the English physiologist Henry Maudsley: "Think of the pains necessary to teach a child to stand, of the many efforts which it must make, and of the ease with which it at last stands, unconscious of even an effort" (*Principle of Psychology*, 118).

43. S. Weir Mitchell, *Roland Blake* (New York: Houghton, Mifflin, 1886), 254.

44. The literary critics Tom Lutz and Cynthia Davis have been attentive to the corporeal nature of Gilman's theorizing about the home and social reform. Analyzing Gilman's domestic writings in terms of the capitalist economy of the Gilded Age, Lutz astutely notes that for Gilman, "women's work as it existed, since it was wasteful, led to neurasthenia" (*American Nervousness*, 230), though he concludes that her vision for reform "helped reshape women as consumers" (230, 243). Davis goes further in examining "The Yellow Wallpaper" in light of Gilman's views about the maddening aspects of women's domestic life, concluding that the literariness of Gilman's gothic prose undermines her commitment to "the healthiness of what we might call a hermeneutics of the overt"; *Bodily and Narrative Forms*, 139.

45. Davis, *Bodily and Narrative Forms*, 133.

46. Charlotte Perkins Gilman, *The Home: Its Work and Influence* (New York: McClure, Phillips, 1903), 6. Subsequent references to this work appear in

parentheses in the text. Concurring with Gilman's belief in the corporeal basis of the mind, one physician explained that "thought exhausts the nervous substance as surely as walking exhausts the muscles"; McClain, "Psychology of Neurasthenia," 82.

47. Walter Felt Evans, *Esoteric Christianity and Mental Therapeutics* (Boston: Carter and Karrick, 1886), 83.

48. Charlotte Perkins Gilman, *Our Brains and What Ails Them*, published in serial form in *Forerunner* 3 (January/October 1910): 249. Subsequent references to this work appear in parentheses in the text.

49. Gilman, *Women and Economics: A Study of the Economic Relation between Men and Women as a Factor of Social Evolution* (New York: Harper and Row, 1966), 155–156.

50. Charlotte Perkins Gilman, "Improved Methods of Habit Culture," *Forerunner* 1, no. 9 (July 1910): 7–9, 7.

51. Ibid., 9.

52. Charlotte Perkins Gilman, "Our Excessive Femininity," Lectures from the 1890s, 22, folder 172, Gilman Papers. Subsequent references to this work are included in parentheses in the text.

53. Stephen Crane, *The Red Badge of Courage* (1895) in Crane, *Prose and Poetry*, ed. J. C. Levinson (New York: Library of America, 1984), 129. Subsequent references to this work appear in parentheses in the text.

54. Lutz, *American Nervousness*, 226–227.

55. Gilman, *The Living of Charlotte Perkins Gilman: An Autobiography* (New York: Appleton-Century, 1935), 91. Subsequent references to this work appear in parentheses in the text.

56. This quotation is from the subtitle to Catherine Golden's essay entitled "'Overwriting' the Rest Cure: Charlotte Perkins Gilman's Literary Escape from S. Weir Mitchell's Fictionalization of Women," in *Critical Essays on Charlotte Perkins Gilman*, ed. Joanne B. Karpinski (New York: G. K. Hall, 1992), 144–158.

57. Walter Benn Michaels, *The Gold Standard and the Logic of Naturalism* (Berkeley: University of California Press, 1987), 3.

58. Mitchell, *Doctor and Patient* (Philadelphia: Lippincott, 1888), 48.

59. Gilman, *The Living*, 330. In contrast to some current critics who construe the narrator's journal-keeping in "The Yellow Wallpaper" as cathartic and therefore potentially therapeutic, Gilman asserted in a 1894 lecture that production not intended for communication is a sign of individual and social ills. For an individual who construes writing as "the relieving of himself," she maintained, it is "as much his business to stop producing—to cease to express himself—as for the consumptive to forbear marrying"; "Art for Art's Sake," 16, 34, folder 171, Gilman Papers. For a useful and historically grounded discussion of the distinction between "empowering and creative" acts of reading and those that are "solipsistic or self-destructive," see Barbara Hochman's analysis of Gilman's tale, "The Reading Habit and 'The Yellow Wallpaper,'" *American Literature* 74, no. 1 (2002): 89–110, 101.

60. Walter Benn Michaels, in his essay treating "The Yellow Wallpaper," emphasizes the phenomenological aspects of work, in particular the "physiological labor of 'self-conquest'" that was the particular occupation of the middle-class nineteenth-century woman; *The Gold Standard and the Logic of Naturalism,* 6.

61. William Dean Howells, *Criticism and Fiction and Other Essays,* ed. Clara Marburg Kirk and Rudolf Kirk (New York: New York University Press, 1959), 72.

62. Charlotte Perkins Gilman, "Stories" (n.d.), in notebook labeled "Thoughts and Figgerings," folder 16, Gilman Papers.

63. Anon., "In Book Land," *Newport (RI) Daily News,* June 27, 1899, 3. Reading Gilman, one contemporary explained, "brings a distinct shock"; Anon., "You Ought to Know," (n.d.), oversize folder 2, Gilman Papers. One newspaper urged that the tale "work[ed] one into an agony of . . . horror"; Anon., *Oklahoman,* January 29, 1928, folder 301, Gilman Papers.

64. Gilman, entry dated June 28, 1908, "Thoughts and Figgerings," folder 16, Gilman Papers. In her personal papers Gilman wrote that the tale "so alarmed" one of the friends of a woman "treated in the same mistaken manner" that "they forthwith altered their methods and the woman got well"; Charlotte Perkins Gilman, "The Yellow Wall Paper—Its History & Reception—Note left by C. P. G.," (n.d.), folder 221, Gilman Papers.

65. Daniel Dennett, *Kinds of Minds: Toward an Understanding of Consciousness* (New York: Basic Books, 1996), 146.

66. Henri F. Ellenberger, *The Discovery of the Unconscious: The History and Evolution of Dynamic Psychiatry* (New York: Basic Books), 142.

67. Wilhelm Griesinger, *Mental Pathology and Therapeutics* (London: New Syndenham Society, 1867), 179, quoted in Ilza Veith, *Hysteria: The History of a Disease* (Chicago: University of Chicago Press, 1965), 195.

68. Perhaps the most notorious instance of hysterical mimicry involved the great Charcot himself, who after placing hysterics in wards alongside epileptics, documented case after case of extravagant physical contortions. Mitchell, for one, never ran into a true case of Charcot's *grande hystèrie* in his own practice, and remained skeptical of Charcot's archetypal hysteria, which looked suspiciously like the stages of an epileptic fit.

69. Smith-Rosenberg, *Disorderly Conduct,* 202.

70. Jean-Martin Charcot, *Charcot The Clinician: The Tuesday Lessons, Excerpts from Nine Case Presentations on General Neurology Delivered at the Salpêtrière Hospital in 1887–88,* trans. with commentary by Christopher G. Goetz (New York: Raven Press, 1987), 107.

71. Davis, *Bodily and Narrative Forms,* 132.

72. Charcot, *Charcot the Clinician,* 106.

73. Janet, "History of a Fixed Idea," 215; emphasis added.

74. Janet Malcolm makes this observation about Freud in "Dora," in *The Purloined Clinic,* 18.

75. David Nordloh, "Late-Nineteenth-Century Literature," *American Literary Scholarship* (2002): 259.

76. Quoted in the introduction to *"The Yellow Wallpaper,"* ed. Thomas L.

Erskine and Connie L. Richards (New Brunswick, N.J.: Rutgers University Press, 1993), 7.

77. Horace Scudder, letter to Charlotte Perkins Gilman, quoted in Gilman, *The Living*, 119.

78. Quoted in Gilman, *The Living*, 120.

79. Charlotte Perkins Gilman, "Why I Wrote *The Yellow Wallpaper*" *Forerunner* 4, no. 10 (October 1913): 271.

80. Stephen Crane, *The Correspondence of Stephen Crane*, ed. Stanley Wertheim and Paul Sorrentino, 2 vols. (New York: Columbia University Press, 1988), 1:115; quoted in Mary Esteve, "A 'Gorgeous Neutrality': Stephen Crane's Documentary Anaesthetics," *English Literary History* 62, no. 3 (1995): 667.

81. Kate Chopin, *The Awakening* (New York: Bedford, 2000), 49.

82. Esteve, "A 'Gorgeous Neutrality,'" 669. Esteve argues that Crane in his fiction produces "anaesthesia" (673) by oversaturating the visual field and pushing realistic representation "to the point of blindness" (671). I argue, by contrast, that Crane enlists and draws attention to the nonvisual sensory rhythms of experience, such that the body could be said to "see" most vividly—and most aesthetically—at those moments when vision is occluded.

83. Crane scholars, both formalists and historicists, have tended to approach *The Red Badge* in terms of cerebration and the visual sense. For instance, Michael Fried, *Realism, Writing, Disfiguration: On Thomas Eakins and Stephen Crane* (Chicago: University of Chicago Press, 1987), argues that Crane makes visible the process of writing through repeatedly figuring faces and effacement. Amy Kaplan links the visual with fixity, urging that "Crane's spectacles isolate discontinuous moments of vision"; "The Spectacle of War in Crane's Revision of History," in *New Essays on "The Red Badge of Courage,"* ed. Lee Clark Mitchell (Cambridge: Cambridge University Press, 1986), 97.

84. James Dawes, *The Language of War* (Cambridge, Mass.: Harvard University Press, 2002), 65.

85. Fleissner, *Women, Compulsion, Modernity*, 66, 68, 69.

86. In an article that is highly critical of what she perceives to be historical and textual inaccuracies in feminist scholarship on Gilman's story, Julia Dock has challenged a central premise of such readings, arguing that nineteenth-century readers actually *did* perceive a feminist subtext in the story; "'But One Expects That': Charlotte Perkins Gilman's 'The Yellow Wallpaper' and the Shifting Light of Scholarship," *Proceedings of the Modern Language Association* 111 (1996): 52–65. A careful reading of reviews shows that the prevailing issue was not gender as such but the then current belief that inharmonious décor (i.e. highly patterned wallpaper) might contribute to nervous illness.

87. Anon., "Books: Light and Serious Stories," *Time and the Hour*, June 17, 1899, 9, folder 301, Gilman Papers.

88. Annamarie Jagose, "Queer World Making," interview with Michael Warner, *Genders* 31 (2000): 1–40, 38.

89. Perhaps the pithiest account of the role played by "The Yellow Wallpaper"

in the rise of academic feminism is written by Jonathan Crewe in his "Queering *The Yellow Wallpaper?* Charlotte Perkins Gilman and the Politics of Form," *Tulsa Studies in Women's Literature* 14, no. 2 (fall 1995): 273–294. He approaches the text "not just as any old text but as a text that has taken on peculiar salience in modern feminist criticism" (274), acknowledging that, as "almost the exemplary literary document of the intellectual movement" (276), it "became an instrument of academic change" (277). Crewe, however, critiques what he sees as academic feminists' misuse of the text's potentially radical, decentering possibilities; similarly, Susan Lanser has faulted critics of Gilman's tale for being "collusive with ideology" insofar as they used the story implicitly to assert themselves as bourgeois white professionals; "Feminist Criticism, 'The Yellow Wallpaper,' and the Politics of Color in America," *Feminist Studies* 15 (1989): 415–441, 422.

90. Charlotte Perkins Gilman, entry dated New Year's Day 1896, "Thoughts and Figgerings," Gilman Papers. In a similar vein, Barbara Hochman has argued that nineteenth-century women readers can be seen as "the forerunners of the 'professional' readers who rediscovered Gilman's tale a century later"; "The Reading Habit," 101.

91. In "Turned," a woman with an inactive Ph.D. discovers that her husband has impregnated their young servant. The wife's solution is to leave her husband, whisk the young woman away, tend her through her pregnancy, help raise the baby, and go back to teaching. I read this story as Gilman's meditation on the rich semantic possibilities of the term *doctor,* which here references reform as well as healing, and education as well as medicine; *The Yellow Wall-paper and Other Writings* (New York: Modern Library, 2000), 78–88.

5. "Mindless" Pleasure

1. John Dewey, "The Psychology of Effort" (1897), in *The Philosophy of John Dewey,* ed. John J. McDermott (Chicago: University of Chicago Press, 1973), 154. Subsequent references to this work appear in parentheses in the text.

2. John Dewey, *Art as Experience* (1934) (New York: Perigee, 1980), 103. Subsequent references to this work appear in parentheses in the text.

3. Harold Frederic, *The Damnation of Theron Ware, or Illumination* (New York: Modern Library, 2002). Subsequent references to this work appear in parentheses in the text.

4. Kate Chopin, *The Awakening,* in *Kate Chopin: Complete Novels and Stories* (New York: Library of America, 2002), 650. Subsequent references to this work appear in parentheses in the text.

5. C[harles] L. Deyo, *St. Louis Post-Dispatch,* "One Hundred Books for Summer" (1899); *Providence Sunday Journal,* "The Newest Books" [unsigned review] (1899), in *Critical Essays on Kate Chopin,* ed. Alice Hall Petry (New York: G. K. Hall, 1996), 55, 15.

6. Pericles Lewis, "James's Sick Souls," *Henry James Review* 22, no. 3 (2001): 248–258, 249. Through a reading of William James's psychology of religion, Lewis argues that Henry James produces a pragmatist aesthet-

ics that is at once ethical and enabling. Henry James in his late novels, Lewis concludes, affirms "the necessity of shared illusion as the only faith on which action can be based" (258).

7. William James, *The Varieties of Religious Experience: A Study in Human Nature* (New York: MacMillan, 1961), 66, 67. Subsequent references to this work appear in parentheses in the text.

8. "Notes from Bookland," *St. Louis Daily Globe-Democrat*, May 13, 1899, 5; "Books of the Week," *Providence Sunday Journal*, June 4, 1899, 15. Since the modern critical rediscovery of Chopin in the 1950s and 1960s, the moralistic evaluation has shifted its terms (if not its edge), insofar as it takes the form, beginning in the 1980s, of critiquing Edna Pontellier as an inadequate feminist heroine. A number of scholars have founded their critiques on the issue of race: see Anna Shannon Elfenbein, "Kate Chopin's *The Awakening:* An Assault on American Racial and Sexual Mythology," *Southern Studies* 26, no. 4 (winter 1987): 304–312; and Elizabeth Ammons, *Conflicting Stories: American Women Writers at the Turn into the Twentieth Century* (New York: Oxford University Press, 1991). Other critiques center on the issue of agency, as in Nancy Walker's discussion of how Edna "is controlled by her own emotions, not by men or society"; "Feminist or Naturalist: The Social Context of Kate Chopin's *The Awakening*," *Southern Quarterly* 17 (1979): 103.

9. Annie Payson Call, *Power through Repose* (Boston: Little, Brown, 1905), Project Gutenberg Literary Archive Foundation e-text, www.gutenberg. org/dirs/etext03/prrps10.txt.

10. For elegant readings of Chopin's novel that are attentive to what Elaine Showalter has called the "rhythm of epiphany and mood," see her "Tradition and the Female Talent: *The Awakening* as a Solitary Book," in *New Essays on "The Awakening,"* ed. Wendy Martin (Cambridge: Cambridge University Press, 1988), 211; and Cynthia Griffin Wolff, "Thanatos and Eros: Kate Chopin's *The Awakening*," *American Quarterly* 25 (October 1973): 449–471. A later essay of Woolf gives a more historicized reading in light of nineteenth-century sex roles; see "An Un-Utterable Longing: The Discourse of Feminine Sexuality in Kate Chopin's *The Awakening*," in *The Awakening: Case Studies in Contemporary Criticism*, ed. Nancy A. Walker (Boston: Bedford, 2000): 376–393.

11. Quoted in Emily Toth, *Kate Chopin* (New York: Morrow, 1990), 344. Subsequent references to this work (abbreviated *Chopin*) appear in parentheses in the text.

12. For an illuminating discussion of the emergence of the writer as medium— such that writing might involve a form of "possession"—see John D. Kerkering, *The Poetics of National and Racial Identity* (Cambridge: Cambridge University Press, 2004), 201–202.

13. *Kate Chopin's Private Papers*, ed. Emily Toth (Bloomington: Indiana University Press, 1998), 205. Subsequent references to this work (abbreviated *Papers*) appear in parentheses in the text.

14. Kate Chopin, "At *Chênière Caminada*," in *A Night in Acadie* (Way and Williams, 1897), in *Chopin: Complete Novels and Stories*, 480.

15. Kate Chopin, "A Mental Suggestion" (uncollected story), reprinted in *Chopin: Complete Novels and Stories*, 877.

16. Arthur Schopenhauer, *The World as Will and Representation*, trans. E. F. J. Payne (New York: Dover, 1969), 1:260. Subsequent references to this work (abbreviated *World*) appear in parentheses in the text.

17. Ralph Waldo Emerson, *Nature; Addresses, and Lectures* (1849) (Cambridge, Mass.: Harvard University Press, 1971).

18. Kate Chopin, *At Fault* (St. Louis: Nixon-Jones, 1890), in *Chopin: Complete Novels and Stories*, 51. Subsequent references to this work (abbreviated *Fault*) appear in parentheses in the text.

19. Chopin, "A Sentimental Soul," in *A Night in Acadie*, 463.

20. Chopin, "A Respectable Woman," in *A Night in Acadie*, 509.

21. Chopin, "Regret," in *A Night in Acadie*, 408.

22. Virginia M. Koudis, "Prison into Prism: Emerson's 'Many-Colored Lenses' and the Woman Writer of Early Modernism," in *The Green American Tradition: Essays and Poems for Sherman Paul*, ed. H. Daniel Peck (Baton Rouge: Louisiana State University Press, 1989), 118.

23. Priscilla Leder, "Land's End: *The Awakening* and Nineteenth-Century Literary Tradition," in *Critical Essays on Kate Chopin* (New York: G. K. Hall, 1996), 246.

24. Chopin, "Lilacs" (uncollected story), in *Chopin: Complete Novels and Stories*, 764.

25. William James, "Energies of Men" (1906), in *Writings, 1902–1910*, ed. Bruce Kuklick (New York: Library of America, 1987), 1234.

26. Richard Dewey, "Mental Therapeutics in Nervous and Mental Diseases," *American Journal of Insanity* 57 (1900–1901): 676, quoted in Eric Caplan, *Mind Games: American Culture and the Birth of Psychotherapy* (Berkeley: University of California Press, 1998), 63.

27. Richard Huber, *The American Idea of Success* (New York: McGraw-Hill, 1971), 131–132, quoted in Gail Thain Parker, *Mind Cure in New England* (Hanover, N.H.: University Press of New England, 1973), 17. Subsequent references to Parker's study (abbreviated *Mind Cure*) appear in parentheses in the text.

28. For thorough discussions of the gender/genre politics of the term "local color," see Richard Brodhead, *Cultures of Letters: Scenes of Reading and Writing in Nineteenth-Century America* (Chicago: University of Chicago Press, 1993); and Judith Fetterley and Marjorie Pryse, *Writing out of Place: Regionalism, Women, and American Literary Culture* (Urbana: University of Illinois Press, 2003).

29. James, "Energies of Men," 1238.

30. For accounts of rhythm in *The Awakening*, which align it not with aesthetics and relaxation, processes tied to living well, but with death, see Cynthia Griffin Wolff, "Thanatos and Eros: Kate Chopin's *The Awakening*," and Elizabeth House, "*The Awakening*: Kate Chopin's 'Endlessly Rocking' Cycle," *Ball State University Forum* 20 (1979): 55–58. Jennifer Fleissner sees Edna as facing the "appalling character of existence" with its

"radical negation" of selfhood; see her chapter entitled "The Rhythm Method: Unmothering the Race in Chopin, Stein, and Grimké," in *Women, Compulsion, Modernity: The Moment of American Naturalism* (Chicago: Chicago University Press, 2004), 242.

31. Quoted in Gordon Epperson, *The Mind of Edmund Gurney* (Madison, N.J.: Fairleigh Dickinson University Press, 1997), 45.

32. Edmund Gurney, *The Power of Sound* (1880) (New York: Basic Books, 1966), 103. Subsequent references to this work (abbreviated *Sound*) appear in parentheses in the text.

33. Charles Darwin, *The Expression of the Emotions in Man and Animals* (New York: Oxford University Press, 1998), 37n6.

34. Lewis, "James's Sick Souls," 250.

35. Readers have long noticed the novel's sick-souled structure, though they haven't labeled it as such. A review in the *Nation* observed that the novel "leads nowhither"; reprinted in *Harold Frederic*, ed. Thomas F. O'Donnell and Hoyt C. Franchere (New York: Twayne, 1961), September 3, 1896. One nineteenth-century reader, Charlotte Porter, wrote of Frederic's "up-to-date" novel, which earned that description by being "so shiftily based on an element in life peculiarly appreciated by the modern mind—relativity"; "Notes on Recent Fiction," *Poet-lore* 8 (August 1896): 459–461, quoted in O'Donnell et al., 181. Even William Dean Howells, who described *The Damnation of Theron Ware* as the "best book" of his "favorite novelist," notes that the ending leaves the reader with no footing for judgment; "My Favorite Novelist and His Best Book," *Munsey's Magazine*, April 17, 1897, 24. These contemporary reviews, collected by Robin Taylor Rogers, are reprinted at a website entitled "Harold Frederic's *The Damnation of Theron Ware*," http://helios.acomp.usf.edu/~rrogers/critreception.html.

36. Critics have tended to select one character as the Mephistopheles figure that provokes the minister's downfall. Donna M. Campbell fingers Ware himself; see her "Frederic, Norris, and the Fear of Effeminacy," in *Resisting Regionalism: Gender and Naturalism in American Fiction, 1885–1915* (Athens: Ohio University Press, 1997): 75–108, 91. Bruce Michaelson focuses on the intellectual trio of priest, doctor, and aesthete, in "Theron Ware in the Wilderness of Ideas," *American Literary Realism* 25, no. 1 (1992): 54–73. David H. Zimmerman censures Father Forbes, in "Clay Feet, Modernism, and Fundamental Option in Harold Frederic's *The Damnation of Theron Ware*," *American Benedictine Review* 45, no. 1 (1994): 33–44. Linda Patterson Miller is particularly eloquent in her castigation of Sister Soulsby; see her "Casting Graven Images: *The Damnation of Theron Ware*," *Renascence* 30 (1978): 179–184.

37. Friedrich Nietzsche, *The Birth of Tragedy from Spirit of Music* (1872), trans. Shaun Whiteside, ed. Michael Tanner (London: Penguin, 1993).

38. Chopin, "A Matter of Prejudice," in *A Night in Acadie*, 408.

39. Willa Cather, in 1899 published a review of Chopin's novel under the pseudonym "Sibert": "A Creole *Bovary* is this little novel of Miss Chopin's"; "Books and Magazines," *Pittsburgh Leader*, July 8, 1899, 6;

reprinted in *The Awakening: A Norton Critical Edition*, ed. Margo Culley (New York: Norton, 1994), 170. See also Sandra M. Gilbert and Susan Gubar, *No Man's Land: The Place of the Woman Writer in the Twentieth Century* (New Haven: Yale University Press, 1989), vol. 2.

40. Chopin, *"Nég Créol,"* in *A Night in Acadie*, 428.

41. James, "The Sentiment of Rationality," in *Writings, 1878–1899*, ed. Gerald E. Myers (New York: Library of America, 1992), 512.

42. Chopin, "Dr. Chevalier's Lie" (uncollected story), reprinted in *Chopin: Complete Novels and Stories*, 728–729.

43. Toth, *Chopin*, 127.

44. Warren Felt Evans, *Mental Medicine: A Theoretical and Practical Treatise on Medical Psychology* (Boston: Carter and Pettee, 1873), 133, 123–124.

45. James, "The Gospel of Relaxation," in *Talks to Teachers on Psychology, and to Students on Some of Life's Ideals* (Boston: Holt, 1899), reprinted in *Writings, 1878–1899*, 835.

46. Call, *Power through Repose*.

47. Quoted in Philip W. Leon, *Walt Whitman and Sir William Osler: A Poet and His Physician* (Oakville, Ontario: ECW Press, 1995), 77.

48. Edward Carpenter, *Days with Walt Whitman* (London: Allen, 1946), 22; quoted in Leon, *Walt Whitman and Sir William Osler*, 80.

49. Horatio Dresser, *Man and the Divine Order* (1903), quoted in Parker, *Mind Cure*, 166.

50. Chopin, "Wiser Than a God," reprinted in *Chopin: Complete Novels and Stories*, 668.

51. Eduard Hanslick, *The Beautiful in Music* (1854), trans. (1891) Gustav Cohen (Indianapolis: Bobbs-Merrill), 1957.

52. Nietzsche, *The Birth of Tragedy*, 116.

53. Patricia Yaeger, "'A Language Which Nobody Understood': Emancipatory Strategies in *The Awakening*," *Novel* 20, no. 3 (spring 1987): 199.

54. Peter Kivy, *Introduction to a Philosophy of Music* (New York: Oxford University Press, 2002), 25.

55. Jean Baptiste du Bos, *Reflexions critique sur la piesie et sur la peinture* (1719), trans. Thomas Nugent as *Critical Reflections* (New York: AMS Press, 1978); quoted in Gurney, *Sound*, 488.

56. Kivy, *Introduction to a Philosophy of Music*, 16.

57. Quoted in Susan Bernstein, *Virtuosity of the Nineteenth Century: Performing Music and Language in Heine, Liszt, and Baudelaire* (Palo Alto, Calif.: Stanford University Press, 1998), 73.

58. Chopin's description of Edna's vision, in fact, partakes of this image from Lucretius, which is featured in Schopenhauer's account of music: "It is a pleasure to stand on the seashore when the tempestuous wind whip up the sea, and to behold the great toils another is enduring. Not that it pleases us to watch another being tormented, but that it is a joy to us to observe evils from which we ourselves are free" (*World as Will*, 320).

59. Bert Bender, "Kate Chopin's Lyrical Short Stories," *Studies in Short Fiction* 2, no. 3 (summer 1974): 257–266.

60. Thomas Y. Levin, "Before the Beep: A Short History of Voice Mail," *Es-*

says in Sound2: Technophobia (September, 1995), www.sysx.org/sound site/csa/eis2content/essays/p59_beep.html; emphasis added.

61. Bernstein, *Virtuosity of the Nineteenth Century,* 73.
62. Charles Sanders Peirce, *Elements of Logic,* para. 248, p. 143, quoted in Kerkering, *Poetics of National and Racial Identity,* 19.
63. Thomas A. Sebeok, "Indexicality," in *Peirce and Contemporary Thought,* ed. Kenneth Laine Ketner (New York: Fordham University Press, 1995), 228; quoted in Kerkering, *Poetics of National and Racial Identity,* 246n54.
64. Max Nordau, *Degeneration* (New York: Appleton, 1895), 19.
65. Quoted in Bryan Magee, *The Philosophy of Schopenhauer* (Oxford: Clarendon Press, 1983), 342. Subsequent references to this work appear in parentheses in the text.
66. James, "What Is an Emotion?" in *Collected Essays and Reviews* (New York: Longmans, Green, 1920), 251, 252. Subsequent references to this work appear in parentheses in the text.
67. Quoted in Epperson, *Mind of Edmund Gurney,* 28.
68. Carl Dahlhaus, *The Esthetics of Music,* trans. William W. Austin (Cambridge: Cambridge University Press, 1982), 21.
69. Adolf Meyer, "The Philosophy of Occupation Therapy," *Archives of Occupational Therapy"* 1 (1922), 17.
70. James assented to Whitman's understanding of "mind" as a verb that entailed caring, attunement, memory, and physical sensation as well as cognition. Nonetheless, James did have one foot in the Victorian world. When in *The Varieties of Religious Experience* (311) he quoted section 5 of "Song of Myself"—asserting that "the well known passage from Walt Whitman is a classical expression . . . of mystical experience"—he omitted the explicitly sexual lines. So James included "I mind how once we (Body and Soul) lay, such a transparent summer morning," and then skipped to the mystical part: "Swiftly arose and spread around me the peace and knowledge that pass all the argument of the earth." He elided these intervening lines, which figure the interpenetration of body and soul: "How you settled your head athwart my hips and gently turn'd over upon me, / And parted the shirt from my bosom-bone, and plunged your tongue to my bare-stript heart, / And reach'd till you felt my beard, and reach'd till you held my feet."
71. Pages 93–94 of her diary, Kate Chopin Papers, Missouri Historical Society St. Louis, quoted in Emily Toth, "Kate Chopin's Music," *Regionalism and the Female Imagination* 3, no. 1 (1977): 28–29.
72. Antonio Damasio, *Looking for Spinoza: Joy, Sorrow, and the Feeling Brain* (Orlando, Fla.: Harcourt, 2003), 3. Subsequent references to this work appear in parentheses in the text.
73. H. L. Mencken, *Prejudices: First Series* (New York: Knopf, 1924), 194; quoted in Parker, *Mind Cure,* 57.
74. Meyer, "The Philosophy of Occupational Therapy," 8.
75. Ibid., 7.
76. Chopin's biographer Emily Toth has suggested that, after the death of Oscar Chopin, the widowed Kate may have had an affair with a married

man, Albert Sampite—whom a number of scholars believe was the model for the various rakish Alcée-characters who appear in Chopin's fiction.

77. James's biographers all report that he had ongoing melancholy that sometimes blossomed into (temporarily) debilitating misery. As Gerald E. Myers describes it, William and Henry James Sr. "were restless, neurotic, and susceptible to depression"; *William James: His Life and Thought* (New Haven: Yale University Press, 2001), 18. But he also notes that "James was a complicated individual; depression alternated with laughter, and an inner loneliness counterbalanced a social charm" (45). Myers then quotes James's own commentary on the joylessness of certain types of Brahmin intellectuals: "So deadly is their intellectual respectability that we can't converse about certain subjects at all. . . . I have numbered my dearest friends persons thus inhibited intellectually, with whom I would gladly have been able to talk freely about certain interests of mind, certain authors, say, as Bernard Shaw, Edward Carpenter, H. G. Wells, but it wouldn't do, it made them too uncomfortable, they wouldn't play, I had to be silent"; "The Energies of Men," 1225. I regret deeply that Robert D. Richardson's biography *William James: In the Maelstrom of American Modernism* (Boston: Houghton Mifflin, 2006), appeared too late for me to tap its wisdom in this study.

6. Corporeal Wonder

1. Kate Chopin, *The Awakening*, in *Kate Chopin: Complete Novels and Stories* (New York: Library of America, 2002), 578. Subsequent references are to this edition; they appear in parentheses in the text.

2. Henry James, *The Spoils of Poynton* (New York: Penguin, 1985), 18.

3. Bill Brown, "A Thing about Things: The Art of Decoration in the Work of Henry James," *Henry James Review* 23, no. 3 (2002), 225.

4. John Dewey, *Art as Experience* (1934) (New York: Perigee, 1980), 107. Subsequent references to this work appear in parentheses in the text.

5. William James, "What Psychical Research Has Accomplished," in *Writings: 1878–1899*, ed. Gerald E. Myers (New York: Library of America, 1992): 680–700, 680.

6. Elaine Scarry, *The Body in Pain: The Making and Unmaking of the World* (New York: Oxford University Press, 1985), 286.

7. Howard Kerr, *Mediums, and Spirit-Rappers, and Roaring Radicals: Spiritualism in American Literature, 1850–1900* (Urbana: University of Illinois Press, 1972); see also Martha Banta, *Henry James and the Occult: The Great Extension* (Bloomington: Indiana University Press, 1972). T. J. Lustig, like Banta, construes James's invocation of the occult as "an important figural resource for James . . . potent as metaphor rather than literality"; *Henry James and the Ghostly* (Cambridge: Cambridge University Press, 1994), 4.

8. Pamela Thurschwell, *Literature, Technology, and Magical Thinking, 1880–1920* (New York: Cambridge University Press, 2001).

9. Susan Gillman, *Blood Talk: American Race Melodrama and the Culture of the Occult* (Chicago: University of Chicago Press, 2003), 6.

10. Lyndall Gordon, *A Private Life of Henry James: Two Women and His Art* (New York: Norton, 1998), 1. Subsequent references to this work appear in parentheses in the text.

11. Colm Tóibín, *The Master* (New York: Scribner, 2004), 105–106. Subsequent references to this work appear in parentheses in the text.

12. See Leon Edel, *The Life of Henry James* (Middlesex, England: Penguin Books, 1977), 2:99–100; and Richard Poirier, *The Comic Sense of Henry James: A Study of the Early Novels* (London: Chatto and Windus, 1960). In her *Suicide in Henry James*, Mary J. Joseph argues that both Minny Temple and Constance Fenimore Woolson "represent two aspects of self-willed death and become archetypal figures in James's fictional treatment of suicide" (New York: Peter Lang, 1994), 80.

13. The critic Osborn Andreas refers to "emotional cannibalism" in the works of Henry James, defining it as "that tendency in human nature to obtain emotional nourishment for indulgence in acts of aggression on other human beings"; *Henry James and the Expanding Horizon: A Study of the Meaning and Basic Themes of James's Fiction* (New York: Greenwood Press, 1969), 2. The "cannibalistic overtones" in the relationship of the Croy family to the appetizing Kate have also been noted by Sallie Sears, *The Negative Imagination: Form and Perspective in the Novels of Henry James* (Ithaca, N.Y.: Cornell University Press, 1969), 66.

14. The *Oxford English Dictionary* states that the term "fetish," in its anthropological sense, refers to "an inanimate object worshipped by primitive peoples on account of its supposed inherent magical powers, or as being animated by a spirit. A *fetish* . . . differs from an *idol* in that it is worshipped in its own character, not as the image, symbol, or occasional residence of a deity" (italics original). Originally, the fetish was a term applied by the Portuguese to the West African belief that gods animated certain objects or charms. For Freud, also, fetishism involved the irrational worshipping of an inanimate object, but he theorized it as a sexual psychopathology. Fetishism for Freud entailed an act of substitution (a shoe for a person, say) and was always driven by fear of female castration. In Freud's account, the fetishist, horrified by the mother's lack of a penis, imaginatively gives her one, albeit in a different form; whatever is substituted then becomes the object of the fetishist's desire; "Fetishism," in *The Standard Edition of the Complete Psychological Works of Sigmund Freud*, trans. James Strachey (London: Hogarth Press, 1953), 21:154.

Also an influential theorist of fetishism, Karl Marx described what he termed *commodity fetishism*, in which the labor of workers is alienated into objects that, despite being animated by their own hands, "rule the producers instead of being ruled by them"; *Early Writings* (New York: Vintage Books, 1975), 431. The literary critic Marcia Ian articulates the unique ontological status of the fetish in modern life: "Fetishism expresses the desire to take . . . symbols literally; it insists violently that symbols not just 'mean,' but 'be.'

Fetishism, therefore, is a kind of materialistic idealism. Fetishism conflates the physiological with the ideal (in Krafft-Ebing's terms), the 'reality' with the 'image' (in Binet's terms), and the signified with the signifier (in current terms) so that the ideal may replace the physiological, the image may replace the reality, and the signifier may replace the signified"; *Remembering the Phallic Mother: Psychoanalysis, Modernism, and the Fetish* (Ithaca, N.Y.: Cornell University Press, 1993), 53–54.

15. W. B. Seabrook, *The Magic Island* (New York: Harcourt, Brace, 1929), 51.

16. Ibid., 103; also, Alfred Metraux, *Voodoo in Haiti* (1959), trans. Hugo Charteris (New York: Schocken Books, 1972), 281.

17. There is a substantial and expanding body of work in this area. Some particularly influential works include Judith Herman, *Trauma and Recovery: The Aftermath of Violence—from Domestic Abuse to Political Terror* (New York: Basic Books, 1992); Bessel A. van der Kolk, Alexander C. Mc-Farlane, and Lars Weisaeth, *Traumatic Stress: The Effects of Overwhelming Experience on Mind, Body, and Society* (New York: Guilford Press, 1996); and Babette Rothschild, *The Body Remembers: The Psychophysiology of Trauma and Trauma Treatment* (New York: Norton, 2000).

18. Important studies include Allan Young, *The Harmony of Illusions: Inventing Post-traumatic Stress Disorder* (Princeton, N.J.: Princeton University Press, 1995); Mark S. Micale and Paul Lerner, eds., *Traumatic Pasts: History, Psychiatry, and Trauma in the Modern Age, 1870–1930* (New York: Cambridge University Press, 2001); and Ruth Leys, *Trauma: A Genealogy* (Chicago: University of Chicago Press, 2000).

19. Cathy Caruth, *Unclaimed Experience: Trauma, Narrative, and History* (Baltimore: Johns Hopkins University Press, 1996), 110. Subsequent references to this work appear in parentheses in the text.

20. Leys, *Trauma*, 284.

21. Ann Cvetkovich, *An Archive of Feelings: Trauma, Sexuality, and Lesbian Public Cultures* (Durham, N.C.: Duke University Press, 2003), 19, 27. Subsequent references to this work appear in parentheses in the text.

22. Philip Fisher, *The Vehement Passions* (Princeton, N.J.: Princeton University Press, 2002), 28–29.

23. My argument is highly compatible with Sharon Cameron's reading of *The Wings of the Dove*, in which she argues that *thinking* in the novel cannot be subsumed to a normal psychological framework. See her *Thinking in Henry James* (Chicago: University of Chicago Press, 1989), esp. 125. Similarly, Pamela Thurschwell insists that the magical potency of thought in James resists a "simplistic Freudian psychodynamics" and is instead deeply (and weirdly) intersubjective; *Literature, Technology, and Magical Thinking*, 107.

24. *William and Henry James: Selected Letters*, ed. Ignas K. Skrupskelis and Elizabeth Berkeley (Charlottesville: University Press of Virginia, 1997), 416.

25. James, "Psychical Research," 680.

26. Théodule Ribot, *The Psychology of the Emotions* (1897) (London: Walter Scott, 1911), 320. Subsequent references to this work appear in parentheses in the text.

27. Millicent Bell, *Meaning in Henry James* (Cambridge, Mass.: Harvard University Press, 1991), 294. The critic Andrew Cutting has helpfully noted that—like a foreordained ritual—"news that Milly dies precedes the reader's experience of the novel" because of "back-cover blurbs" and other critical commentaries; see his *Death in Henry James* (New York: Palgrave Macmillan, 2005), 84.
28. F. O. Matthiessen, *Henry James: The Major Phase* (New York: Oxford University Press, 1963), 67. Edward Wagenknecht in *The Novels of Henry James* echoes Matthiessen when he writes, "The great girl killer of the nineteenth century . . . would seem the most likely candidate for Milly's complaint" (New York: Frederick Ungar, 1983), 213.
29. *The Complete Notebooks of Henry James*, ed. Leon Edel and Lyall H. Powers (New York: Oxford University Press, 1987), 102.
30. Ruth Bernard Yeazell is here representative when she writes, "Never knowing to what literal disease Milly Theale succumbs, we may assume that she dies of betrayal; almost as easily, however, we may choose to believe that what kills Milly in the end is not the lovers' ambiguously kind deception, but Lord Mark's brutal truth"; *Language and Knowledge in the Late Novels of Henry James* (Chicago: University of Chicago Press, 1976), 84.
31. Quoted in Jean Strouse, *Alice James: A Biography* (Boston: Houghton Mifflin, 1980), 287.
32. Upon receiving Henry's telegram ("Alice just passed away painless. Wire Bob"), William wrote, "Poor little Alice! What a life! I can't believe that that imperious will and piercing judgment are snuffed out with the breath. . . . Of course we all live in the expectation of your letters telling the details. I had expected no slow agony but rather some sudden syncope. I telegraphed you this A.M. to make sure the death was not merely apparent, because her neurotic temperament & chronically reduced vitality are just the field for trance-tricks to play themselves upon, and she might possibly" [end of letter missing]. March 7, 1892, *William and Henry James: Selected Letters*, 264–265. Henry James's response is quoted in Linda Simon, *Genuine Reality: A Life of William James* (New York: Harcourt Brace, 1998), 241. For an illuminating feminist reading of Alice James, see Diane Price Herndl, *Invalid Women: Figuring Feminine Illness in American Fiction and Culture, 1840–1940* (Chapel Hill: University of North Carolina Press, 1993), esp. 126.
33. Quoted in Gordon, *A Private Life of Henry James*, 110.
34. Catherine Lutz, *Unnatural Emotions: Everyday Sentiments on a Micronesian Atoll and Their Challenge to Western Theory* (Chicago: University of Chicago Press, 1988), 11; emphasis added.
35. Josef Breuer and Sigmund Freud, *Studies on Hysteria* (1893–1895), trans. James Strachey with Anna Freud (New York: Basic Books, 1957), 181.
36. Charles Darwin, *The Expression of the Emotions in Man and Animals* (New York: Oxford University Press, 1998), 239. Subsequent references to this work appear in parentheses in the text.
37. A number of essays on James's novel explicitly treat the medical questions raised by Milly's illness and treatment by Sir Luke. See Lawrence Roth-

field, *Vital Signs: Medical Realism in Nineteenth-Century Fiction* (Princeton, N.J.: Princeton University Press, 1992), esp. 174; Rita Charon, "The Great Empty Cup of Attention: The Doctor and the Illness in *The Wings of the Dove*," *Literature and Medicine* 9 (1990): 105–124; and Joan Lescinski, "Fierce Privacy in *The Wings of the Dove*," *Literature and Medicine* 9 (1990): 125–133.

38. Quentin Anderson, *The American Henry James* (New Brunswick, N.J.: Rutgers University Press, 1959), 237.

39. William James, *The Principles of Psychology* (Cambridge, Mass.: Harvard University Press, 1983), 374. Subsequent references to this work appear in parentheses in the text.

40. Henry James, *Roderick Hudson* (New York: Penguin, 1986), 207. Marcia Ian treats the idea of the fetish in this early James novel in *Remembering the Phallic Mother*, 63–68.

41. Quoted in Ralph Barton Perry, *The Thought and Character of William James*, 2 vols. (Boston: Little, Brown, 1935), 1:216.

42. John Auchard makes a similar observation when he writes, "Science abandons empiricism in *The Wings of the Dove* and this excellent medical man offers clairvoyance"; *Silence in Henry James: The Heritage of Symbolism and Decadence* (University Park: Pennsylvania State University Press, 1986), 106.

43. Sir Spenser St. John, *Hayti; Or, the Black Republic* (London: Smith, Elder, 1884), vi, 225. Subsequent references to this work appear in parentheses in the text.

44. William James, *The Will to Believe and Other Essays in Popular Philosophy* (New York: Longmans Green, 1899), 25.

45. Henri F. Ellenberger, *The Discovery of the Unconscious: The History and Evolution of Dynamic Psychiatry* (London: Basic Books, 1970), 55. Subsequent references to this work appear in parentheses in the text.

46. R. Osgood Mason, *Telepathy and the Subliminal Self* (New York: Holt, 1897), 30.

47. See Jean-Martin Charcot, *Charcot the Clinician: The Tuesday Lessons, Excerpts from Nine Case Presentations on General Neurology Delivered at the Salpêtrière Hospital in 1887–88*, trans. with commentary by Christopher G. Goetz (New York: Raven Press, 1987), 109–121; *Discovery of the Unconscious*, Ellenberger, 89–101; and Roy Porter, "The Body and the Mind, the Doctor and the Patient," in *Hysteria beyond Freud*, Sander L. Gilman et al. (Berkeley: University of California Press, 1993): 225–285; 256–260.

48. Hippolyte Bernheim, *Suggestive Therapeutics: A Treatise on the Nature and Uses of Hypnotism* (New York: Putnam, 1890), ix. Subsequent references to this work appear in parentheses in the text.

49. Frederic W. H. Myers, *Human Personality and Its Survival of Bodily Death* (London: Longmans, Green, 1907), 127. Subsequent references to this work appear in parentheses in the text.

50. Sigmund Freud, *The Origin and Development of Psychoanalysis*, with an

introduction by Eliseo Vivas (New York: Henry Regnery, 1967), 6. This text comprises a series of five lectures that Freud delivered at Clark University on September 7 through 12, during his first visit to the United States in 1909; they were originally published in the *American Journal of Psychology* 21 (April 1910), 181–218.

51. See James, *Principles of Psychology*, 222–2; Ellenberger, *Discovery of the Unconscious*, 358–359, 372–374.

52. James, "Psychical Research," 692. Subsequent references to this work (abbreviated "Psychical") appear in parentheses in the text.

53. Freud writes in *An Autobiographical Study*, "In every analytic treatment there arises, without the physician's agency, an intense emotional relationship between the patient and the analyst which is not to be accounted for by the actual situation. . . . We can easily recognize it as the same dynamic factor which the hypnotists have named 'suggestibility' which is the agent of hypnotic rapport"; quoted in Mikkel Borch-Jacobsen, *The Emotional Tie: Psychoanalysis, Mimesis, and Affect* (Palo Alto, Calif.: Stanford University Press, 1992), 70. Subsequent references to this work appear in parentheses in the text.

54. *The Letters of William James*, vol. 2, edited by his son Henry James (Boston: Atlantic Monthly Press, 1920), 327–328.

55. William Sargant, *The Mind Possessed: A Physiology of Possession, Mysticism, and Faith Healing* (Philadelphia: Lippincott, 1973), 14.

56. Quoted in Linda Simon, *Genuine Reality*, 189.

57. William James, *The Varieties of Religious Experience: A Study in Human Nature* (New York: Macmillan, 1961), 101. Subsequent references to this work appear in parentheses in the text.

58. These letters are reprinted in *William James on Psychical Research*, 101.

59. Pamela Thurschwell refers to this moment in a footnote to her very interesting discussion of Henry James's relationship with his typist, Theodora Bosanquet. See her *Literature, Technology, and Magical Thinking*, 172n71.

60. For illuminating accounts of how Henry James's ideas about women's speech pertained to nation-building, see Lynn Wardley, "Woman's Voice, Democracy's Body, and *The Bostonians*," *English Literary History* 56 (1989): 639–655; and Caroline Levander, *Voices of the Nation: Women and Public Speech in Nineteenth-Century American Literature and Culture* (Cambridge: Cambridge University Press, 1988), 12–34.

61. Henry James, *The Question of Our Speech; The Lesson of Balzac: Two Lectures* (Boston: Houghton, Mifflin, 1905), 10.

62. William Dean Howells, "Editor's Study," *Harpers*, May 1886, 973; emphasis added.

63. William James, "Report on Mrs. Piper's Hodgson-Control," *Proceedings of the Society for Psychical Research*, pt. 58, vol. 23 (June 1909), 32. Subsequent references to this work appear in parentheses in the text.

64. William James, "The Psychology of Belief," in *Writings: 1878–1899*, 1021–1056, 1045; emphasis added. For a very helpful discussion of the

corporeal effects of belief in James's writings, see Franklin G. Miller, "William James, Faith, and the Placebo Effect," *Perspectives in Biology and Medicine* 48, no. 2 (2005), esp. 278–280.

65. Simon, *Genuine Reality*, 192.

66. Eugene Taylor, *Shadow Culture: Psychology and Spirituality in America* (Washington, D.C.: Counterpoint, 1999), 168.

67. William James, "What Makes a Life Significant," in *Writings: 1878–1899*, 861.

68. William James, "Emotion," in *Psychology: The Briefer Course*, in *Writings: 1878–1899*, 359.

69. Denis Diderot, *The Paradox of Acting* (1830) (New York: Hill and Wang, 1957), 19.

70. For a fascinating and pertinent discussion of antebellum poetics, spirit mediumship, and the "cooperative aesthetic" modeled by the new technology of the telegraph, see Eliza Richards, "Lyric Telegraphy: Women Poets, Spiritualist Poetics, and the 'Phantom Voice' of Poe," *Yale Journal of Criticism* 12, no. 2 (fall 1999): 284.

71. Uriah Clark, *Plain Guide to Spiritualism* (Boston: W. White, 1863), 172, quoted in Taylor, *Shadow Culture*, 138.

72. William James, "Is Life Worth Living?" in *The Will to Believe and Other Essays in Popular Philosophy*, 97. Subsequent references to this work appear in parentheses in the text.

73. William James, "The Sentiment of Rationality," in *Writings: 1878–1899*, 529.

74. Marcia Ian has written a probing article on this topic, "Immaculate Conceptions: Henry James and the Private Sphere," *Henry James Review* 22, no. 3 (2001): 239–247. I would, however, amend her conclusion that "Henry James's secular religion was founded upon the continuity of consciousness alone" (244); as I argue, belief for the Jameses was intersubjective and tended to emerge in collaborative acts of embodied consciousness.

75. Henry James, "Is There a Life after Death?" in *After Days: Thoughts on the Future Life* (New York: Harper, 1910), 217.

76. Similarly, Ross Posnock has written of Henry James's "extreme commitment to the self as social process"; see his *The Trial of Curiosity: Henry James, William James, and the Challenge of Modernity* (New York: Oxford University Press, 1991), 182.

77. Bell, *Meaning in Henry James*, 16.

78. *William and Henry James: Selected Letters*, March 26, 1870, 71.

79. One can discern in the writings of Henry James seeds of the virtual logic of sex on the internet. Earl Jackson, associate professor of communications at University of California, Santa Cruz, has described the "new metaphysics of sexuality" as a "three-tiered system," which casts sexual encounters along a continuum, from "cybersex," which transpires online, through "real sex," which is mediated by the telephone, to "ultra-real sex," which involves "slow-time interface, which means actual physical contact"; Na-

tional Public Radio, *This American Life*, program no. 66, "Tales from the Net," aired June 6, 1997.

80. For a terrific account of the sexual politics of the terrorizing gaze in *Wings*, see Michael Moon, "Sexuality and Visual Terrorism in *The Wings of the Dove*," *Criticism* 28, no. 4 (fall 1986): 427–443.

81. Walter Cannon, "Voodoo Death," *American Anthropologist* 44, no. 2 (April/June 1942): 170. Subsequent references to this work appear in parentheses in the text.

82. Emile Durkheim, *The Elementary Forms of the Religious Life* (1915), trans. and ed. Karen E. Fields (New York: Free Press, 1995), 397.

83. A. G. Leonard, *The Lower Niger and Its Tribes* (London, 1906), 257.

84. *The Placebo Effect: An Interdisciplinary Exploration*, ed. Anne Harrington (Cambridge, Mass.: Harvard University Press, 1997), 1.

85. Brown, "A Thing about Things," 228. Subsequent references to this article appear in parentheses in the text.

86. Serge Leclaire, *A Child Is Being Killed: On Primary Narcissism and the Death Drive*, trans. Marie-Claude Hays (Stanford, Calif.: Stanford University Press, 1998), 8. My thanks to Caroline Levander for bringing Leclaire's work to my attention.

87. Caruth, *Unclaimed Experience*, 111.

88. Amy Hungerford, "Memorizing Memory," *Yale Journal of Criticism* 14, no. 1 (2001): 67–92. In this article, Hungerford excavates the radical account of language that underpins the trauma theory, in which texts (especially survivor accounts of the Holocaust) are imagined not as representations of their authors' experiences to which a reader might have intellectual and emotional access but as embodiments (and transmitters) of that experience. Hungerford argues that Caruth and Felman, influenced by deconstruction's notion of the materiality of the signifier, end up conflating writing and persons and thereby invest texts with "the pathos of life and death" (88) that properly belongs to actual human beings.

89. Caruth, *Unclaimed Experience*, 111.

90. Janet Malcolm, *Psychoanalysis: The Impossible Profession* (New York: Vintage, 1982), 6, quoted in Kenneth Kidd, "'A' is for Auschwitz: Psychoanalysis, Trauma Theory, and the 'Children's Literature of Atrocity,'" *Children's Literature* 33 (2005): 125.

91. Hungerford, "Memorizing Memory," 73, 78.

92. Walter Benn Michaels, in *The Shape of the Signifier: 1967 to the End of History* (Princeton, N.J.: Princeton University Press, 2004), has eloquently and disturbingly described the consequences of a "powerful but incoherently reductive materialism" (15) that entails "the redescription of communication as penetration" (68). I part with him in attributing this state of affairs to the Affective Fallacy, as well as his argument that the way to correct it is to affirm a conception of language that reduces the experience of reading to a purely cognitive activity. This, of course, makes the same mistake that Kate Croy does in *Wings*: of imagining that one's mind can be en-

listed without one's affective engagement. This state of being is what Rei Terada appropriately terms "zombie-like"; see *Feeling in Theory: Emotion after the "Death of the Subject"* (Cambridge, Mass.: Harvard University Press, 2001), 156.

93. William James, *Human Immortality* (1898), in *Writings: 1878–1899*, 1124.

94. Jeffrey Williams, "The Last Generalist: An Interview with Richard Powers," *Cultural Logic* 2, no. 2 (spring 1999): 1–16, 8.

Acknowledgments

It has been a pleasure to think back over the inspiring mentors who have helped me to write this book. First among these is Walter Benn Michaels. I am grateful for his guidance, insight, and liberality during my time in graduate school, and for his continued support of this project. A brilliant teacher, he is for me a model of intellectual intensity and professionalism. My heartfelt thanks to Larzer Ziff, whose encyclopedic knowledge of American literature made him an animating presence from the very beginning; and to Sharon Cameron, under whose impeccable tutelage I first encountered Henry James's late novels. The meticulous scholarship and stimulating guidance of Frances Ferguson and Mary Poovey were important influences as I embarked on this project. Lindsay Waters provided the vital force to bring this book's long evolution to a conclusion: I am thankful to him and to his terrific assistant Phoebe Kosman for their tireless enthusiasm, and to the readers for Harvard University Press for their generous, immensely constructive reports.

During a decade-long journey from Baltimore to Cambridge and then to Chapel Hill, many friends and fellow scholars have fertilized my thinking, cheered me on, and kept me excited about the project. My thanks to Scott Black, Andy Franta, Liz Kelleher, Oren Izenberg, Stacey Margolis, and Steve Newman for their intellectual companionship during our days at Johns Hopkins. When I moved back north, my community expanded to include Ann Keniston, Laura Johnson, Peter Lurie, and Lisa Rodensky, with whom I traded chapters as well as tales of our elaborate efforts to balance scholarship and family. Three people in particular have, from early on, been unflagging fellow travelers and scholarly comrades: Tyler Curtain, Jack Kerkering, and Jeanne Follansbee Quinn. I am grateful for their friendship, and for their myriad contributions, practical and conceptual, to help bring the project to its final shape.

I have many wonderful colleagues at the University of North Carolina, Chapel Hill, who have made work a pleasure. For their insight and advice at key moments, I am especially grateful to Joy Kasson, John McGowan, and James Thompson. Trudier Harris and Jane Danielewicz have supported and encouraged me since I joined the department. I deeply appreciate the time, attention, and acumen of those readers, at UNC and beyond, who made their way through portions (or all!) of the book in manuscript: my thanks to Dale Bauer, Cynthia Davis, Rebecka Fisher, Mary Floyd-Wilson, Randall Knoper, Elizabeth Kramer, Tim Marr, Eliza Richards, and Priscilla Wald. Much of the thinking for this project was tested out and refined in discussions with graduate students, particularly those in the 2005 Literature and Emotion seminar: my thanks for their interest in and contributions to this book. Two splendid research assistants helped me prepare the book for publication, Jason Maxwell and especially Allison Bigelow, who wore a path between Greenlaw Hall and Davis Library as she hunted down and gathered sources and assisted with footnotes. Ashley Reed did yeowoman's work as a proofreader; my thanks to her.

One of the delights of academic work is that one can hash out ideas around the dinner table, and I'm lucky to have a group of friends who are great cooks and sparkling conversationalists: my fond thanks to Daniel Jurayj, Alan Keenan, Jon Kranes, Sonya Mead, Rich Monastersky, Ira Paneth, Kate Silbaugh, Alice Truax, Alex Whiting, Sarah Whiting, Cheri Wiggs, and Ron Witte. My wonderful extended family has provided levity, sustenance, and lovely distractions over the years, as well as plenty of room—including a beautiful house in the Berkshires—when I needed to work. My deep thanks to my parents, Jane and Dave Thrailkill, and Elizabeth and George Kramer, for their potent combination of optimism and patience. As I wrote this book, it was gratifying to witness the growth of two ardent young readers, Olivia and Naomi Truax; they provide a daily reminder of just how thrilling stories can be. My thanks to the extraordinary young women who have cared for my girls over the years, without whom this book could not have been written.

For that essential resource—time—I thank the English Department and the Institute for the Arts and Humanities at UNC: each, at key moments, provided a semester leave from teaching. Portions of Chapters 2 and 4 have appeared, in different form, in "Killing Them Softly: Childbed Fever and the Novel," *American Literature* 71, no. 4 (fall 1999); and "Doctoring 'The Yellow Wallpaper,'" *English Literary History* 69, no. 2 (summer 2002). Chapter 1 was published in an earlier form with the title "Emotive Realism" in *JNT: Journal of Narrative Theory*, 36.3 (2006). The essay appears here by permission of *JNT* and Eastern Michigan University. I am grateful to the editors of these journals for granting permission to reprint here material from these essays.

Working on this project has been at times daunting. I have been fortunate to have two soul mates who have given me steady support from start to finish. Cathy Kerr's unconventional wisdom has so informed my thinking that I consider her a collaborator in the creation of this book: the current of her friendship runs deep through these chapters. At every turn Hawley Truax gave me the courage to proceed and—especially as my notes and papers seemed to blossom all over our house—the space to do so. He has kindled my ideas and nourished my spirit for more than half a lifetime. I dedicate this book to him.

Index

306 · Index

Hobbes, Thomas, 263n95; on laughter, 48–50
Hochman, Barbara, 279n59, 282n90
Hodge, Hugh L., 267n32
Hodges, R. M., 271n45, 271n46
Hodgson, Richard, 227, 229, 232, 233, 245
Holmes, Oliver Wendell, Sr., 9, 10, 11, 14, 25, 39–40, 55–57, 84, 115–116, 261nn71,73, 267n24, 268nn36,39,41,269nn45,47,52 270nn2,4,5,6, 273n35; algebra of human nature, 70–74; on corporeal processes, 88; *Elsie Venner*, puerperal fever, and, 54–83; *Mortal Antipathy, A*, 89–94, 95, 103, 105, 108, 111, 112; railway effects and, 98–99, 114–115; on technology and body, 85; on unconscious embodied memory, 86–87
Homeopathy: art, 12
Homeostasis, 41, 42
Hooker, Worthington, 268n42
House, Elizabeth, 284n30
Household aesthetics, 202–203
House of the Seven Gables, The (Hawthorne), 84
Howells, William Dean, 73, 89, 134, 226, 257–258n19, 269n46, 271n15, 275n4, 280n61, 285n35, 293n62
Huber, Richard, 284n27
Hughlings Jackson, John, 42–43, 58, 97, 98, 103, 255n31, 262n81, 273n37
Humanities: vs. sciences, 25
Human Personality and Its Survival of Bodily Death (Myers), 223
Hume, David, 103
Humor. *See* Laughter
Hungerford, Amy, 247, 248, 295nn88,91
Hunter, Kathleen Montgomery, 254n11, 269n54
Hutton, James, 37, 258n57
Hypnosis, 122, 222–223
Hypotheses, 223
Hysteria, 86, 95–96, 135–136, 213, 222; female, 136; male, 103–104

Ian, Marcia, 289n14, 292n39, 294n74
Identification, 64, 95
Illumination (Frederic). *See Damnation of Theron Ware, The* (Frederic)

Intelligence: mimetic representation and, 81–82
Intentionality, 57, 58; without intention, 81, 99
Interior environment, 41–42
Interpretation, 2; cognition and, 4; experience and, 3
Interpretations of Dreams (Freud), 247
Interrogative criticism, 124–125, 146
Introduction to the Study of Experimental Medicine (Bernard), 42
"Is There Life after Death?" (Henry James), 240, 249

Jackson, Earl, 294n79
Jackson, James, 265n14
Jacobus, Mary, 277n19
Jagose, Annamarie, 281n88
James, Alice, 212, 291n32
James, B. W., 278nn33
James, Henry, 14, 36, 49, 117, 118, 141, 225–226, 240–241, 255n2, 256n5, 260n55, 263n100, 267n23, 275n2, 288n2, 289n13, 291nn32, 292n40, 293n57,61, 294nn75; as artist, 246; on laughter, 51; occult and, 201–218; on possession, 233; *Roderick Hudson* and, 18–21, 34, 59, 217; on social self, 234; *Spoils of Poynton*, 201, 217, 243; *Wings of the Dove, The*, 203, 208, 209, 211–218, 234–246, 248–249
James, Henry (son of William), 293n54
James, Henry, Sr., 288n77
James, William, 7, 8, 9, 13, 22, 28, 37, 38, 43, 58, 128–129, 157, 163, 165, 174, 175, 177, 185, 190, 192, 194, 195, 199, 220, 223, 224, 225, 241, 242, 252nn14,18, 254n7, 256n20, 259n31, 260nn53,60,62, 261nn65,67,67, 262n84,85,86,89, 266n18, 278n40, 283n7, 284n25, 286nn41,45, 287n66, 288n5, 292nn39,44, 293n57, 294nn63,64, 294nn67,68,72,73; 296n93; on aesthetics, 203; on duality of experience, 36–37; on emotion, 40–41, 54; on experience, 43–44; hypnosis and, 222–223; on persuasive notions, 236; on possession, 217, 233; on religion, 157, 163–164; on social self, 234; on soul,